# BETTER
# BASICS
## FOR THE HOME

———— ❧ ————

MORE PRAISE FOR **BETTER BASICS FOR THE HOME**

"This book is so rich in good sense, sound advice, and fascinating tips that it should be a handbook in every home."

DIANNE DUMANOSKI, environmental journalist
and coauthor of *Our Stolen Future*

"An excellent, practical manual of alternatives to the toxic consumer goods sold commercially. It belongs in the home of every health-conscious family."

LEO GALLAND, M.D., author of *Power Healing*

"Annie Berthold-Bond has a passion for the environment that is deep and true. With this book she is giving the rest of us the chance to join her. Thank you, Annie."

JANE L. WOLFSON, PH.D., Director,
Environmental Studies and Science, Towson University

# BETTER BASICS
# FOR THE HOME

## Simple Solutions
## for Less Toxic Living

ANNIE BERTHOLD-BOND

THREE RIVERS PRESS
NEW YORK

The author has included cautions and general guidelines for using the formulas in this book. However, each individual, fabric, or material may react differently to a particular suggested use. For this reason, the author cannot assume responsibility for personal or property damage resulting from the use of the formulas found here. It is recommended that before you begin to use any formula, you read the directions carefully and test it first. If you have any questions or concerns regarding the safety or health effects of any formula, consult first with a physician or other appropriate professional.

Published by Three Rivers Press, 201 East 50th Street, New York, New York 10022. Member of the Crown Publishing Group.

Random House, Inc. New York, Toronto, London, Sydney, Auckland
www.randomhouse.com

THREE RIVERS PRESS is a registered trademark of Random House, Inc.

Printed in the United States of America

Design by Maggie Hinders

Library of Congress Cataloging-in-Publication Data
Berthold-Bond, Annie.
    Better basics for the home: simple solutions for less toxic
living / by Annie Berthold-Bond. — 1st ed.
    1. House cleaning—Environmental aspects. 2. Household
supplies—Toxicology. 3. Indoor air pollution. 4. Housing and
health. I. Title.
    RA77.5 .B47   1999
    640—dc21                                        98-48649

ISBN 0-609-80325-5

10   9   8   7   6   5   4   3   2   1

First Edition

*To Danny and Lily*

# Acknowledgments

**B**OOKS this hard to write become family efforts—everyone has to pitch in doing the laundry, making do with too many dinners of tacos or spaghetti, and handling all the other details of day-to-day life. I offer a heartfelt thank-you to my husband, Daniel, for keeping it all together for so many weeks on end, and to Lily for choosing to understand and accept the ebbs and flows of her mother writing a book. Without this from both of them, *Better Basics for the Home* would never have been finished.

My friends and extended family have helped sustain me, too, both with their love and support and as readers and testers of recipes. A special thanks to Pat Beecher, my daily phone friend and to my herbalist friend Josie Delgado-Freany, who generously gave me a great deal of her time and expertise. Others include my mother, Nancy Prosser; my sisters, Kathy Gibbons, Carolyn Keck, and Yari Bond; my sister-in-law Megan Berthold; Erin Schulman, Carol Merrill, Anna Brudvig, Maryann Despopo Barrett, my stepbrother Jamie Prosser, Lyn Itskovitz, James Steinberg, Deb Bansemer, Carl Frankel, Amy Algieres, and Phillip Frazer. For help with the Mayan Formula, a thanks to Dr. Rosita Arvigo, Christopher Lindner, John Bierhorst, and Ruth Ketay.

It would be remiss of me not to thank all the health practitioners whose hard work and dedication to healing got me well enough from Lyme disease so I could write: Dr. Richard Horrowitz, Bonnie Tarttier-Railing, and Dr. Wu Yi Zhang.

The professional team that helped launch this book deserves much of the credit for its reaching the public's hands. I thank my agent, Lisa Ross, of the Spieler Agency, for her clear thinking and unending support. The production team at Crown did excellent work: Thank you to production editor Vincent La Scala, and designer Maggie Hinders. And I take my hat off to Margot Schupf and Pam Krauss, the editors at Crown who are responsible for *Better Basics for the Home* reaching a level I dreamed and hoped it would but never imagined could actually happen. The book wouldn't have gotten here without them. Pam's overall enthusiasm for the project was always steadfast and encouraging, and Margot's editing was the best that one could ever wish for—perceptive, demanding yet friendly, and sharp as a tack.

# Contents

# Contents

# BETTER
# BASICS
## FOR THE HOME

# Introduction

*The frog does not drink
up the pond in which it lives.*

—CHINESE PROVERB

I T IS EARLY JUNE in upstate New York, and I am sitting on the front porch in our old wicker love seat. A flock of Canada geese just flew overhead—a big V of them—heading directly north. Compass perfect. The morning dew is still on the grass, and the birds haven't quieted down yet for the day. There are still a few wood thrushes singing, my favorite birds with their jazzy melodies. The tidy look of our gardens reflects Sunday's hard work by my husband and daughter. The snow peas are ready to eat, and the first lily is in bloom, a bright golden yellow. The chimney swift that made her nest on top of one of the porch posts is a nervous Nellie with me sitting

out here. She alternates between perching on the wheelbarrow handle, the hummingbird feeder, and the cold frame, waiting for me to leave.

My father loved to garden, as did his father before him. I am linked to them by the glory of this cool June day. They too sat as I am sitting now, in different homes in different places, wondering how the raspberries will do this year, if the deer will eat the garden the weekend when the dogs are in the kennel, if the tomatoes will get that blight. And our neighbors down the road have similar things on their minds; I see their window boxes planted with petunias and the gardens tended. We glean from one another a few insights as the summer season unfolds, such as exactly how much rain has fallen, or where to find a patch of jewelweed to help a poison ivy rash.

The other night my family and I spent an hour in our dusty, cluttered basement because a tornado was bearing down on us. That was a first for me, and I'll be forty-five next week. This never happened in my parents' lifetime, or my grandparents'. My nine-year-old spent the following morning down there fixing up a place for us that would be more comfortable for the next time. Global warming supposedly makes for wild weather. Could that be the cause? Other strange things are happening. The land I can see from my porch is infested with ticks where ten years ago there were none. It seemed to get this way after the gypsy moth spraying. And the summers are so warm now that it seems like we are living in Tennessee— we finally broke down and bought an air conditioner. In winter the snow isn't on the ground for long anymore either. The last decade we've been able to cross-country ski only two or three times a year, whereas before we always had a few months' stretch. I feel these changes break a bond with the past and the old lifeways. We look to a future without familiar markers.

It is unimaginable, as I look out at the beauty of this day, to think that our natural world is in jeopardy. How did such a thing happen? I well up with grief thinking of it. There is no land left free of pesticide drift. The oceans' coral reefs are dying. Frogs and songbirds are disappearing. Our very biosphere is heating up from too much logging and burning of fossil fuels. It's unclear who is actually perpetrating the violation, hard to fix the blame. Maybe at first just one man-made chemical was produced that hadn't stood the test of time, and somehow the brakes never were put on, even after we learned about DDT. We keep manufacturing the toxic products by the thousands and then the millions, despite the "unintended consequences," the hidden costs. Who thought of our entire planet as a testing ground?

Years ago Robert Frost began his poem "Directive" by writing, "Back out of all this now too much for us. . . ." But now there is no place left for us to back out to. We exist only as part of the earth.

Frost leads you to his directive "if you're lost enough to find yourself. . . ." Are we lost enough yet? I have my doubts when I hear about resistance to the global warming treaty and about biotechnology news of scorpion genes spliced into soybeans. But maybe we're lost just enough to start finding ourselves. Frost's conclusion, some fifty years past, was that our collective salvation would come by turning our individual backs to the world in a solitary sort of way and by finding our roots in the past. That won't work now, not the turning our backs to the world part. Not with the strange things that are happening, irretrievably interconnecting us to the rest of the world. Contaminated air, water, and food are a loss of liberty and hard to accept without a fight, especially if you have a child. Even so, Frost was onto something with returning to our roots.

I've had the feeling for a long time that the way toward finding ourselves has to do with putting everyday life into focus and paying attention. It has to do with what goes on in my front yard and with my neighbor's petunias. I realized this after becoming extremely sensitive to even low levels of chemicals in the environment, after being poisoned by gas and pesticides in 1980. What happened to me could happen to anyone. I worked at a restaurant that had a gas leak; seventy people were hospitalized. A month later our apartment building was exterminated with a pesticide that has since been taken off the market due to its neurotoxicity. This one-two punch to my central nervous system damaged my immune system, and the sensitivities developed. That's when day-to-day living got really hard. It wasn't until I *had* to be away from chemicals that I began to realize how many we live with.

The extent of the contamination is startling—from hair spray and floor wax to dandelion killers and plastic shower curtains and other products that line our hardware store and supermarket shelves. We moved ten times in four years in a desperate search for clean air. Then I realized that the pollution was coming from everyday products: pollution that is causing high ozone at ground level, low ozone in the stratosphere, and hormone disruption in wildlife. Who'd ever have believed that the products we use daily for mundane chores would change the course of life, on both a personal and a planetary scale?

It is also here, in the day-to-day world, that we find an astonishing abundance of multifaceted gifts from nature providing us with safe materials, the alternative products with which to do our chores. These natural alternatives are nourishing and life-giving, a stark contrast to those dead chemicals that line the supermarket shelves. The cucumbers growing in our gardens or that we buy at a farmers' market can soften and tone the skin, because they have the same pH as our skin. Our neighbor's patch of nettles will make a tea that can help us stay healthy into old age. The plentiful herb thyme can kill bacteria on our cutting boards. That beautiful barn-red color still seen on some New England farms was made with milk and raspberries, or maybe milk and local dirt rich in iron oxide, and can be easily re-created. And we can harness the wind and sun for energy, clean up toxic waste sites with bacteria, and use soybeans instead of petroleum to make plastics, fusing new technology with old and

safe materials. Learning old ways of doing things based on natural formulas is one way to incorporate safe materials that have stood the test of time in daily life.

In the old days, a household recipe book would be passed down from mother to daughter. A survival guide for much more than just cooking, the compendium of helpful hints would offer solutions for removing laundry stains, formulas for paints, herbal lore, and more, all relating to ingredients found in the kitchen cupboard, local fields, and the family herb garden. From these simple staples, poultices could be made that would sooth burns, and herb mixtures could be created to repel flies.

It is within this tradition that I have written *Better Basics for the Home.* It is a book of simple ingredients for simple tasks. I've tried to retrieve from near oblivion the know-how that was abandoned with the advent of the chemical age. All formulas have been looked at with a discerning eye. Those containing lead or other toxic materials that we no longer consider safe have been weeded out, as have recipes that never seemed to work no matter how many different ways I tested them. And I've put them through the filter of our perspective at the threshold of the new millennium. *Better Basics for the Home* is a different kind of survival guide, one in which concern about the environment beyond our home is an urgent priority. If we establish healthy homes, we'll go a long way toward establishing a healthy planet.

Gathering and using back-to-basics know-how can be rewarding in many ways. Life is simplified, money is saved, and there is pride in acquiring this knowledge. I enjoy being out here on the porch puzzling how to use our ever-abundant mint, which mice avoid, to keep them out of the house this fall. I bet my grandfather knew. The mint won't harm anybody. I don't have to buy anything. Using it makes good sense. And did you know that mint will soothe an upset stomach?

I'm not advocating being rooted in the past but rather putting down healthy, deep roots in the natural world, collectively establishing an abiding partnership with nature, and spurning that which conquers and exploits the earth. If we focus our considerable intelligence on integrating our everyday life with nature, we may reclaim our reverence for life. We may find what the Sioux leader Luther Standing Bear called the "great unifying force that flows in and through all things."

# The Commonsense Rule of Thumb

It is a great relief to establish a healthy home. Two-thirds of us cite healthy air and water as an extremely important local priority, second only to safety from crime, according to Roper Starch Worldwide. National Wildlife Federation research has noted that up to 80 percent of us are concerned about how pesticides and indoor air pollution affect our health. Other polls show that a natural lifestyle is one that women, mothers in particular, overwhelmingly want because it protects the health of their families.

Yet polls ever since Earth Day 1990 consistently show a significant gap between wanting

a more healthful environment and knowing how to create it. We are realizing that the government doesn't fully protect us from toxic products, leaving an uneasy and pervasive feeling that we have to take charge of safeguarding our families' health. The stumbling blocks seem insurmountable.

Having lived in a healthy home for more than a decade, I've learned that after some initial adjustment, the way to establish such a home is quite simple. The most important guideline for choosing safe materials is to follow this basic rule of thumb: Use only materials that have been around so long, and been used by people without harm for so long, that they are "generally regarded as safe" (GRAS for short), otherwise they would have long since been abandoned. Using only GRAS substances will take us back to the time before plastics and forward to new technology using old and safe materials. It will introduce us to plants and healing herbs; minerals such as baking soda, borax, and washing soda; and products from animals and insects such as milk, honey, shellac, and royal jelly. We may not have realized that these natural materials could clean, disinfect, moisturize, or make paint. This discovery will open up a new way of looking at our world.

Our alternative is to get a combined degree in toxicology and environmental studies in order to do a simple risk analysis of bathtub cleansers that won't cause harm, or to go shopping armed with research files. That's a stretch for even the most well intentioned among us.

Help also comes from something we all

already have, even if we need to clear out cobwebs to find it, and that is our common sense. If the choice for polishing furniture is between polish in a can that reads "fatal if swallowed" or using a simple but effective recipe of lemon juice and raw linseed oil, common sense and the GRAS rule guide us to the lemon and raw linseed oil.

Mixing up face creams or wood stain isn't much different than cleaning the windows with vinegar, soap, and water instead of using Brand Name X, or making a cake with flour, eggs, and milk instead of buying a mix. And it seems amazing, although true, that we can make paint ourselves using milk and lime. With a few simple staples we can clean our houses, wash our hair, rid the dog's bed of fleas, and do many other things too.

As we learn to live in a simpler, less polluting, easier way, we will be reminded of the nearly forgotten know-how of our grandparents, or maybe our *great*-grandparents. In his book about the Civil War South, *Cold Mountain*, Charles Frazier sums up as well as anyone how to learn to make do by using common sense and back-to-basics know-how. With her commonsense survival skills, Ruby, an illiterate girl who grew up in a dirt-floored hovel, ran circles around highly educated Ada.

*"How do you come to know such things?" Ada had asked.*

*Ruby said she had learned what little she knew in the usual way. A lot of it was grandmother knowledge, got from wandering around the settlement talking to any old*
*woman who would talk back, watching them work and asking questions. Some came from Sally Swanger, who knew, Ruby claimed, a great many quiet things such as the names of all plants down to the plainest weed. Partly, though, she claimed she had just puzzled out in her own mind how the world's logic works. It was mostly a matter of being attentive.*

Looking for cause and effect is another way of choosing safe products. Sometimes I wonder if we've allowed consumer products to deplete the earth's resources or to be so toxic because the products don't look like the raw materials used to make them. We don't see the connections. A can of pretty robin's-egg blue paint in a hardware store isn't visibly connected to its ingredients of fungicides and petroleum or to the smokestacks of the factory where it was made. Seeing the loss and damage that occurs in its creation might incline us to purchase a more ecological brand or to buy a little less. Or having access to the old-timers' recipe for milk paint might inspire us to try it out ourselves.

Just because a formula is old, or its ingredients are natural, doesn't mean it is safe, of course. Some old paint recipes call for white lead. A musty-smelling 1951 housekeeping book I found recently at a yard sale recommended using DDT paint on screens and windows. DDT paint! For those of you not familiar with DDT, it is a pesticide, now banned, that is symbolic of the worst of the industrial age's impact on the environment. Natural materials such as turpentine, citrus solvents, and tung oil can cause health problems for many. Needless to say, we need to look at the old recipes with a discerning eye. The key is to integrate the best of the old—the simplest, most wholesome ingredients and methods—with the best of the new—information about the effect of poisons on our collective health, and how to replace them with safe alternatives.

## SIGNAL WORDS

Besides choosing GRAS materials, the next best way to protect yourself and the world at large from toxic products is to read labels and pay particular attention to "signal words." They are placed on products by order of the federal government, with the primary purpose of protecting you, but sometimes to tell you about the products' potential impact on the environment. POISON/DANGER means something very toxic; only a few drops could kill you. WARNING means moderately toxic; as little as a teaspoonful can kill. CAUTION denotes a product that is less toxic; two table-spoons to a cup could kill you. There are a few others, such as STRONG SENSITIZER, which means the product can cause multiple allergies. I'd suggest that everyone get over the "it will never happen to me" way of thinking and read labels, believe them, and simply avoid toxic products. Calamity might not happen to you, but it could happen to a child, or a neighbor, or a fish or a dog.

## CHEMICALS AND MATERIALS TO AVOID

The Environmental Health Foundation, in its book *Toxic Turnaround,* compiled a list of the top four chemical groups we should reject and eliminate. The guidelines are an excellent starting point. If we eliminate these chemicals, we will go a long way toward solving our environmental and health problems. I add plastics as a fifth category because of the increasing evidence that many plastic components are endocrine disrupters, synthetic chemicals that our bodies receive as if they were natural hormones. The switch can cause havoc in processes dependent on hormones, such as reproduction. The first four chemical groups of the list, given below, are from *Toxic Turnaround;* the descriptions are mine.

**1. PESTICIDES.** Pesticides are toxic poisons designed to kill. The list of pesticides that are probable or possible carcinogens is extensive. Of the pesticides legally allowed to be used on food crops, the EPA considers to be potentially carcinogenic 60 percent of the registered herbicides, 90 percent of the fungicides, and 30 percent of the insecticides. Evidence is mounting that pesticides can alter the immune system's normal structure, reducing resistance to disease. There is also increased documentation of endocrine disruption in wildlife caused by pesticides. Other concerns include central nervous system depression and the fact that organochlorine pesticides are long-lasting in the environment.

**2. TOXIC GASES, SUCH AS CHLORINE AND AMMONIA.** Most household bleach is sodium hypochlorite, a moderately toxic chlorine salt. Chlorine bleach is dangerous when combined with ammonia or acids such as vinegar, because toxic gases are released. In the wastewater stream, household bleach can bond with other chemicals to form simple organochlorines. Organochlorines can cause cancer and endocrine disruption. Ammonia is a suspected mutagen; is poisonous, corrosive, and explosive; and can cause chronic inflammation.

**3. HEAVY METALS.** Heavy metals are highly toxic. Lead, a common example, is a carcinogen, mutagen, and neurotoxic poison. Exposure can result in loss of IQ, headache, fatigue, sleep disturbances, aching bones and muscles, convulsions, brain and kidney damage, and death. Mercury poisoning can cause brain damage, irritability, memory loss, tremors, kidney disease, decreased fertility, and death.

**4. VOLATILE ORGANIC COMPOUNDS (VOCs).** Volatile organic compounds are chemicals that evaporate into the air and react with sunlight to form ground-level ozone. Formaldehyde and solvents are VOCs and are some of the most dangerous pollutants in household building products. Volatile organic compounds include carcinogens, endocrine disrupters, central nervous system disrupters, and sensitizers.

**5. PLASTICS.** The first clue that plastics could cause endocrine disruption came when it was discovered that the plastic tubing used in laboratories leached chemicals that mimicked the hormone estrogen. To make plastics flexible, phthalate is added. Phthalates are endocrine disrupters and are used in most plastics. Styrene is another endocrine disrupter that is used in the manufacture of many plastics.

# Putting Better Basics into Practice

Most people have some practical concerns about living without toxic chemicals. Just how much of a change is it going to be? Does living this way take more time? Is it more expensive? How do I begin? My answers to these legitimate questions follow. But basically, I suggest you just jump in and try it. I've never once had a person tell me they've regretted it. Some people want to switch to less toxic living on the spot; others stop restocking toxic cleansers as they run out, learning about the alternatives as they go along. Most start switching to natural body care gradually. Choose any way that will work for you. To make it easier to start the process of changing over, I have placed an icon (✘) at particularly easy recipes, hoping this will offer you the encouragement you need to give *Better Basics for the Home* a try.

## DOES IT TAKE MORE TIME?

Most recipes in this book can be mixed in less than a minute. That is all the time it takes to mix up cleaning products from scratch the day you need them. The quality of time spent grabbing a spray bottle of commercial product with toxic materials compared to a homemade mix is different, too. You have peace of mind knowing exactly what you are putting into that spray bottle, and knowing it is safe. Who knows, that commercial product could give you a headache and you could have to spend the afternoon on the couch. What kind of a time-saver is that?

**CLEANING.** You need to take the time to learn the basics about using less toxic materials, but after that it takes no more time to pick up a bottle of homemade cleanser than it does one that is store-bought. Many of the recipes take literally seconds to whip together. If you choose to make your own wax polish, you need fifteen minutes, but the polish smells wonderful, buffs to a high shine, doesn't pollute your home, and is well worth the effort.

**BODY CARE.** Using body care "simples" such as lemon juice for cleaning the face, followed by aloe vera gel for moisturizing, takes no more time than unscrewing a jar or cutting and squeezing the lemon. Creams and lotions take some time to make, but only when you are first learning how. After that they can be whipped up as quickly as, say, making mashed potatoes. The key is simply having the ingredients around. Making soap is a project, like making bread. Save it for a rainy or winter day when you have time to putter around in your slippers. I make a couple of batches a year, one for my family and one for holiday gifts. Home spas can take from hours to all day to complete, as well they should.

**GARDENS, PET CARE, AND PEST CONTROL.** Organic gardening and pest control products are entirely different from their chemical counterparts: You watch, think, do a little of this and that, and watch some more. The herbal repellents take a few minutes to make, then they are the same as putting on any repellent. Natural pet care takes about the same amount of time as natural body care.

**HOUSE CARE AND HOBBIES.** As with the other areas of less toxic living, safer renovating and building doesn't take longer, it just takes a different way of thinking, and adjusting to that takes time. Crafts and hobbies are meant to take time, and the *Better Basics for the Home* recipes don't add or subtract any.

## COST SAVINGS

For years I have compared the cost of products most people might have under their kitchen sink and in their medicine cabinet with formulas I make myself, matching the products ounce for ounce. Although prices fluctuate with the years, my general finding has always been that homemade formulas cost about one-tenth the price of their commercial counterparts—and that includes expensive essential oils and concentrated, all-purpose detergents for homemade recipes. Our family saves so much money living this way that we still save money overall when we buy expensive essential oils such as tea tree oil, which is the best for certain jobs, such as killing mold and treating an eczema rash. Without those additions, homemade products would cost closer to one-twentieth the price of store-bought products.

## BUT DO THESE FORMULAS WORK?

The answer is yes, because they are based on simple chemistry. After studying thousands of formulas, I've concluded that most modern chemical companies copy the old folk recipes, using synthetic ingredients instead of natural ones. The folk recipes were based on good science and had the special ingredients—fresh lemon juice in a furniture polish, compared to a synthetic acid, or real lemon oil compared to petroleum oil with synthetic lemon fragrance. For skin care, the old formula would have an emollient vegetable or nut oil for the skin, for example, whereas the modern product usually contains pore-clogging mineral oil. The healing, protective, and antibacterial properties of beeswax used in old-fashioned creams have been lost to paraffin, a petroleum wax that gives the skin nothing.

Folk recipes were often intuitively based on the pH scale of acids and alkaline bases. On the pH scale, 7 is neutral, with anything above that being an alkaline base (baking soda, washing soda, borax, and lye are examples), and anything under 7 being an acid (vinegar, lemon juice, silk, and wool, for example). Baking soda would be used in cleaning to neutralize acidic materials, and vinegar would be used for those that were alkaline. Vinegar would be used to make a substance more acidic, such as a solution for washing wool, where an alkaline material such as soap would damage the fibers.

My daughter was taught about acids and bases in third grade in a way that is easy for any of us to do at home. Simply boil a red cabbage cut into wedges in just enough water to cover. Let cool, then strain the blue-purple juice into a jar. Cabbage juice has a neutral pH—a blue-purple color. When it is added to acids, it turns pink; when added to alkalines, it turns yellowish green. If you want to neu-

tralize an odor or a stain but don't know its pH, use the red-cabbage-juice test. Our cutting board turned pink with the test and I grabbed the baking soda. A grass stain turned yellowish green, so I soaked the garment in vinegar.

Using minerals for household chores is an astonishing discovery, and once you use them you can forgo dangerous chemical solvents for good. Highly alkaline, minerals neutralize and deodorize a lot of odors; they also dissolve grease and are safe, mild abrasives. Mixing baking soda with liquid soap until creamy makes my all-time favorite recipe, a soft scrubber for the bathtub. Washing soda is so strong it will curl wax right up off the floor—handy if you want to remove wax. My friend Pat runs a daycare center in her home, and she cleans with simple homemade formulas and always passes state inspections.

Some of the most sophisticated skin care ingredients are simple plants that hydrate, heal, and nourish. The famous Queen of Hungary Water, an herbal vinegar used as an astringent and hair rinse, and Cleopatra's famed milk baths were alpha-hydroxy acids, which naturally exfoliate dead skin cells and leave the skin soft and supple. Sweet birch is full of salicylates, acids that are anti-inflammatory. A basic birch-water formula can be used for many purposes. It is powerfully antiseptic and was a staple ingredient in nineteenth-century personal care products for clear complexions and is an excellent shampoo and conditioner (for dandruff in particular). It also cuts body oils and grease in the kitchen sink. Native Americans use birch water as a parasite remedy. Many old recipes are full of such helpful "secret" ingredients.

After fifteen years of cleaning without toxic chemicals, I can report unequivocally that less toxic cleaning works. My home is at least as clean as any working parent's—fastidious sometimes and a disaster at others—but my windows are as clear as my neighbors' (when I clean them), the bathroom tiles shine, and the refrigerator sparkles.

# A Simpler, Healthier Way of Life

I should warn you, using common sense and choosing what is generally regarded as safe will result in your rejecting the vast majority of consumer products. But what you gain is a simpler, cheaper, and healthier way of life.

All of us come at a concept such as simplicity from different angles. Finding simplicity in our lives is like peeling an onion—there are many different layers. There is the simplicity of decor, for example. Or the simplicity of movement. Listening to the water of a fountain, or the rain on the roof of a tent, seems to calm and simplify one's thinking. Things that are simple seem to give a sense of ease. Usually when we think of simplicity, we think of things that are pared down.

*Better Basics for the Home* pares down simple tasks of day-to-day living to just a few basic, safe materials. There is less to worry about, our pace can become less frenetic, we have an eas-

ier way of life, and we have peace of mind knowing that the ingredients we are using for our daily chores won't cause harm. This can improve the quality of our lives.

There is another aspect of simplicity to be discovered when using simple ingredients. Just as in planting a seed and seeing it come up, there is a visible connection between mixing a few ingredients and seeing the resulting product emerge. Such a relationship is genuinely straightforward. There is nothing intangible, no cause for worry about packages, trucks, warehouses, smokestacks, chemists, or life cycles. When we grab a commercial product, there is, I think, a false sense of simplicity.

I have gained good health by living in a healthy home. But the deepest gratification in living a less toxic way of life is knowing that my family's health is protected from unnecessary chemical overload. I worry a lot less because I know our home is a haven, a natural sanctuary, a place for our bodies to rest and recuperate. The quality of our lives is improved because our bodies are under less stress. In addition to causing cancer, many synthetic chemicals affect our central nervous systems, and that can leave us cranky, irritable, or with a headache. By contrast, fresh, clean air renews and rejuvenates. People tell me all the time that living in a less toxic home improves their sleep, makes their babies less fussy, improves their children's concentration, and improves their sense of well-being. Step-by-step, you too can make a healthy home, and I urge you to try your hand at it.

# CHAPTER 1

# The Basics

THIS is the nuts and bolts chapter of *Better Basics for the Home.* Here is where you will find practical information for putting a less toxic lifestyle into practice: a glossary of ingredients; helpful equipment and accessories; the basic formulas for creams, lotions, herbal infusions, soap,

and other mixtures; how to package your homemade products and even turn them into gifts; how to find ingredients; and guidelines for buying commercial products.

Many of the ingredients called for in this book's recipes are found in the kitchen cupboard and outdoors in nearby woods, even in city parks. Others are found in the produce section of the supermarket or in the garden. *Better Basics for the Home* introduces a new world of uses for herbs and essential oils, fruits and vegetables, minerals and stones. Putting

these natural ingredients together in useful ways is a process of discovery that can be fun and interesting. It is an exciting feeling to make your first skin cream or bar of soap, and it is reassuring to discover how quickly these preparations can be assembled.

There is a great deal of leeway in making the recipes in *Better Basics for the Home.* Experiment and find out what works for you. I've read thousands of formulas and often seen the same ingredients used fifteen different ways, with changed ratios every time. And all of the resulting products worked. Follow your intuition— explore the way different materials feel on your skin and hair, how well they clean your countertops or make your garden grow, then adapt them by adding a little more of this or less of that if you think it might make a product more appealing to you. Get a feel for the process and be flexible. The only rule to follow is to be safe—don't burn yourself, misuse essential oils, or take risks with lye when making soap.

# GLOSSARY OF INGREDIENTS

## PLANTS

### HERBS

Herbs have many attributes that make them useful in household formulas. They may repel insects; they may be antiseptic, fragrant, or preservative; or they may provide powerful therapeutic benefits to body care products. Many herbs can be used in formulas simply for their pleasing fragrance, such as a lavender-scented soft scrubber, for example. But most herbs used in the recipes given here do double or multiple duty. The lavender that scents the soft scrubber also gives the product disinfectant properties, preserves it, and repels insects.

NOTE: The medicinal attributes of herbs are legendary, but they are not detailed under the specific herbs listed below because medical remedies are beyond the scope of this book.

*A Note on Harvesting Herbs:* It is important to pick wild herbs ecologically (to "wild craft"). Use only herbs that grow abundantly in many areas, and leave rare and overharvested plants alone. Take only what you need. Contact Jean's Greens for guidelines on ecological harvesting (see Sources and Resources).

**Alkanet.** Alkanet is a plant of the borage family.
> *Part Used:* Bright maroon root, dried and pulverized.
>
> *Attributes:* Alkanet's red pigment is the constituent primarily sought after, but alkanet is also soluble in oil and has protective qualities for the skin.
>
> *Uses in BETTER BASICS FOR THE HOME:* As a pigment in wood stain formulas and in body care products such as lipstick.

Available in health food stores and from herb suppliers.

**Allspice.** An aromatic evergreen tree.
> *Parts Used:* Berries (dried and powdered), essential oil.
>
> *Attributes:* Rich in nutrients; fragrant and antiseptic.
>
> *Uses in BETTER BASICS FOR THE HOME:* In men's body care products and in baths.

Powdered allspice berries are available in any supermarket; essential oil is available from herb suppliers.

**Aloe Vera.** A plant with succulent leaves native to Africa. Aloe is easily grown as a houseplant.

*Part Used:* Clear gel contained in the leaf.

*Attributes:* Aloe vera is antibacterial, antifungal, antiseptic, anti-inflammatory, and astringent. Heals burns, acne, age spots, sunburn, and rashes. Contains the immune system stimulant aloectin B. Aloe penetrates all three layers of the skin and is deeply hydrating and moisturizing.

*Uses in BETTER BASICS FOR THE HOME:* Aloe is used for the skin and hair in body care formulas.

Available in health food stores and from herb suppliers.

**Arrowroot.** Perennial cultivated mainly in South America and the Caribbean.

*Part Used:* Roots (dried and powdered).

*Attributes:* The roots contain up to a quarter of their weight as starch.

*Uses in BETTER BASICS FOR THE HOME:* As a thickener in body care products and as a body powder.

Available in supermarkets and from herb suppliers.

**Birch (Sweet or Black).** A tall woodland tree native to the northeastern United States and Canada.

*Parts Used:* Inner bark or twigs made into an infusion; birch bud essential oil.

*Attributes:* Contains high amounts of salicylic and tannic acid. (Salicylate is the active ingredient in aspirin.) It is anti-inflammatory, healing for tissue, astringent, antiviral, and antiseptic. It also cuts grease.

*Uses in BETTER BASICS FOR THE HOME:* In cleaning for its grease-cutting and antiseptic qualities, and in body care for the skin and hair.

Available from herb suppliers.

**Black and Green Tea.** Both teas are made from the evergreen shrub family Theaceae (not to be confused with the *Melaleuca* tree, source of Australian tea tree oil). Tea grows in Asia and Africa.

*Part Used:* Black tea is made by drying and fermenting tea leaves. Green tea is dried but not fermented. The leaves are infused to make tea.

*Attributes:* Black tea contains strong tannins, making it a useful dye, dust mite repellent, and astringent. Green tea contains potent flavonoids and polyphenolic catechins, antioxidants that play an important roll in the prevention of skin cell damage. It has documented anticarcinogenic effects, soothes and moisturizes skin, and protects from the dangers of UVB rays.

*Uses in BETTER BASICS FOR THE HOME:* Black tea is used in housekeeping for repelling dust mites, in body care as an astringent, and in house care as a dye in paints and stains. Green tea is used in body care products for its healing and soothing qualities, and in sunscreen and antiaging skin-care formulas.

Available in supermarkets and health food stores.

**Black Walnut.** Oily nuts from the black walnut tree, which grows in eastern North America.

*Parts Used:* Shells (pulverized) and oil from the nuts.

*Attributes:* The shells make an excellent brown dye; the oil is powerfully antifungal.

*Uses in BETTER BASICS FOR THE HOME:* As a hair and furniture dye, and for skin problems including athlete's foot, eczema, and acne.

Available in health food stores and from herb suppliers.

**Calendula.** Also known as pot marigold, calendula is a plant with bright yellow flowers native to Europe.

*Part Used:* Flowers (infused or crushed).

*Attributes:* Calendula flowers are highly emollient, antibacterial, anti-inflammatory, antifungal, and antiviral. They are immune system stimulants and are rich in carotenoids.

*Uses in BETTER BASICS FOR THE HOME:* In body care, calendula is useful for skin problems including eczema, psoriasis, varicose veins, diaper rash, burns, and acne. It brings out blond highlights in hair and is a stimulant in baths. Calendula also repels garden pests such as cabbage maggot, corn earworm, cucumber beetle, Mexican beetle, and rabbits.

Available in health food stores and from herb suppliers.

*Caution:* Do not use calendula when pregnant. Use with caution if you are allergic to ragweed.

**Camphor.** An evergreen tree native to Japan and China.

*Part Used:* Volatile essential oil.

*Attributes:* Pest repellent; also healing for skin problems such as cold sores.

*Uses in BETTER BASICS FOR THE HOME:* Camphor is an excellent moth and mole repellent. In body care, camphor is used occasionally for skin problems.

Available in health food stores and from herb suppliers.

*Caution:* Don't take camphor internally or when pregnant. Don't buy synthetic camphor oil; it is toxic.

**Carnauba Wax.** Wax made from the leaves of a Brazilian palm tree.

*Part Used:* Wax.

*Attributes:* Carnauba wax is the hardest of waxes.

*Uses in BETTER BASICS FOR THE HOME:* Carnauba is used in floor, furniture, and car waxes.

Available in some hardware stores and from mail order supply houses.

**Chamomile (Roman or German).** An herb that grows wild in Europe and other temperate regions. It resembles a daisy.

*Part Used:* Flowers (infused or crushed).

*Attributes:* Chamomile is anti-inflammatory, antiseptic, antimicrobial, antiallergenic, astringent, and antioxidant. It contains tannins, flavonoids, and salicylates and is rich in minerals.

*Uses in BETTER BASICS FOR THE HOME:* In body care, chamomile is used in skin care (it is particularly good for sensitive skin, helps reduce and prevent wrinkles, helps eczema, is astringent and cleansing, and is healing and moisturizing) and to lighten hair. Chamomile is used to repel pests such as wasps and flies. In housekeeping, it is useful as a strewing herb: It helps freshen the air. Available in health food stores and from herb suppliers.

*Caution:* Chamomile is a member of the ragweed family and should be avoided by those sensitive to ragweed.

**Chickweed.** Chickweed is a low-growing perennial weed with small leaves. It grows in the wild and in gardens in Europe and North America.

*Part Used:* Leaves (infused or crushed).

*Attributes:* Contains saponins and antioxidants. It is emollient and healing for the skin.

*Uses in BETTER BASICS FOR THE HOME:* In body care, chickweed is used to help heal skin problems such as psoriasis, eczema, and diaper rash.

Available in yards and gardens and from herb suppliers. Chickweed doesn't dry well, so it is best to find a fresh, local supply.

**Cinnamon.** A spice that is extensively cultivated throughout tropical regions.

*Part Used:* Inner bark (powdered or broken in bits and decocted).

*Attributes:* A highly aromatic bark. It is astringent (being rich in tannins), antifungal, antiseptic, and antibacterial.

*Uses in BETTER BASICS FOR THE HOME:* In body care, cinnamon is used as an antiseptic astringent primarily in men's products such as aftershave.

Available in supermarkets and health food stores.

**Cleavers (Goosegrass).** A wild weed common to temperate areas such as Europe, Australia, and North America.

*Part Used:* Leaves (infused or crushed).

*Attributes:* Contains glycosides, tannin, and citric acid. It reportedly is a detoxifying herb, cleansing the lymph system and thereby helping to treat skin diseases.

*Uses in BETTER BASICS FOR THE HOME:* In body care, for the treatment of skin diseases.

Available in health food stores and from herb suppliers.

**Comfrey.** A leafy perennial herb native to Europe and naturalized around the world.

*Parts Used:* Leaves (infused or crushed) and roots (decocted).

*Attributes:* Rich in allantoin, a cell proliferant that helps repair damaged tissue. Comfrey leaves contain tannins and saponins; the roots are rich in allantoin mucilage. Comfrey also contains alkaloids, which are toxic to the liver and may be carcinogenic.

*Uses in BETTER BASICS FOR THE HOME:* Comfrey is used in body care to stimulate new skin growth, as an antiwrinkle agent, to heal wounds, and to treat dandruff and varicose veins.

Available in health food stores and from herb suppliers.

*Caution:* Do not use comfrey internally or when pregnant, and use for only limited times externally. Do not boil comfrey; heat can destroy the allantoin.

**Echinacea.** Also known as coneflower, this plant is native to the United States and has bright lavender daisylike flowers with a rust-colored center.

*Part Used:* Roots (decocted).

*Attributes:* Echinacea stimulates the immune system. It is also known to be anti-inflammatory, antibacterial, and antiallergenic.

*Uses in BETTER BASICS FOR THE HOME:* Used in body care for skin problems such as burns and athlete's foot.

Available in health food stores and from herb suppliers.

**Eucalyptus.** Evergreen native to Australia and Tasmania with blue-gray leaves.

*Parts Used:* Leaves (infused) and essential oil.

*Attributes:* Highly antiseptic, germicidal, and repellent to insects.

*Uses in BETTER BASICS FOR THE HOME:* Used in body care in menthol formulas and as an antiseptic and astringent for the skin.

Available in health food stores and from herb suppliers.

**Henna.** Flowering shrub native to the Middle East, India, and North Africa.

*Parts Used:* Leaves (infused) and bark (decocted).

*Attributes:* Primarily used as a hair dye. Henna is antifungal, antibacterial, and a humectant.

*Uses in BETTER BASICS FOR THE HOME:* Used in body care for the hair as a reddish brown dye, although neutral henna is also used as a hair conditioner.

Available in health food stores and from herb suppliers.

**Horsetail.** A weed common to North America and other temperate climates, horsetail has fernlike leaves and grows to about 18 inches high.

*Part Used:* Leaves (infused).

*Attributes:* Strengthens nails and hair because of its high (as much as 70 percent) silica content. The silica also makes it useful as an abrasive for cleaning metal and wood.

*Uses in BETTER BASICS FOR THE HOME:* In cleaning and body care.

Available in damp woods and roadsides and from herb suppliers. Avoid *E. palustre* horsetail.

**Irish Moss.** A reddish brown seaweed found on the Atlantic coast.

*Part Used:* Dried moss (infused or crushed).

*Attributes:* Contains large amounts of polysaccharides and nutritious minerals. Commonly used as an emulsifier and binding agent because it becomes gel-like.

*Uses in BETTER BASICS FOR THE HOME:* In body care, for creams, lotions, and baths.

Available in health food stores and from herb suppliers.

**Lavender.** A fragrant herb easily grown in temperate climates.

*Parts Used:* Flowers (infused or crushed) and their essential oil.

*Attributes:* Lavender flowers contain a volatile oil, flavonoids, tannins, and essential oils that include the constituent linalool. Lavender is astringent, antiseptic, and antibacterial.

*Uses in BETTER BASICS FOR THE HOME:* Highly prized for its fragrance and disinfectant properties, lavender oil is used in many cleaning and body care products. Lavender is also used in skin care and baths. As an insect repellent, lavender is particularly useful against mosquitoes and clothing moths. Available in health food stores and gardens and from herb suppliers.

**Lemon Balm.** Includes citronella and other members of the mint family such as pennyroyal, peppermint, and spearmint (although spearmint doesn't contain menthol). A fragrant herb easily grown in temperate climates.

*Parts Used:* Leaves (infused or crushed) and their essential oil.

*Attributes:* Contains menthol, volatile oils, antioxidants, flavonoids, and tannins. The mints are antiviral, antibacterial, and antiseptic.

*Uses in BETTER BASICS FOR THE HOME:* Cleansing and stimulating for the skin, the mints are used in everything from eczema lotions to facial steams and as an astringent for oily skin. Lemon balm can be used as a substitute for lemon oil for furniture polish, and mints in general freshen the air. Mints are excellent pest repellents—pennyroyal and citronella are famous examples—and especially repel mice, mosquitoes, and fleas.

Available in health food stores and from herb suppliers.

*Caution:* Pregnant women should not use pennyroyal. The essential oil of pennyroyal is highly toxic and should not be taken internally.

**Licorice Root.** A plant native to the Mediterranean region and parts of Asia.

*Part Used:* Roots (decocted).

*Attributes:* Emollient, anti-inflammatory, and mildly estrogenic. Contains saponins.

*Uses in BETTER BASICS FOR THE HOME:* Licorice is used in body care for facial steams because it is emollient and cleansing.

Available in health food stores and from herb suppliers.

**Neem.** A large evergreen tree whose trunk exudes a gum.

*Part Used:* Bark gum.

*Attributes:* Neem is an all-purpose, natural pesticide.

*Uses in BETTER BASICS FOR THE HOME:* Pest control.

Available from herb suppliers.

*Caution:* Pregnant women should not use neem.

**Nettle.** A weed growing wild in temperate climates.

*Part Used:* Leaves (infused or crushed) and roots (decocted), although the recipes in *Better Basics for the Home* call only for the leaves.

*Note:* Fresh nettle leaves sting—you must dry or boil them before use. To diminish the sting, rub the skin with jewelweed.

*Attributes:* Nettle is rich in nutrients, silica, and flavonoids. The root contains phenol and is antiseptic. Nettle is also antifungal, astringent, anti-inflammatory, and antihistamine.

*Uses in BETTER BASICS FOR THE HOME:* Nettle is used in body care formulas. It is good for skin problems, promotes hair growth, and is highly nutritious for skin and hair. For gardening, nettle is an excellent addition to compost, and nettle tea is nutritious for houseplants.

Available from health food stores and herb suppliers.

**Orris Root.** A flowering perennial native to the Mediterranean region.

*Part Used:* Roots (powder).

*Attributes:* The root has the fragrance of violets and is used as a fixative in perfumes and potpourri because its resinous oils stay strong for a long time. It is antibacterial and high in tannin and resin.

*Uses in BETTER BASICS FOR THE HOME:* Orris root is used as a fixative in perfumes, sachets, and potpourris.

Available from herb suppliers.

**Pennyroyal.** See Lemon Balm (page 17).

**Pyrethrum.** Including pyrethrin, pyrethrum, and pyrethroids. Pyrethrum powder comes from ground chrysanthemum flowers and contains the active ingredient pyrethrin, which kills many insects. Don't confuse pyrethrum with pyrethroids. The latter are synthetic pesticides and should be avoided.

*Part Used:* Flowers (infused or crushed).

*Attributes:* A natural pesticide.

*Uses in BETTER BASICS FOR THE HOME:* As a pesticide.

*Caution:* Pregnant women should not use pyrethrum. Many people are allergic to pyrethrum, so use it with caution.

Available in organic gardening stores.

**Rose.** A garden shrub native to the Middle East but naturalized throughout the world.

*Part Used:* Flower petals.

*Attributes:* Rose petals are rich in tannin and terpenes. They are astringent, anti-inflammatory, antiseptic, and aromatic. Rose hips are high in vitamin C.

*Uses in BETTER BASICS FOR THE HOME:* Rose water is often used as a fragrance and as a skin softener. In housekeeping, rose petals make excellent additions to potpourris and sachets.

Available in gardens and from herb suppliers.

**Rosemary.** An evergreen shrub with needle-like, aromatic leaves.

*Part Used:* Leaves (infused or crushed).

*Attributes:* An herb rich in flavonoids, camphor, phenol, resins, and saponin. Its volatile oil is anti-inflammatory, astringent, antibacterial, and antifungal.

*Uses in BETTER BASICS FOR THE HOME:* In cleaning, rosemary is an aromatic, disinfectant cleanser. Rosemary is used a great deal in body care recipes; it helps keep hair healthy and promotes growth, and it is healing and antiseptic for skin disorders. It is an excellent cleanser and astringent. In gardens, rosemary attracts beneficial insects and repels carrot flies, Mexican bean beetles, slugs, and snails.

Available in supermarkets and health food stores and from herb suppliers.

**Sage.** A silver-green herb native to the Mediterranean region and naturalized worldwide.

*Part Used:* Leaves (infused or crushed).

*Attributes:* Rich in tannin, volatile oils, terpene, camphor, antioxidants, flavonoids, and phenol. Sage is antibacterial and antiseptic.

*Uses in BETTER BASICS FOR THE HOME:* For body care, sage makes a good antibacterial gargle and mouthwash; darkens gray hair; is astringent, cleansing, and good for acne; is a particularly good deodorant; and is moisturizing and softening for the skin. Sage is disinfectant and good for cleaning. It attracts bees and is a good companion plant with carrots, strawberries, and tomatoes. As an insect repellent, sage works well against flies, cabbage moths, and carrot flies.

Available in supermarkets and health food stores and from herb suppliers.

*Caution:* Do not use sage when pregnant because of the phenol content.

**Soap Bark (Quillaja Bark).** Evergreen native to Peru and Chile.

*Part Used:* Bark (decocted).

*Attributes:* Rich in saponin, a soapy constituent.

*Uses in BETTER BASICS FOR THE HOME:* Soap-free cleansing of skin and hair. Soap bark literally foams and lathers.

Available from rain forest herb suppliers.

**St. John's Wort.** Hardy perennial native to Europe and naturalized in North America.

*Part Used:* Flowers (infused or crushed).

*Attributes:* Natural antibiotic, full of volatile oil, flavonoids, tannins, and resins. Contains hypericin, a strong antiviral ingredient. Astringent, antiseptic, anti-inflammatory, and an immune system stimulant.

*Uses in BETTER BASICS FOR THE HOME:* Used extensively in body care creams and salves for skin problems and disorders.

Available in local fields and meadows and from herb suppliers.

*Caution:* Do not use if pregnant.

**Stevia.** A plant native to the Americas, with sweet leaves and buds.

*Parts Used:* Leaves and buds (powdered).

*Attributes:* The plant has thirty times the sweetness of sugar and no calories.

*Uses in BETTER BASICS FOR THE HOME:* To disguise the taste of baking soda in toothpaste.

Available in health food stores and from herb suppliers.

**Thyme.** An aromatic shrub native to the Mediterranean region and naturalized throughout the world.

*Parts Used:* Leaves (infused or crushed) and essential oil.

*Attributes:* Thyme's high phenol content makes it one of the most antiseptic of all the essential oils. The oil is toxic and must be used with caution.

*Uses in BETTER BASICS FOR THE HOME:* Because of thyme's phenol content, it can be used in cleaning as a disinfectant. It is sometimes used as a natural fumigant. For body care, thyme is used for its antiseptic and antibacterial qualities.

Available in supermarkets and health food stores and from herb suppliers.

*Caution:* Do not use if pregnant. Also, you should only buy thyme essential oil that has had its irritating properties removed by being distilled twice.

**Witch Hazel.** A tree that has been naturalized throughout North America.

*Parts Used:* Leaves (infused); twigs and bark (decocted); as a store-bought extract.

*Attributes:* Witch hazel contains tannic and gallic acid as well as volatile oils. It is highly astringent, cleansing, antioxidant, and anti-inflammatory.

*Uses in BETTER BASICS FOR THE HOME:* Witch hazel is used as a cleanser and an astringent in body care recipes. It is good for eczema. Available in supermarkets (as an extract) and health food stores and from herb suppliers.

## OTHER PLANT-BASED INGREDIENTS

### ESSENTIAL OILS

Essential oils are aromatic liquids extracted from flowers, grasses, fruits, leaves, roots, and trees. There are hundreds of essential oils, and they are used for everything from insect repellents to aromatherapy and fragrance. Be sure to use 100 percent pure oils, and use with caution. Essential oils can burn the skin and should not be ingested. All the terpene essential oils are disinfectants; they include thyme, sweet orange, lemongrass, rose, clove, eucalyptus, cinnamon, rosemary, orris root, birch, tea tree, and lavender. These oils serve many purposes because of their antiseptic and antifungal properties. *Better Basics for the Home* uses these oils as disinfectants, mold eradicators, and air fresheners and in body care products. They are also used as preservatives. Essential oils are commonly used for fragrance in potpourris, air fresheners, sachets, and even as a rinse for clothes.

Available in health food stores and from herb suppliers.

*Caution:* When pregnant, avoid the essential oils of pennyroyal, sage, wintergreen, basil, myrrh, and thyme. Also, essential oils can harm the eyes, so be sure not to get shampoos, rinses, or conditioners in the eyes. Don't add more than 3 drops of essential oil per ounce of base preparation used near the eyes.

## PLANT EXTRACTS AND DERIVATIVES

**Glycerin.** Glycerin is formed when vegetable oils such as olive and coconut are combined with an alkali to make soap. It is a thick, sweet, fatty liquid, soluble in water and alcohol. Soap made at home will contain glycerin, but it has been removed from most commercial soap.

*Attributes:* Glycerin is a humectant: It absorbs 50 percent of its weight in moisture from the air. It is used in many cream and polish formulas because it helps oil mix with water. Glycerin also dissolves many forms of dirt and has antifreeze properties.

*Uses in BETTER BASICS FOR THE HOME:* In body care formulas, glycerin is used because it is a humectant, emollient, and lubricant. For cleaning, glycerin is known to help prevent hardening and cracking of leather; it is lubricating because it retains moisture. Pure vegetable glycerin is available in health food stores.

**Grapefruit Seed Extract.** An extract made from grapefruit seeds.

*Part Used:* Liquid extract of grapefruit seeds.

*Attributes:* Powerfully antibacterial.

*Uses in BETTER BASICS FOR THE HOME:* As a preservative.

Available in health food stores.

**Vinegar.** Vinegar is an acid made from the fermentation of dilute alcoholic liquids. Historically, it was made by the natural souring of wine or apple cider.

*Attributes:* The acid in vinegar neutralizes alkaline substances such as scale from hard water. Vinegar is also disinfectant and anti-fungal.

*Uses in BETTER BASICS FOR THE HOME:* Vinegar is used extensively in cleaning formulas because it dissolves gummy buildup, eats away tarnish, and removes dirt from wood surfaces. White distilled vinegar is used to avoid stains while cleaning. In body care, vinegar is an ingredient in many formulas because it is an alpha-hydroxy acid and astringent. Organic apple cider vinegar is recommended for body care.

Available in supermarkets; organic apple cider vinegar is available in health food stores.

## OTHER OILS

**Almond Oil.** An oil extracted from the almond nut.

*Attributes:* High in protein, it is also lubricating and moisturizing for the skin.

*Uses in BETTER BASICS FOR THE HOME:* Used in creams and lotions, particularly for dry skin, and as a base for herbal infusions.
Available in health food stores.

**Apricot Kernel Oil (Persic Oil).** Natural oil from the kernel of an apricot pit.

*Attributes:* Lubricating and moisturizing.

*Uses in BETTER BASICS FOR THE HOME:* Used in creams and lotions, especially for sensi-

tive or older skin, for its rich, lubricating qualities.
Available in health food stores.

**Avocado Oil.** Derived from the avocado.

*Attributes:* High in vitamins A, D, and E. One of the most moisturizing oils, it is rich and penetrating for the skin.

*Uses in BETTER BASICS FOR THE HOME:* Used in dry-skin creams and lotions and for eczema and scalp problems.
Available in health food stores and from herb suppliers.

**Carnauba Wax.** Wax made from the leaves of a Brazilian palm tree.

*Part Used:* Wax.

*Attributes:* Carnauba wax is the hardest of waxes.

**Castor Oil.** From the seeds of the castor oil plant.

*Attributes:* This lubricating oil is soluble in alcohol, making it useful for some applications, such as aftershave. It is a good enough lubricant to be used in airplane engines.

*Uses in BETTER BASICS FOR THE HOME:* As a lubricant and in some skin care salves.
Available in pharmacies.

**Cocoa Butter.** Obtained from the cacao plant, cocoa butter is a semisolid vegetable fat with a low melting point.

*Attributes:* Used as a stabilizing ingredient in creams. Cocoa butter is water repellent and protective of the skin.

*Uses in BETTER BASICS FOR THE HOME:* Cocoa butter is used in body care formulas in creams, particularly sunscreens. It is also used in some moisturizers and is particularly useful for dry and dehydrated skin, cradle cap, and eczema.

Available in health food stores and from herb suppliers.

**Coconut Oil.** Extracted from fresh coconuts, coconut oil is a white vegetable fat.

*Attributes:* Coconut oil is the most lathering of oils; it is semisolid and serves as a stabilizer, which is why it is preferred in soaps. It also washes off easily and doesn't stain towels, making it an oil of choice for massage therapists.

*Uses in BETTER BASICS FOR THE HOME:* Coconut oil is used in soap and some creams and as a massage oil.

Available in health food stores and from herb suppliers.

**Jojoba.** A liquid wax from the jojoba tree that never goes rancid.

*Attributes:* High in essential fatty acids, jojoba is antiseptic, a good lubricant, and an excellent substitute for the old formulas that called for sperm whale oil.

*Uses in BETTER BASICS FOR THE HOME:* Used as an engine lubricant and in body care products such as cold creams and lotions.

Available in health food stores and from herb suppliers.

**Linseed Oil.** Linseed oil is made from flax seeds.

*Attributes:* High in essential fatty acids, linseed oil is a good lubricating oil for wood and is soluble in turpentine. It will harden when exposed to air, which is why it is the base in many paints. Most commercial linseed oil is boiled to shorten the drying time.

*Uses in BETTER BASICS FOR THE HOME:* Linseed oil and flax seeds are used in numerous body care products because they are softening. Taking linseed oil internally is recommended to treat dry skin. Linseed oil is also used in paints, stains, polishes, and waxes.

*Note About Shopping for Linseed Oil:* Most if not all linseed oil found in hardware stores has chemical dryers and should be avoided. Instead, buy pure boiled linseed oil from a wood-finishing supply catalog (see Sources and Resources). Or buy pure linseed oil at health food stores.

*Note:* To make your own bleached and thickened linseed oil (to use instead of boiled linseed oil for wood care), set flax oil in the sun for three to four days uncovered. Cover at night. To purify rancid linseed oil (for wood care only), add baking soda (5 percent of the weight of the oil).

**Peanut Oil.** A colorless or yellow, fatty, nondrying oil obtained from peanuts.

*Attributes:* Peanut oil is nutritious and good for all skin types.

*Uses in BETTER BASICS FOR THE HOME:* Peanut oil is used in creams, lotions, and massage oils.

Available in health food stores and from herb suppliers.

**Sesame Oil.** The oil of sesame seeds.

*Attributes:* Sesame oil is anti-inflammatory, a natural sunscreen, and rich in lecithin and protein.

*Uses in BETTER BASICS FOR THE HOME:* Used for skin problems such as psoriasis and eczema; good for all skin types.

Available in health food stores.

**Shea Butter (Karite Butter or African Butter).** A butter from the nuts of the magnolia tree of central Africa.

*Attributes:* Shea butter is high in triglycerides; it is an emollient and a natural sunscreen.

*Uses in BETTER BASICS FOR THE HOME:* Used in moisturizers, sunscreens, and hair conditioners.

Available in health food stores and from herb suppliers.

**Walnut Oil.** The oil pressed from walnut meat.

*Attributes:* A light oil high in essential fatty acids. It has traditionally been used for paints and varnishes because it dries clear, unlike linseed oil, which can yellow. Like linseed oil, walnut oil hardens when exposed to air.

*Uses in BETTER BASICS FOR THE HOME:* In furniture finishes and paint.

Available in health food stores.

**Wheat Germ Oil.** Extracted from wheat germ (the embryo of the wheat kernel separated in milling).

*Attributes:* High in vitamin E and many other vitamins and minerals.

*Uses in BETTER BASICS FOR THE HOME:* Used as a preservative because of its vitamin E content, and in nutritious, antioxidant creams for aging or injured skin.

Available in health food stores and from herb suppliers.

## MISCELLANEOUS PLANTS

**Peat Moss (Sphagnum).** Large genus of mosses that grow only in wet, low-pH areas where they become compacted with other plant materials and debris to form peat.

*Part Used:* Moss.

*Attributes:* Nutritious topsoil substitute.

*Uses in BETTER BASICS FOR THE HOME:* Soil amendment.

Available in gardening centers.

## MINERALS

Minerals that are alkaline, such as baking soda and washing soda, work like magic for cleaning because they neutralize acid-based odors and stains. With their help you can eliminate the need for toxic solvents. You can effectively clean the oven with nothing more than baking soda and water, for example. And minerals are unsurpassed in their ability to deodorize and clean the air. Add to these attributes the fact that they are nonabrasive cleansers, and you have a powerful line of defense for many heavy-duty cleaning challenges.

**Alum.** White mineral salt from clay or root, which contains aluminum.

*Attributes:* Alum is a strong astringent.

*Uses in BETTER BASICS FOR THE HOME:* Used as a preservative. It is not included in body care formulas because of the controversy about whether aluminum contributes to Alzheimer's disease.

Commonly used for pickling, alum is available in the spice section of the supermarket.

**Baking Soda.** Mineral made from soda ash.

*Attributes:* Baking soda is slightly alkaline (pH about 8.1; 7 is neutral), so it neutralizes acid-based odors in water, and it adsorbs odors from the air.

*Uses in BETTER BASICS FOR THE HOME:* For cleaning, baking soda can be used as a gentle, nonabrasive cleanser for kitchen countertops, sinks, bathtubs, ovens, and fiberglass. For laundry, it eliminates perspiration odors and even neutralizes the smell of many chemicals (add up to a cup per load to the washing machine). It is a useful air freshener and a fine carpet deodorizer.

Available in the baking supplies section of the supermarket.

**Borax.** Alkaline mineral that is toxic in high doses.

*Attributes:* Used as a preservative in many formulas, such as wallpaper paste. It is also used as an emulsifier, stabilizer, and deodorizer.

*Uses in BETTER BASICS FOR THE HOME:* Borax is used in cleaning and pest control.

Available in the laundry supplies section of the supermarket.

*Caution:* Some borax is contaminated with arsenic where it is mined, according to the Washington Toxics Coalition. For this reason I use borax sparingly and not in body care.

**Chalk.** Calcium carbonate; see Whiting, page 26.

**Clays.** Clay is an earthy material that hardens when dry. Clay comes in a variety of naturally occurring colors (red, yellow, green, gray, white). Green clay is particularly drying to the skin. White kaolin (fuller's earth) is a fine-textured natural clay.

*Attributes:* Used for masks because it draws oils, impurities, and toxins from the skin.

*Uses in BETTER BASICS FOR THE HOME:* As a skin mask.

Available in health food stores and from herb suppliers.

**Cornstarch.** Starch made from corn.

*Attributes:* A thickener, cornstarch absorbs moisture.

*Uses in BETTER BASICS FOR THE HOME:* Used for spot removal and as a thickener in creams.

Available in the baking supplies section of the supermarket.

**Cream of Tartar.** Purified and crystallized bitartrate of potassium; a residual by-product of fermentation that is scraped out of the barrels used to make wine.

*Attributes:* An acid.

*Uses in BETTER BASICS FOR THE HOME:* Used as an acid-based abrasive cleanser, and in children's craft supplies as a stabilizer. It is also an alpha-hydroxy acid and can be used as a skin exfoliant.

Available in the spice section of the supermarket.

**Emery.** Dark, granular mineral that consists of corundum.

*Attributes:* A hard, abrasive powder.

*Uses in BETTER BASICS FOR THE HOME:* Used as an abrasive.

Available in hardware stores and from wood-finishing supply catalogs.

**Lime.** See Mini-Glossary on page 284 for mason's lime (used in milk paint); see page

222 for uses for agricultural lime. Lime is highly alkaline and neutralizes acids.

Mason's lime is available in lumber supply stores; agricultural lime is available in gardening centers.

**PABA (Para-aminobenzoic Acid).** Water-soluble B vitamin derived from plants and animals.

> *Attributes:* Acts as a skin nutrient and sun protector by screening out damaging UV rays.
>
> *Uses in BETTER BASICS FOR THE HOME:* In sunscreens.

Available in powder form from herb suppliers.

**Perlite.** Volcanic glass that has a concentric shelly structure, usually grayish in color.

> *Attributes:* When expanded by heat, perlite forms a lightweight aggregate used in concrete and plaster.
>
> *Uses in BETTER BASICS FOR THE HOME:* For concrete and as a medium for potting plants.

Available in gardening supply centers.

**Plaster of Paris.** White, powdery, slightly hydrated calcium sulfate made by heating gypsum. When mixed with water, it forms a quick-setting paste.

> *Attributes:* It sets quickly.
>
> *Uses in BETTER BASICS FOR THE HOME:* House care and craft projects.

Available in hardware and craft supply stores.

> *Caution:* Do not inhale the powder, and buy additive-free plaster of paris.

**Pumice.** Volcanic glass full of cavities and light in weight.

> *Attributes:* Abrasive and moisture absorbing.

> *Uses in BETTER BASICS FOR THE HOME:* Polishing and smoothing surfaces.

Available in hardware stores and from wood-finishing supply catalogs.

> *Caution:* The fine powder should not be inhaled.

**Rottenstone.** Decomposed siliceous limestone.

> *Attributes:* Abrasive.
>
> *Uses in BETTER BASICS FOR THE HOME:* In polishes.

Available in hardware stores and from wood-finishing supply catalogs.

**Washing Soda.** A chemical relative of baking soda, washing soda (sodium carbonate) is soda ash that is processed differently than baking soda.

> *Attributes:* Washing soda is much more strongly alkaline than baking soda, with a pH around 11. It releases no harmful fumes and is far safer than commercial solvents, but you should wear gloves when using it because it is caustic.
>
> *Uses in BETTER BASICS FOR THE HOME:* Washing soda is an excellent solvent that cuts grease; removes petroleum oil, wax, or lipstick; and neutralizes odors in the same way that baking soda does. Don't use it on fiberglass or aluminum, or on waxed floors unless you intend to remove the wax. It is also an adequate paint stripper.

Available in the laundry supply section of the supermarket.

**Waterglass.** Sodium silicate, made by the fusing of washing soda (soda ash) and clean sand. It can be dissolved in water by prolonged exposure.

*Attributes:* A sealant.

*Uses in BETTER BASICS FOR THE HOME:* Used for sealants in areas where moisture is not a serious problem.

Available in hardware and lumber supply stores.

**Whiting.** Powdered calcium carbonate; chalk.

*Attributes:* White alkaline substance.

*Uses in BETTER BASICS FOR THE HOME:* Used as a base for whitewash and some milk paints.

Available in hardware and lumber supply stores.

**Zeolite.** Hydrous silicates (feldspars), which occur as secondary minerals in cavities of lava.

*Attributes:* Zeolite can act as an ion exchanger (naturally absorbing pollutants from the air).

*Uses in BETTER BASICS FOR THE HOME:* Zeolite is used as an air cleaner.

Available from mail order suppliers.

**Zinc Oxide.** White powdered derivative of pure zinc.

*Attributes:* Zinc oxide is soluble in acids and alkalines. It is mildly antiseptic, antifungal, antibacterial, and astringent, and it blocks UVA and UVB radiation.

*Uses in BETTER BASICS FOR THE HOME:* Zinc oxide is used in body care products, particularly for diaper rashes and as a sunblock.

Available as a powder from herb suppliers and as a ready-made cream in pharmacies.

## ANIMAL PRODUCTS

With the possible exception of hide glues and gelatin, no animal product discussed in *Better Basics for the Home* requires an animal to be killed. Hide glue and gelatin are usually made from animals that have died from other causes and are not killed simply for the purpose of making these products. Hide glues and gelatin are included because no other materials are as effective for keeping wood from cracking, so they are ideal for making wood musical instruments. Vegetarians should avoid gelatin protein creams, and vegans will want to avoid milk- and egg-based skin care products.

**Anhydrous Lanolin.** Oil from sheep's wool that can be removed with no harm to the sheep. An excellent waterproofer.

*Attributes:* A rich, oily cream that can easily be rubbed into leather or skin. It is commonly used by nursing mothers for cracked and sore nipples.

*Uses in BETTER BASICS FOR THE HOME:* As a water repellent for leather and in creams for skin problems.

Available in pharmacies.

**Beeswax.** Beeswax is a product of the worker bee for constructing the cell walls of the honeycomb. A yellow solid insoluble in water, it has a rich, distinctive aroma.

*Attributes:* Beeswax is used to add stiffness to creams and waxes and as an emulsifier. Beeswax protects the skin by sealing in moisture; it also has preservative properties.

*Uses in BETTER BASICS FOR THE HOME:* Beeswax is used in creams, lotions, waxes, and polishes.

Available in health food stores and from herb suppliers.

**Cochineal.** Red dye consisting of the dried bodies of female cochineal insects (small bright-red cactus-feeding scale insects).

*Attributes:* The dye.

*Uses in BETTER BASICS FOR THE HOME:* As a dye in paints and stains.

Available from artist, craft, and wood-finishing supply catalogs.

**Diatomaceous Earth (DE).** Made from the skeletons of prehistoric algae.

*Attributes:* An all-purpose pesticide powder.

*Uses in BETTER BASICS FOR THE HOME:* As a pesticide.

*Note:* Use natural diatomaceous earth, not the type sold for swimming pools.

Available in garden supply centers and from natural-pet catalogs.

**Gelatin.** Glutinous material obtained from boiling animal hooves and hides.

*Attributes:* An excellent glue for wood instruments because it contracts and expands with wood, keeping it from cracking. It is also a source of protein.

*Uses in BETTER BASICS FOR THE HOME:* Used in glues.

Available in the baking supplies section of the supermarket.

**Hide Glue.** Glutinous material obtained from boiling animal hooves and hides.

*Attributes:* An excellent glue for wood instruments because it contracts and expands with wood, keeping it from cracking. It is also a source of protein.

*Uses in BETTER BASICS FOR THE HOME:* Used in glues and in protein creams.

Available in wood-finishing supply catalogs.

**Honey.** Sweet, sticky substance made by honeybees from the nectar of flowers.

*Attributes:* Honey is a thickener, antibacterial, and humectant.

*Uses in BETTER BASICS FOR THE HOME:* Honey is used in many skin care formulas. Because it is a natural humectant (it attracts moisture to the skin), it is an excellent moisturizer. It is also nutritive and kills bacteria.

Available in supermarkets, health food stores, and specialty food markets.

**Royal Jelly.** Highly nutritious secretion of the pharyngeal glands of honeybees.

*Attributes:* One of the most nutritious substances known.

*Uses in BETTER BASICS FOR THE HOME:* Royal jelly is included in some face masks and moisturizers.

Available in health food stores; be sure to buy active royal jelly, found in the refrigerated section.

## MILK PRODUCTS

**Casein.** Milk protein used for milk paints and some face creams. Casein is made by curdling milk; the curdle is the casein. For more on casein, see page 282.

Available from artist supply and paint catalogs.

**Milk.** White substance secreted by the mammary glands of mammals for feeding their young.

*Attributes:* Nourishing, rich in calcium, and an alpha-hydroxy acid.

*Uses in BETTER BASICS FOR THE HOME:* In body care, milk is used as an alpha-hydroxy acid in skin care products.

**Shellac.** Sealant made from a scale insect excretion called lac, from India. Alcohol is used as a solvent.

*Attributes:* Lac is a naturally hard resin resistant to ultraviolet rays.

*Uses in BETTER BASICS FOR THE HOME:* Shellac is used on wood, particularly instruments and fine furniture.

Available from wood-finishing supply catalogs.

# Creating Creams and Other Formulas from Scratch

## EQUIPMENT

T I P S *Use glass, stainless steel, enamel, or—as a last choice—plastic equipment. Avoid cast iron, Teflon, and aluminum, because they can react with ingredients. Yard sales are an abundant source of cheap supplies.*

* Glass or stainless steel measuring cups and spoons (make sure you have at least one measuring cup that holds two to four cups)
* Scale (one that clearly shows ounce gradations less than one pound)
* Double boiler
* Mixer for making polishes, creams, and lotions (electric handheld mixer, blender, food processor, Vitamix, hand blender, or manual handheld mixer; I like to use an electric handheld mixer or a blender)
* Bowls
* Crock-Pot (optional)
* Coffee-bean grinder, spice mill, or mortar and pestle
* Chopsticks or wooden spoons (You will reach for a chopstick over any other stirrer

once you make your first product using beeswax.)
* Strainer
* Funnel
* Large mixing tub (for big renovating jobs such as mixing concrete)
* Rubber spatulas
* Rubber gloves
* Eyedropper

**Accessories**
* Natural-fiber exfoliating scrubbers (loofah, bristle body brush, sisal-ramie buffer)
* Natural sea sponge
* Cotton tea bags or old, clean socks (for herbal baths)
* Natural-fiber towels and washcloths
* 100 percent cellulose sponges (avoid those claiming to kill bacteria; they contain a long-lasting pesticide)
* Natural-bristle brushes
* "Green" pads made of recycled materials

### PACKAGING AND CONTAINERS
* Spray bottles

   You will need a number of spray bottles in different sizes. I'd suggest a few straightforward utility spray bottles plus some small "designer" spray bottles in pretty colors for essential oil sprays and personal care products.
* Glass jars with lids

   It is fun to place your homemade body care products in small cosmetic-sized jars; they make appealing gifts when packaged that way. Cases of six to twelve are available from herbalists' catalogs. See Sources and Resources.

Collect gallon-sized glass jars with secure lids to hold herbal vinegars such as Queen of Hungary Water. Restaurants go through great quantities of large glass jars and are usually happy to part with them.

Mason jars are excellent choices for infusing herbs and storing finished products. I bought one case each of pint- and quart-sized mason jars (they are often on sale in winter) and use them all the time.

Collect an assortment of glass jars that had food in them, washed for reuse. Wide-mouthed jars are especially useful, as are small jars such as those holding artichoke hearts.

Unless otherwise noted, avoid packaging your creams and lotions in plastic, because the plastics can leach into the ingredients and you can absorb them into your skin. For more on plastics, see page 7.

### CLEANLINESS AND CLEANUP

Rancidity of kitchen cosmetics is the biggest concern when you make your own. A clean work environment is key to avoiding spoilage by contamination with bacteria. (See page 36 for preserving kitchen cosmetics and where appropriate for other products.)

Pans, mixers, and other equipment used for making creams and other products that contain beeswax should be washed right away; once beeswax hardens, it is difficult to remove. If this happens, reheat the utensils and, once the beeswax has softened again, wipe it off with a paper towel.

### THE SHELF LIFE OF PRODUCTS

Cleaning products can be mixed on the spot for the day's cleaning. Make just enough for your use at that time. Spray cleaners with minerals, vinegar, and detergent will last indefinitely, as will those with essential oils.

Lotions, creams, infused oils, and polishes can go rancid, especially those with herbs. Add natural preservatives as described on page 36. Refrigerate the preparations when possible, and make only small batches—enough for a month. Use distilled water to prevent the addition of unwanted bacteria. Follow directions carefully. Use cosmetic "simples" (see page 34) whenever possible, and make only the amount you need at a time. Sometimes a cream or lotion will separate. That doesn't necessarily mean the product has gone bad; it may just need remixing.

Use common sense in determining if a product has gone bad. Use all your senses. If the product smells bad or if mold is growing on it, toss it out.

# The Basic Formulas

### HOW TO MAKE CREAMS

Cream formulas are used in *Better Basics for the Home* recipes for solvent-free car, furniture, floor, and leather waxes and polishes, and for skin creams such as moisturizers and sunblocks.

## BASIC CREAM FORMULA

*Many recipes I came across specified small amounts*
*of either borax or lecithin to help blend (emulsify)*
*the oils, beeswax, and water. With this formula,*
*I don't need either, so I skip them in favor*
*of simplicity.*

4 ounces oil (2½ ounces blended oils,
1½ ounces coconut oil or cocoa butter;
see Note About Oils)
½ ounce beeswax (see Note About Beeswax)
4 ounces distilled water
(see Note About Water)
Natural preservative (optional, see page 36)
Natural fragrance (optional, see page 37)

Combine the oils and beeswax in a double boiler over medium heat. Once the wax is melted (10 to 15 minutes), remove from the heat and add the water. Mix with an electric handheld mixer until thick and creamy. If you are using a blender, fill it with the liquid, then drizzle in the melted oils and wax mixture while the blender is on. Add the optional ingredients (if using), and stir to blend.
**Makes 1 cup**

*Preparation Time:* 25 minutes
*Shelf Life:* 6 months refrigerated; a few weeks with an herbal water infusion; discard if you see mold; refrigerate
*Storage:* Glass jar with a screw top
NOTE ABOUT OILS: One-third to one-half of the oil should be a saturated fat (solid at room temperature), such as coconut oil or cocoa but-

ter. The rest of the oil can be a blend of oils and/or oils infused with healing, astringent, or emollient herbs.
NOTE ABOUT BEESWAX: This amount of beeswax makes a slightly stiff cream. If you want it lighter, add less beeswax; for a stiffer cream, add more.
NOTE ABOUT WATER: Always use distilled water, to reduce the risk of bacterial contamination. Use less water for thicker creams. Aloe vera gel, herbal tinctures, and even alcohol can be used as part of the measurement.

### HOW TO MAKE LOTIONS

Lotions are thinner than creams. Often a folk recipe for a lotion is like that for cream except it calls for about twice as much water. This makes an unsatisfactory product—kind of a spongy-feeling cream. My capable herbalist friend Josie, president of Hermana Herbal Products, came to my rescue after many failed attempts with that approach, suggesting I follow my cream recipe but halve the beeswax and add a little glycerin. What a lovely lotion that makes. Lotions do not need to contain beeswax, though; the word *lotion* can mean a wide range of liquid skin-care products. Many commercial lotions have high amounts of alcohol, which is why they may dry out or sting the skin.

## BASIC LOTION FORMULA

4 ounces oil (2½ ounces oil or blended oils,
1½ ounces coconut oil or cocoa butter;
see Note)

¼ ounce beeswax

4 ounces distilled water

1 tablespoon pure vegetable glycerin

Natural preservative (optional,
see directions on page 36)

Natural fragrance (optional,
see directions on page 37).

Combine the oils and beeswax in a double boiler over medium heat. Once the wax is melted (10 to 15 minutes), remove from the heat and add the water and glycerin. Mix with an electric handheld mixer until creamy. Add the optional ingredients (if using), and mix to blend. For a more liquid lotion, decrease the beeswax, but don't use less than ⅛ ounce or the lotion won't emulsify. If it doesn't emulsify, add 1 teaspoon borax.

**Makes 1 cup**

*Preparation Time:* 25 minutes
*Shelf Life:* 6 months; a few weeks with an herbal water infusion; discard if you see mold; refrigerate
*Storage:* Glass jar with a screw top
NOTE: You can use all coconut oil or all cocoa butter.

## HOW TO MAKE SALVES

Salves are traditionally used as medicine for the skin. The oil is infused with healing herbs such as comfrey and calendula to remedy burns, cuts, bruises, and sores of all kinds. Nonpetroleum jelly is in fact a commonly used salve. One of the nicest uses of this salve is in making lubricating and waxy lip balms.

## BASIC SALVE FORMULA

*Similar to petroleum jelly, or thicker depending on the amount of oil.*

1 ounce beeswax

2 to 8 ounces oil (more for soft salve,
less for hard; see Note)

Liquid vitamin E capsules (one 200-i.u.
capsule for every 2 ounces oil)

Melt the beeswax with the oil in a double boiler over medium heat. Remove from the heat, add the contents of the vitamin E capsule, and cream with an electric handheld mixer.

**Makes ¼ to 1 cup, depending on the oil content**

*Preparation Time:* 25 minutes
*Shelf Life:* 6 months; 1 month with herb-infused oils; discard if you see mold; refrigerate
*Storage:* Glass jar with a screw top
NOTE: Herb-infused oils are recommended. Choose herbs appropriate to a particular problem (see the glossary starting on page 12), and infuse the oils as described below.

### Variation

NONPETROLEUM JELLY: Follow directions above, using the ratio of 2 ounces oil (more oil for less thick salve) to ½ ounce beeswax.

## HOW TO MAKE INFUSIONS

Herbal infusions—herbs steeped in boiling water—are a time-honored way of extracting the powerful nutritional and medicinal value of herbs. Infusions can be drunk as tea or used as the liquid ingredient in creams and lotions.

## BASIC INFUSION FORMULA

Heaping handful leaves and flowers
(about 1 ounce herbs to 1 quart water)
Boiling water

Place the herbs in a mason jar, add boiling water to cover, seal the jar tightly, and let it set overnight or for at least 4 hours. Some herbalists place a metal knife or spoon in the jar to eliminate the risk of breakage, but mason jars withstand high temperatures. Strain, and discard the herbs.

*Preparation Time:* About 15 minutes
*Shelf Life:* 1 week refrigerated
*Storage:* Glass jar with a screw top

### HOW TO MAKE DECOCTIONS
Decoctions are similar to herb infusions except that the ingredients from roots and barks are extracted by simmering them in water. Licorice root (for facial steams) or ginger root (for arthritis rubs) are good examples of suitable plant materials for a decoction, as are soap bark (for skin and hair washing) or walnut shells (for dyes and stains). The plant materials tend to be hard and need to be simmered to help release their beneficial constituents.

## BASIC DECOCTION FORMULA

Heaping handful roots and/or bark
4 cups water

Break the roots or bark into small pieces (2 to 3 inches long), place in a pan, and cover with the water. Bring to a boil, then reduce the heat and simmer the ingredients for 1 hour, replenishing the water as it evaporates. Let cool, then strain thoroughly.
**Makes 4 cups**

*Preparation Time:* About 5 minutes
*Shelf Life:* About 1 week refrigerated
*Storage:* Glass jar with a screw top

### HOW TO MAKE TINCTURES
Although tinctures are used more medicinally than for personal care products, a dropperful of a tinctured herb added to a skin or hair care preparation can be an easy way to impart its hair- or skin-healing properties.

## BASIC FORMULA FOR TINCTURES

Fresh herb
Enough 90-proof vodka, rum, bourbon, or
brandy to cover

Pack the herb tightly into a clean glass jar. *Completely* cover with alcohol. Set the covered jar in a cool, dark place for 3 to 6 weeks. Strain, then pour into amber or blue tincture bottles.
*Preparation Time:* About 15 minutes
*Shelf Life:* Up to 2 years
*Storage:* Colored tincture bottles kept in a cool, dark place

Variation
HERBAL VINEGAR TINCTURE: Substitute organic apple cider vinegar for the alcohol.

## HOW TO MAKE ESSENTIAL OILS

For those of you with the inspiration and energy, here are directions for making your own essential oils. Otherwise, it is a great deal easier to buy essential oils; just make sure they are pure.

## BASIC ESSENTIAL OIL DISTILLATION FORMULA

Fragrant herb (such as rose petals)
Distilled water
Ice

1. Obtain about 5 feet of plastic hose of a diameter that snugly fits the spout of a teakettle. Set up the hose to go from the spout of the teakettle while it is on the stove to a lower level, such as a table, where there is a bowl of ice over which the hose should lay, then continue to a lower level (such as a chair seat) where the hose empties into another bowl.
2. Fill the kettle with a generous handful of the herb, cover with water, bring to a boil, then reduce the heat and let simmer. The steam will carry the essential oil through the hose. Add more water as it evaporates from the kettle.
3. Once the condensed steam is in the lowest bowl, use an eyedropper to carefully remove the essential oil, which will have floated to the top. Store the oil in dark glass containers.
**Amounts vary with different herbs**

*Preparation Time:* About 1 hour
*Shelf Life:* Indefinite
*Storage:* Dark glass containers
NOTE: Distill thyme twice to remove irritants.

## HOW TO MAKE INFUSED OILS

Infusing healing herbs in oil is an excellent method for extracting the benefit of herbs for use in body care products such as homemade soap, shampoo, creams, and lotions. Water and air degrade infused oils, because they increase the chance of spoilage. For this reason many herbalists prefer to use dried herbs. I like infusing oils in a Crock-Pot because it is effective and quick, which reduces the chance of the oils going rancid. However, there are many ways of infusing oils, not the least of which is filling a glass jar with herbs, covering the herbs with olive oil, sealing the jar tightly, and setting it in the sun.

## BASIC FORMULA FOR INFUSED OIL

2 ounces dried herbs
8 ounces olive oil or jojoba oil (or other oil with a long shelf life)
Liquid vitamin E capsules (one 200 i.u. capsule for every 2 ounces oil)

Place the herbs in a Crock-Pot and cover completely with the oil. Place over low heat for 6 hours. For a strongly infused oil, let cool, strain out the herbs and discard, add another 2 ounces herb to the already infused oil, and heat again for 6 hours. Let the mixture cool in the Crock-Pot for a few hours. Strain the herbs thoroughly from the oil, discard the herbs, and add the contents of a vitamin E capsule to the oil.
**Makes 1 cup**

*Preparation Time:* 20 minutes
*Shelf Life:* 2 months refrigerated
*Storage:* Dark glass jars

## BETTER BASIC SIMPLES

Traditionally, a simple is a product using only one herb, usually a tincture but sometimes a tea. The beauty of simples, in the words of the Green Terrestrial Herbal Products catalog, is that you can "feel the effects of an individual herb working on your body, thus gaining deeper understanding and relationship to the herb." In *Better Basics for the Home,* I have expanded the use of the term *simple* to include homemade products made of one or two ingredients. Ironically, simples often can be the most sophisticated solution to a problem. Milk, for example, used by famous beauties for centuries, is now known to be a fruit acid, or an alpha-hydroxy acid; using milk for body care reflects an understanding of its unique attributes and current cosmetic research. Experiment with simples for body care or cleaning to find the ones that are best for you. You can't beat the price. Start by putting aloe vera gel—a wonderfully hydrating and healing substance—on your face, and feel your skin drink it up and ask for more.

## HOW TO MAKE SOAPS

Just wait until you wash your hands with your own homemade olive oil castile soap. Who would have believed that soap could be so emollient and leave skin feeling so soft without the drying effects inherent in most commercial soaps? I like making soap more than making bread. I put on my slippers, listen to music, and enjoy one of the most relaxing, satisfying, and useful craft projects I know.

Making a couple batches of soap takes about the same amount of time as making two loaves of bread. Homemade soap costs more than store-bought soap, but it lasts for months, and gifts of it are well appreciated.

Fats and lye combined in a chemical process called saponification result in soap and glycerin. Fats are melted and lye is dissolved in water. Once the two materials reach the same temperature, they are combined and saponified; the result is a glycerin-rich soap. In saponification, about 10 percent of the fat is split into glycerin. Unfortunately, much commercial soap has been processed to remove the glycerin, which is an excellent humectant and moisturizer.

## SPECIAL EQUIPMENT FOR MAKING SOAP

* Two glass or metal thermometers with good visibility in the 95 to 105°F range
* Large glass, stainless steel, or hard plastic container that holds up to 32 ounces water
* Enamel or stainless steel (not aluminum) cooking pot that holds up to 1½ gallons
* Molds in which to pour the liquid soap (I use plastic Tupperware-type storage units available in supermarkets and department stores)
* Protective goggles
* Cooling sinks or tubs big enough to hold the cooking pots

NOTE: When working with lye, be sure to have vinegar handy; it will neutralize a lye spill.

### Ingredients Needed

* Fats

Almost any fat can be used for soap, although most recipes specify two-thirds of the fat to be saturated (such as coconut oil or beef tallow) or hydrogenated (such as Crisco) and one-third to be a liquid fat such as olive oil or canola oil. The solid fats help speed the hardening process of the soap, although if the correct amount of lye is used the oils will harden eventually. If you want to experiment with fats not called for in the recipes below—such as earthnut oil or herring oil—search the Internet for "soap recipes" and you will find charts that give the ratio of fat to lye.

Fats and oils commonly used for soap are animal tallow and grease, coconut oil (promotes good lathering), and cottonseed, corn, soy, palm, palm kernel, and olive oil. A standard home soap recipe uses about one-third olive oil to two-thirds coconut oil and vegetable shortening.

* Lye

Sodium hydroxide is a highly alkaline and caustic material found in the supermarket drain cleaners aisle. The brand name Red Devil is 100 percent lye (don't substitute other drain cleaners). Sodium hydroxide is also available from Chem Lab Supplies (see Sources and Resources). In the old days, lye was made by putting wood ashes in a vessel, pouring boiling water on them, covering securely, and letting the mixture sit. If an egg was cracked into the mixture and it didn't sink, the product was a highly alkaline material called potash, caustic soda, or, more recently, lye.

*Caution:* The downside in making soap is that lye is so alkaline that it is dangerous to work with. It can be fatal if swallowed, and when mixed with water it gives off powerful fumes for thirty seconds. If it spills on the skin it will burn. Wear protective goggles and gloves. Mix lye and water outdoors even in winter, and don't allow children or pets in the vicinity. There is less chance of splashing if you add the water to the container after the lye. If you get any lye on your skin, flush immediately with water and vinegar.

* Water

Soft water is needed to make soap; rainwater is perfect. Distilled water is fine, too. If you have hard water, add 1 teaspoon washing soda or borax to every 10 ounces or so of water.

## BASIC DIRECTIONS FOR MAKING SOAP
### (Also Known as Creamy Castile Soap)

16 ounces water
6 ounces lye
16 ounces olive oil
8 ounces coconut oil
17½ ounces shortening

1. Put on protective glasses and gloves, and mix the water and lye in a large glass, stainless steel, or hard plastic container that holds up to 32

ounces. Once the lye and water are combined, the water gets very hot—more than 200°F.

2. Heat the oils and shortening over low heat in an enamel or stainless steel cooking pot (not aluminum) that will hold up to 1½ gallons. Heat the oil to 95 to 105°F (this will take about 35 minutes).

3. Constantly check the temperatures of the lye and water mixture and the oil mixture. They should reach 95 to 105°F at the same time. If necessary, cool the lye or oil by placing the container in a pan of cold water.

4. Add the lye to the oil, stirring constantly.

5. Once the soap starts to "trace" (dragging a spoon through it produces an indentation that remains for a few seconds)—anywhere from 10 minutes to 1 hour—add plant materials and/or essential oils.

6. Pour the soap into molds (I use rectangular Tupperware containers that are about 4 inches deep), place the tops on, and cover with blankets for 24 hours. Once the soap has hardened, it will pop out of the molds. Air-dry the soap on baking racks for 3 to 4 weeks.

**Makes about 24 bars**

*Preparation Time:* About 2 hours
*Shelf Life:* Indefinite
*Storage:* Wrap in pretty wrappers such as colored or waxed paper tied with raffia.
NOTE: Sometimes a white powder forms on the soap while it is drying. You can scrape this off. If the soap doesn't harden, reheat the mixture to 140°F, then stir while it cools. It should harden. Some soap batches don't seem to saponify properly. Let the soap dry for 4

weeks, then mold the mixture into soap balls. Wear gloves while molding the soap. For more soap recipes, see Chapter Three.

## HOW TO PRESERVE KITCHEN COSMETICS

If you will be using your cream, lotion, or infused oil within a few weeks, you do not need to include ingredients to retard spoilage. Otherwise, you can choose among a number of natural materials that will extend the shelf life of the products, usually by a few months.

**ANTIOXIDANT VITAMINS A, E, AND C.** My herbalist friend Josie successfully uses the antioxidant vitamins A, E, and C in her products, which need to be fresh because her Hermana line of personal care products is sold in stores and through her mail order catalog.

DIRECTIONS: For 8 ounces cream or oil, add 1 teaspoon (1 gram) vitamin C powder, ¼ teaspoon vitamin A powder, or 1 tablespoon wheat germ oil (for its vitamin E).

**GRAPEFRUIT SEED EXTRACT.** This method of preserving is easy, and the extract is odorless and blends well into creams. This preservative would be expensive for producing gallons of creams and lotions, but for small batches it is by far the most convenient. Grapefruit seed extract is available in health food stores.

DIRECTIONS: Use 6 drops per ounce cream or oil, or ⅓ teaspoon per cup.

**ANTISEPTIC ESSENTIAL OILS.** Sweet orange, lemongrass, rose, clove, rosemary, and lavender essential oil are all more antiseptic than phenol, the industry standard of disinfectants, according to research by Jean Valnet, M.D., author of *The Practice of Aromatherapy.* The skin is sensitive to these oils, however, so only small amounts should be used; they also are very fragrant, so choose aromas you can live with.

DIRECTIONS: Per ounce of cream or oil, use 3 drops or less (eye area), 5 drops or less (face), or 25 drops or less (body).

### HOW TO ADD FRAGRANCE

If you plan to add straight essential oils or essential oil blends as a fragrance for creams, lotions, shampoos, or even cleaning products, follow the directions above for using antiseptic essential oils. If you plan to use a perfume dilution (see page 180), add up to 2 teaspoons (¼ ounce) per cup (8 ounces) cream; reduce the perfume to ⅓ teaspoon for eye creams.

# Labeling and Packaging Your Products

We spend a lot of money for labeling cachet, and we pay a lot for the allure of pretty bottles and elegant labels. Large department stores make their biggest profit at the cosmetic counter. Pay attention to what compels you to buy a product, then make your own labels with your own sense of glamour. Design them on a computer, print them out in color if you can, and tape them on. If you can't think of anything inspiring, choose lines of poetry.

### LABELING FOR SAFETY

Always label homemade formulas, and keep them out of the reach of children.

### PACKAGING AND GIVING GIFTS

Many of the preparations found in *Better Basics for the Home* make wonderful gifts. Bath oils can be packaged in fluted colored-glass bottles with round stoppers. Creams can be given for holiday gifts in cosmetic jars ordered through herbalists' catalogs. Homemade oatmeal and calendula soap wrapped in cloth and tied with satin ribbon is a great stocking stuffer or a fine gift any time of year. Mason jars are easily decorated by gluing calico onto the lids. Antiseptic lavender cutting-board spray placed in a small, colored plastic spray bottle is an unexpected surprise. Raffia and homemade paper can be used to wrap dry ingredients for milk paint. Creative gift wrapping with cloth, as perfected by the Japanese, is memorable and reusable. Preparations that are particularly suitable for gift giving are brought to notice with this icon:

# Sources of Supplies

Baking soda, washing soda, vinegar, milk, borax, and other basics are readily available in the supermarket; washing soda and borax are in the laundry section. Herbs, essential oils, all-purpose soaps and detergents, cold-pressed vegetable oils, and a few basic ingredients such as aloe vera gel and apple cider vinegar are available in health food stores. Hardware stores often have carnauba wax, rottenstone, and other raw materials for polishes. You'll want to get on the list of a few mail order suppliers, depending on your interests. Herbalists' catalogs are full of interesting ingredients and accessories. A few wood-finishing supply houses offer hard-to-find shellacs and waxes, and a number of catalogs offer milk paint protein (casein) and natural earth pigments. Don't forget the Internet; simply type in a key word such as *lime* at a search engine. For specific sources, see Sources and Resources.

## Testing

Always spot-check the preparations in this book for colorfastness and allergic sensitivity, whether the product is for your carpet, skin, or the wall of the house.

## Guide to Commercial Products

I know that everyone who reads this book will not forgo buying ready-made products. But carefully supplementing commercially available products (environmentally safer ones, of course) with those that are homemade considerably reduces consumption of toxic products. I'll tell you about my shopping habits to show you how making things from scratch results in needing just a few commercial products, most of which are detergents. One woman wrote a magazine article about the cupboard under my kitchen sink, because there is almost nothing there. She couldn't believe it. The only commercial items I buy are laundry detergent, automatic dish detergent, all-purpose detergent, paint and sealants (although I am a convert to homemade milk paint and whitewash for small jobs), white glue, lipstick, and shampoo (and even this I am waffling on).

Everything else I make with staples such as baking soda, vinegar, aloe vera gel, and a few essential oils. I am thinking hard for exceptions. Maybe toothpaste: I like baking soda sweetened with the herb stevia, but I can't convince my family to make the switch.

### WHERE TO FIND ENVIRONMENTALLY SAFER COMMERCIAL PRODUCTS

Where do I find the few commercial products I buy? I shop for them at health food stores and through mail order catalogs. In the natural product arena there is tough competition and scrutiny, which makes for high-quality products that are biodegradable and use renewable resources. Most of the cleaning products found in health food stores are excellent. I can't say the same for body care products; there is a wide range available, and the composition varies greatly from synthetic to pure. But health food stores are a good source for ingredients to make body care products at home. Catalogs are an excellent source of natural fibers, essential oils, nontoxic building supplies, and hard-to-find natural materials such as earth pigments and casein for making milk paint.

### A NOTE ABOUT SOLVENTS AND CITRUS SOLVENTS

Washing soda is the best solvent substitute. You can make waxes and polishes by emulsion instead of using solvents (see Basic Cream Formula, page 30). Avoid all petroleum-based solvents; they are toxic and long-lasting in the environment. Citrus solvents are an improvement over long-lasting petroleum-based solvents, but the American Industrial Hygiene Association set a Workplace Environmental Exposure Level of thirty parts per million for d-limonene, the main ingredient in citrus solvents. This is more restrictive than those set for turpentine, toluene, n-hexane, and other toxic solvents. If you use citrus solvents, be sure to use adequate ventilation, and keep them out of the reach of children.

## BUYER'S GUIDE

There are times when all of us need to buy a ready-made product, and for this the Buyer's Guide is designed. Throughout this book, you'll find recommendations for a few commercial products that work effectively and are considered safe according to current research. Only a few recommendations are offered, because this book is about reducing consumption. One drawback of recommending products is that the formulations change, and companies come and go. To address this, I will periodically post such changes at my web site: http://www.betterbasics.com.

If you follow the GRAS (generally regarded as safe) rule, you'll reject toxic chemicals, so the guide doesn't detail those chemicals to avoid. Instead it highlights the good news: companies that have worked hard to provide safe products made with renewable resources. I've concluded that you will gain the most from this approach. If you want the long list of toxic products, see some of the excellent books on the subject, for example, *Toxics A-Z: A Guide to Everyday Pollution Hazards* by John Harte (see Sources and Resources).

I am not a chemist but have arrived at my product recommendations after almost twenty years of learning to live without toxins, reading labels, and studying reports from such proven organizations as Green Seal, the Washington Toxics Coalition, the Center for Clean Products and Clean Technologies at the University of Tennessee, Seventh Generation, and The Healthy House Institute. For body care I have relied heavily on one of the most trusted chemists in the field, Aubrey Hampton, of Aubrey Organics, and in particular his wonderfully informative book, *Natural Organic Hair and Skin Care.*

I highly recommend that you subscribe to the publications *Rachel's Environment and Health Weekly, News on Earth, The Green Guide,* and *Alternatives.* I'd also recommend that you become a member of Green Seal, a nonprofit organization that gives a green seal of approval to products that have met their high standards. *Rachel's Environment and Health Weekly* gives excellent overviews of new research on toxins. *News on Earth* provides updates on how everyday product choices affect the environment. The Washington Toxics Coalition newsletter, *Alternatives,* comes out four times a year, and the group frequently publish helpful booklets.

# CHAPTER 2

# Housekeeping

**W**ITH your first step into my friend Pat's house, you are enfolded in the rich, deep fragrance of vegetable oil soap, a trace of eucalyptus from a wild herb wreath, and the fruity, spicy scent of an orange and clove pomander hung on the door. The bright colors of couch pillows are juxtaposed with blue glass and white lace curtains, and there are bowls of lavender and rosebud potpourri on the radiators. Undoubtedly the ironing board will be up in the kitchen so Pat can tend to her family's natural-fiber clothes and linens (she loves ironing). If you are really lucky, muffins or cookies will be coming out of the oven.

People of all generations like to come to Pat's house—her children's friends, her friends, her friends' children, neighbors—they're always dropping by. Who wouldn't want to be there?

It's such a natural setting, a place of life, nature, and nurturance. Isn't that what a home should be? The environment is well matched, of course, by Pat's welcoming and accepting self. But there is another secret to the allure of such a home: There are no jarring chemical fumes from Brand Name X and Brand Name Y, no synthetic air fresheners, nothing that will sneak up on you and give you a headache. Pat's home is cleaned without toxins.

As far back as ancient Egyptian and Greek times, people used lavender, rosemary, tansy, and other herbs for cleaning. They freshened their linens by placing fragrant sachets, herbs, and flowers in drawers and closets. Homes were "sweetened" with garlands of lavender and mint. These days, herbs are once again becoming mainstays of cleaning—less toxic cleaning, that is. We are rediscovering the benefits of essential oils. Many, such as orange blossom and lavender, are antibacterial; others, such as tea tree, can kill mold; still others protect wool clothing with their fragrance. You don't need much more than a few essential oils, white distilled vinegar, soap, and baking soda to clean and care for your house with great success.

## New Cleaning Basics

Just as *integrated pest management* means to solve pest problems at their source and in the least toxic manner, so *integrated cleaning* means to think about the cleaning jobs in your home, to determine if they can be minimized and the chemicals reduced or eliminated. This new method of cleaning is catching on in schools and industrial settings across the country, and we can implement the idea in our homes. To do smart cleaning, you should choose the least toxic approach, use as little cleaning product as possible, and see if you can reduce the need to clean. For example, you will wash the floor less often if you have a doormat to collect mud from shoes.

There is a myth that cleaning with natural materials takes more elbow grease. This belief is just that, a myth. I have found that some materials, such as baking soda, need time to loosen grease and grime, thereby taking no

elbow grease at all (and allowing you to do other things such as have a nap while the mineral does its work). Sometimes you need to rinse more than you would otherwise, but that just takes a little extra time, not more muscle.

## Better Basic Housekeeping Materials

Believe it or not, cleaning from scratch is easier than cooking from scratch, because it takes almost no time at all to combine the simple ingredients that most formulas require, and of course there is no cooking time. If you keep your pantry stocked with the few basic items described below—most of which you probably have on hand anyway, such as white distilled vinegar and baking soda—you are all set to go.

### THE FIVE BASIC INGREDIENTS FOR LESS TOXIC CLEANING

With five ingredients—baking soda, washing soda, liquid soap or detergent, distilled vinegar, and an antiseptic essential oil—you can clean everything in the house.

**MINERAL MIGHT: BAKING SODA AND WASHING SODA.** The magic of minerals is that they neutralize many stains and odors. They are alkaline, cut grease, and can even dissolve wax. Baking soda and washing soda in particular are indispensable to the less toxic cleaning kit. Baking soda also serves as a mild abrasive. Washing soda is the best heavy-duty scourer and an excellent substitute for toxic solvents. It is slightly caustic, so you need to wear gloves when using it. If minerals don't solve a cleaning problem, it is probably because not enough of the mineral was used or it wasn't left on long enough (such as overnight for oven cleaners).

**LIQUID SOAP OR DETERGENT.** Liquid soap or detergent removes stains and cuts grease. Soaps and detergents are not the same thing. In fact, detergents are chemically different from soaps. Both soaps and detergents are surfactants, or surface active agents, which basically means a

washing compound that mixes with grease and water. Soaps are made of materials found in nature. Detergents are synthetic (although some of the ingredients are natural); they were developed during World War II when oils to make soaps were scarce. There is little doubt that soap is better for your health and the environment than are detergents. Nonetheless, a big drawback of washing with soap is that the minerals in water react with those in soap, leaving an insoluble film. This can turn clothes

## BUYER'S GUIDE

### DETERGENT SURFACTANTS AND LIQUID SOAP

DETERGENTS are toxic to fish and wildlife and should never be used when the effluent goes directly into lakes and streams. Seventh Generation, Earth Friendly Cleaner, Life Tree, and Ecover are four brands of detergent that are made with renewable materials instead of petroleum-based ingredients, and with natural essential-oil fragrance and no dyes or optical brighteners. There is one good, biodegradable, vegetable-based surfactant called alkyl polyglycoside surfactant (APG) found in mainstream products, but you have to call the manufacturer of your brand to find out if they use it. (Most supermarket brands specify only "anionic and nonionic surfactants.") A detergent ingredient to avoid because it is a endocrine disrupter is nonionic nonylphenol ethoxylate, which is still found in some commercial products. For more information on this, read *Troubling Bubbles,* by Philip Dickey, published by the Washington Toxics Coalition (see Sources and Resources).

Phosphates cause algae bloom and foam in lakes and streams. Studies have shown that products with phosphates also have much higher levels of heavy metals—in particular, arsenic. Unless you know if your state has banned phosphates, buy liquid laundry detergents, because they are all phosphate free.

An excellent liquid soap for cleaning is the Dr. Bronner's brand of liquid castile soaps. Some of the Dr. Bronner's soaps contain small quantities of antiseptic essential oils, such as in the popular peppermint castile soap.

grayish, and the film can leave a residue. Detergents react less to minerals in water and for all practical purposes are the product of choice for laundry, unless you have very soft water. Those of you with hard water—which has a high mineral content—already know about this, I am sure. If you choose to wash your clothes with detergent, you can ensure the least possible damage to the environment by selecting the most biodegradable products (see the Buyer's Guide, page 42).

**VINEGAR AND ESSENTIAL OILS.** Vinegar neutralizes many stains and odors, dissolves scale, and pulls dirt out of wood. Use only white distilled vinegar for cleaning; apple cider vinegar could stain some materials, such as upholstery. Antiseptic essential oils—such as tea tree, sweet orange, lemongrass, rose, clove, eucalyptus, cinnamon, birch, or lavender—kill bacteria and mold. For more information about these products, see the Glossary of Ingredients, starting on page 12.

## ACID OR BASE?
### SOME BASIC CHEMISTRY

In the Introduction, I talked a little bit about acids and bases and how to use these chemical properties to suit your needs. It helps a lot to know when and why to use baking soda or white distilled vinegar, two mainstays of less toxic cleaning. Baking soda is alkaline and white distilled vinegar is acidic: They neutralize each other. From there you can extrapolate to realize that baking soda will neutralize an acidic stain or odor, and white distilled vinegar will neutralize alkaline stains, such as grass.

A neutral pH is 7. Anything above 7 is alkaline; anything below it is acid. In terms of the basic materials you need for nontoxic cleaning, the pH levels break down as follows: washing soda, 11; borax, 9.25; baking soda, 8.2; white distilled vinegar, 3.

GENERAL CAUTIONS

* Label all bottles carefully.
* Keep all products away from children (detergents are toxic).
* Make sure to spot-check fabrics for color-fastness before using any cleanser.
* Do not mix ammonia with bleach or vinegar. Note that ammonia and bleach are not ingredients in any recipe in this book. Ammonia gives off harmful gases and should be avoided.
* Washing soda can scratch fiberglass (use baking soda instead). Marble is also easily scratched. Don't use "green" pads for either of these materials.
* Use only white distilled vinegar for formulas in this chapter.

# HOUSEKEEPING FORMULAS

Following are low-toxic formulas, organized alphabetically, with which to tackle most housekeeping chores. Included are easy-to-make air fresheners; all-purpose household cleaners; cleansers and deodorizers for carpets; carpet stain removers; disinfectants; dish detergents; drain cleaners; floor cleaners, polishes, and waxes; furniture dusters, polishes, and waxes; laundry products; metal cleaners; mold and mildew removers; oven cleaners;

plastic and vinyl cleaners; herbal sachets, pot-pourris, and pomanders; scouring powders and soft scrubbers; tub and tile cleaners; upholstery cleaners; and window and glass cleaners.

# Air Fresheners

I have never used a commercial air freshener. They've always seemed counterintuitive to me: If the air smells bad, shouldn't you just remove the source? Nonetheless, I know that a lot of people use air fresheners frequently, and for your benefit this section is written. You can freshen the air with any naturally fragrant herbs, bark, or flowers that appeal to you. Many combinations are possible. Pine needles simmered in water would be much better than synthetic pine fragrance (but many people are allergic to pine); rose petals can be used in season, as can clover blossoms and lavender.

There are many ways to freshen the air that don't require mixing a formula.
* Open a window.
* Eliminate the source of the odor (which may require persistence).
* Invest in an activated carbon air filter.
* Purchase an ozonator, a machine that uses ozone to neutralize odors. People, plants, pets, and even electronic equipment need to be removed when an ozonator is in use. Be sure to follow the manufacturer's direc-

## BUYER'S GUIDE
### FRESHENING THE AIR

I WENT to my local supermarket to see what is in air fresheners these days, and the label on the first product I looked at read: "This product is banned in California because it causes cancer." It contained dichlorobenzene, a chemical that is extremely toxic, a central nervous system depressant, a kidney and liver poison, and one of the chlorinated hydrocarbons that is long-lasting in the environment and is stored in body fat. Who would buy such a thing if they thought about it for just one minute? On top of that, air fresheners not only mask odors that we should attend to—a musty carpet that should be dried out, for example—but they affect the nose so we simply don't smell the offending odors. The problems will still be there in a few hours after the nose has adjusted. There are much healthier alternatives: Baking soda neutralizes acid odors, and vinegar neutralizes alkaline odors. You don't need much more than these two ingredients to solve most odor problems. Health food stores sell air fresheners that are 100 percent natural. You can also buy zeolite, a mineral that absorbs odors: Buy zeolite bags and place them where needed (see Sources and Resources).

tions carefully. (See N.E.E.D.S. in Sources and Resources.)

* Use plants, which can help clean the air by neutralizing pollution. Research at the National Aeronautics and Space Administration (NASA) has revealed that, especially in enclosed places, plants can significantly reduce pollutants such as formaldehyde. Plants can be placed in problem areas, such as a kitchen with cabinets made of formaldehyde-releasing particleboard or pressed wood. Plants and the pollutants they can reduce include aloe vera (many toxic materials), English ivy (petroleum-based products), fig trees (formaldehyde), chrysanthemum (many toxic materials), and spider plants (formaldehyde). Chinese evergreen, bamboo palm, and lilies are also useful.
* Put one drop of 100 percent pure essential oil on a lightbulb (to achieve a specific scent).
* Put a few drops of essential oil in a bowl of water and place the bowl on a radiator.
* Place five to ten drops of essential oil in two cups of water in a spray bottle.
* Use antiseptic essential oils such as sweet orange and lavender in the bathroom by mixing a room spray containing four or five drops of essential oil to one cup of water.
* Burn sage, rosemary, or juniper in a glass or bowl. Hospitals in France during World War II burned rosemary and juniper for their antiseptic benefit. Sage is often used in Native American traditions as a purifier.
* Burn herbs in a wood fire.

## DEODORIZING SPRAY

*While reducing odors, this spray also leaves a lingering light fragrance in the air.*

8 drops lavender oil
4 drops each bergamot and clove oil
2 drops oil of peppermint
½ cup vodka
½ cup distilled water

Combine the ingredients in a spray bottle and shake well. Spritz into the air four or five times in areas you feel need freshening, being careful to avoid your eyes when spraying.
**Makes 1 cup**

*Preparation Time:* About 1 minute
*Shelf Life:* Indefinite
*Storage:* Leave in the spray bottle

### Variation
HERBAL DEODORIZING SPRAY: You can choose other essential oils for your deodorizing spray if you prefer a different scent. Another combination is 8 drops lavender oil, 4 drops rose geranium oil, 2 drops bergamot oil, ½ cup vodka, and ½ cup distilled water.

## WINTER HOLIDAY MULLED CIDER AIR FRESHENER

*I like to use this spicy air freshener during the holiday season. It makes our home smell welcoming.*

2 sticks cinnamon
5 or 6 whole cloves
8 cups apple cider, or as needed

Combine the spices and 4 cups of the cider in a nonaluminum pan and simmer over low heat for 3 to 4 hours, adding more cider as the mixture evaporates (about 1 cup every hour). The simmering releases the spices' aromatic oils.

**Makes 4 cups**

*Preparation Time:* About 1 minute
*Shelf Life:* The mixture can be reused two or three times, providing you add fresh cider to maintain 4 cups cider in the pan
*Storage:* Leave in the pan, or cool and store in a mason jar with a screw top

Variations

HOT AND HUMID SUMMER DAY AIR FRESH-ENER: This preparation is a refreshing pick-me-up for hot and muggy days. Substitute 10 to 20 sprigs fresh mint and 8 cups water for the above ingredients.

STUFFY HOUSE FRESHENER: A light, lemony air freshener that is particularly good for hot days, this is also good for reducing cooking odors. Substitute 4 or 5 citrus peels and 8 cups water for the above ingredients.

MULLED HERB ROOM SWEETENER: Simmering herbs releases some of their aromatic oils into the air, cleansing your home of many odors and leaving a subtle, natural, and earthy aroma. For the above ingredients substitute a small handful each of rosemary, bay leaves, and sweet marjoram; a few whole cloves; 1 cup organic apple cider vinegar; and 7 cups water.

## VIVA VANILLA

*Vanilla extract shows up as an air freshener in many nineteenth- and early-twentieth-century housekeeping books.*

Natural vanilla extract

Place 1 tablespoon natural vanilla extract in each of three or four ceramic bowls and place them, uncovered, in the kitchen or bathroom. After a few hours, a light, refreshing vanilla scent will waft into the surrounding air. Replace every day.

## FOR ALKALINE ODORS

2 tablespoons white distilled vinegar,
or as needed
2 cups water

Add the vinegar and water to a spray bottle. Shake to blend. Spray stains or problem areas generously. Don't rinse for 15 minutes or so. If the odor persists, add another 2 tablespoons vinegar to the bottle and spray again.

**Makes 2 cups**

*Preparation Time:* 30 seconds
*Shelf Life:* Indefinite
*Storage:* Leave in the spray bottle

## FOR ACID-BASED ODORS

*Keep a box of baking soda handy; it will quickly and completely neutralize odors such as urine, sour milk, vomit, and rotten fruit.*

2 tablespoons baking soda

2 cups hot water

Dissolve the baking soda in the hot water and pour into a spray bottle. Shake to blend. Spray problem areas generously. Don't rinse unless there is a residue.

**Makes 2 cups**

*Preparation Time:* 30 seconds
*Shelf Life:* Indefinite
*Storage:* Leave in the spray bottle

Variation

BORAX: Substitute 1 tablespoon borax, another alkaline mineral, for the baking soda.

### CUTTING BOARD ODOR REMOVER

*Because vinegar neutralizes alkaline odors and baking soda neutralizes acid odors, one or the other of these ingredients will eradicate virtually all cutting board odors.*

½ cup white distilled vinegar or

½ cup baking soda

½ cup water

For a vinegar wash, combine the vinegar and water in a spray bottle, and generously spray onto the cutting board. Let the mixture rest on the board for 30 minutes before rinsing. For a baking soda cleanser, sprinkle the cutting board with the baking soda. Spray with water until the baking soda is moist; let it set on the board for 30 minutes before rinsing.

**Makes 1 cup**

*Preparation Time:* 30 seconds
*Shelf Life:* Indefinite
*Storage:* Leave in the spray bottle; shake to blend before reusing

# All-Purpose Household Cleaners

Having an acidic cleanser and an alkaline cleanser in the house makes a lot of sense. I have mixed and labeled two bottles and keep them both handy. Alkaline minerals and soap are excellent and safe substitutes for harmful solvent-based all-purpose cleaners. They neutralize odors, dissolve grease, and remove soils and stains. If you need a slight abrasive for difficult jobs such as removing crayon marks, mix the minerals with liquid soap or detergent until creamy, then rub gently until the crayon marks disappear. Alternatively, melt the crayon marks with a hair dryer, then wipe clean.

Acidic cleansers containing vinegar or lemon juice can be used for sinks and bathrooms to cut soap scum and dissolve the mineral buildup (scale) that comes from hard water. Don't mix the alkaline minerals with vinegar in hopes of creating a more powerful cleanser, because the minerals will neutralize the acid and vice versa.

Antibacterial essential oils are included in some of the formulas for their antiseptic and antifungal properties. Most smell good and can add enjoyment to the drudgery of cleaning.

* Use hot water to dissolve minerals such as borax and baking soda.

* Don't use washing soda on fiberglass, because it can scratch.

* If you have hard water, use liquid detergent instead of liquid soap to avoid soap scum.
* To avoid white streaks that accompany too high a concentration of washing soda and baking soda, use ½ teaspoon per cup of water.

*Caution:* Always be sure to spray away from people's faces, because spray cleaners can harm the lungs and eyes.

## BASIC FORMULA FOR ALL-PURPOSE CLEANSER

*Use all-purpose cleansers along baseboards and on walls, fixtures, and countertops. These are also the products of choice for scuffs, crayon marks, spills, and spot cleaning. (For cleaning glass, see Window and Glass Cleaners, page 100; for dusting, see Furniture Care, page 73.)*

### ALKALINE CLEANER
*This is the all-purpose cleanser you should reach for first, because it works on most dirt.*

½ teaspoon washing soda
2 teaspoons borax
½ teaspoon liquid soap or detergent
2 cups hot water

Combine the washing soda, borax, and soap in a spray bottle. Pour in the hot water (it will dissolve the minerals), screw on the lid, and shake to completely blend and dissolve. Spritz every 6 inches or so of surface once or twice, wiping off the cleanser with a rag as you go.

For tough dirt, leave the cleanser on for a few minutes before wiping it off. Shake the bottle each time before using.
**Makes 2 cups**

*Preparation Time:* About 1 minute
*Shelf Life:* Indefinite
*Storage:* Leave in the spray bottle

### Variations
BASIC BORAX SPRAY: Eliminate the washing soda.
BAKING SODA SPRAY: Substitute baking soda for the washing soda for a gentler, less caustic spray cleaner.
EPSOM SALTS SPRAY: To make a spray full of alkaline but noncaustic minerals, substitute Epsom salts for the washing soda.
CLUB SODA SPRAY: Use only enough hot water as needed to dissolve the minerals, and substitute club soda for the rest of the water. Club soda is rich in alkaline minerals.

### ACID CLEANER
*If you have hard water, pets, young children, or an ill person in your home, this all-purpose cleaner will be useful. The acid will dissolve mineral buildup and neutralize and deodorize many body fluid odors.*

¼ cup white distilled vinegar or lemon juice
½ teaspoon liquid detergent
¾ cup warm water

Combine the ingredients in a spray bottle. Shake to blend before use. Spray the problem area generously (three or four spritzes per foot), then wipe with a clean cloth.

**Makes 1 cup**

*Preparation Time:* Less than 1 minute
*Shelf Life:* Indefinite with vinegar; a few days with lemon juice
*Storage:* Leave in the spray bottle, or store in a glass jar with a spray top. If the cleaner is made with lemon juice, store it in the refrigerator.

## PLAIN OL' SOAP AND WATER ✕

*It is easy to forget to use soap, one of the oldest and best cleansers there is. This formula is particularly good for greasy dirt.*

1 ounce castile soap (bar or liquid)
2 cups warm water

If you are using bar soap, place the soap and water in a jar. Let set overnight, or until the soap dissolves, shaking occasionally. If you are using liquid soap, place it and the water in a spray bottle. Use as you would any all-purpose cleaner. Shake to blend before each use.

**Makes a generous 2 cups**

*Preparation Time:* About 1 minute
*Shelf Life:* Indefinite
*Storage:* Leave in the spray bottle

## BASIC FORMULA FOR ANTISEPTIC ALL-PURPOSE CLEANSER 🎁

*Not only does this preparation clean, but the essential oils disinfect and provide a natural fragrance.*

Up to 1 teaspoon antiseptic essential oil
(thyme, sweet orange, lemongrass, rose, clove,
eucalyptus, cinnamon, rosemary, birch,
lavender, or tea tree)
1 teaspoon washing soda
2 teaspoons borax
½ teaspoon liquid soap or detergent
2 cups hot water

Combine the ingredients in a spray bottle. Shake to dissolve and blend the minerals. I like to spray this cleanser onto a surface, then leave it for 15 minutes or so before I wipe it up with a rag, to give the essential oil's antiseptic qualities time to work.

**Makes 2 cups**

*Preparation Time:* About 1 minute
*Shelf Life:* Indefinite
*Storage:* Leave in the spray bottle, or store in a glass jar with a screw top

Variations
CLOVE AND CINNAMON HOLIDAY CLEANSER: Use ½ teaspoon each clove and cinnamon essential oils.
LIGHTLY LAVENDER ANTISEPTIC SPRAY: Use 1 teaspoon lavender essential oil.
SWEET ORANGE: Use 1 teaspoon sweet orange oil.
NOTE: Pine oil is an essential oil disinfectant, and you can use that here instead of other essential oils. However, many people are allergic to pine, so use with caution.

## TEA TREE OIL ANTIMILDEW ANTISEPTIC SPRAY ✗ 🎁

*Tea tree oil works wonders against mildew.*

2 teaspoons tea tree oil
½ teaspoon liquid soap or detergent
2 cups water

Combine the ingredients in a spray bottle. Shake before using. Do not rinse off for a few days to allow the tea tree oil to do its work. The strong odor of the tea tree oil will dissipate after a few days.
**Makes 2 cups**

*Preparation Time:* About 1 minute
*Shelf Life:* Indefinite
*Storage:* Leave in the spray bottle, or store in a glass jar with a screw top

## BLACK BIRCH BRANCH WATER ANTISEPTIC GREASE-CUTTING ALL-PURPOSE CLEANER

*I like to use this cleanser for the kitchen sink and stove. Drink a bit of the birch infusion before you combine it with soap in the spray bottle. Birch water has a slight wintergreen flavor, and it is refreshing on a hot summer day.*

Black birch twigs packed into a quart mason jar and filled with boiling water
1 teaspoon liquid soap or detergent

Steep the black birch in the mason jar overnight. Strain out the liquid and pour it into a spray bottle. Add the soap. Shake to blend

before each use. Spray the cleaner on surface and wipe up with a sponge or cloth as you go.
**Makes 2 cups**

*Preparation Time:* About 10 minutes, plus time to collect the birch (about 30 minutes if it is nearby)
*Shelf Life:* About 1 month refrigerated
*Storage:* Leave in the spray bottle, or store in a glass jar with a screw top

## CLUB SODA SPRAY ✗

*This formula shows up in all the do-it-yourself, back-to-basics books. It couldn't be easier, and it really does work, because club soda is full of alkaline minerals.*

## BUYER'S GUIDE
### ALL-PURPOSE CLEANERS

MANY commercial all-purpose cleaners contain ammonia, butyl cellusolve (a neurotoxic solvent), and bleach (sodium hypochlorite), all of which you should avoid. Dr. Bronner's peppermint castile soap is a good alternative all-purpose cleaner. Health food stores also carry Seventh Generation's all-purpose household cleaner, which comes in a spray bottle. It is made with renewable resources and works well.

2 cups club soda

Pour the club soda into a spray bottle. Spray and wipe up with a clean rag as you go.

**Makes 2 cups**

*Preparation Time:* Less than 1 minute
*Shelf Life:* Indefinite
*Storage:* Leave in the spray bottle

## TWO-STEP, HEAVY-DUTY, ALL-PURPOSE CLEANSER

*Use this formula for tough stains and grease, such as engine oil.*

2 teaspoons washing soda
2 teaspoons borax
½ teaspoon liquid soap or detergent
1 cup hot water

Combine the ingredients in a spray bottle and shake well. Spray the stain. The high concentration of washing soda can result in white residue, so rinse well with water. Wipe dry.

**Makes 1 cup**

*Preparation Time:* About 1 minute
*Shelf Life:* Indefinite
*Storage:* Leave in the spray bottle

## ALL-PURPOSE CLEANER FOR BIG JOBS

*If you are inspired to wash walls, or have some big cleaning project that needs doing, this preparation will be useful.*

¼ cup each washing soda, borax, and liquid soap or detergent
2 gallons hot water

Combine the ingredients in a pail and stir to dissolve. Wearing gloves, saturate a sponge with the mixture, wring out the excess liquid, and wash the area. Resaturate the sponge frequently as you go. Rinse well.

**Makes 2 gallons**

*Preparation Time:* 3 to 4 minutes
*Shelf Life:* Discard

## PLAIN OL' SOAP AND VINEGAR FOR BIG JOBS ✗

*This is a particularly good all-purpose formula for bathrooms, because the vinegar will help fight mildew and mineral buildup in shower stalls. It is also a good choice for areas where rinsing is difficult, because it is free of minerals, such as washing soda, that can leave a white residue.*

¼ cup liquid soap or detergent
½ cup white distilled vinegar
2 gallons water

Combine the ingredients in a pail and stir to dissolve. Follow the directions for the all-purpose cleaner above.

**Makes 2 gallons**

*Preparation Time:* 3 to 4 minutes
*Shelf Life:* Discard

# Cleaning and Deodorizing Carpets

I recommend avoiding the use of carpets if you can, especially those that are wall to wall. Carpets are repositories of biological contaminants such as dust mites, mold and mildew, animal dander, bacteria, pollen, and viruses. In addition, the chemical fumes from carpets and their backing can have serious consequences for your health. Studies at Anderson Labs, international experts in testing toxics in consumer products, report that mice have dropped dead after breathing some new carpet fumes. Most natural wool carpets have been pretreated with powerful chemical moth deterrents. Studies have shown that carpets are commonly contaminated with lead and pesticides that are carried in from the outside on shoes. The best solution is to have a few area rugs—preferably cotton—that can be cleaned easily.

Yet for all that, it is the rare home that doesn't have a big carpet somewhere. I myself have a beautiful Oriental rug that I inherited and have struggled for years to keep clean, especially after each additional puppy we've had to house-train. Regular deep cleaning of carpets is crucial for keeping down biological contaminants, but it is difficult to keep carpets clean. I once spilled bright yellow medicine all over my mother's white carpet, and . . . I mean . . . who ya gonna call? We finally got it off with 3 percent hydrogen peroxide solution.

## PRACTICAL POINTERS FOR CLEANING CARPETS

In the old days, the usual way to clean rugs was to take them outside and beat them with a baseball bat or a broom handle. For small area rugs, the best method is still to give them fresh air, sun, and a good beating. In winter you can put them outside to freeze; once the dirt and dust are frozen, it is much easier to beat them off. For big carpets, where this is impractical, nothing is better than a deep steam cleaning and of course a good vacuuming. Hiring someone to come in and steam clean gives the best results, but you need to carefully question the company about the detergent they use. I haven't yet found a company that uses a detergent without perfumes and antimicrobial chemicals (pesticides) in the shampoos, or one that will use my detergent—a concentrated all-purpose formula called Infinity Heavenly Horsetail, available in health food stores. The one time I sent out my Oriental rug to be cleaned, the man agreed to use my detergent, and he said it worked better than his industrial brand.

A safe do-it-yourself method for deep cleaning your carpet—and one I have used successfully many times—is to rent a steam cleaning water-extraction machine from your local hardware store or supermarket, and shampoo the carpet yourself using your own perfume- and additive-free detergent. You need to rinse out the machines thoroughly before you start, because the previous renter might have used a shampoo containing pesticides. I wouldn't recommend using soap on a carpet, because the soap scum that develops with hard water could leave a dull residue. Another reason I like renting machines and shampooing carpets at home is that I can use antifungal essential oils in the rinse water: a teaspoon or two of tea tree oil to a bucketful (about 2 gallons) of water.

## DUST MITES AND ANIMAL DANDER IN CARPETS

One of the oldest carpet cleaning formulas I found while researching this book required infusing galls with water and sprinkling the mixture over the carpet, then rubbing it off with a clean cloth. Pure gall was specified for particularly dirty spots. Gall, a ball-like swelling on trees caused by insects, bacteria, or fungi, is rich in tannic acid, as are many herbs, such as thyme. An eastern acorn gall contains 50 percent tannic acid, for example; Chinese sumac gall contains more than 60 percent tannic acid. In the nineteenth century, galls were so popular for their tannin that they were cultivated using particular insects. Why were galls so popular for carpets, I wondered? More investigation revealed that tannic acid neutralizes the allergens in dust mites and animal dander. Some tannic acid powders on the market (see Sources and Resources) are simply sprinkled on the carpet, then vacuumed up. You could also experiment with making very strong black tea (also rich in tannic acid) and spraying it on, but do this only on a dark carpet.

## A TOXIC CARPET

I have met many people over the years who became chemically sensitive when they started living or working in an environment with new wall-to-wall carpet. I now believe that if you suspect a new carpet is toxic (not all are), the situation warrants nothing less than the following decisive measures. Testing is not definitive. You can purchase a spray carpet sealant that seals in carpet fumes (it is invisible). A friend used it while he was living in a temporary apartment with a brand-new carpet that smelled strongly of chemicals, and I thought it worked well. It didn't eliminate the odor completely, but my friend stopped getting headaches. (See Sources and Resources.) The next best thing you can do is remove the carpet or move. Health is too precious to lose because of a carpet.

Even old Oriental carpets can cause problems, because the wool often has been treated with chlorinated hydrocarbon pesticides for mothproofing. You may not smell the chemicals until the carpet is wet.

## NEUTRALIZING ODORS

The best weapons at our disposal for deodorizing carpets and neutralizing offensive biologically based odors are minerals such as baking soda, borax, and washing soda. You could even use Epsom salts in a pinch. White distilled vinegar works well for some odors, too. Between the two—alkaline minerals or acidic vinegar—you can tend to many odors, including those of some chemicals.

*Caution:* Always spot-test a cleaning product on a hidden part of the carpet, to make sure it doesn't do anything harmful to the fibers and dyes.

## BASIC CARPET CLEANER

*Many hardware stores and even large supermarkets rent steam extraction carpet cleaners, which can be used with this formula.*

¼ cup concentrated all-purpose liquid detergent (perfume free)
4 gallons water

Fill the machine's water and detergent dispenser. Follow the manufacturer's directions.
**Makes 4 gallons**

*Preparation Time:* A few minutes
*Shelf Life:* Discard

### Variation

HEAVY-DUTY CLEANER: Sometimes the addition of alkaline minerals helps remove dirt.
Dissolve 2 teaspoons each borax and washing
soda in about 4 cups hot water, then add the
mixture to the water dispenser in the machine.
Be sure not to add too many minerals; they can
leave a white residue that will require extra
rinsing to remove.

## BASIC CARPET ANTIFUNGAL SPRAY ✗

*Carpets can get musty for a number of reasons. Tea
tree oil, a powerful antifungal essential oil, is a
real boon in such circumstances.*

2 teaspoons tea tree oil
2 cups water

Combine the ingredients in a spray bottle, and
shake to blend. After testing the formula on an
inconspicuous area of the carpet to ensure that
it doesn't stain, generously spritz the mixture
onto the rest of the carpet. Don't rinse. The
strong smell will dissipate within a few days.
**Makes 2 cups**

*Preparation Time:* 30 seconds
*Shelf Life:* Indefinite
*Storage:* Leave in the spray bottle, or store in a
glass jar with a screw top

### Variation

BASIC CARPET ANTIMICROBIAL SPRAY: Substitute 2 teaspoons sweet orange oil for the tea
tree oil.

## BASIC CARPET DEODORIZER
## AND ODOR REMOVER ✗

*Nothing works like baking soda to remove odors from
a carpet. It literally neutralizes them on the spot.*

### BUYER'S GUIDE

#### CARPET CLEANERS

THE liquid detergent I use for
cleaning carpets is Infinity
Heavenly Horsetail, available
in health food stores and from
N.E.E.D.S. (see Sources and Resources). Call N.E.E.D.S. or Nontoxic Environments to ask about
other carpet cleaners, such as
Granny's Old Fashioned Products,
which are free of synthetic perfume
and toxic chemicals.

## Baking soda

Sprinkle baking soda over the carpet. Sometimes you will need a box or two of baking soda to really do the trick. Leave it on overnight. To avoid clogging your vacuum cleaner, sweep off as much baking soda as you can, then vacuum up the rest. If some of the baking soda is damp and has left a residue, wash it off with 1 cup water mixed with $\frac{1}{4}$ cup white distilled vinegar.

### Variations

BORAX DEODORIZER: Substitute borax for the baking soda if the carpet is slightly musty.
HERBAL CARPET DEODORIZER: To make a fragrant carpet deodorizer, add some ground herbs, such as rose petals, to the baking soda. As a rule of thumb, add about 1 tablespoon ground herbs to 2 cups baking soda.
URINE NEUTRALIZER: Use borax or baking soda (following the directions above) or a spray of straight club soda (do not rinse; soak up moisture with a sponge, if necessary).
SPILLED MILK, WINE, AND ALCOHOL NEU-TRALIZER: Follow the directions for Urine Neutralizer, above.

## WHIPPED DETERGENT

*The texture of this formula—like egg whites that are stiff but not dry—makes it fun to work with, and it helps disperse the detergent so it isn't too thick and concentrated on the carpet. This cleanser is a good choice when you need to clean the carpet but aren't able to obtain a steam cleaner.*

Equal amounts water and liquid detergent ($\frac{1}{2}$ cup each water and detergent should cover 10 square feet)

Whip the water and detergent together with a hand beater until frothy. With a sponge, scoop some mixture onto a section of carpet, rub in, and wipe dry with a clean rag. Continue over the entire carpet.

*Preparation Time:* A few minutes
*Shelf Life:* Indefinite, but rewhip before reusing
*Storage:* Tupperware container with a lid

### CARPET STAIN REMOVERS

HANDS-ON

* Blotting is a good way to clean up stains quickly. Blot with white paper towels or clean fabric; stand on the absorbents so they penetrate more deeply into the stain, then remove. Don't rub the carpet with the paper towels or fabric; just repeat using clean absorbent material.
* Scoop as much of the stain as possible onto a spoon or appropriate implement.
* Don't use salt on carpet stains; it can leave a residue.
* If you spray water over minerals (such as baking soda, washing soda, or borax) sprinkled on a carpet—something I have done often, especially for pet stains, to try to activate the minerals more—the residue becomes its own problem to remove. Let the minerals dry completely, then vacuum them up as much as possible. If there is still some residue, spray white distilled vinegar and water ($\frac{1}{2}$ cup each in a spray

bottle) on the hardened minerals to dissolve them; let dry, then vacuum.

For more on stains, see Laundry Products, page 82.

## CORNSTARCH POWDER STAIN ABSORBER

Cornstarch

Pour cornstarch onto the stain and let it set for 15 minutes or so. Cornstarch absorbs moisture, so it will lift a lot of the stain. To remove, sweep up as much cornstarch as possible, then vacuum.

## VINEGAR AND WATER

*Vinegar makes this formula a good antiseptic deodorizer, which can be sprayed or sponged onto stains to neutralize odors such as urine. It also draws out dirt and can be used as an effective rinse following a detergent.*

About 1 cup each white distilled vinegar and water

Combine the ingredients in a spray bottle or a bowl. Spray or sponge the mixture onto the carpet, making sure not to splash the vinegar in your eyes. Let it set for 10 minutes or so before blotting the mixture with a sponge or paper towel. The vinegar odor will dissipate after a few hours.
*Preparation Time:* Less than 1 minute
*Shelf Life:* Indefinite
*Storage:* Glass jar with a screw top, lidded plastic container, or spray bottle

## GLYCERIN AND WATER STAIN SOFTENER

*Glycerin softens dried-on stains and is a good presoak for problem areas before washing the carpet with a detergent.*

¼ cup vegetable glycerin
¼ cup warm water

Blend the glycerin and water; rub on the stain, then let set for 15 minutes. Wash out the stain with a detergent.
**Makes ½ cup**

*Preparation Time:* Less than 1 minute
*Shelf Life:* Indefinite
*Storage:* Glass jar with a screw top

## 3 PERCENT HYDROGEN PEROXIDE SOLUTION

*Ever since problems with chlorine have been reported, hydrogen peroxide has been a popular bleach substitute. This formula should be used for stains on a light carpet, not a dark one, because it could bleach the carpet dye. Be sure to test the formula carefully before using.*

1 part 3 percent hydrogen peroxide solution to 6 parts water

Dab the mixture onto the stain. If you need a stronger dilution of hydrogen peroxide, use 3 percent hydrogen peroxide solution straight from the bottle (if tests show that it doesn't discolor the carpet).

*Preparation Time:* 30 seconds
*Shelf Life:* Make only the amount you will use at a time

## CLUB SODA

*Club soda is a good all-purpose stain remover for acid stains such as coffee, wine, tomatoes, and fruit juice.*

Club soda

Sprinkle club soda over stains straight from the bottle, or pour it into a spray bottle and spray the stain. Blot dry with a clean, absorbent cloth.

*Preparation Time:* None
*Shelf Life:* Indefinite

## ENZYME CLEANER

*Enzyme cleaners, found in health food stores, can be used on protein stains such as blood.*

Enzyme cleaner

Follow the manufacturer's directions.

## BAKING SODA, BORAX, OR PULVERIZED CHALK

*These minerals neutralize unpleasant odors and absorb liquid stains. Chalk is known to absorb grease.*

Baking soda, borax, or pulverized white chalk

Sprinkle over the stain. Let set for 30 minutes before sweeping up. Vacuum any residue.

# Cleaning Dishes

All sorts of studies have been done on which is better for the environment, washing dishes in a dishwasher or by hand; usually the dishwasher wins due to energy and water conservation issues. One exception is the research by Philip Dickey at the Washington Toxics Coalition, who found that automatic dish detergents are contaminated with arsenic. Dickey's research revealed that where there are phosphates, arsenic is sure to follow, and virtually all dishwasher detergents contain phosphates. Both arsenic and phosphates cause problems in the wastewater stream. Liquid dish detergents, for washing dishes by hand, have minimal arsenic and no phosphates.

### HAND-WASHING LIQUID DISH DETERGENTS

Dishpan hands were the scourge of the housewife of the 1950s, or so advertisers would have us believe. I don't know where the ads have gone, but the problem of dishpan hands remains—although thankfully the ranks of males doing the dishes have grown. Dish detergents pull natural oils from your skin as easily as they pull salad dressing from a dirty plate or hamburger grease from a skillet. Wearing gloves is an option not relished by most of us, but it is to be recommended, especially if you use commonly available dish

## BUYER'S GUIDE

### DISH DETERGENTS

THE most difficult product to substitute for an environmentally preferable one is automatic dish detergent. Most commercial products have phosphates and chlorine, and I'm sorry to say that, if you have hard water, you'll have trouble getting your dishes sparkling clean without those ingredients. I speak from experience. However, Life Tree and Seventh Generation products, available in health food stores, are good formulations that are worth a try. For washing dishes by hand, be sure to buy a product that is free of dyes and synthetic fragrances. Ecover has some good choices; the one I use has lemon and aloe and cuts grease well.

detergents with antibacterial agents (pesticides), artificial fragrances, and dyes. Health food store brands don't have synthetic additives, but they still strip the oils from your skin. Liquid soaps can also be caustic and drying to the hands. If you don't wear gloves, be sure to treat your skin with something like the aloe and glycerin moisturizer described on page 142.

## TIPS

* If you don't plan to wash dishes right away, sprinkle nonaluminum cookware with baking soda, and soak dishes with burned-on food in baking soda and water. It makes cleanup easier.

* Add white distilled vinegar to the rinse water; it will help remove hard-water spots, as will a little borax.

* Washing soda is an excellent choice for pots and pans with burned-on food. Add a few tablespoons to the pans, fill with enough water to cover the problem areas, and soak for a few hours or overnight. Don't use washing soda on aluminum.

* Clean electric drip coffeemakers with white distilled vinegar. Add ¼ cup vinegar to 8 to 10 cups water, and run the machine through one cycle.

* Clean nonstick pans by soaking the burned-on food with a mixture of baking soda and water.

* Remove coffee and tea stains by soaking with a teaspoon or so of baking soda.

* Always wash utensils exposed to raw meat in very hot water to reduce bacteria.

* Try any combination of the following mostly acidic materials for dirty vases and mineral buildup on glass and china: black tea, vinegar, salt, lemon juice, and Coca-Cola.

* For stubborn buildup on white porcelain, try 3 percent hydrogen peroxide solution as a bleach.

## BASIC DISHWASHING SOAP FORMULA

*It is easy to make your own dishwashing liquid. It works well except with hard water, in which case it can cause soap scum.*

1 ounce liquid castile soap
2 cups water
1 teaspoon vegetable glycerin
5 to 10 drops lavender essential oil (optional—
lavender is antibacterial)

Combine the soap and water in a jar. Add the glycerin and lavender (if using). Stir to blend. Pour some on a sponge and wash the dishes, or add a few teaspoons to a sink full of warm water.

# Cleaning Drains

HANDS-ON
Plunger
Plumber's snake
Pang pressure gun

T I P *To keep drains clean, pour 1 cup washing soda down them every week or so.*

## BAKING SODA OR WASHING SODA AND BOILING WATER ✄

If water won't go down the drain in your sink, pour 1 cup washing soda into the water surrounding the drain, as close to the drain as possible. Within a minute, the water should go down. If water hasn't yet backed up, and you don't have any washing soda, pour 1 cup baking soda down the drain followed by 3 cups boiling water. The boiling water chemically changes the baking soda to a more washing soda–like chemical.

Variation
BUBBLE, BUBBLE, TOIL, AND TROUBLE: Follow the baking soda and boiling water, or

## BUYER'S GUIDE
### DRAIN CLEANERS

MANY commercial drain cleaners are very caustic. Some are nothing more than straight lye, a dangerous material you don't want in your home, especially if you have PVC pipes, which can be easily damaged. The only time I have lye in our home is when I make soap, and then only with the strictest safety precautions. Other drain cleaners are acids. All seem to be bad news for the wastewater stream, and their efficacy is in doubt, according to *Consumer Reports.* The safest commercial products, if you don't want to use the manual methods listed in Hands-On (see above), are bacteria-based enzyme cleaners, available in health food stores.

the washing soda, with 1 cup vinegar. There will be a great bubbling from the drain as the alkaline and acidic ingredients react with each other. Sometimes the bubbling works to dislodge whatever is blocking the drain.

# Cleaning Fixtures

All-purpose cleaners work well for cleaning fixtures. For a multitude of other choices, see page 47.

## CLUB SODA

*Club soda is full of alkaline minerals, which dissolve and loosen stains and remove discoloration.*

Club soda

Add about 2 cups club soda to a spray bottle. Spray on fixtures. Wipe dry, then polish with a soft, clean rag.
**Makes 2 cups**

*Preparation Time:* Less than 1 minute
*Shelf Life:* Indefinite

# Cleaning Floors

The fragrance of vegetable oil soap on wood floors is as wholesome as bread baking in the oven. I use a German brand of all-purpose vegetable oil soap—Sodasan—that smells particularly rich and nutty because it contains linseed oil. You can make your own linseed oil soap (see page 34) by substituting linseed oil for some of the olive and coconut oil. So-called vegetable oil soaps available commercially are usually

detergents, but detergents may be necessary to avoid soap scum if you have hard water.

## TIPS

* Use a damp mop, not a broom, to sweep, because it keeps flying dust to a minimum. You can add a few drops of oil to the mop as a dust collector.
* Consider using a doormat, especially during mud season.
* Before you mop, spritz the floor with water to dampen the dust.

## BASIC FLOOR CLEANER FORMULA

*You can use this preparation on all floors except when directed by the manufacturer to avoid even mild detergents.*

¼ cup liquid soap or detergent
Up to ½ cup white distilled vinegar
or lemon juice
2 gallons warm water

Combine the ingredients in a large plastic bucket. Use with a mop or sponge.
**Makes about 2 gallons**

*Preparation Time:* About 1 minute
*Shelf Life:* Discard

### Variations
HEAVY-DUTY GREASE-CUTTING FLOOR CLEANER: Add ¼ cup washing soda to the bucket before adding the warm water. Stir to dissolve. Do not use on waxed floors.

MY favorite soaps and detergents for washing floors include Life Tree Home Soap (a concentrated detergent), Murphy's Oil Soap (a detergent; the appealing scent is a natural essential oil), Sodasan soap (noted above, this is a wonderful-smelling, real vegetable oil soap), and Infinity Heavenly Horsetail (a concentrated detergent). Murphy's Oil Soap is available in supermarkets; the rest are found in health food stores and green, or ecologically minded, stores.

ANTISEPTIC FLOOR CLEANER: Add 10 to 20 drops (depending on how strong a fragrance you want) lavender, rosemary, or other antiseptic essential oil.

DEODORIZING FLOOR CLEANER: Borax helps eradicate musty odors and lift dirt. Add ¼ cup borax to the bucket before adding the warm water. Stir to dissolve.

HERBAL TEA FLOOR SOAP: For scent, add a few cups strong peppermint tea or lavender infusion.

## FLOOR OIL

*Jojoba is an excellent choice for floors, because it is a liquid wax that never goes rancid. But it is expensive. Additive-free linseed oil is expensive too but works well as a floor oil because it dries. Two sources of additive-free boiled linseed oil are Natural Choice and Auro (see Sources and Resources).*

Jojoba or additive-free boiled linseed oil

Rub jojoba or linseed oil into wood floorboards sparingly. Remove any excess oil with a cotton towel, then buff.

*Preparation Time:* None
*Shelf Life:* Indefinite

## FLEA-KILLING FLOOR SOAP ✗

*Citrus peel extract kills all stages of the flea. Using this floor soap once or twice a week during flea season will go a long way toward eliminating any infestation.*

¼ cup citrus solvent
¼ cup liquid soap or detergent
2 gallons warm water

Combine the ingredients in a pail, and wash the floor as usual. Please see cautions about citrus solvents on page 38.
**Makes about 2 gallons**

*Preparation Time:* About 1 minute
*Shelf Life:* Discard

## WOOD SOAP

*Adding glycerin to soap or detergent makes it more lubricating, reducing the risk of drying out the wood.*

¼ cup liquid vegetable-oil soap (see Note)
or detergent
½ teaspoon glycerin
2 gallons warm water

Combine the ingredients in a pail, and stir to blend. Wash the floor as usual.
**Makes about 2 gallons**

*Preparation Time:* About 1 minute
*Shelf Life:* Discard
NOTE: If you are using soap instead of detergent and have hard water, add ¼ cup white distilled vinegar to the rinse water, or add 1 teaspoon citric acid to the soap, glycerin, and water.

## LINOLEUM CLEANERS

### BASIC LINOLEUM FLOOR CLEANER ✗

¼ cup liquid soap or detergent
2 gallons water

Combine the ingredients in a pail, and wash floor as usual.
**Makes about 2 gallons**

*Preparation Time:* About 1 minute
*Shelf Life:* Discard

### LINOLEUM SPOT SHINE

*Cornstarch shines linoleum really well but needs hand polishing. Use this preparation for scuffs and spots or, if you're feeling energetic, make enough to polish the whole floor.*

½ cup cornstarch
Enough water to make a paste

Combine the ingredients in a bowl, scoop onto a sponge, and hand-polish the floor. Rinse.
**Makes enough for about 4 square feet**

*Preparation Time:* Less than 1 minute
*Shelf Life:* After a few hours, the cornstarch will have absorbed all the water, and the formula will dry out.

### Variation

LINOLEUM CREAM CLEANER: If you prefer not to get down on your hands and knees, try this cream cleaner: It can be applied with a mop. Combine ¼ cup each water and liquid soap or detergent; stir to make a creamy mixture. Spread some of the mixture on a mop with a knife, then push the mop over the scuffed area vigorously until the dirt disappears. Rinse.

### CLUB SODA LINOLEUM SPRAY ✗

*The alkaline minerals in club soda work wonders against dirt.*

2 cups club soda

Pour the club soda into a spray bottle, spray onto the linoleum, and mop dry.
**Makes 2 cups**

*Preparation Time:* Less than 1 minute
*Shelf Life:* Indefinite

## LINOLEUM MARK REMOVER ✂

*The baking soda in this preparation makes it slightly abrasive.*

½ cup baking soda
Liquid soap, dish soap, or detergent

Pour the baking soda into a bowl. Stir in the soap a bit at a time until the texture is like frosting. Scoop onto a sponge and wash the floor. Rinse well.
**Makes about ¾ cup**

*Preparation Time:* About 1 minute
*Shelf Life:* It dries out after a day

## SOLVENT-FREE FLOOR WAX REMOVER

*I once used washing soda to remove floor wax that contained a horrible-smelling synthetic perfume.*

Washing soda
Water

If you need to remove a lot of floor wax, sprinkle large amounts of washing soda on the floor and spray liberally with water. Moisten frequently so the paste doesn't dry out. Wear gloves. The more washing soda and water you use, and the longer you leave it on the floor, the easier the wax will peel off. Washing soda leaves a carbonate deposit that needs to be thoroughly rinsed off. You can use plain warm water or Basic Floor Cleaner Rinse Formula (below) to do this.

*Preparation Time:* None

## FLOOR WAX REMOVER II

*Because citrus solvents cause indoor air pollution, this formula should be used only as a last resort, and then only with adequate ventilation.*

1 cup citrus solvent
2 quarts water

Combine the ingredients, pour on the floor, and mop up. (See cautions about citrus solvents, page 38.)
**Makes about 2 quarts**

*Preparation Time:* A few minutes
*Shelf Life:* Discard

## BASIC FLOOR CLEANER RINSE FORMULA ✂

*Vinegar makes an effective rinse because it pulls up dirt and neutralizes any residual baking soda, borax, or washing soda that may have been used for cleaning.*

½ cup white distilled vinegar
2 gallons water

Combine the ingredients in a bucket. After the floors have been washed, rinse with this mixture. The smell of the vinegar will dissipate quickly.
**Makes about 2 gallons**

*Preparation Time:* About 1 minute
*Shelf Life:* Discard

## BUYER'S GUIDE

### FLOOR AND FURNITURE WAXES

### AND POLISHES

ALTHOUGH I've looked far and wide, I can't find commercially available floor and furniture waxes without toxic solvents. I was discouraged until I finally made a successful face cream by emulsifying waxes and oils—and you know you can't put solvents in a face cream—and it dawned on me that I could use the homemade cream for waxing floors, furnitures, and cars, too. The recipes here are variations on the Basic Cream Formula found on page 30.

FLOOR WAX

## BASIC POLISHING CREAM
## WAXING FORMULA

*This creamy wax is lovely to work with and pure enough to be used as a skin moisturizer.*

4 ounces oil (2½ ounces olive oil or jojoba,
1½ ounces coconut oil)
1 ounce beeswax
1 ounce carnauba wax
4 ounces distilled water

Natural preservative of choice
5 to 10 drops essential oil of lemon (optional)

Melt the oils and waxes in a double boiler over medium heat. Remove from the heat, pour in the water, and mix with a hand mixer until thick and creamy. (If you are using a blender, first add the water, then drizzle in the oils and melted waxes while the blender is on so they emulsify.) Add the preservative and essential oil as desired, then blend. Dab some cream onto a soft cotton rag and rub into the floor. Buff and polish the floor until the oils have been well worked.
**Makes 1⅛ cups**

*Preparation Time:* About 25 minutes
*Shelf Life:* 6 months or more
*Storage:* Glass jar with a screw top

## BASIC WATERLESS WAX FLOOR SALVE

*If you fear that water might damage a wood floor, polish it with this cream.*

4 ounces olive oil or jojoba
½ ounce beeswax
½ ounce carnauba wax

Melt the oil and waxes in a double boiler over low heat (about 5 minutes). Remove from the heat and blend with a hand mixer until creamy.
**Makes ⅝ cup**

*Preparation Time:* About 25 minutes
*Shelf Life:* Indefinitely with jojoba (which doesn't go rancid); 1 year with olive oil.

Discard when the wax smells stale or rancid.
*Storage:* Glass jar with a screw top

## JOJOBA POLISH ✗

*Jojoba is a liquid wax that offers some sealant properties and never goes rancid. The only drawback is that it is expensive.*

Jojoba

Simply dab some on a soft cotton cloth, and buff into the wood.

*Preparation Time:* None
*Shelf Life:* Indefinite

### Variation
CLEANER POLISH: This is less oily than straight jojoba. Add a few teaspoons jojoba to 1 cup organic apple cider vinegar, and use to lubricate, shine, and clean a wood floor.

# Cleaning Formica

## CREAMY CLEANER ✗

*This is a good alternative to commercial soft scrubs.*

½ cup baking soda
Enough liquid soap or detergent to make
a creamy paste

Combine the ingredients with a spoon, then scoop a generous amount onto a sponge and use it to clean the countertop. Rinse well.
**Makes about ½ cup**

*Preparation Time:* Less than 1 minute
*Shelf Life:* Make only as much as you need at a time; the mixture will dry out

## CLUB SODA SPRAY ✗

*See page 50 for recipe.*

# Cleaning Metal

Nothing made my father feel as though the house was in order as much as having the silver polished. I've since inherited some of that silver, and I have to agree with him: Tarnished silver makes the house feel untended. Fortunately, my generation doesn't seem to own much silver—except for what we inherit—because polishing silver is time-consuming. But metal is beautiful when it is shined and buffed, reflecting light and mirroring surrounding objects. Your chemistry lessons will come in handy for metal cleaning. One metal cleaner works like a magnet: Salts dislodge the tarnish, which then attaches to aluminum foil. Other formulas utilize acids to neutralize alkaline tarnishes; still others use alkaline and mildly abrasive minerals such as baking soda. Sometimes the solution is as simple as using a tomato. Use a soft, natural-fiber cloth to polish dry metals after rinsing.
ALL-PURPOSE METAL CLEANERS
**ASHES:** Gather together wood ashes, sprinkle on a damp rag, and polish. Rinse with hot water, and wipe the metal dry with a soft cloth.
**BAKING SODA:** Mix ½ cup baking soda with enough water to make a paste. Scoop some

paste onto a sponge, and buff the metal. Rinse with hot water, and wipe the metal dry with a soft cloth. Discard leftovers.

**CHALK:** Sprinkle pulverized chalk on a damp rag, and polish. Rinse well.

**DIATOMACEOUS EARTH:** Combine $\frac{1}{2}$ cup diatomaceous earth with enough water to make a paste. Scoop some paste onto a sponge, and buff the metal until clean. Rinse with hot water, and wipe the metal dry with a soft cloth. Discard leftovers.

**TOOTHPASTE:** A little dab will do ya. Rub on white toothpaste with your hand until the tarnish is removed.

**VINEGAR:** Soak metal in a mixture of water and at least $\frac{1}{4}$ cup white distilled vinegar. For very tarnished metal, soak in straight vinegar. (You can substitute lemon juice for the vinegar.) Rinse in hot water, and wipe the metal dry with a soft cloth.

## ALUMINUM

Follow the directions below for brass, bronze, and copper cleaners. Don't use baking soda or washing soda on aluminum, or it will pit.

## BRASS, BRONZE, AND COPPER

### TIPS

* Use natural acids to clean these metals.
* Remove the lacquer cover on new brass, bronze, and copper by submerging in boiling water with a few teaspoons each baking soda and washing soda. Once the lacquer has peeled off, polish dry.

## VIM AND VINEGAR ABRASION

*The acid in vinegar eats off tarnish, and the salt is mildly abrasive.*

3 teaspoons salt
1 tablespoon flour
Enough white distilled vinegar
to make a paste

Combine the ingredients until a paste is formed. Scoop the paste onto a clean sponge and polish the metal clean. Rinse with hot water, and buff dry with a soft cloth.
**Makes 2 tablespoons**

*Preparation Time:* About 1 minute
*Shelf Life:* Discard leftovers

### Variation

LEMON OR LIME JUICE, TOMATO JUICE, OR MILK: Substitute any of these acids for the vinegar.

## ACID RUB

*In a pinch, open your refrigerator or cupboards and look for catsup or Worcestershire sauce. Who doesn't have catsup?*

Catsup, Worcestershire sauce, or lemon or lime slices

Dab on a clean cloth, and rub the metal. Rinse with hot water, and wipe the metal dry with a soft cloth.

## Variation

CREAM OF TARTAR PASTE: Add enough water to a few teaspoons cream of tartar to make a paste.

## ACID SOAK

*Soaks are an easy way to clean metal: You can go off and have fun while the acid does the work of eating off the tarnish.*

Enough white distilled vinegar, lemon or lime juice, tomato juice, or milk to cover the metal (see Note)

Soak the metal in the acidic solution for several hours or overnight. Rinse in hot water, and wipe dry with a soft cloth.

NOTE: You can dilute the acid with water for large objects, but make the solution no less than half acid.

## GOLD AND SILVER

### TIPS

* Place a piece of chalk in the silver drawer to absorb moisture.
* Wrap silver in felt to store.

## MAGIC MINERAL CLEANER FOR SILVER

*You can smell this formula work: The odor of rotten eggs is released as the tarnish is pulled off the silver.*

1 tablespoon salt
1 tablespoon baking soda
A few sheets of aluminum foil
Water

Place the foil in a pan large enough to hold the silver. Combine the salt and baking soda and add to the pan. Add water to cover and let set for a couple of hours. Pour out the water; rinse the silver thoroughly in hot water and wipe dry with a soft rag.

NOTE: Do not use this cleaner for pieces that have parts joined by glue, such as candlesticks.

## PERFECT TOOTHPASTE POLISH

*Toothpaste polishes silver beautifully.*

White toothpaste

Rub silver with a dab or two or three (as much as you need), then polish with a soft, clean cloth.

## BAKING SODA POLISH

¼ cup baking soda
Water

Pour the baking soda into a bowl and add enough water to make a paste. Scoop onto a sponge, and rub the silver until the tarnish is removed. Rinse in hot water and wipe dry with a soft cloth.

**Makes ¼ cup**

*Preparation Time:* Less than 1 minute
*Shelf Life:* Make only as much as you need at a time; this mixture will dry out

### Variations

POLISHING PASTE: Substitute 1 teaspoon each cream of tartar and salt for the baking soda.
OLD-TIMER'S TECHNIQUE: Place a few teaspoons cream of tartar in a pan large enough to hold the silver or gold. Add water to cover. Bring to a boil, lower the heat, and simmer until the tarnish is removed. Let cool. Rinse in hot water and wipe dry with a soft cloth.

### ACID SOAK

*Acid works well for silver and gold, but the results aren't perfect. Touch up with white toothpaste or baking soda, as needed.*

White distilled vinegar, lemon juice, or another natural acid such as milk or tomato juice

Soak the silver or gold overnight in straight vinegar or other natural acid. Rinse thoroughly in hot water and wipe dry with a soft cloth.

#### PEWTER

Removing the tarnish from pewter is difficult, and I haven't found a method that really works. I suppose part of pewter's charm is the tarnished look. Choose recipes from the silver and gold section, above, to clean pewter, or use this chalk formula.

### CHALK IT UP!

Ground chalk (either pulverize a piece of chalk, or use whiting)
Enough vodka, rum, or brandy to make a paste

Make a paste of the ingredients. Scoop some onto a sponge and polish clean. Rinse and rub dry. Discard leftovers.

# Cleaning Ovens

Most people have self-cleaning ovens these days. You simply lock the oven shut and turn the knob to self-cleaning. There are no chemicals involved; the grease is just incinerated with high heat. Follow the manufacturer's directions, and be sure to have the windows open.

If you don't have a self-cleaning oven, the following preparation is for you.

### BAKING SODA OVEN CLEANER

*Baking soda has never failed me for oven cleaning. Even heavy grime lifts off with this formula.*

Small to medium box baking soda
Water

Sprinkle the bottom of the oven with baking soda to cover. Spray with water until very damp, and keep moist by spraying every few hours. Let set overnight. In the morning, simply scoop out the baking soda—all the grime will be loosened—and rinse the oven well. Baking soda needs a lot of rinsing, but it is well worth the effort because it produces no toxic fumes.

## Variation

WASHING SODA FOR TOUGH JOBS: Substitute half washing soda for half the baking soda. Washing soda is a little more heavy-duty than baking soda, but it needs more rinsing, so bring it out just for really tough jobs.

# Disinfectants

I knew the times were changing when my no-nonsense, northern New Englander mother threw out her sponges in exchange for counter-wiping cloths because she could wash the cloths every few days in the washing machine, thereby keeping them hygienic. The media had convinced even her that the kitchen was a harborer of disease. Although that may be right, the solutions that many advertisers and manufacturers propose may not be. Just like antibiotics, common disinfectants may contribute to drug-resistant bacteria, according to Stuart B. Levy, M.D., director of the Center for Adaptation Genetics and Drug Resistance at the Tufts New England Medical Center. Furthermore, many commercial disinfectants are ineffective to begin with, just like antibiotics, according to the Government Accounting Office of the U.S. government, if they are used in the wrong place at the wrong time.

Did my mother need to throw out her sponges? Assuming the sponges were pure cellulose, they would have been okay—sterilized, in fact, if she had boiled them for three to five minutes. My casual stroll through a supermarket recently turned up antibacterial agents—pesticides—impregnated in sponges, cutting boards, dishwashing liquid, hand soaps, and more. Neither my mother nor the rest of us can sterilize our homes even if we use a lot of disinfectants. Buying disinfectants is a waste of money. Our focus should not be on disinfectants as much as on good handling practices of meat and cleanliness of high-risk areas such as bathrooms.

Disinfectants have to be registered as pesticides with the Environmental Protection Agency (EPA) in order to make a disinfectant claim on packaging. If you don't need to have a registered disinfectant—for example, if you don't have to clean a medical facility but simply want to clean your home—there are a lot of workable options that are much less toxic. Boiling sponges is based on common sense. And using essential oils as disinfectants doesn't appear to cause drug-resistant bacteria, as do synthetic triclosan-based disinfectants and antibacterial soaps.

## ANTISEPTIC HERBS AND ESSENTIAL OILS

Using herbs as antiseptic agents is an old art. It used to be called keeping your home "sweet." Not only were herbs such as lavender, mint, lemon balm, and thyme strewn on floors, they were potted up and placed on windowsills, and boughs were hung from rafters. Window boxes sprang from this tradition, I am sure, with potted herbs keeping away germs and flies and freshening the air. The antiseptic qualities of essential oils can be impressive. Studies have shown that many are more antiseptic than phenol, an industry disinfectant standard. Thyme oil is particularly powerful and has been found to kill bacteria including *E. coli* more effectively than brand-name disinfectants. However, thyme oil contains natural phenol and must be used with caution.

Doctors during the time of the Black Death of 1348 wore big cloaks over their heads; protruding from the cloak was a canoe-shaped beak about ten inches long full of antiseptic herbs. The herbs, we believe today, were meant to kill the germs that caused the disease. Another legendary use of herbs from that time concerns the Vinegar of the Four Thieves. A family of perfumers robbed the victims of the Black Death. For most people, that would have meant their own death, but these men knew well the antiseptic essential oils, and they infused them in vinegar and rubbed them on their bodies, thereby protecting themselves.

## DISINFECTING COMMON PROBLEM AREAS

**BATHROOM SINKS.** Always leave a bar of soap by the sink so people can wash their hands. To clean your sink, scrub with an antibacterial soft scrubber (see page 96).

**CUTTING BOARDS.** Wood cutting boards have been found to have natural antibacterial prop-

erties, *but* some plastic and wood cutting boards are porous enough that bacteria can fall into the tiny holes and cause a health hazard. A good rule of thumb is to not cut meat on cutting boards but rather on plates or pans that can be washed in soapy water at high temperatures, such as in a dishwasher. This will avoid cross-contamination. Or have two cutting boards, one of a size that fits easily into the dishwasher for meat only. I rinse my cutting boards frequently with straight white distilled vinegar. You can also pour boiling water on a cutting board.

**SPONGES.** Place them in boiling water for three to five minutes.

**TOILETS.** Spray toilet bowls with straight white distilled vinegar or with an antibacterial spray that contains an antiseptic essential oil (see Tea Tree Deodorizer, page 97).

**TOILETS WHEN TRAVELING.** Soak paper towels (tear them apart and cut into fours) in an antibacterial solution (see page 71), then place the saturated towels in a small plastic container or plastic bag to take with you. Wipe the toilet seat before sitting down.

HANDS-ON

*UV light:* Ultraviolet light kills bacteria. Fit a gooseneck lamp with a UV lightbulb, place it over your cutting board, and turn it on for 24 hours. Never look at the light; it can damage your eyes.

*Boiling Water:* This works well for washing sponges, cutting boards, stainless steel, and a variety of household utensils.

*Steam:* Although expensive, disinfectant steamers are now reaching the consumer market. They can be used to temporarily disinfect countertops, cutting boards, toilets, and so forth.

*Freezers:* You can freeze fabric to retard bacterial growth. Diapers, for example, can be cleaned, wrapped, and placed in the freezer overnight.

NOTE: Essential oil of thyme, sweet orange, lemongrass, rose, clove, eucalyptus, cinnamon, rosemary, birch, lavender, and tea tree are all more antiseptic than phenol. Herbs that are especially antiseptic include myrrh and bay.

## ANTIBACTERIAL SPRAY I 🎁

*I love the smell of essential oil antibacterial spray, particularly one with lavender oil, and I keep a spray bottle with this mixture near the cutting board. I thoroughly clean the board, then spray it two or three times a week.*

1 cup water
20 drops sweet orange essential oil
10 drops lavender essential oil
10 drops eucalyptus essential oil

Pour the water into a spray bottle. Blend the essential oils in a glass jar. With an eyedropper, add 8 drops of the essential oil base to the spray bottle. Spray on and let set for at least 15 minutes, or don't rinse at all (my preference). **Makes 1 cup spray and enough essential oil base mixture for 5 cups spray**

*Preparation Time:* A few minutes
*Shelf Life of Base Mixture:* Indefinite (if properly stored, essential oils last for years)
*Shelf Life of Spray:* Indefinite
*Storage of Base Mixture and Spray Bottle:* In a cool, dark place; screw tops on securely

### Variation

ANTIBACTERIAL SPRAY II: For a different blend of essential oils, substitute 20 drops sweet orange oil, 10 drops lavender oil, 5 drops eucalyptus oil, and 5 drops lemongrass oil.

## VINEGAR OF THE FOUR THIEVES 🎁

*This fourteenth-century formula has been passed down through the generations. The antibacterial herbs change from time to time depending on what herbs are locally available, but the formula has worked to prevent illness so successfully that it has never been abandoned.*

Handful each dried lavender, rosemary, sage,
wormwood, rue, and mint
Enough organic apple cider vinegar to cover
(about 4 quarts)

Follow the directions for vinegar infusions
(page 32), making sure that the vinegar completely covers the herbs throughout the setting
time. Let the mixture set for 4 to 6 weeks.
Strain. Pour as needed into a spray bottle.
Spot-test before using on fabrics.
**Makes about 4 quarts**

*Preparation Time:* About 10 minutes, plus 4 to
6 weeks setting time
*Shelf Life:* Indefinite
*Storage:* Glass container with a screw top, in a
cool, dark place

### Variations

GRAVE ROBBERS' BLEND: Substitute pine,
frankincense, balsam, clove, cinnamon, and
rosemary for the herbs.
VODKA AND HERBS: For an even more antiseptic formula, substitute vodka, rum, or
brandy for the vinegar.
SICKROOM SPRAY: Pour 2 cups of any of the
above completed formulas into a spray bottle.
Spritz into the air, being sure to avoid the eyes
and mouth.

## SOAP AND WATER ✗

*The EPA recognizes soap as a perfectly fine
disinfectant in its own right.*

Bar of olive oil castile soap
Water

Place a bar of soap near the sink. Encourage
people to wash their hands with it. To make
your own soap, see page 34.

### Variation

TEA TREE OIL ANTISEPTIC SOAP: Tea tree oil
is antifungal and antibacterial. Add 10 drops
tea tree oil to 4 ounces liquid castile soap in a
jar. Shake or stir to blend.

## VIM AND VINEGAR ✗

*On an airplane I happened to sit next to a vinegar
expert. I learned a lot about vinegar, including
that it is an excellent disinfectant. Use white
distilled vinegar, as it doesn't stain.*

White distilled vinegar

Use straight vinegar on cutting boards, in toilets, and on bathroom fixtures.

*Preparation Time:* None
*Shelf Life:* Indefinite

### Variation

ALCOHOL: Substitute rum, vodka, or brandy
for the vinegar; alcohol is one of the best disinfectants known. (Remember those cowboy
movies when they splashed whiskey on the
gunshot wound?)

## GRAPEFRUIT SEED EXTRACT ✗

*Grapefruit seed extract is used as a preservative
in natural cosmetics because it kills molds and*

*bacteria. It doesn't have much odor—helpful for those sensitive to essential oils.*

25 drops grapefruit seed extract
1 cup water

Combine the ingredients in a spray bottle. Spray onto the problem area; don't rinse.
**Makes 2 cups**

*Preparation Time:* Less than 1 minute
*Shelf Life:* Indefinite
*Storage:* Leave in the spray bottle

## BORAX ✗

*Borax has deodorizing properties. Use it generously in pastes or as a powder for toilets, carpets, and pet odors.*

Borax

See Scouring Powders and Soft Scrubbers, page 94.

# Furniture Care

Gothic romances such as *Jane Eyre* and *The Mayor of Castorbridge* always had servants of the great houses buffing the furniture to a high polish. The fragrance I imagine in these references is the rich, deep, honey-nut smell of beeswax and linseed oil. Oh, to have the time to bring my furniture to life like that. The simple recipes in this section will bring out the natural beauty of your wood furniture without hours of work.

## DUSTING

I once had an excellent cleaning woman named Terry who used to roar through the entire house of eight rooms—and I mean roar—in three hours. By the end of a day, there were about twenty dusting rags (no exaggeration) piled on the washing machine, and the house looked about three shades lighter simply because of the dust she had picked up on her rags (my husband and I are often too busy to dust regularly). As soon as a rag was dirty enough to threaten getting dirt back onto the surfaces, she'd drop it in a pile and grab a clean one. Her rag technique was an excellent one to learn.

### TIPS

- Wool dusting cloths work well because static electricity draws dust to wool, and lanolin in the wool causes the dust to stick to the wool.
- Next best to wool is a soft, 100 percent cotton rag such as a well-worn T-shirt or old diapers.
- Keep a rag bag handy; every time you have clothes to give away or toss into the trash, look at them with an eye for dusting, and toss suitable ones into the rag bag.
- Spritz rags with water before dusting so dust collects on the rag instead of puffing into the air.

## WOOD FURNITURE DUSTER ✗

*Traditional do-it-yourself formulas for furniture dusters are greasy, using mostly oil with just a few drops of vinegar. These products are unpleasantly* oily and make the furniture gummy. I turn the formulas upside down and use mostly vinegar with a few drops of oil. This makes a wonderful formula, and you get an added benefit because vinegar draws dirt out of wood.

¼ cup white distilled vinegar or lemon juice
A few drops jojoba or olive oil
3 to 5 drops fragrant essential oil (optional)

Combine the ingredients in a bowl, dab some on a soft natural-fiber rag, and use it to dust. The smell of vinegar will dissipate in a few hours.
**Makes ¼ cup**

Preparation Time: Less than 1 minute
Shelf Life: Indefinite with vinegar; if you use lemon juice, make only as much as you will use at one time
Storage: Glass jar with a screw top

## LEMON OIL DUSTER

10 drops lemon oil
2 tablespoons lemon juice
A few drops raw linseed oil or jojoba

Combine the ingredients in a jar. Shake to blend. Dab some on a cloth (about ½ teaspoon at a time), and dust.
**Makes about 2 tablespoons**

Preparation Time: 1 to 2 minutes
Shelf Life: Make only as much as you need at a time (lemon juice can turn rancid)

## CLEANING WOOD

## BASIC WOOD CLEANING FORMULA

This is a good formula for well-used furniture. Our old harvest dining room table is used for everything from homework to sewing projects to eating our meals, and it needs more of a wash than other furniture in the house.

¼ cup white distilled vinegar
¼ cup water
½ teaspoon liquid soap or detergent
A few drops jojoba or olive oil
3 to 5 drops fragrant essential oil (optional)

Combine the ingredients in a bowl, saturate a sponge with the mixture, squeeze out the excess, and wash surfaces. The smell of vinegar will dissipate in a few hours.
**Makes ½ cup**

Preparation Time: Less than 1 minute
Shelf Life: Indefinite
Storage: Glass jar with a screw top

Variations
LEMON LIGHTENER: Lemon is a mild bleach and can be substituted for vinegar to lighten wood. Only make as much as you need at a time.
ANTISEPTIC ROSEMARY WOOD CLEANSER: Add 5 to 10 drops rosemary essential oil. Rosemary adds an earthy scent and provides antiseptic qualities.

## CITRUS SPRAY CLEANSER

*This is a good spray cleaner for cutting grime. Just be sure to use it in an area with adequate ventilation (see page 38).*

2 teaspoons citrus solvent
2 cups water
A few drops jojoba or olive oil

Combine the ingredients in a spray bottle, and shake to blend. Spray dirty furniture, wiping dry with a soft cloth as you go. Spot-test for colorfastness before you use the spray on fabric.
**Make 2 cups**

*Preparation Time:* Less than 1 minute
*Shelf Life:* Indefinite
*Storage:* Leave in the spray bottle

### FURNITURE WAXES AND POLISHES
Polishing uses friction to make a surface glossy and smooth, and wood polishes use oils to aid this process. A wax polish leaves a protective layer of wax in addition to shine. See page 30 for more details about making wax creams.

## BASIC POLISHING CREAM WAXING FORMULA

*You can bring furniture to a high polish with this natural wax, and it smells wonderful whether or not you add the lemon oil.*

4 ounces oil (2½ ounces olive oil or jojoba,
1½ ounces coconut oil)

1 ounce beeswax
1 ounce carnauba wax
4 ounces distilled water
Natural preservative of choice (see page 36)
5 to 10 drops essential oil of lemon (optional)

Melt the oils and waxes in a double boiler over medium heat. Remove from the heat, pour in the water, and mix with a hand mixer until thick and creamy. (If you are using a blender, first add the water, then drizzle in the melted oils and waxes while the blender is on so they emulsify.) Add the preservative and essential oil as desired, then blend. Dab some cream onto a soft cotton rag, and rub into the furniture. Buff and polish until the oils have been well worked into the wood.
**Makes 1¼ cups**

*Preparation Time:* 25 minutes
*Shelf Life:* 6 months or more
*Storage:* Glass jar with a screw top

### Variations
COCOA BUTTER CREAMY WAX: Substitute cocoa butter for the coconut oil if you like the distinctive cocoa butter scent.
CARNAUBA CREAM WAX: Substitute carnauba (available in hardware stores) for half the beeswax. Carnauba wax, the hardest wax around, is useful for heavily used furniture.
CARNAUBA COCOA BUTTER WAX: For a rich, nutty-scented wax, follow directions above for Carnauba Cream Wax, substituting cocoa butter for the coconut oil.

LEMONY LAVENDER WAX: For a light flower-scented wax, add 5 to 20 drops essential oil of lavender.

### WATERLESS WAXES

The advantage of waterless waxes is that water doesn't bead in the polish. The trade-off is that the wax requires more oil and can be slightly greasy, and it takes more time to rub the wax into the wood. To reduce this problem, I suggest you make a very hard wax (use less oil)—say, 3 ounces oil to 1 ounce beeswax. (The recipe calls for 1 to 8 ounces oil.) If the wax seems too hard to be worked well into the furniture, rub it on, then soften it with a hair dryer, rubbing the wax into the furniture with a soft cloth as it melts. Be sure not to overheat the furniture. As with creamy waxes, you can substitute carnauba for half of the beeswax to make a harder wax. You can also substitute a "hard" oil such as coconut oil or cocoa butter for some of the liquid oil.

## BASIC WATERLESS WAX FORMULA

*This is an easy cream wax to make.*

2 to 8 ounces olive oil or jojoba (more for a
soft wax, less for hard)
1 ounce beeswax
1 capsule (200 i.u.) liquid vitamin E per 2
ounces of oil

Melt the oil and beeswax in a double boiler over medium heat. Remove from the heat, add the contents of the vitamin E capsule, and blend with a hand mixer until creamy.
**Makes up to 1 cup**

*Preparation Time:* 25 minutes
*Shelf Life:* 6 months or more
*Storage:* Glass jar with a screw top

## BASIC BEESWAX ✖

*Pure beeswax is a good sealant for wood.*

Small chunk beeswax
(about 1 inch by 2 inches)

Rub the beeswax into the wood as if you were using a crayon. Follow lightly with a hair dryer (not hot enough to scorch the wood) to soften the beeswax, and buff as you go with a soft cotton cloth.

### SIMPLE WAX-FREE POLISHES

## OLD FOLK FORMULA FOR FURNITURE POLISH ✖

*This is an old recipe that originally called for stale beer. I've used vinegar instead, because I was afraid that beer might leave the house smelling like a bar.*

4 cups white distilled vinegar
Handful of salt

Combine the ingredients in a nonaluminum pan and simmer for 1 hour, checking frequently to make sure that the liquid hasn't evaporated, and if it has, add more vinegar. Cool. Dab the mixture onto a cloth, and polish.

**Makes 4 cups**

*Preparation Time:* 1 hour
*Shelf Life:* Indefinite
*Storage:* Glass jar with a screw top

## BASIC RUBBED OIL FINISH ✗

*Linseed oil is the first choice for a furniture oil because it dries completely over time. Jojoba and olive oil don't dry as well, but they also do not go rancid as do many vegetable oils, making them good alternatives to linseed oil.*

Food-grade linseed oil, jojoba, or olive oil

Dribble a bit of oil onto the wood, and rub in deeply with a soft cloth, adding more oil as needed. Reapply over the following months as needed.

*Preparation Time:* None

### Variations

OIL AND LEMON: For a lemony smelling polish, add 5 drops pure lemon essential oil per ounce of oil.

TART POLISH: With a vinegary polish you don't have to worry about how well an oil dries, because there is not enough oil to cause a gummy buildup. Combine ¼ cup white distilled vinegar and a few drops oil.

ABRASIVE POLISH FOR ROUGH-SURFACED FURNITURE: Pour about ¼ cup rottenstone into

a bowl, and add linseed oil bit by bit to make a paste. Scoop some of the paste onto a soft cloth, and rub gently over the furniture, working with the grain.

## SHELLAC (ALSO CALLED FRENCH POLISH)

See page 294.

### Problem solving

We tend to damage good wood furniture at the worst times—visiting a wealthy aunt or the in-laws—but with these tips you'll be able to handle most disasters.

**BURNS.** Polish away burns by making a slightly abrasive rottenstone or pumice powder paste using jojoba or olive oil. Pour about ¼ cup rottenstone or pumice powder into a bowl, and add the oil bit by bit to make a paste. Scoop some of the paste onto a rag, and rub repeatedly over the burn.

**CANDLE-WAX REMOVER.** You'd be amazed at how often people ask me how to remove candle wax from furniture and carpets. Nothing works as well as a hair dryer—a handy solution if there ever was one. Soften the wax with the hair dryer, making sure not to burn yourself or the furniture. As the wax melts, wipe it up with a cloth.

**STAIN, SPOT, AND CUP RING REMOVER.** There are two good approaches to this problem. Start with an oil—nut oil, vegetable glycerine, or an actual nut—rubbed onto the stain, spot, or ring. Often this will do the trick. If the mark is deeper in the wood, try baking soda, white toothpaste, or pulverized chalk (if possible, use chalk that matches the color of the wood). Sprinkle on the baking soda or chalk, or squirt toothpaste onto the stain, spot, or ring, and rub back and forth with your finger.

### LEATHER FURNITURE CLEANER AND POLISH

Lemon juice or vinegar will pull dirt out of leather but may also dry it out. Adding a bit of jojoba or olive oil (a few drops per tablespoon or so) to these preparations will help prevent that problem.

## LAVENDER LEATHER CREAM

*This lush leather cream is very lubricating.*

1 ounce beeswax
1 cup walnut oil
½ cup glycerin
½ cup water
2 or 3 drops lavender essential oil
4 capsules (200 i.u.) liquid vitamin E

Melt the beeswax and oil in a double boiler over medium heat. Remove from the heat and add the glycerin, water, lavender oil, and the contents of the vitamin E capsule. Blend immediately with an electric beater until emulsified.
**Makes 2 cups**

*Preparation Time:* 25 minutes
*Shelf Life:* 6 months
*Storage:* Glass jar with a screw top, in a cool, dark place

## DRESSED IN JOJOBA ✗

*Vinegar will give leather a good cleaning. The liquid wax in this formula will keep the vinegar from drying out the leather.*

½ cup white distilled vinegar or lemon juice
A few drops jojoba or olive oil

Combine the ingredients in a bowl. Saturate the end of a soft rag with the mixture, and rub over the leather.
**Makes ½ cup**

*Preparation Time:* Less than 1 minute
*Shelf Life:* Indefinite with vinegar, 1 week with lemon juice

## SOAPY POLISH

*A liquid version of saddle soap, this polish cleans and lubricates.*

½ cup jojoba
½ teaspoon liquid castile soap

Combine the ingredients in a bowl and blend with a wire whisk. Dab a soft natural-fiber cloth into the mixture, and rub onto the leather. Do not rinse, but wipe off any residue.
**Makes ½ cup**

*Preparation Time:* About 1 minute
*Shelf Life:* Indefinite
*Storage:* Glass jar with a screw top

## LEATHER WASH

*Alcohol and vinegar combine to make this a strong disinfectant.*

¼ cup each vodka, white distilled vinegar,
and water
A few drops jojoba or olive oil

Combine the ingredients in a glass jar. Shake to blend. Pour some of the mixture onto a soft rag, and rub onto the leather. Do not rinse, but follow with Lavender Leather Cream (page 78) or Lanolin (page 79) to lubricate the leather.
**Makes ¾ cup**

*Preparation Time:* About 1 minute
*Shelf Life:* Indefinite
*Storage:* Glass jar with a screw top

## EGG WHITE WHIP SPOT REMOVER

1 or 2 egg whites, depending on the size of
the spot

Beat the egg whites until stiff. Scoop onto a clean sponge, and dab the area. Let set. Rinse with warm water.
**Makes 1 to 2 cups**

*Preparation Time:* A few minutes
*Shelf Life:* A few hours

## GLYCERIN GREASE STAIN LOOSENER

*A humectant, glycerin is very lubricating.*

Up to 1 teaspoon vegetable glycerin

Saturate the stain with glycerin, and let it set for 10 minutes or so. Wipe up with a soft cloth. Rinse away the residue thoroughly with warm, soapy water.

*Preparation Time:* None
*Shelf Life:* Indefinite

## CORNMEAL RUB

*Cornmeal absorbs some spots and stains.*

A few tablespoons cornmeal

Rub the stain with the cornmeal. Let it dry completely, then brush off.
**Makes a few tablespoons**

*Preparation Time:* None
*Shelf Life:* A few months in a cupboard; 1 year in the freezer
*Storage:* Glass jar with a screw top, or small plastic container

## LANOLIN ✕

*Lanolin adds waterproofing as well as lubrication to leather. It is available in tubes from pharmacies.*

Anhydrous lanolin

Simply apply some lanolin to your leather furniture and buff to a high shine.

## SADDLE SOAP

*As the name implies, saddle soap is a leather cleaner and polish. In the old days when most peo-*

*ple had a horse, they used saddle soap, and the recipes weren't much different than this.*

2 ounces jojoba
2 ounces olive oil
1 ounce beeswax
1 ounce grated soap or liquid castile soap
3 ounces water
1 ounce vodka, rum, or whiskey

Melt the jojoba, oil, beeswax, and soap over medium heat. Once the beeswax has melted (about 5 minutes), remove from the heat, add the water and alcohol, and blend immediately with an electric beater until emulsified.

**Makes 1¼ cups**

*Preparation Time:* 25 minutes
*Shelf Life:* 6 months or more
*Storage:* Glass jar with a screw top, in a cool, dark place

# Herbal Sachets, Potpourri, and Pomanders

Sachets and potpourris use the same ingredients—fragrant flower petals, leaves from aromatic herbs, spices, pine cones (optional), and fixatives such as orris root or citrus peels—but the plant matter is processed and packaged differently. Sachets are used in drawers to freshen linens, wool sweaters, and underwear and are hung in closets to repel clothing moths or add fragrance. In the olden days women often tucked small herbal sachets into their bras.

Potpourri is used more as an air freshener and to disperse flower, herb, or spice fragrance into the air. A good time to collect ingredients for these herbal crafts is on a summer vacation, on walks, or when tending a garden. A nice benefit of collecting your own ingredients for a potpourri on a vacation or a special walk is that it will remind you of that time and place. Otherwise, find materials in garden centers, herb supply catalogs, and health food stores.

## SUGGESTED INGREDIENTS FOR SACHETS AND POTPOURRI

*Petals and Buds:* Roses, jasmine, phlox

*Fragrant Herbs:* Rosemary, basil, bay, mint, lady's mantle, thyme, lemon balm, lavender, chamomile, sage

*Roots, Spices, Seeds, and Berries:* Allspice, cloves, star anise, cinnamon sticks, licorice, juniper berries, ginger, whole nutmeg, caraway, vanilla, bayberry, cardamom pods

*Fragrant Essential Oils:* Gardenia, rose, clove, cinnamon, lemon, sweet orange, myrrh, ylang-ylang, lavender, neroli, sandalwood

*Fixatives:* Orris root powder (many people are allergic to orris root), dried citrus peel (orange, lemon, lime, et cetera) ground in a coffee grinder or spice mill, plants with fixative qualities (clary sage, mint, bay, oakmoss, violet roots, cloves, coriander seeds, patchouli), cedar chips, ground corncobs

## SOME SCENT COMBINATIONS

*Woodsy:* Lemon balm, thyme, nutmeg, rosemary, sandalwood, sage, black pepper, cloves, cinnamon

*Lemony:* Lemon balm, geranium, lemongrass, lemon thyme, bergamot, lemon verbena, citrus peel, pennyroyal, mint

*Summery:* Rose, lavender, mint, lemon balm, orris root

*Lavendery:* Lavender, rose

*Mothproofing Sachet:* Rosemary, mint, thyme, lavender, cloves

*Herbs That Repel Clothing Moths:* Lavender, lemon, cloves, camphor, hyssop, winter savory, rosemary, cassia bark, cedar, sassafras

*Fruity:* Gardenia; carnation; peony; lemon balm; lemongrass; orange, lemon, and lime peel; vanilla

*Vacuum Sachet:* In the *Herbal Home Companion,* Theresa Loe recommends putting sachets in the vacuum cleaner bag. Include ½ cup or so of zeolite to absorb odors.

## GUIDELINES FOR MAKING SACHETS AND POTPOURRI

## BASIC FORMULA FOR SACHETS AND POTPOURRI 🎁

2 cups flower petals
1 cup herbs (more or less, depending on how aromatic they are)
2 tablespoons total (or less so as not to overwhelm other fragrances) roots, spices, seeds, and berries
8 to 10 drops essential oil
2 teaspoons fixative (see page 80)

Combine the ingredients gently so as not to bruise the petals. Store in an airtight container to dry for 6 weeks, gently shaking and turning upside down and back every few days during the drying time.

**Makes 3 cups**

*Preparation Time:* About 10 minutes
*Shelf Life:* 6 months
*Storage:* Glass jar with a screw top, in a cool, dark place

### SACHETS (SWEET BAGS)

Prepare the sachet following the directions above. After the plant mixture has dried thoroughly (6 weeks or so), crumble the petals and herbs, and use a coffee grinder to grind the spices and seeds.

**FABRIC CHOICES.** Choose a natural fiber with a tight weave, such as silk. A good idea for small sachets for drawers and linens is to fill cotton teabags sold for making your own tea (check health food stores). Another easy option is a cotton bandana, scarf, or handkerchief; place the plant mixture in the middle, gather the edges together, and tie with a ribbon.

**SIZES AND SHAPES.** Sachets traditionally come in two or three basic sizes, although in fact anything goes. One traditional size placed among undergarments (an old-fashioned tradition, particularly for a bride at her wedding) is about 2 inches by 2 inches; the other is a pillowcase shape about the size of a piece of paper (8½ inches by 11 inches) to be hung in closets and placed in drawers. Sachets about 4 inches by 4 inches are ideal for mothproofing when storing sweaters and other woolens.

## POTPOURRI

Follow the directions for making potpourri and sachets above, paying particular attention to the shape and color of the petals, herbs, and spices. Unlike sachets, in which the plant matter is ground and crumbled, plants in potpourri should be kept as intact as possible. Once the plant matter has dried the requisite six weeks or so, place the mixture in glass bowls, baskets, or other attractive containers.

## POMANDERS

### BASIC POMANDER

Scotch tape
1 orange, lemon, or lime
About 2 ounces whole cloves
Up to 1 tablespoon each ground cinnamon,
nutmeg, and ginger
1 teaspoon orris root (optional)
4 feet ribbon

Attach a strip of Scotch tape around the orange from top to bottom. Do the same thing around the circumference. The two strips will cross squarely in two places. With a hammer and a small nail, make holes along both edges of the strips. Stick the cloves into the holes. Then make nail holes all over except where the strips and cloves are. Place the studded fruit in a bowl, and dust the ground spices into the empty holes. Some people then fill the holes with cloves (so more than 2 ounces are needed); others leave them as is. You choose. Place the bowl in a dark, dry place for about 4 weeks; the fruit should be exposed to the air so it can dry. Dust the dried fruit with orris root as a fixative. Then wrap half the ribbon around the fruit from top to bottom, following the tape strips; tie it at the top. With the other half of the ribbon, follow the other tape strip around the circumference, and tie. Hang from the top tie, or give as a gift.
**Makes 1 pomander**

*Shelf Life:* If it dries properly, indefinite; otherwise discard

# Laundry Products

The combined effect of 250 million Americans (and billions more worldwide) washing their clothes once a week—or more—has a staggering effect on the environment. Understanding why laundry products are formulated the way they are is important to help you make informed choices about the environment, while at the same time meeting your lifestyle needs.

## CHOOSING SOAP OR DETERGENT

In most supermarkets and even health food stores, all commercial laundry-cleaning products are detergents, not soaps. Whereas most soaps are better for the environment than all but one detergent, soap can cause soap scum and graying of clothing unless you have soft water (see Buyer's Guide, page 42). There was a time when I was willing to shave my own soap bars and use an old-fashioned wringer washer—I loved that machine—but these days, as a working parent with chronically overflowing laundry baskets, it's no longer possible, even for me.

## IF YOU DO CHOOSE SOAP

**WATER SOFTENING: HOW TO DO IT.** The best way to soften water for washing laundry with soap is to add a water softener—baking soda works well—to the water in the washing machine, leave it for 10 minutes, then add the laundry and soap. I highly recommend experimenting on your own, because water has varying amounts of minerals. Start out with $\frac{1}{4}$ cup, and increase to $\frac{1}{2}$ cup or more if you have very hard water. The benefits of baking soda are its ability to neutralize odors and soften clothes. One caution: Baking soda can leave deposits on clothes if used in too high concentrations.

**THE OLD WAY: MAKING YOUR OWN LAUNDRY SOAP SHAVINGS.** My neighbor's mother had twelve children and washed every-thing, including the diapers, in castile soap, with excellent results. She made her own soap shavings from bar soap. Castile soap is a mild soap originally made from olive oil. Today castile soap can be made from other vegetable oils as well, and the soap can be found in liquid or bar form. You can make your own "flakes" to use in your washing machine by shaving the soap with a grater. My neighbor's mother used to shave her soap on an old-fashioned soap board. Try to make the thinnest shavings possible so they will dissolve well. A little trial and error might be needed to get the right amount. If you do use soap shavings, you need to use hot water to melt the soap for the wash cycle. Always rinse the clothes in cold water, however, to stop the soap from sudsing.

**LAUNDRY BLUING.** Bluing was used in the old days, before optical brighteners and detergents, to counteract the yellowing and graying of fabric washed with soap. Prussian blue was usually used, because it reacted with the alkaline residue left by soap. The blue would make the fabric look white. If you are using a detergent with optical brighteners (most have them), don't bother to try bluing. However, for those of you using soap, give it a try.

## BASIC BATCH OF LAUNDRY BLUING

3 cups baking soda
$\frac{1}{2}$ teaspoon Prussian blue

Combine the ingredients. Add 1 teaspoon of the mixture per load of laundry.
**Makes 3 cups**

## BUYER'S GUIDE

### LAUNDRY PRODUCTS

ECOVER, Seventh Generation, Life Tree, and Earth Friendly Cleaner provide concentrated, vegetable-oil-based (as opposed to petroleum-based) laundry detergents without synthetic fragrances. They are available in health food stores. If you buy laundry detergents in your supermarket, be sure to choose those that are dye and perfume free.

*Preparation Time:* Less than 1 minute
*Shelf Life:* Indefinite
*Storage:* Glass jar with a screw top

TIPS

* Detergents and soaps leave a film on clothes, although the film from the detergent is invisible. Before switching from detergent to soap, or from soap to detergent, wash the clothes first with ½ cup white distilled vinegar for a full load, ¼ cup for a small load.
* Your choice of detergent or soap for washing silk and wool is important. Please see the recommendations for specific natural fibers starting on page 88. The wrong product can leave the fabric stiff and brittle.
* Polyester and synthetic fibers are harder to clean than naturally derived fibers; therefore, detergents are advised to clean these fabrics. Natural fibers need less powerful laundry products.

WHITENERS

## LET THERE BE LIGHT AND LEMONS

*Lemons lightly bleach everything from hair to wood to clothing.*

½ cup lemon juice

Add the lemon juice to the rinse cycle. This works best if you hang the clothes to dry in the sun.
**Makes ½ cup**

*Preparation Time:* None
*Shelf Life:* 3 to 4 days refrigerated
*Storage:* Glass jar with a screw top or a lidded plastic container

## MINERAL MIGHT

*Minerals are called laundry boosters; they generally brighten clothing and help keep laundry from graying. Don't use this formula if the fabric could shrink in warm or hot water.*

½ cup borax or washing soda

Add the mineral to the wash cycle, using warm to hot water so it dissolves.
**Makes enough for 1 load**

*Preparation Time:* None

## HYDROGEN PEROXIDE

*Commercially available hydrogen peroxide comes in a standard 3 percent solution.*

½ cup hydrogen peroxide

Add to the rinse cycle.
**Makes enough for 1 load**

*Preparation Time:* None

FABRIC SOFTENERS AND STATIC CLING
Fabric softeners are designed to reduce static cling. If you wear natural fibers, you usually won't have that problem. Add ¼ to ½ cup baking soda to the wash cycle to soften the fabric.

## ODOR REMOVAL

Minerals neutralize many odors, from perspiration to the smell of some new clothing. The longer you soak the clothes in minerals, the better they work, although one simple wash with minerals works well for most odors. If you need to soak the clothes overnight, do not add the detergent until right before you wash the clothes. If the odor isn't completely gone, use more minerals and keep soaking, agitating the washing machine occasionally to blend.

Acids neutralize alkaline smells. The well-known example of this is using tomato juice (acidic) on dogs after they have been sprayed by a skunk.

**THE "NEW" SMELL.** All new clothing and fabric except those that are organic have undoubtedly been coated with a formaldehyde-based material to keep them from wrinkling. Formaldehyde is a suspected carcinogen, and you should try to wash out the new smell before wearing the clothing. To do this, soak it overnight (or at least for an hour or two) in a washing machine, with 1 cup baking soda added to the water. Agitate the machine occasionally. To wash, add your normal detergent and proceed as usual. Another approach is to neutralize the new smell with an acid such as white distilled vinegar. Soak new fabric overnight in up to 2 cups white distilled vinegar per wash load of water. To wash, add detergent or soap and 1/4 cup baking soda to the washing machine and launder as usual.

Some imported clothes are now impregnated with long-lasting disinfectants; you can identify these clothes by the smell alone. It is very hard to remove it. If the fabric is rayon, you can learn from my hard-earned experience that soaking in baking soda and washing will invariably shrink the fabric. Baking soda doesn't work well against disinfectants, and too strong a vinegar solution can damage rayon fibers. I've started asking catalog companies if their clothes are disinfected, and I won't buy the clothes if they have been.

## BUYER'S GUIDE

### BLEACH

MOST household bleach is sodium hypochlorite, a moderately toxic chlorine salt. In the wastewater stream, household bleach can bond with other chemicals to form simple organochlorines. Organochlorines can cause cancer and endocrine disruption. Seventh Generation offers an effective alternative bleach, which you can find in health food stores and some supermarkets.

## MINERAL MAGIC

*You'd be amazed at how many chemical odors your clothing picks up in everyday life. Nothing works as well to remove the odors as this formula: I've used it to remove even pesticides.*

½ cup baking soda or washing soda
(see Note)

Add to the wash cycle with your normal deter-gent. Let the machine fill with water and the agitation begin, then turn it off and let the clothes soak for a few hours, or better yet overnight. Agitate for a minute or so every few hours during the day and before going to bed. Then continue the cycle. Repeat if the odor still lingers (I often have to repeat the process twice to completely rid new bedsheets of formaldehyde, for example).

NOTE: If you have very hard water, washing soda can leave a carbonate deposit on clothes. Substitute borax instead.

## SPOT REMOVERS AND PRESOAKS

### TIPS

* Be sure to spot-test for colorfastness.
* Note that acid- and protein-based stains are removed with alkaline materials such as washing soda, baking soda, and borax; alkaline stains such as grass, tarnish, and minerals are removed with acids such as vinegar, citrus, and cream of tartar.
* Absorbent materials work for some stains. Try blotting the stain with paper towels, or with cornmeal, chalk, or cornstarch (cover the stain with the powder, and wipe off as it absorbs).
* For stains on colored fabric, try a paste made with water and cream of tartar.
* Glycerin is excellent for softening older stains before washing.

* Wool and silk can be ruined with alkaline materials. Choose an acidic or neutral detergent, such as Heavenly Horsetail, and rinse with ¼ cup white distilled vinegar to a pail of water, to ensure reestablishment of the acidic environment of the fabric.
* Pour boiling water from a height of 2 to 3 feet onto fabric stretched taut over a bowl in the sink. This works well for removing wine, coffee, and tea from cotton and linen.
* If the dyes in your clothing are bleeding, add 1 cup salt to a filled washing machine and let the clothes soak for an hour or so before washing. The salt will act as a fixative. Test first.

## GENERAL DIRECTIONS:

**PASTES.** Combine dry material with enough water to make a paste. Rub into the stain, and launder as usual.

**SOAKS.** Soak tough stains overnight if necessary.

**DAB SOME STAIN REMOVER ON THE STAIN.** Dab some recommended cleanser, such as glyc-erin, on the stain, then launder.

**SPRAYS.** Liquid ingredients, such as club soda or 3 percent hydrogen peroxide solution, can be put in a spray bottle and sprayed onto fabric.

### STAIN REMOVERS

*All-purpose:* Washing soda, cornstarch

*Baby Formula:* Washing soda, borax, strong soap or detergent

*Berries:* Washing soda, borax, strong soap or detergent, club soda, white wine, 3 per-cent hydrogen peroxide solution, glycerin. See Tips, above, for pouring boiling water on fabric from a height.

*Blood:* Washing soda, borax, club soda, 3 percent hydrogen peroxide solution, strong soap or detergent, cold water, cornstarch and cold water, saltwater

*Butter and Grease:* Washing soda, glycerin as a prewash, soap or detergent

*Chewing Gum:* Freeze it, then pull it off

*Chocolate:* 3 percent hydrogen peroxide solution, washing soda

*Coffee and Tea:* Washing soda, borax, club soda, 3 percent hydrogen peroxide solution

*Crayons:* Mixture of baking soda and detergent; glycerin as a prewash; heat with a hair dryer, then wipe off

*Decals:* Vegetable oil or glycerin; heat with a hair dryer, then pull off

*Egg:* Cold water, washing soda, cream of tartar paste

*Food:* Washing soda, borax, club soda, strong soap or detergent

*Fruit:* Washing soda, borax, club soda, strong soap or detergent

*Grass:* White distilled vinegar, citrus solvent, cream of tartar, milk, glycerin

*Grease:* Washing soda (loosen first with glycerin, white distilled vinegar, baking soda paste)

*Ink:* Milk, white distilled vinegar or lemon juice and salt, cream of tartar, white wine, soap and water. For ballpoint ink, soak in vodka

*Lipstick:* Glycerin, baking soda and detergent soft scrub

*Mold and Mildew:* Borax, 3 percent hydrogen peroxide solution

*Mustard:* Washing soda (loosen first with vegetable glycerin or strong soap or detergent)

*Oil:* Washing soda, glycerin, vegetable oil

*Paint:* White distilled vinegar, milk, lemon juice, citrus solvent, cream of tartar, glycerin

*Perspiration:* Shampoo, washing soda, borax; older perspiration stains may respond to white distilled vinegar

*Petroleum Oil:* Washing soda

*Protein Stains:* See Blood

*Ring Around the Collar:* Shampoo, chalk, cream of tartar paste

*Rust:* White distilled vinegar, borax, milk, lemon juice, citrus solvent, cream of tartar

*Sugar:* Use cold water only, so as not to set the stain

*Tomato Sauce:* Washing soda, borax, cream of tartar, baking soda

*Urine:* Washing soda, borax, baking soda

*Wax:* Washing soda

*Wine:* See Berries

## CLEANING DIAPERS

Soak diapers in a covered pail with water and 1 cup borax. Don't let the diapers sit more than a day or so. After washing, add 1 cup white distilled vinegar to the rinse water to remove all detergent or soap residue.

## LAUNDRY STARCH

## CORNSTARCH

*There are a few diehards who still starch shirts. This formula is for them.*

2 teaspoons cornstarch

1 cup water

Combine the ingredients in a spray bottle; shake to dissolve. Spray on clothing before ironing.

**Makes 1 cup**

*Preparation Time:* Less than 1 minute
*Shelf Life:* Make only as much as you'll need at a time. The recipe can be halved.
NOTE: Hide the white cornstarch residue on dark clothes by adding ¼ cup steeped and strained black tea to the rinse water.

### NATURAL FLAME RETARDANTS

Flame retardants are used on clothing and bedding intended for people who are immobilized for one reason or another: babies and the elderly, for example. Wool is naturally flame retardant; mattresses made of all wool pass state requirements for flame retardant qualities.

## NATURAL NONPERMANENT FLAME RETARDANT

*The flame retardant has been mostly washed out of secondhand baby clothes. This preparation will provide some protection.*

5 ounces borax

4 cups hot water

Combine the ingredients in a spray bottle. Shake to dissolve. Spray the clothes and don't rinse. Reapply after each wash.

**Makes 4 cups**

*Preparation Time:* About a minute
*Shelf Life:* Indefinite

### RINSES

* Baking soda is a good fabric softener.
* ¼ cup white distilled vinegar added to the rinse water will remove soap or detergent residue.
* Add 10 drops or so lavender or rose essential oil to the rinse water. Lavender provides some insect repelling qualities, and rose imparts a lovely and lingering fragrance.

### DRY CLEANING

Clothes are dry-cleaned instead of washed to prevent them from shrinking. It is the agitation of "wet" cleaning that often causes fabric to shrink. This is especially true of wool and rayon. The cleaner used by 80 percent of the industry is perchlorethylene, a highly neurotoxic chemical and possible carcinogen. If you have your clothes dry-cleaned in shops that use "perc," be sure to air them well before wearing.

Guidelines for washing specific types of fabric successfully without dry cleaning are found below.

### GUIDE TO WASHING NATURAL FIBERS

NOTE: Much of the information here about how to clean fibers is derived from *Fiber Facts,* by Bette Hochberg. The booklet is written for weavers but is helpful for anyone interested in caring properly for natural fibers.

PROTEIN FIBERS

*Caution:* Never use bleach on wool, silk, or other protein fibers.

### *Wool (Sheep)*

* Wool should not be left in direct sunlight, because it disintegrates more quickly.
* Wool is resilient and recovers quickly from wrinkling if hung (particularly in a steamy bathroom).
* Wool is naturally flame retardant.

*Wet Cleaning*

* Hand-wash gently; agitation can cause the fibers to contract. Never twist or wring out wool; gently swirl the wool in the water, then rinse and press water out.
* Use mild soap or detergent with as close to a neutral pH as possible. Alkaline materials destroy wool: Any soap or detergent with a pH above 8 will harm wool. Infinity Heavenly Horsetail all-purpose cleaner (available in health food stores) has a pH of 4.5, ideal for cleaning protein fibers such as wool and silk. To lower the pH of a soap or detergent, add 1 tablespoon white distilled vinegar or lemon juice before washing. In general, soaps are better to use than detergents for wool, because they strip less of the wool's natural oil.
* Water temperature when washing wool should be 100° F.
* If you need to remove a soapy film, use a white distilled vinegar or lemon juice rinse.
* Block the wool—lay it flat and stretch it to the correct size and shape—before drying; it will dry to the blocked size.

*Ironing*

* Always iron with steam, not dry heat, and at a medium setting.

*Storage*

* Make sure that wool is clean when you store it to prevent moth damage.
* For an old and famous weaver's herbal sachet to store with your woolens, see page 81.

*Wool for Bedding*

Wool is an excellent material for comforters and mattresses. The average person gives off a pint of water vapor as perspiration during an eight-hour sleep period under a comforter. Wool has the ability to absorb large amounts of moisture under warm and cool sleeping conditions, so you don't feel wet and clammy. Be sure to buy organic wool batting (see Sources and Resources) for making comforters and mattresses, because most wool is heavily sprayed with pesticides. Chemical-free wool comforters and mattresses are expensive, but if well cared for they will become heirlooms, passed on from generation to generation.

### *Silk*

* Cultivated silk (mulberry silk) and so-called raw or wild silk (tussah silk) are made from different silkworms, with the coarser raw silk derived from wild or partially wild silkworms. Raw silk is much stronger than silk from cultivated silkworms.
* As a rule, silk is a strong, durable fiber resistant to tearing.
* Use peroxide, not bleach, to whiten silk.

*Wet Cleaning*

* Silk should not be exposed to the agitation of a washing machine or the fabric will shrink. It is less able to withstand abrasion than most wools, so hand-wash gently.

* As with wool and rayon, never twist or wring out silk; gently swirl it in the water, rinse, then press the water out.

* Wash silk in water that is 100 to 120°F.

* It is much better to use a soap than a detergent for silk. Detergents can strip the natural oil from silk and leave it stiff and brittle. Use a gentle castile soap with as close to a neutral pH as possible. Avoid harsh lye soaps, because they have a high pH that can harm silk; anything with a pH above 10 will destroy silk. Never use washing soda on silk. If you are concerned about the alkalinity of your soap, neutralize some of the lye by adding vinegar or lemon juice to the soap.

* To combat dulling due to soap scum— common in hard-water areas—rinse in water in which a few tablespoons of white distilled vinegar have been added.

*Ironing*

* Use a cool to medium iron.

* Silk is resistant to wrinkling and resumes its shape easily; hanging silk in a steamy bathroom may be all it needs.

*Storage*

* Silk is vulnerable to damage from sunlight and should be stored in a cool, dark place.

*Hair or Fur (Alpaca, Angora, Camel, Goat, Llama, Mohair)*

* Follow the directions for washing and caring for wool.

*Down (Cashmere)*

* Follow the directions for washing and caring for wool.

### NATURAL FIBERS: CELLULOSE FIBERS

*Cotton (Seed Fiber)*

* Cotton is a moderately strong fiber.

* All cotton except organic cotton is usually heavily sprayed with pesticides. To reduce possible pesticide residue, soak the cotton overnight in cool water and 1 cup baking soda. Rinse thoroughly.

* Dyes used on cotton can bleed if not applied with a proper fixative. To reduce bleeding, soak the fabric in cool water with ¼ cup salt and 1 tablespoon white distilled vinegar. Don't wash colored cotton clothing with white fabrics.

*Wet Cleaning*

* Unless the garment is preshrunk, wash it in cold water. If the garment is preshrunk, washing in warm water (120°F) is recommended.

* Wash with an alkaline material (pH over 7) such as most soaps and detergents. Strong soaps and detergents shouldn't harm cotton.

* Do not add vinegar or lemon juice to the rinse; these acids can weaken the fibers.

*Ironing*

* Use a hot iron.

* Cotton is moderately resistant to wrinkling

but not as much so as wool or silk.

*Storage*

* Although cotton resists damage from sunlight better than wool or silk, cotton should still be stored away from direct sunlight, especially because the sun will fade the dyes.

* Because cotton wrinkles, hanging is better than folding.

*Flax/Linen, Ramie, and Hemp (Bark Fibers)*

* Bark fibers make the strongest, most sturdy fabric available if they are well woven.

* Although a bit stiff when new, bark fibers soften with repeated washings.

*Wet Cleaning*

* Washing bark fibers such as linen in a washing machine on the gentle cycle is okay because they are not damaged or shrunk by agitation.

* Bark fibers can handle strong alkaline soaps, detergents, and even washing soda.

* Wash bark fibers in water that is around 120°F.

* Avoid rinses with vinegar or lemon juice.

* Hang linen and other bark fibers to dry, then finish in a cool dryer to soften.

*Ironing*

* Use a hot iron.

*Storage*

* Bark fibers wrinkle easily, so hang whenever possible.

MANUFACTURED FIBERS: CELLULOSE FIBERS

*Rayon (Regenerated Cellulose Fibers—Man-Made)*

Rayon feels a lot like cotton but is much weaker and shrinks significantly in the agitation and abrasion of a washing machine. It took me a long time and many ruined garments before I learned that it wasn't the temperature that caused the fabric to shrink—although rayon must be washed in cool water—but the agitation of the washing machine.

*Wet Cleaning*

* The key to washing rayon without shrinkage is to not use the washing machine but to hand-wash.

* As with wool, never twist or wring out rayon; gently swirl it in the water, then rinse and press the water out.

* Wash rayon in cool water (around 100°F).

* Don't use vinegar or lemon juice in the rinse water for rayon; they can damage the fibers. If an acid-based material such as fruit juice or tomato sauce is spilled on rayon, immediately rinse in cold water. If you have hard water, use a detergent instead of a soap to avoid soap scum and the subsequent need for a vinegar or lemon juice rinse.

* Even strong soaps and detergents are okay to use on rayon.

*Ironing*

* Rayon wrinkles more easily than cotton but less so than linen.

* Use medium-high heat.

*Storage*

* Store away from sunlight.

*Acetate (Cellulose Fiber Derivative)*

* Follow the directions for rayon.

*Synthetic Fibers (Nylon, Polyester, Acrylic)*

* Synthetic fibers don't breathe well. If in summer you feel as though you are wrapped in a plastic bag, check the fabric of your clothing. Undoubtedly it is polyester, or at least partially so.

* Synthetic fibers are not sustainable for the environment. They are derived from petroleum.

* Little fiber balls known as pills can form easily on synthetic fibers and are a sure sign of wear. Try to clip them off with sharp scissors.

*Wet Cleaning*

* Synthetic fibers should be washed with soaps and detergents that are mildly alkaline—pH 8 or 9—but not strongly so, or the fabric will weaken.

* Wash synthetics in cool water (between 100 and 110°F); heat can cause permanent wrinkles in synthetic fabric.

* Using a washing machine is fine for synthetics, although a lot of agitation may cause fiber balls, or pills.

* Mild white distilled vinegar or lemon juice rinses are fine for synthetic fibers.

*Ironing*

* A hot iron will melt synthetic fibers. Use a low temperature.

* One of the best (and only) reasons to wear synthetics is that they do not wrinkle easily, although high heat can permanently set wrinkles.

*Storage*

* Polyester and acrylic hold up against sun-

light better than do natural fibers, but it's best to store them away from direct sunlight.

# Mold and Mildew

Mold can be dangerous to your health, and it detracts from property value. It should be eradicated as soon as it appears. Dry out anything that is damp, such as basements and carpets. Fix leaks in the plumbing and roof. Wipe up spills. Vigilance will pay off.

HANDS-ON

* Remove the water source.

* Use a dehumidifier.

* Make sure the air in your home is circulating properly. Use fans if necessary.

* Use an ultraviolet lightbulb anywhere mold appears. It works particularly well in the basement. Called a germicidal UV light by one manufacturer, it can kill up to 100 percent of the mold. Never look directly at the light; it can damage your eyes.

* Cover the mold with cornstarch to remove moisture. Dust off.

* Place zeolite bags in moist area to remove odors.

* Place an open bag of lime in a damp area; the lime will absorb moisture.

## TEA TREE TREASURE ✄ 🎁

*Nothing works to eradicate mold and mildew as well as this spray. I've used it successfully on a* moldy ceiling from a leaking roof, a musty bureau, a musty rug, and a moldy shower curtain. Tea tree oil is expensive, but a little goes a long way. Unless you have frequent mold crises, this mixture can last for months.

2 teaspoons tea tree oil
2 cups water

Combine the ingredients in a spray bottle, shake to blend, and spray on problem areas. Do not rinse. The strong odor will dissipate in a day or so.
**Makes 2 cups**

*Preparation Time:* Less than 1 minute
*Shelf Life:* Indefinite
*Storage:* Leave in the spray bottle

## CITRUS SEED EXTRACT

*The advantage of this formula over Tea Tree Treasure is that it is odorless.*

25 drops citrus seed extract
1 cup water

Combine the ingredients in a spray bottle, shake to blend, and spray on problem areas. Do not rinse.
**Makes 2 cups**

*Preparation Time:* About 1 minute
*Shelf Life:* Indefinite
*Storage:* Leave in the spray bottle

## HYDROGEN PEROXIDE SPRAY

*This spray is odorless.*

½ cup 3 percent hydrogen peroxide solution
1 cup water

Combine the ingredients in a spray bottle. Spray on the moldy area. Do not rinse.
**Makes 1½ cups**

*Preparation Time:* Less than 1 minute
*Shelf Life:* Make only as much as you need at a time; hydrogen peroxide loses its potency when exposed to the air

### Variation
VINEGAR SPRAY: Substitute white distilled vinegar for the hydrogen peroxide. The odor will dissipate quickly, and vinegar's shelf life is indefinite.

## BORAX SCRUB

*Borax works well for must. I once significantly reduced the musty smell on the walls of a bedroom by covering them with a thick borax paste, leaving it on the walls for a few days until the borax dried, then dusting the borax off the wall.*

Borax

Scoop some borax onto a sponge and scrub the area. Leave on overnight to dry. Dust off borax by sweeping or vacuuming.

# Plastic and Vinyl Cleaners

Some plastics made from a chemical soup of petroleum products are hormone disrupters. Avoid plastic and vinyl whenever possible by buying fabric shower curtains, cars with cloth or leather seats, and wood outdoor furniture. For existing plastic or vinyl, the release of toxic fumes, called outgassing, should be minimized by frequent washing with the preparations listed below. A shower curtain, for example, could be left to bake in the sun.

### MINERAL MAGIC FOR PLASTICS

*If you wash new plastics, such as vinyl car seats, once a week, the outgassing will be reduced.*

½ cup baking soda
Water

Place the baking soda in a bowl, and add enough water to make a paste. Scoop some paste onto a sponge, and scrub the plastic surface. Rinse well. (This will need a lot of rinsing. If you want to do a quick clean, use 1 tablespoon baking soda to 3 cups water.)
**Makes ½ cup**

*Preparation Time:* About 1 minute
*Shelf Life:* Make only as much as you need at a time; this mixture will dry out

Variations
WASHING SODA WASH: Substitute washing soda for the baking soda. Washing soda is caustic and will reach deeper into the plastic than baking soda.
BORAX BLAST: Substitute borax for the baking soda. Borax will need less rinsing than baking soda or washing soda.
SOAP FLAKES: Use 1 tablespoon soap flakes to 2 cups water to make a liquid cleanser. Scoop onto a sponge and scrub the plastic. Rinse well.

# Scouring Powders and Soft Scrubbers

Taking a bath in my childhood invariably included sitting in grit from the scouring powder used to clean the bathtub. Scouring powder was always hard to rinse off completely. That may explain why I was so excited when I figured out how to make a soft scrubber that rinsed off easily and didn't smell unpleasantly of chemicals. As you will see, all the variations I suggest for soft scrubbers are adaptations of my original recipe—mixing enough liquid soap or detergent into baking soda so that it has the texture of cake frosting. You can easily mix and match the ingredients listed below to customize your own soft scrub and scouring powders.

T I P *Be nice to your back and use a long brush to clean the bathtub and shower stall.*

### SCOURING POWDERS
NOTE: Washing soda shouldn't be used on fiberglass because it can scratch. Confectioners'

sugar shakers, available in most hardware stores, are convenient containers for scouring powders. You can decorate them with colorful stickers.

## BASIC BAKING SODA SCOURING POWDER SIMPLE

*Baking soda makes a mildly abrasive cleanser that deodorizes as it cleans.*

Baking soda

Lightly sprinkle baking soda onto a surface, scour with a sponge, and rinse thoroughly.

*Preparation Time:* None
*Shelf Life:* Indefinite
*Storage:* Keep dry

## BORAX DEODORIZING SIMPLE

*Borax is a good choice for shower stalls, because it helps eliminate mildew.*

Borax

Lightly sprinkle borax onto a surface, scour with a sponge, and rinse thoroughly.

*Preparation Time:* None
*Shelf Life:* Indefinite
*Storage:* Keep dry

## ANTIBACTERIAL DEODORIZING SCOURER

*Salt has been used for centuries to preserve food because of its antibacterial qualities. Combine it*

*with herbs for their fragrance and additional qualities, and with borax for its deodorizing ability, and you have a good antiseptic product for bathtubs, shower stalls, and sinks. Grind the dried herbs in a coffee or spice grinder.*

1 cup each salt and borax
2 to 4 tablespoons dried and ground
antiseptic herbs such as thyme,
rosemary, and lavender

Combine the ingredients and stir to blend. Sprinkle onto the surface, scour with a sponge, then rinse thoroughly.
**Makes 2 cups**

*Preparation Time:* About 5 minutes
*Shelf Life:* Aromatic oils in the herbs will dry out after a few months
*Storage:* Glass jar with a screw top

## HEAVY-DUTY SCOURING POWDER

*This scourer will need extra rinsing, so use it only when you really need the power of washing soda.*

½ cup each baking soda and washing soda

Combine the ingredients, sprinkle onto the surface, scour with a sponge, then rinse thoroughly.
**Makes 1 cup**

*Preparation Time:* Less than 1 minute
*Shelf Life:* Indefinite
*Storage:* Glass jar with a screw top, confectioners' sugar shaker, or Tupperware container

## PORCELAIN STAIN REMOVER SCOURER

*Try this for rust stains in the bathtub.*

### Cream of tartar

Sprinkle cream of tartar directly from the container onto the surface or onto a sponge. Scour the area thoroughly, then rinse.

## MARBLE SCOURER

*You can grind chalk with a mortar and pestle.*

### ½ cup pulverized chalk

Sprinkle the ground chalk onto the surface or onto a sponge, and scour thoroughly. Rinse, then wipe dry with a soft cloth.
**Makes ½ cup**

*Preparation Time:* None
*Shelf Life:* Indefinite
*Storage:* Glass jar with screw top

### SOFT SCRUBBERS

## BASIC SOFT SCRUBBER FORMULA

*This is one of my most favorite recipes in the book. I use it on the bathtub, sinks, Formica countertops, and the shower stall. I like to make this with Heavenly Horsetail, which is a thick, concentrated liquid detergent.*

### ½ cup baking soda
Enough liquid soap or detergent to make a frostinglike consistency

5 to 10 drops fragrant essential oil, such as 5 drops each rose and lavender (optional)

Place the baking soda in a bowl; slowly pour in the liquid soap, stirring all the while, until the consistency reaches that of frosting. Add a few drops essential oil (if using). Scoop the creamy mixture onto a sponge, wash the surface, and rinse.
**Makes ½ cup**

*Preparation Time:* About 1 minute
*Shelf Life:* Make only as much as you need at a time; natural soft scrubbers dry out

### Variation
ANTIBACTERIAL SOFT SCRUBBER: Substitute borax for half of the baking soda, and add about 15 drops antibacterial essential oil, such as thyme, sweet orange, lavender, clove, rosemary, tea tree, or cinnamon.

## HEAVY-DUTY GREASE-CUTTING SOFT SCRUBBER

*This formula will take more rinsing than those made with borax and baking soda, so use it only for tough jobs; wear gloves, because washing soda is caustic. Don't use this on fiberglass, because it can scratch.*

### ½ cup washing soda
Enough liquid soap or detergent to make a frostinglike consistency

Follow the directions for Basic Soft Scrubber Formula above.

## MILDEW-REMOVING SOFT SCRUBBER

Borax
Enough liquid soap or detergent
to make a paste
A few drops tea tree oil

Follow the directions for Basic Soft Scrubber Formula, page 96.

## ANTIBACTERIAL SALT SCRUBBER

Salt
Enough liquid soap or detergent
to make a paste

Follow the directions for Basic Soft Scrubber Formula, page 96.

## WHITENING SOFT SCRUBBER

*Use this formula for small areas or stains.*

2 tablespoons cream of tartar
Enough 3 percent hydrogen peroxide solution
to make a paste

Follow the directions for Basic Soft Scrubber Formula, page 96.

# Toilet Bowl Cleaners

Buy a good toilet bowl brush to help reduce the time spent doing this chore.

## VINEGAR DEODORIZER

*Vinegar is an effective disinfectant.*

$\frac{1}{4}$ cup white distilled vinegar
2 cups water

Combine the ingredients in a spray bottle, shake, and spray along the inside rim of the toilet. Leave on for 15 minutes or so before scrubbing with a toilet brush.
**Makes 2$\frac{1}{4}$ cups**

*Preparation Time:* About 1 minute
*Shelf Life:* Indefinite
*Storage:* Keep in spray bottle

## TEA TREE DEODORIZER

*Tea tree oil kills bacteria, and the strong smell of the oil will dissipate in a few days.*

2 teaspoons tea tree oil
2 cups water

Combine the ingredients in a spray bottle, shake, and spray along the inside rim of the toilet. Leave on for 30 minutes or so before scrubbing with a toilet brush.
**Makes a little more than 2 cups**

*Preparation Time:* About 1 minute
*Shelf Life:* Indefinite
*Storage:* Keep in spray bottle

## BORAX EASY CLEAN

*Iron rings will disappear effortlessly
with this technique.*

1 cup borax

Pour borax into the toilet and let it set overnight. Swirl with a toilet brush in the morning. Flush.

## SOAP AND BRUSH

*Peppermint adds some antibacterial benefit
to this cleaner.*

About 1 tablespoon peppermint
liquid castile soap

Squirt the soap into the bowl; scrub and flush. If you have hard water, add ¼ cup white distilled vinegar before flushing.

## TOILET BOWL SIZZLER

*This is my favorite toilet cleaner because it sounds
as if powerful cleaning is going on.*

About ½ cup each baking soda and
white distilled vinegar

Pour the ingredients into the toilet. Let sizzle, then scrub. Flush.

## VITAMIN C MAGIC

1,000 milligrams vitamin C crystals

Follow the directions for Borax Easy Clean, above.

# Tub and Tile Cleaners

* Washing soda can scratch fiberglass, so substitute baking soda or borax.
* You can't sterilize a bathroom, so it is a waste of money to buy disinfectants to do so. Reduce bacteria by lowering the lid before flushing, and encourage family members to wash their hands with soap and water before meals. Wash the hot- and cold-water faucet handles frequently with soap and water, or spray with Lightly Lavender (below).
* If you have hard water, soak a washcloth in white distilled vinegar and rest it on the mineral buildup for a few hours, then rinse the area.
* Excessive mold and mildew in your bathroom is a sign that more air circulation is needed. Invest in a fan vented to the outdoors.
* Reduce bathroom moisture by wiping down the shower stall with a squeegee after a shower.
* For tub and tile cleaners, see All-Purpose Household Cleaners (page 47) and Soft Scrubbers (page 96).
* To remove mold, see the preparations given under Mold and Mildew, page 92.

## LIGHTLY LAVENDER

*I like to have this spray in the bathroom to use as
a final rinse on the vanity countertop or after*

*cleaning the toilet. It has a lovely scent, and laven-
der is highly antiseptic.*

1 teaspoon essential oil of lavender
2 cups water

Combine the ingredients in a spray bottle, shake
to blend, then spray. There's no need to wipe off.
**Makes 2 cups**

*Preparation Time:* Less than 1 minute
*Shelf Life:* Indefinite
*Storage:* Leave in the spray bottle

## TUB STAIN REMOVER

*Hydrogen peroxide is a natural bleach; cream of
tartar, an acid, has been used for years to remove
rust stains from porcelain.*

1 tablespoon cream of tartar
Enough 3 percent hydrogen peroxide solution
to make a paste

Combine the ingredients in a bowl. Scoop the
mixture onto a sponge, cover the stained area,
and let rest for a few hours. Scrub clean, then
rinse.

*Preparation Time:* 1 minute
*Storage:* Discard leftovers

## SOAP AND WATER

*The EPA recommends simple soap to kill germs.*

1 ounce liquid castile soap
8 ounces water

Combine the ingredients in a bowl or pail.
Scoop the mixture onto a sponge and wash.
Rinse.

## MIRROR DEFOGGER

*If fogged mirrors bother you, try this
preventative formula.*

½ teaspoon vegetable glycerin
½ cup water

Combine the ingredients in a spray bottle, and
spray on the mirror before baths and showers.
Do not rinse.
**Makes ½ cup**

*Preparation Time:* About 1 minute
*Shelf Life:* Indefinite
*Storage:* Glass jar with a screw top, or Tup-
perware

## SOAP SCUM SPRAY

*The vinegar in this formula is the key ingredient
because its acid content eats up soap scum.*

1 teaspoon borax
½ teaspoon liquid detergent
¼ cup white distilled vinegar
2 cups hot water

Combine the ingredients in a spray bottle, and
shake to blend. Spray. Follow with a sponge.
Rinse.
**Makes 2¼ cups**

*Preparation Time:* About 1 minute
*Shelf Life:* Indefinite
*Storage:* Keep in spray bottle

## Upholstery Cleaners

See Cleaning and Deodorizing Carpets (page 51) and Laundry Products (page 82).

## Window and Glass Cleaners

Around Earth Day 1990, every newspaper in the country (or so it seemed) offered recipes for nontoxic cleaners made with basic ingredients that we all have in our kitchen cupboards. The recipe for window cleaner was invariably plain white distilled vinegar and water; the method of drying was with old newspapers. People by the thousands tried this, and many swore off cleaning with homemade products for good because the formula left streaks on their windows. Actually the problem was that the commercial products they had used for years had left a wax buildup, and vinegar alone wouldn't remove the residue. A dab of dish soap with the vinegar and water would have done the trick, and from then on they could have used plain vinegar. Try this at home, and you may never go back to commercial glass cleaners again.

### TIPS

* Buy a little squeegee at a hardware store to avoid wasting paper towels. Squeegee the water to the corners of the glass, then wipe with a cotton rag.

* Be careful not to add too much detergent, or you will have to rinse it off. Halve the amount of detergent if it is concentrated.
* To remove all the smudges when you are cleaning both sides of a window, wipe vertically on one side and horizontally on the other.

### ALL-PURPOSE WINDOW CLEANER

¼ cup white distilled vinegar
½ teaspoon liquid soap or detergent
2 cups water
A few drops essential oil, for scent (optional)

Combine the ingredients in a spray bottle, and shake to blend. Spray on, then remove with a squeegee, paper towel, or newspaper.
**Makes 2¼ cups**

*Preparation Time:* About 1 minute
*Shelf Life:* Indefinite
*Storage:* Leave in the spray bottle

### VINEGAR STRAIGHT UP

*This preparation will work well after you have cleaned off the residue of commercial products with the all-purpose cleaner above.*

½ cup white distilled vinegar
2 cups water

Combine the ingredients in a spray bottle, and shake to blend. Spray on, then remove with a squeegee, paper towel, or newspaper.
**Makes 2½ cups**

*Preparation Time:* Less than 1 minute
*Shelf Life:* Indefinite
*Storage:* Leave in spray bottle

### Variation

LIGHT AND LEMONY: Substitute lemon juice for the vinegar. Freshly squeezed lemon juice does not last more than a few days and needs to be kept in the refrigerator.

## CLUB SODA

*Club soda is full of alkaline minerals that help dissolve dirt.*

2 cups club soda
A few drops essential oil, for scent (optional)

Pour the club soda (and essential oil if used) into a spray bottle. Spray on, then remove with a squeegee, paper towel, or newspaper.
**Makes 2 cups**

*Preparation Time:* Less than 1 minute
*Shelf Life:* Indefinite
*Storage:* Leave in spray bottle

## CORNSTARCH CLEANER

¼ cup cornstarch
1 cup hot water

Blend the ingredients together in a bowl; let cool. Saturate a soft, natural-fiber rag in the mixture, and wash over the window. Rub until the window is clean.
**Makes 1 cup**

*Preparation Time:* A few minutes
*Shelf Life:* Make only as much as you need at one time

## SUPER-DUPER DIRTY-WINDOW CLEANER

¼ teaspoon washing soda
½ cup hot water
¼ teaspoon liquid soap or detergent
2 cups club soda

Dissolve the washing soda in the hot water, then pour into a spray bottle. Add the liquid soap and club soda. Shake to combine, then spray and wipe clean.
**Makes 2½ cups**

*Preparation Time:* 1 minute
*Shelf Life:* Indefinite
*Storage:* Leave in the spray bottle

# CHAPTER 3

# Skin Care

**W**ALKING down the steps from the front porch of my house

one day, I brushed against a weed with burrs. It suddenly

dawned on me that the weed was burdock, the roots of which

I had been drinking every morning to help my hair grow back after my bout

with Lyme disease. The plant was pushing up through the front steps. I'd yanked those weeds out of the ground and thrown them on the compost pile for years without thinking about it. Now, because I was learning how to identify herbs, I recognized that that irritating weed was, in fact, one of the most powerful healing herbs of all time. The experience opened my eyes to my natural surroundings. I'd been so dulled by getting things out of a package that I couldn't even see what was at my front door. I've since discovered (within a hundred yards of

my house) witch hazel, one of the world's best astringents; black birch, which is full of salicylates that soften the skin and condition hair; St. John's wort; and nettle—all herbs that you will read about in this chapter as having healing and beneficial effects on the body. Few experiences have been more gratifying or have integrated my life more with nature than learning how to make herbal body care products with "weeds" I have found on my own land.

You don't even need to harvest the herbs to feel the rejuvenation and connection with nature that comes from pure, natural body care products. I gave my friend and yoga teacher Erin a few homemade herbal wares to test for me. She is a young-hearted and beautiful woman who just turned fifty, someone who pays close attention to her skin and hair and admits to spending a lot of money at cosmetic counters. I gave her a fruit acid (alpha-hydroxy acid) astringent lotion for the skin and another equally easy-to-make hydrating moisturizer. She called me a few days later to rave about how her skin felt as soft as a baby's, how it glowed in a most luminous way, and how connected to nature she felt, as if she had collected the ingredients in the woods herself.

It *is* hard to explain to people how fresh and almost alive these homemade body care products can make them feel. The products nourish, replenish, and rejuvenate. They give a high level of nutrients to the body, a far cry from the petroleum-based, synthetic, dead-in-a-bottle cosmetics that most of us have used for so many years. And they smell like nature—like the wild and gardens—not the mall; you feel connected to an aloe vera leaf, a calendula blossom, an almond tree, an avocado; you don't feel connected to a smokestack in a factory.

## IDEAL BEAUTY VERSUS REAL BEAUTY

At its heart, natural body care is an issue of health and healing for our bodies, minds, and the world around us. To choose natural products over synthetic products is to take steps toward enhancing our individuality, expressing our real selves. We can begin to break away from the media's omnipresent exhibit of impossible beauty standards. And isn't it time? After all, these days the beauty ideal for a woman is to look like a boy—tall, thin, with no hips or breasts. Could anything be more ill-founded? There aren't many girls and women who fit the image, and as a result the self-confidence of girls in our society is at a record low. There are equally impossible demands on boys. Let's counter the trend with valuing the beauty of a laugh, a smile in the eye, or a kind word. Or the great vitality that comes from a healthy diet, skin that is luminous without makeup, hair that shines with luster without sprays and chemicals. These attributes transcend physical imperfections—who doesn't have some?—and celebrate instead the essential beauty within.

## THE HOME SPA

This chapter and the next are packed with recipes to cleanse, rejuvenate, and relax, so take a day or two and treat yourself and friends or family to facial steams and masks, body soaks and scrubs, hair treatments, and more. Help your home environment enhance the healing effect of a spa by reducing indoor air pollution with nontoxic cleaning, natural building supplies, and oxygen-giving houseplants. Keep an eye out for yard sales that sell pretty bottles and jars for storing herb blends and bath salts. Listen to music you love. Share the experience with a friend by giving each other pedicures, foot rubs (try them with beach sand and rosemary), and manicures. Cover your face with a mask of avocado and yogurt, and take some time off from your routine.

# New and Old Better Basic Materials

## CHOOSING NATURAL BODY CARE

Do we miss out on anything that modern chemistry has to offer by using fruits, vegetables, and herbs found in gardens, woods, and the supermarket? It is natural to be concerned that we'll deprive ourselves of some spectacular beauty secrets by mixing up body care products instead of buying those that are ready-made. But most modern cosmetic companies copy the best of the old folk recipes and use synthetic ingredients in place of natural ones. Beeswax, with its healing, protective, and antibacterial properties, is replaced with petroleum-based wax, which gives the skin nothing. The natural essential oils used as fragrance in the old recipes are often powerfully antibacterial and healing in their own right, compared to the complex synthetic perfume mixtures that cause 40 percent of the population to have allergic reactions and have no benefits for the skin. *Better Basics for the Home*'s body care products return to the original formulas, using the true ingredients, enabling you to reap all the rewards.

The most exquisite skin care regimen I've come across is an ancient Mayan one. Simple herbs and vegetables were combined with a sophisticated understanding of the needs of the skin. The results are dazzling. Since I discovered the Mayan formulas, I've never used anything else on my skin. The Mayan formulas are the best of the best, a week doesn't go by that I am not complimented on my skin. I've adapted the Mayan formulas in *Better Basics for the Home* so that they are easy to make with ingredients found in North America.

The five basic ingredients used throughout history for body care are herbs; distilled water or organic apple cider vinegar; fruit and nut oils and their by-products (such as vegetable glycerin); products from bees such as royal jelly, honey, and beeswax; and fruits and vegetables. With some agony, I have narrowed down to sixteen the number of herbs and plants used for most *Better Basics for the Home*'s recipes for body care. It isn't that there aren't many more that aren't wonderful. But they can be overwhelming to learn about, and it is more important to know when and why to use the proper ones. From this perspective, sixteen is a lot; one wise herbalist suggested that I try to learn only four or five herbs a year. If you learn how and why to use the herbs I've listed in the table on page 106, you will be well equipped to make most body care products with herbal healing benefits, and you can add more to your repertoire throughout your lifetime.

The sixteen plants and herbs are aloe vera, birch, calendula, chamomile, comfrey, horsetail, lavender, lemon balm (and other mints), nettle, orris root, soap bark, rose, rosemary, sage, St. John's wort, and witch hazel. They have surprising effects on the skin and hair. Those with emollient properties soften and lubricate; others hydrate and moisturize. Many are antibacterial, making them excellent choices for skin and hair problems. And from time immemorial, herbs have been used for their anti-inflammatory benefit—to heal wounds, rashes, and other skin irritations. The table highlights the specific body care benefits of these sixteen herbs, which are used in formulas throughout Chapters Three and Four, for everything from skin care to pedicures.

# MINI-GLOSSARY

**Alkaloid.** Derived from plants that contain pharmacologically active ingredients with medicinal value, although alkaloids are often deadly poisonous.

**Allantoin.** Allantoins help renew cells. Comfrey, the allantoin source in *Better Basics for the Home,* is used in skin care preparations for its healing and antiaging properties.

**Alpha-hydroxy Acid.** An acid derived naturally from substances such as citrus fruits, sugarcane, sour milk, and apples. These acids help to dissolve the bond, or "glue," that holds dead cells on the surface of the skin; they help control the aging process at the cellular level by firming underlying tissue, thus enhancing elasticity; and they tighten pores and help control age spots, lines, wrinkles, sun damage, and dry and oily skin problems.

**Anti-inflammatory.** Counteracting swelling, pain, or redness.

**Antibacterial.** Counteracting bacteria; that is, antiseptic.

**Antioxidant.** Substance that prevents the formation of free radicals in the body. Antioxidants can be vitamins, minerals, enzymes, amino acids, or synthetic chemicals.

**Antiseptic.** Destroying the growth of bacteria or germs that cause decay and infection.

**Astringent.** Tightening and closing the pores. A dramatic demonstration of this is to put a leaf of blackberry or colt's foot in your mouth and start to chew. Your mouth will pucker up as if you ate a lemon.

**Bioflavonoid.** Anti-inflammatory nutrient found in many plants that is useful for healthy circulation. Bioflavonoids are aromatic compounds (many contain pigments) that are used for making natural dyes.

**Emollient.** Softening, lubricating, and moistening the skin and hair. They also provide a protective barrier to hold moisture in.

**Free Radical.** A molecule that creates oxidation and contributes to the aging process, leading to health problems and decreased immunity. Antioxidants work to defend the cells from free radicals. Your body produces its own antioxidants; foods rich in vitamins and minerals are another source.

**Humectant.** Drawing moisture from the surrounding environment and helping the skin retain water.

**Infusion.** A mixture that is steeped, not boiled. Herbal infusions consist of herbs that are covered with boiling water, then steeped for a minimum of four hours.

**Moisturizing.** Hydrating the skin with water and oils.

**pH.** The pH of skin and hair ranges from 4.5

to 5.5. The pH scale ranges from 1 to 14, with 7 being neutral. Anything below that is acidic; anything above it is alkaline. Knowing about the pH of the skin and hair is important for body care: Soap and many body care products are alkaline, and the skin and hair should be returned to their natural acidic state by rinsing the hair with lemon juice or organic apple cider vinegar or using an acidic toner on the skin after washing with soap.

**Salicylic Acid.** Popular in aspirin, acne, and dandruff treatments, salicylic acid is an organic acid that occurs in several plants (such as cloves, cocoa, birch, and yarrow). It is antiseptic and anti-inflammatory and a counterirritant.

**Saponin.** Very soapy ingredient found in some plants, particularly soap bark.

**Tannin.** Tannins are produced by plants such as tea and witch hazel. Tannins contract the tissues of the body—they draw the tissues closer together and improve their resistance to infection—and are used in astringents and for dyeing and tanning.

## HERB BENEFITS

| HERB | Antibacterial Antiseptic Cleanser | Astringent | Anti-inflammatory | Emollient | Moisturizing | Heals Skin |
|---|---|---|---|---|---|---|
| ALOE VERA | YES | YES | YES | YES | YES | YES |
| BIRCH | YES | YES | YES | | | YES |
| CALENDULA | YES | YES | YES | YES | YES | YES |
| CHAMOMILE | YES | YES | YES | YES | YES | YES |
| COMFREY | YES | YES | YES | YES | YES | YES |
| HORSETAIL | | YES | | | | YES |
| LAVENDER | YES | YES | YES | | YES | YES |
| LEMON BALM | YES | YES | | | | |
| NETTLE | YES | YES | YES | | | |
| ORRIS ROOT | YES | | | | | |
| SOAP BARK | YES | | | | | |
| ROSE | YES | YES | YES | | YES | |
| ROSEMARY | YES | YES | YES | | | YES |
| SAGE | YES | YES | | | | |
| ST. JOHN'S WORT | YES | YES | YES | | | |
| WITCH HAZEL | YES | YES | YES | | | |

## GOOD HERBS AND ESSENTIAL OILS FOR DIFFERENT SKIN AND HAIR TYPES

*Dry Skin and Hair:* Lavender, orange blossom, chamomile, rose, aloe vera, comfrey root, St. John's wort, mint, orris root, nettle, licorice, calendula, kelp, Irish moss, horsetail

*Sensitive Skin and Hair:* Calendula, chamomile, comfrey, licorice

*Oily Skin and Hair:* Lavender, rose, witch hazel, lemon balm, mint, licorice, rosemary, sage, neutral henna, horsetail

*Antibacterial Essential Oils:* The following essential oils have been found to be more antiseptic than phenol, the industry standard: thyme, sweet orange, lemongrass, rose, clove, eucalyptus, orris root, cinnamon, rosemary, birch, lavender, and tea tree. Thyme has a high phenol content and should be used with caution.

### FRUIT ACIDS (ALPHA-HYDROXY ACIDS, OR AHAS)

Alpha-hydroxy acids exfoliate by dissolving the glue that holds dead skin cells together. They cleanse the top layer of skin, allowing the body's natural emollient oils to reach the surface cells and help moisturize and relieve dryness. They help cleanse oily skin and remove blackheads. By aiding new cell growth, they help reverse the process of aging. A 1997 study at Massachusetts General Hospital found that 70 percent of those using AHAs showed fewer symptoms of sun damage, versus 41 percent using the placebo. The famed beauty Cleopatra unknowingly used the benefit of AHAs on her skin when she bathed in milk.

Store-bought creams and lotions with AHAs have up to 10 percent acidity. Doctors now provide AHA chemical peels of between 20 and 70 percent acidity, which are so strong they can leave scabs that scar. The FDA believes that these strong peels could expose the skin to an increased risk of sunburn. Vinegar (organic apple cider vinegar is best for this purpose) is an all-natural AHA that you can use at home (avoid the eyes) that has 7 percent acidity and is a safe and sure way to get the benefit of fruit acids without danger to the skin (although even at this lower level, you should be aware of the increased risk of sunburn). The benefits of homemade fruit acids become evident as soon as you start using them; your skin starts feeling soft and smooth.

### ANTIOXIDANT- AND ENZYME-RICH FRUITS AND VEGETABLES

Fruits and vegetables are nourishing for the skin and hair because they are full of vitamins, minerals, and free-radical-fighting antioxidants such as bioflavonoids. Antioxidants protect against free-radical damage caused by the sun, smoking, aging, and pollution. Some fruits and vegetables, such as cucumbers, bananas, persimmons, peppers, and watermelon, have the general pH of skin and hair (between 4.5 and 5.5—on the acidic side) and help restore their natural acid mantle after the use of more alkaline substances such as soap.

### HOW TO FIND THE BEST COSMETIC
### FATS AND OILS FOR YOUR SKIN

Formulas for creams, lotions, rubs, and soaks usually call for an oil to keep the skin supple and soft. Finding the right oils for your skin is one of the most satisfying aspects of making your own creams, lotions, lip balms, and so forth. Try out three or four on your skin, and you will instantly feel which ones are best for you. I put a few drops of avocado oil in aloe vera gel for a custom-made moisturizer for the crow's feet around my eyes, and that worked well. But keep in mind that avocado oil is a lush, rich oil, so use only a smidgen in a cream. If you make a cream using too much greasy oil, it will feel heavy and suffocating on the skin. When choosing which oil to use in a lip balm, I found apricot kernel oil to be the most soothing and emollient, surpassing all the others for this specific purpose. Grapeseed oil is a wonderful choice for creams, because it is one of the least greasy. Many herbalists blend a lot of oils together for their products, such as almond, canola, grapeseed, jojoba, and peanut. By using this approach, you can obtain the diverse benefits of different oils, although it is harder to come up with just the oils that are a perfect match for your skin.

**Oils and Rancidity.** Jojoba (a liquid wax) does not go rancid; it is highly antiseptic.

# BUYER'S GUIDE

## COSMETIC FATS AND OILS

A GOOD giveaway about how natural a product is is its fat and oil content, which is listed on the label. If petroleum jelly, petrolatum, or mineral oil is listed as an ingredient, you know that the product has been derived from petroleum. If you find instead almond oil, apricot kernel oil, jojoba, or wheat germ oil, for example, you may have found a natural product.

Although "natural" oils from animals are sometimes found in cosmetics, you need to decide for yourself how you feel about killing animals for such a purpose. Emu oil, currently popular, is acquired by "processing" (killing) the bird. Castor oil is made from castor beans and muskrat and beaver genitals. Castor oil derived from the animals is used primarily in perfumes and incense. Oil is sometimes derived from animals that are endangered species. If squalene oil is listed, determine if you can (call the company if necessary) whether it is derived from olive oil, rice bran, wheat germ, or sharks. Sharks are quickly becoming an endangered species, because they are being overfished for medicinal and cosmetic purposes. Avoid shark-derived squalene oil if you can. In the old days, spermaceti, made from the oil of sperm whales, was used as a cosmetic oil. It might still be found in the rare product. Don't buy it; this whale is now seriously endangered. You will also occasionally find sea turtle oil in cosmetics. It is necessary to kill the turtle to acquire the oil, so avoid these products.

Olive oil has a long shelf life and never dries out. On the other hand, flax seed oil and other oils with a high omega-3 content can go rancid within hours of exposure to air. Add preservative essential oils or antioxidants (see Chapter One) to oils to reduce their rate of oxidation.

Oils infused with vegetable matter pose an even greater risk, because there is an increased chance of bacteria such as botulism. Infuse oils in a Crock-Pot to speed up the process (infusing in sunlight can take a few weeks), and strain out the vegetable matter completely before adding preservatives.

See Chapter One for details on preservative formulas and instructions.

## WATER

Use only distilled water when making cosmetics at home. Bacteria is removed from distilled water through a filtering process, and products made with it will have a longer shelf life than those made with tap water.

### VINEGAR

Always use organic apple cider vinegar for body care as opposed to white distilled vinegar, which is used for cleaning.

## Making Kitchen Cosmetics

There is a great deal of leeway in making personal care products. I have often seen the same product made fifteen different ways, with different ratios of ingredients every time. Follow your intuition: Explore the way different materials feel on your skin and hair and adapt the recipes by adding a little more of this or less of that if you think it might make a product more appealing to you. Experiment and be flexible. The only rule to follow is to be safe:

Don't burn yourself, misuse essential oils, or splash anything into your eyes.

### EQUIPMENT FOR MAKING KITCHEN COSMETICS

For a complete list of equipment needed for making kitchen cosmetics, see page 28.

### PRESERVING KITCHEN COSMETICS

To learn everything you need to know about preserving kitchen cosmetics, see page 36.

### USING ESSENTIAL OILS ON THE SKIN AND BODY

As already mentioned, the skin is very sensitive to essential oils, so don't use high quantities. Follow these proportions for essential oils per ounce of cream or oil: eye area, 3 drops or less; face, 5 drops or less; body, 25 drops or less.

### ADDING FRAGRANCE

If you plan to add straight essential oils or essential oil blends into the product you are making, follow the directions for using anti-septic essential oils on page 36. If you have made a perfume (see "Fragrances," page 180), you can use up to 2 teaspoons (¼ ounce) per cup (8 ounces) of cream, reducing the amount of perfume used to ⅓ teaspoon for eye creams.

### MAKING CREAMS AND LOTIONS

For the basic formulas for cream, lotion, salves, nonpetroleum jellies, herbal infusions, essential oils, infused oils, and tinctures, please see Chapter One.

### HERB-INFUSED WATERS AND OILS

Infusing healing herbs in oil or water is an excellent way to obtain the benefits of herbs in body care products such as homemade soaps, shampoos, creams, and lotions. See Chapter One for directions on how to do this, then substitute the herb water for tap water or distilled water in the following formulas.

NOTE: When rose water is called for in a recipe, I mean a rose infusion. Commercial rose water often contains glycerin.

### RAW EGGS

Until salmonella-free eggs are on the market, raw egg should be used on the skin or hair only by those without a compromised immune system or at your own risk. Although salmonella poisoning from eggs on the skin is rare, it could happen. Some organic farms now test their eggs for salmonella, and it is only from such farms that you should buy eggs for *Better Basics for the Home*'s formulas.

# Caring for Your Skin

The beauty of my newborn daughter's skin left me in awe. Her roly-poly arms and legs and belly were as soft as silk and actually glowed with a luminous quality. A cut would heal at what seemed the speed of light. Despite the beauty industry's promises, I have never seen an adult with such exquisite skin. Part of the reason for this, of course, is because the natural aging process changes our skin, as does exposure to the sun and elements. But I am positive that you don't need to have the best skin care specialists of Hollywood available to you to have healthy and incandescent adult skin, or spend hundreds of dollars on expensive creams. One reason for damaged skin is that most of us are simply never taught the basics of proper skin care. For decades the only readily available commercial products have been made with petroleum and formaldehyde—hardly skin-enhancing chemicals. Treating your skin to emollient plant materials, natural fruit acids, moisture, and nutrients can be transforming after only a few days. Many of my friends and family have dutifully tested formulas found in this chapter on their faces and bodies, and they all rave about how their skin glows and how soft and pliable it feels.

## UNDERSTANDING THE SKIN'S LAYERS

Skin regulates body temperature, produces vitamin D, and provides a remarkably effective barrier against injury and disease. It absorbs, secretes, excretes, and breathes and is nearly waterproof. Healthy skin is a sign of a healthy body, and it is important to keep it well nourished and hydrated so you stay healthy.

The skin has three layers. The outer layer, the epidermis, consists of dead and dying cells; these need to be exfoliated frequently so the dead cells don't block the protective and lubricating benefits of the oils generated by the second layer of skin, the dermis. This exfoliating process is accomplished with steams, fruit acids, scrubs, soaps, and cleansers. The dermis contains the sweat glands, oil glands, hair follicles, and more. It lubricates the epidermis and is responsible for the skin's elasticity. Blocked oil and sweat glands cause skin problems. The innermost layer is the fatty layer, which determines the firmness of the skin. It needs to be hydrated, lubricated, nourished, and protected. Lack of any of these—brought on by smoking, too much sun, or insufficient water, for example—cause premature aging of the skin. Aloe vera gel is one material that hydrates, lubricates, nourishes, and protects. For more ingredients and formulas, see Moisturizers on page 141.

## DIET TIPS FOR HEALTHY SKIN

* Drink two quarts of water a day.
* Make sure your diet is rich in omega-3 essential fatty acids, which are found in such foods as salmon and walnuts. If it isn't,

take 1 tablespoon pure cold-pressed linseed oil a day. Skin that doesn't have enough of these fats has trouble retaining moisture.
* Eat a healthy diet rich in enzymes and antioxidants, such as found in fresh fruits and vegetables.

## RECOMMENDED DAILY SKIN CARE ROUTINES

The following three-step routine is used and recommended by skin care experts: cleaning; toning and exfoliating; and moisturizing, hydrating, and nourishing.

## RECOMMENDED WEEKLY OR MONTHLY SKIN CARE ROUTINE

Complete six-step natural facials are good to do once a week or month. The benefits to your skin are enormous. Make adjustments when you change your cleansing, exfoliating, or moisturizing routine. For example, in switching from the astringent Queen of Hungary Water (an herbal vinegar, see page 137) to a papaya enzyme exfoliant, I needed to change my moisturizer, because the herbal vinegar dried my skin more than did the papaya enzyme. And although the moisturizer was perfect for dry skin, it was too oily for my skin when it retained more oils using enzymes.

*Caution:* If your skin hasn't experienced the deep cleansing of steams and masks, don't start them the morning of your wedding or the day of an important meeting, because the skin can become temporarily irritated.

**STEP ONE: CLEANSE.** Washing off the dead and dying skin cells on the outer layer of the skin is important to do every day so that the dead cells don't block the oils underneath. Most people think of soap as the only skin cleanser, but in fact there are many approaches to cleaning the skin on a daily basis. Formulas found here include soap; soap-free cleansing "simples," such as witch hazel extract, AHAs, enzymes, and oils; traditional cold creams and vanishing creams; scrubs; and cleansing creams, milks, and lotions, with and without soap. Always wash the face with warm water.

**STEP TWO: STEAM.** Steam opens the pores and deeply cleanses the skin, hydrating it at the same time. The simplest way to steam your face is to heat a pan of distilled water to a boil, remove it from the heat and, with a towel tent over your head, lean over the pan, allowing the steam to waft over your face for about ten minutes. More complex steams include specific herbs, such as licorice, for their emollient and healing benefits.

**STEP THREE: USE MASKS.** Masks are used to draw impurities from the skin, but they also draw oils and moisture. There are many types of masks, including those that moisturize and hydrate the skin. Clay masks are best for oily skin because they can dehydrate the skin. Ingredients used for nonclay masks run the gamut from mashed avocado to royal jelly. Masks should always be applied to damp skin and rinsed off with cold water.

**STEP FOUR: TONE.** A toner smooths the skin by closing the pores, adjusting the pH (soap is alkaline, and the skin's pH needs to be returned to its naturally acidic state), removing oils and soaps, and even nourishing the

skin. There are three kinds of toners, and the ingredients are usually strong. Clarifying and exfoliating lotions include AHAs such as lemon juice and are wonderfully softening. Astringents close the pores with ingredients such as witch hazel extract and organic apple cider vinegar and are particularly useful for oily skin. Skin fresheners tend to be antiseptic and hydrating.

**STEP FIVE: MOISTURIZE.** Moisturizing returns oils and moisture to the skin after they have been stripped away by cleansing. Some moisturizers are thick creams that protect the skin from the elements. Others found here include simple ingredients such as glycerin and vitamin-E-rich wheat germ oil and honey, which hydrate, nourish, and soften the skin. Lotions are another big category of lubricating moisturizers. Formulas for glycerin lotion and creamy lotions without alcohol are included in this chapter.

**STEP SIX: HYDRATE.** The innermost layer of the skin is the fatty layer. It needs to be hydrated; otherwise there will be premature aging of the skin. If the skin is cleansed, toned, and moisturized, then moisture will reach deep into the fatty layer, protecting it. Splash water on your face whenever you think of it. Or spritz your face with one of the refreshing herbal spritzer preparations described in this chapter.

# Skin Cleansers

All skin care experts agree that cleaning your face every day—even if you have dry skin—is

# THREE-PART MAYAN FORMULA

I THINK I was meant to find this Mayan skin care formula so I could put it in *Better Basics for the Home* and we could all benefit from it. The discovery couldn't have been more strange. I was in the sauna at my local gym and met Ruth Ketay, a woman who had the skin of a forty-year-old, except that she must have been in her mid-sixties. She didn't look as though she'd had a face-lift, either. We started chatting, as people in saunas do, and I asked her the secret of her beautiful skin. She told me the following story. In the early part of this century, a Mexican archaeologist decoded an old Mayan text of beauty formulas. He gave the formulas to a chemist, who made up a batch, then he sold them through an obscure outlet in Los Angeles, where my sauna friend found them. She was so impressed that she bought out the store and has been using them ever since. I tried them, and I have never felt such things on my skin. It became instantly baby soft. Unfortunately, the chemist died and the exact formulas he used were lost. But we know many of the ingredients and can understand the biology of the skin as a result of using the formulas.

This is the point at which my winding trail of research began. I searched first for translations of Mayan words, exchanging faxes with an herbalist in a Central American rain forest. With the help of archaeologist Christopher Lindner at Bard College, I consulted with John Bierhorst, a scholar of Aztec languages, and with many herbalists. Carol Merrill (of *Let's Make a Deal*) helped me find a source of pure plumeria! The result of this path of discovery has led to a close approximation of the original three-part Mayan formula, using ingredients that are more easily available in North America. Using this adaptation of the formulas will cleanse and soften the skin with fruit acids and herbal soaps, correct the pH of the skin, fight free radicals with antioxidants including vitamin A, give a natural and nutritious face-lift, and moisturize and hydrate the skin.

PART ONE

## AGUA DE MAYA CLEANSER

*The original formula called for extracts of herbs, salts of potassium oleate, salts of potassium palmilizaite, quillaja bark (soap bark), and filtered water. Here is my adaptation.*

Small handful soap bark
2 cups water

Make a decoction by adding a handful of soap bark to a pan and adding water to cover. Bring to a boil, then reduce the heat and simmer for an hour, adding more water if needed. Let cool and strain. Soap bark is very soapy. Pour some on your hands, work it into a lather, and wash your face. Rinse.
**Makes: 2 cups**

*Preparation Time:* 5 minutes
*Shelf Life:* About 1 week refrigerated
*Storage:* Glass jar with a screw top
NOTE: Soap bark is available from Raintree Marketing, Inc. (see Sources and Resources).

PART TWO

## ZAZIL TONER

*The original formula called for yerba buena plant (spearmint), lemon juice, cucumber juice, distilled water, chamomile flowers, and carrot juice. Here is my adaptation. A good time to make this toner is when the harvest is bountiful in August and September. If you don't own a juicer, borrow one and make large batches, freeze the mixture in ice cube trays, and pop out a cube as needed. Cucumber juice could be made in a blender. Or you can make just a week's worth of this toner at a time.*

¼ cup cucumber juice
⅛ cup carrot juice
½ cup spearmint infusion
¼ cup chamomile infusion
½ cup lemon juice

Make the cucumber juice and carrot juice in a juicer. Make strong infusions of spearmint and chamomile, and let cool. Combine the ingredients in a glass jar, and shake to blend. If you freeze the mixture in ice cube trays, just pop out a cube and rub it over your face, then put the cube in the refrigerator and use the toner over the next few days. Otherwise, dab some of the toner on your fingers and massage into your face. Rinse.

**Makes 1¾ cups**

*Preparation Time:* About 30 minutes

*Shelf Life:* 1 year frozen; 1 week refrigerated

*Storage:* Ice cube trays in the freezer, or glass jar with a screw top in the refrigerator

PART THREE

## FLORA DE MAYO "CREAM"

*The original formula, meaning frangipani cream, called for hydrolyzed gelatin, royal jelly, honey, extracts and essences from Cacaloxochitl (cactus plant and flowers—translated as raven flower, nicte, or frangipani, and more commonly known as plumeria), Kabah leaves, and filtered water. One adaptation is to add 1 teaspoon each of royal jelly and plumeria flower essence to 8 ounces of cream. Here is another.*

½ cup aloe vera gel

⅛ cup glycerin

½ to 1 teaspoon royal jelly

1 teaspoon plumeria flower essence (see Essential Applications in Sources and Resources)

Combine the ingredients in a bowl, and stir vigorously to blend. Dab some on your fingers, and massage into your face.

**Makes ⅝ cup**

*Preparation Time:* A few minutes

*Shelf Life:* 6 months refrigerated

*Storage:* Glass jar with a screw top

A toner will remove any residual oil that may be left on your skin from your cleanser, so don't be too concerned about choosing only oil-free materials. The toner will also return your skin's pH to normal.

### SOAP

You will be amazed at how emollient homemade soap is compared to most commercial soaps, which have been stripped of their glycerin and as a result can be drying for the skin. Glycerin is a colorless, sweet, syrupy liquid obtained from animal and vegetable oils and fats during the soap-making process (saponification). Even people with dry skin might get away with washing their face daily with a good castile soap that hasn't had the glycerin removed. If you'd like to try making your own soap, see below. Otherwise, to avoid dryness, choose a castile soap, preferably one from a cottage industry or one that is superfatted (it con-

an important part of maintaining healthy skin. But fearing the drying and harsh qualities of soap, many people skip facial cleansing, unaware that there are many gentler, soap-free ways to cleanse the skin. Even using just warm water and a washcloth or natural sea sponge is much better than nothing, because the water will hydrate the skin and the washcloth will remove the top layer of dirt. Try a few of the following cleansers and find those you like for your skin.

tains an extra amount of oil). Buy your soap at health food stores to avoid soaps made with biocides, petroleum oil, and synthetic perfumes.

Soap is very alkaline (lye is just about the most alkaline substance you can find); to return your skin to its normal acidic state, it is important to use an acid-based astringent after washing with soap.

**HOMEMADE BAR SOAPS.** Making soap is a wonderfully relaxing task, and the results are beautiful and surprisingly softening for the skin. The soap seems to last forever. I have offered a few variations of the basic formula for castile soap here, but in truth the variations are endless. The ratios of fat to lye to water must always remain the same, but you can mix and match ingredients for infusing in the oil and water, and you can add dry ingredients, such as oatmeal, seaweed, and even flower petals, that will impart healing qualities. For the basic soap formula, see page 35.

The soaps offered here are vegetarian soaps, made without tallow or other animal fats. They are also considered glycerin soaps, because the glycerin hasn't been removed.

## BASIC CREAMY CASTILE SOAP FORMULA 🎁

*My husband says that no other soap he has ever used has been nicer for washing his hair. One batch will make enough for you and for gifts alike. I find I need to make two batches a year: one in fall, much of which I give away during the holidays, and one in spring, to keep my own family of three in soap for the year.*

16 ounces olive oil

8 ounce coconut oil

17½ ounces hydrogenated oil such as Crisco

6 ounces lye

16 ounces water

⅛ to ½ ounce fragrant essential oil(s) of choice (optional)

Follow the soap-making directions on page 34.
**Makes 24 bars**

*Preparation Time:* About 2 hours, then 3 weeks to harden
*Shelf Life:* Indefinite
*Storage:* Wrap in pretty paper

### Variations

**OATMEAL LAVENDER SOAP:** Oatmeal adds softly abrasive qualities to the soap, good for scrubbing your body in the shower. Oatmeal is also softening and emollient for the skin. Lavender adds a lovely, light fragrance. After saponification but before pouring the soap into molds, add the essential oil lavender (as much as desired), and stir in up to 1 cup oatmeal flour (you can make this easily in a blender). Add a few whole oatmeal flakes to give the soap a wholesome appearance.

**COMFREY CALENDULA SOAP:** Comfrey and calendula are healing herbs for the skin. This formula is particularly advised for anyone with skin problems such as eczema or psoriasis. The day before making the soap, infuse a few handfuls of calendula flowers in the 16 ounces olive oil in a Crock-Pot for 7 hours or so, and infuse the comfrey in the 16 ounces water overnight.

Substitute the calendula-infused oil for the olive oil, and the comfrey infusion for the water in the formula. Right before pouring the soap into molds, stir in a few tablespoons ground comfrey leaves and calendula petals as desired.

ROSE WATER SOAP: Rose water is renowned for its skin softening benefits, and it also has a lovely, flowery fragrance. The day before you plan to make the soap, infuse 2 handfuls rose petals in the 16 ounces water, and steep overnight. Strain, and substitute for the water in the formula.

SEAWEED MINERAL SOAP: Seaweed adds a highly nutritious element to your soap, as well as slight abrasion. Seaweeds also have a slight briny odor, so choose another formula if the scent might bother you. Grind Irish moss and/or kelp and add up to 1 cup to the saponified soap mixture right before pouring it into molds, stirring a few times to blend.

WINDSOR SOAP: This traditional English soap is easy to make, and its distinctive quality is the caraway fragrance. Substitute canola oil for the olive oil, and add up to ½ teaspoon essential oil of caraway.

DEAD SEA MINERAL SOAP: Another soap rich in nutrients, this is an excellent soap for psoriasis. Add up to 1 cup Dead Sea minerals (available in health food stores) and 2 teaspoons vitamin E powder.

FLAX SOAP: Many old-fashioned formulas for soap specify linseed oil, which is rich in omega-3 essential fatty acids—good for the skin. Linseed oil is expensive; it is available in health food stores. Substitute linseed oil for half of the olive oil, or less, and add ½ to 1 cup flax seed, ground or whole, to the soap mixture.

CLEANSING BAR FOR OILY SKIN: Clay draws oil from the skin. Add up to ½ cup green clay (see Masks, page 154) and as much essential oil of lemon (or rosemary or sage) as desired.

CLEANSING BAR FOR DRY SKIN: Almonds are emollient and softening for the skin. Add up to ½ cup almond meal and up to ½ teaspoon cleansing essential oil such as lavender.

CINNAMON SPICE ANTIBACTERIAL SOAP: Not only does this soap have antibacterial properties, it makes a fun-smelling soap that is well suited to the winter and holiday season. Add up to ½ teaspoon antibacterial essential oils such as cinnamon and clove.

EMOLLIENT BAR SOAP: Infuse emollient herbs such as calendula and yarrow in the oil and water. The day before you plan to make the soap, infuse 2 handfuls rose petals in the 16 ounces water, and steep overnight. Strain, and substitute for the water in the formula.

TRADITIONAL SOAP FOR MEN: To make this version of Windsor Soap, add some or all of these spicy, woodsy-smelling essential oils: cinnamon, caraway, lavender, thyme, peppermint, and bergamot.

CORNMEAL AND CALENDULA SCRUBBING SOAP: A good soap to use for helping your skin sluff off dead skin cells. Infuse calendula in the oil, and add up to 1 cup cornmeal just before pouring the soap into molds, stirring to blend.

SUPERFATTED SOAP: Superfatted soaps are good for dry skin. The extra oil makes the soap more emollient and moisturizing. Add up to 4 tablespoons additional oil. Avocado oil is particularly recommended for this purpose, because it is so emollient.

## "GENTLED" SOAP 🎁

*A "gentled" soap contains emollients and has been diluted with water. Gentled soaps dry out the skin less than those without added glycerin and honey. Grate the soap with a kitchen grater.*

1 ounce grated homemade bar soap (or commercial castile bar soap)
¾ cup distilled water
¼ teaspoon honey
½ teaspoon glycerin
5 to 10 drops antiseptic essential oil such as rosemary or lavender (see Note)

Place the grated soap in the water overnight to dissolve. Add the other ingredients and stir to blend. The consistency should be that of a thick, creamy soup. Dab a washcloth into the mixture and use for washing the skin. Rinse with warm water.
**Makes about ¾ cup**

*Preparation Time:* About 5 minutes
*Shelf Life:* Indefinite, although the soap and water will separate
*Storage:* Glass jar with a screw top, or a dispenser
NOTE: If your skin is very dry, add 1 to 2 teaspoons avocado or almond oil.

## BASIC CLEANSING WATER ✂

*Cleansing water is much less soapy and much thinner than a "gentled" soap. I use this formula a lot, because it doesn't dry out my skin.*

½ ounce grated soap or liquid castile soap
1 cup water

Place the soap in the water overnight to dissolve. Stir to blend. Dab a washcloth into the mixture and use for washing the skin.
**Makes 1 cup**

*Preparation Time:* A few minutes
*Shelf Life:* Indefinite
*Storage:* Glass jar with a screw top

### Variations

HERBAL SOAPWATER: This formula uses water that has been infused with antiseptic herbs such as rose petals and lavender. You need to preserve such a mixture (the flowers can start to rot) with 20 drops lavender oil (or other antiseptic oil) per ounce. It will keep for 1 to 2 months.

ANTISEPTIC SOAPWATER: You can easily make your own antibacterial soap to keep by your sink (use it especially for hand-washing). Add up to 5 drops antibacterial essential oils such as lavender, rose, cinnamon, clove, and/or tea tree oil per ounce. Stir to blend. It will last indefinitely.

EMOLLIENT SOAPWATER: Glycerin is a humectant, which helps your skin retain moisture. Add 1 teaspoon glycerin to the formula. Shake or stir to blend. It will last indefinitely.

OILY SKIN SOAPWATER: Witch hazel is wonderful for cleansing oily skin. Add 3 tablespoons witch hazel extract to the water. Shake or stir to blend. It will last indefinitely.

### CLEANSING SOAP-FREE "SIMPLES"

Time-honored simple cleansers such as glycerin, aloe vera gel, and milk clean, moisturize, and nourish skin at the same time. Many of them are, not surprisingly, alpha-hydroxy acids, which naturally exfoliate the dead cells on the surface of the skin. Often commercial products have about six supporting ingredients just to preserve and emulsify but only one important constituent, such as glycerin.

## PURE VEGETABLE GLYCERIN SIMPLE ✂

*Although thick and sticky, glycerin cleanses the skin, leaves it satiny smooth, and it hydrates.*

1 teaspoon glycerin
3 teaspoons water

Combine the ingredients in a small glass jar. Shake or stir to blend. Dab your fingers into the mixture and massage onto your face. If the mixture feels too thick, place it over low heat until warm, let cool until tolerable, then spread on your face with your fingertips. Rinse well with warm water and pat dry.
**Makes 1⅓ tablespoons, enough for 1 week**

*Preparation Time:* Less than 1 minute if unheated; about 3 minutes if heated

*Shelf Life:* Indefinite (or until most of the water evaporates)
*Storage:* Glass jar with a screw top

### Variation

GLYCERIN AND ROSE WATER CLEANSER: Rose water is an excellent antiseptic cleanser. Combine half glycerin and half rose water in a pan and heat until warm (do not boil). Let cool until tolerable, then spread on your face with your fingertips or cotton balls. Rinse with warm water. The shelf life is 1 to 2 months.

## WITCH HAZEL EXTRACT

2 teaspoons witch hazel extract

Pour the witch hazel extract into a bowl. Dab a washcloth or cotton ball into the liquid, and wash over your face. Rinse with warm water.
**Makes enough for 1 washing**

*Preparation Time:* Less than 1 minute
*Shelf Life:* Indefinite

### Variations

ALOE AND WITCH HAZEL EXTRACT: Substitute 1 teaspoon each aloe vera gel and witch hazel extract. Aloe moisturizes and heals the skin.
WITCH HAZEL EXTRACT AND TEA TREE OIL ANTISEPTIC CLEANSER: Add 5 drops tea tree oil to the 2 teaspoons witch hazel extract. Tea tree adds additional antibacterial action to this simple cleanser.

## SOAP BARK CLEANSER
### (Part One of the Mayan Formula)

See page 114.

## CAMPING CLEANSER

It is not uncommon to find yourself on a camping trip and discover that you left the soap at home. Collect surrounding weeds, burn them, and use their ashes for an old-fashioned skin cleansing formula. Take care with nettles; they can sting when they are fresh.

> 1 tablespoon weed ashes, such as those of
> nettles and ferns
> Water

Burn the weeds on the edge of a campfire. Gather the ashes, add water, and combine to form a paste. Rub gently on your face, then rinse.

**Makes 1 tablespoon**

*Preparation Time:* About 10 minutes
*Shelf Life:* Indefinite
*Storage:* Glass jar with a screw top

## FRUIT ACID (ALPHA-HYDROXY ACID, OR AHA) CLEANSING "SIMPLES."

The cleansing effect of fruit acids is so deep that you will feel compelled to include your neck. Then you might even want to bathe in a tub full of the solution, as Cleopatra did with her famous sour milk beauty baths.

*Caution:* Avoid the eyes when using AHAs on the face.

## CLEOPATRA'S FAMED MILK CLEANSER ✗

*Used for hundreds of years to soften skin, milk is a source of lactic acid, one of the AHAs.*

> ¼ cup milk, buttermilk, yogurt, or sour cream

Using your fingertips, "wash" your face with the milk. Rinse. (Add milk to your bath, too, for the same effect.) For gifts or traveling, when packaging fresh milk is impractical, you can use powdered milk.

**Makes enough for 1 bath**

Variation

ENHANCED MILK CLEANSER: Add any or all of the following to the milk: rose water (a cup or so); nut or vegetable oil of choice (½ teaspoon or less); glycerin (1 teaspoon or less); 1 or 2 cucumbers, mashed; 2 to 3 tablespoons grated orange or lemon peel; 2 to 3 tablespoons lemon juice; ¼ cup aloe vera gel; herb tea; honey; witch hazel extract; herbal water.

## FRUIT AHA CLEANSER ✗

*Lemon juice is a particularly good fruit-acid face cleanser; strawberries are known as good cleansers of oily skin.*

¼ cup juice or mashed pulp of apples (organic apple vinegar or cider okay), strawberries, blackberries, grapes (wine is okay), citrus fruits (lemon, lime, orange, or grapefruit juice), or tomatoes

Squeeze or mash the fruit to obtain the juice. Dab onto your fingers and pat on your face, being sure to avoid your eyes. Leave on for 10 minutes or so before rinsing. When I use lemon juice on my face, I often don't rinse it off at all. **Makes ¼ cup**

*Preparation Time:* A few minutes
*Shelf Life:* Up to 1 week refrigerated
*Storage:* Glass jar with a screw top

## Variations

ENHANCED FRUIT ACIDS: Add 1 tablespoon of any or all of the following: witch hazel extract (good for oily skin), aloe vera gel (good for dry or injured skin), honey or glycerin (good for dry skin), calendula or chamomile-flower tea, a few drops avocado oil (for very dry or aged skin).
CREAM OF TARTAR: An excellent AHA, this is found inside wine barrels but is available in the spice section of your local supermarket. Make a watery paste of cream of tartar and cool water, and dab it on your face and neck with your fingertips. It is a good skin cleanser because the grainy texture provides a slight scrubbing effect, so the skin is left feeling particularly clean.

### ENZYME CLEANSING SIMPLES

Enzymes fight free-radical damage and are known to reduce age spots and fine lines. They cleanse the skin by dissolving dead cells from the skin's surface. Enzyme cleansers also leave the skin soft and unusually supple.

## GREEN PAPAYA ✗

1 slice green papaya or 1 tablespoon papaya juice

Rub the fruit or juice onto your face. Let set until dry. Rinse with warm water and pat dry. **Makes enough for 1 cleansing**

*Preparation Time:* Less than 1 minute
*Shelf Life:* Discard leftovers

### Variation

RIPE PINEAPPLE ✗: Pineapple is sometimes easier to find than papaya, and its enzymes work as well. Substitute 1 slice ripe pineapple or 1 tablespoon pineapple juice.

### CLEANSING OIL SIMPLES

Oddly enough, oil removes oil. Many herbalists recommend cleaning your face with an oil that has been enriched with antiseptic essential oils such as cinnamon, clove, or lavender. Be cautious about using essential oils on the face, making sure that no more than five drops are added per ounce of the oil base, and only three drops per ounce around the eyes. Be especially careful—even fastidious—to avoid getting any oil in the eyes.

Because coconut oil lathers well, it is found in many cleansing recipes. In lotions without beeswax, such as cleansing milks, coconut oil will separate from the liquid, so you will need to stir the mixture each time before use. If the separation bothers you, substitute your choice of fruit or nut oil such as grapeseed or avocado for the coconut.

## CLEANSING OIL BASIC FORMULA ✂ 🎁

*Coconut oil is a good base because it isn't greasy. Choose the antiseptic oil—lavender, rose, cinnamon, clove, tea tree, rosemary, or sweet orange— with the fragrance you like the most.*

1 ounce coconut oil
¼ ounce vegetable oil of choice
5 drops antibacterial essential oil, such as rosemary or lavender

Combine the ingredients in a bowl and stir well. The coconut oil will soften when stirred. Dab a bit on your fingertips and massage into your face. Rinse well with warm water.
**Makes about ¼ cup**

*Preparation Time:* A few minutes
*Shelf Life:* A few months refrigerated, or until the oil smells rancid
*Storage:* Small glass jar with a screw top

### Variations
ALL-LIQUID OILS: Coconut oil is semihard; if you prefer a thinner cleanser, substitute a liquid oil, such as avocado, for the coconut oil.

SEAWEED CLEANSER: Seaweed adds nutritional minerals to this cleanser. Add ¼ ounce ground seaweed to the oils. It will keep about a week.

CUCUMBER ALMOND MILK: Cucumber is softening for the skin and has the same pH as the skin. Substitute ½ ounce almond oil, 2 ounces cucumber juice, and ¼ teaspoon ascorbic acid for everything but the essential oils. Place in a glass jar, cover, and shake. It will keep about a week refrigerated.

OILY SKIN CLEANSER: Witch hazel extract is a strong astringent cleanser. Add 2 tablespoons witch hazel extract, lemon juice, or strawberry juice to the oils. If you add lemon juice or strawberry juice, add ¼ teaspoon ascorbic acid. It will keep about a week refrigerated.

EMOLLIENT ALOE AND COCONUT CLEANSING MILK: Aloe is wonderfully healing for the skin. Add 2 ounces aloe vera gel, 1 ounce witch hazel extract, and ¼ teaspoon ascorbic acid to the oils. It will keep about 4 months.

## COLD CREAMS, VANISHING CREAMS, AND MAKEUP REMOVERS

Cold creams are heavy, thick creams that sit on top of the skin and absorb makeup, dirt, and oils; they are then wiped off with cotton balls or washcloths. They should always be followed by an astringent to remove excess grease.

Conventional cold cream recipes call for mineral oil and/or stearic acid (a fatty acid derived from animal or vegetable sources) and petroleum-based waxes. Many of the older recipes called for spermaceti, the oil from sperm whales. These conventional creams aren't greasy, but the mineral oil will clog pores. I've successfully adapted these recipes to be more healthful and ecological but still not too greasy by substituting jojoba, known to have properties similar to sperm whale oil, and by using one of the least greasy oils, grapeseed.

## BASIC COLD CREAM VANISHING FORMULA 🎁

*Here is a rich, thick cream that isn't too greasy.*

1 ounce jojoba
1 ounce grapeseed oil
½ to 1 ounce beeswax (less for a thinner cream)
2 ounces water (preferably rose or lavender water)
1 teaspoon vegetable glycerin
1 teaspoon borax
Antioxidant preservative (1 teaspoon vitamin C powder, ¼ teaspoon vitamin A powder, or 1 tablespoon wheat germ oil)
10 drops essential oil of choice, for fragrance (optional; see Note)

Melt the oils and beeswax in a double boiler over medium heat. Remove from the heat and pour in the water, glycerin, borax, preservative, and fragrance (if desired). Mix with an electric handheld mixer until thick and creamy. Scoop about ½ teaspoon onto your fingers and massage into your face. Wipe off with a washcloth or cotton ball. Rinse well with warm water.
**Makes about ³⁄₄ cup**

*Preparation Time:* 25 minutes
*Shelf Life:* 6 months; less with herbal waters
*Storage:* Glass jar with a screw top
NOTE: A classic essential oil combination is 5 parts neroli and 3 parts oil of rose.

### Variations

CREAMY LAVENDER CLEANSER: The organic apple cider vinegar in this formula adds some AHA benefit. Use lavender water; add 1 tablespoon organic apple cider vinegar and use lavender oil as a fragrance.
RICH AND CREAMY VANISHING CREAM: Lanolin is rich and healing for the skin; it is so therapeutic that it is recommended to breastfeeding women to heal cracked and sore nipples. Substitute 1 ounce anhydrous lanolin for the grapeseed oil.

## BASIC FORMULA FOR COLD CREAM WITHOUT BEESWAX ✂

*Although an untraditional formula, this is far and away my favorite cold cream—not because it is any less thick but because it feels less suffocating, is the easiest to wipe off, and leaves my skin soft. It is also easy to make.*

1 tablespoon each jojoba, glycerin, and cornstarch

Combine the ingredients in a bowl and stir until creamy. Dab some on your fingers and massage into your skin. Wipe off with a washcloth or cotton ball. Rinse well with warm water.
**Makes about ¼ cup**

*Preparation Time:* About 1 minute
*Shelf Life:* 4 months
*Storage:* Glass jar with a screw top

## CLEANSING CREAMS

Cleansing creams are similar to cold creams except they contain soap and sometimes alcohol. The oils in cleansing creams help counteract the drying aspects of the soap.

## BASIC CLEANSING CREAM FORMULA 🎁

1 ounce grated soap
1 ounce vodka
1 tablespoon borax
2 ounces water
2 ounces jojoba
2 ounces grapeseed oil
1 ounce almond oil
1 ounce beeswax
Natural preservatives and optional fragrances
(see Chapter One)

The day before you make this cream, combine the soap, vodka, borax, and water, and set aside to dissolve. To make the cream, combine the oils and beeswax in a double boiler, and place over low heat until the beeswax is melted (about 10 minutes). Remove from the heat, add the soap mixture, preservatives, and optional fragrance, and combine with a hand or electric mixer until creamy. The texture should be that of Hollandaise sauce. Scoop about ½ teaspoon onto your fingers and massage into your skin. Wipe off with a wash-

cloth or cotton ball. Rinse well with warm water.

**Makes 1¼ cups**

*Preparation Time:* About 25 minutes
*Shelf Life:* 6 months
*Storage:* Glass jar with a screw top

### Variation

FRUIT ACID CLEANSING CREAM: Substitute organic apple cider vinegar for the water.

## SOAP-BASED CLEANSING MILKS AND WATERS

Cleansing milks, increasingly popular as face cleansers, are called "milks" not because milk is necessarily an ingredient but because they are thin lotions.

## BASIC CLEANSING MILK LOTION ✄ 🎁

1 cup antiseptic herbal water (such as rose, lavender, rosemary, or thyme)
1 ounce grated or liquid soap
1 tablespoon vodka
1 teaspoon sweet almond oil
Antioxidant or essential oil preservative (see page 36)

The day before making the milk, make the herbal infusion: Put a handful of herbs such as lavender flowers or rose petals in a mason jar, cover with boiling water, and set the jar aside for 8 hours or overnight; strain. To make the lotion,

combine the ingredients in a jar and shake to blend. (If you are using grated soap, let the soap dissolve in the mixture overnight before using.) Dab some lotion on your fingers and massage into your skin. Rinse with warm water.
**Makes about 1 cup**

*Preparation Time:* About 15 minutes
*Shelf Life:* 1 to 2 months
*Storage:* Glass jar with a screw top

## Variations

OATMEAL CLEANSING MILK: Oatmeal softens the skin and provides some abrasion. Add 1 tablespoon oatmeal flour to the mixture. Shelf life is about 2 weeks.

ROSE WATER MILK: Rose is astringent and antiseptic. Substitute rose water for other herbal waters.

FRUIT ACID MILK: Substitute Queen of Hungary Water (page 137) for the herbal water. The shelf life of this product is indefinite.

CUCUMBER-LAVENDER CLEANSING MILK: The shelf life of this formula is only 3 to 4 days, but it is a good product—astringent, the same pH as the skin, and antiseptic—and worth making on a regular basis. Substitute half cucumber juice and half rose water for the water, and use lavender as an essential oil.

CUCUMBER CLEANSING MILK: Cucumber is an astringent toner with the same pH as the skin. Substitute cucumber juice for the water. Refrigerate after using; discard after 3 to 4 days.

HERBAL CLEANSING MILK: This product is welcomed by men who prefer not to use floral scents. Infuse the water with herbs such as sage, rosemary, and mint.

## WITCH HAZEL EXTRACT CLEANSING WATER

*An emollient cleansing water, this formula is particularly good for dry skin.*

¼ cup sweet almond oil
¼ cup witch hazel extract
1 tablespoon vegetable glycerin
2 teaspoons liquid soap
Natural preservatives and optional fragrance
(see Chapter One)

Combine the ingredients in a glass jar. Shake to blend. Dab some on your fingers and massage into your skin. Rinse with warm water.
**Makes about ½ cup**

*Preparation Time:* About 1 minute
*Shelf Life:* About 1 year (discard when the oil begins to smell rancid)
*Storage:* Glass jar with a screw top

## BIRCH BUD WATER

*Birch is renowned for its skin-softening properties.*

¼ cup birch water
1 tablespoon vodka
1 teaspoon liquid soap
1 teaspoon glycerin
A few drops essential oil of birch (optional)

Make a birch infusion by packing a quart mason jar with birch twigs, covering with boiling water, sealing, and letting it set overnight. Strain. Combine ¼ cup birch water (drink the rest; it is very refreshing) with the other ingredients in a glass jar. Shake to blend. Dab some on your fingers and massage into your skin. Rinse with warm water.

**Makes about ¼ cup**

*Preparation Time:* About 10 minutes
*Shelf Life:* About 4 months refrigerated
*Storage:* Glass jar with a screw top

## HERBAL CLEANSING WATER

### ROSE CLEANSING WATER (DRY SKIN)
½ cup rose water
½ ounce liquid castile soap (or grated soap)
½ cup aloe vera gel
1 teaspoon avocado oil
10 to 20 drops lavender essential oil

The day before, make a rose water infusion. Strain. Combine the ingredients in a glass jar and shake to blend. If you are using grated soap, let it set overnight to dissolve. Dab some on your fingers and massage into your skin. Rinse with warm water.

**Makes about 1 cup**

*Preparation Time:* About 10 minutes
*Shelf Life:* Up to 4 months refrigerated, or until the oil smells rancid
*Storage:* Glass jar with a screw top

### LEMON BALM AND LAVENDER CLEANSING WATER (OILY SKIN)
½ cup water infused with lemon balm and lavender
1 ounce castile soap (or grated soap)
½ cup witch hazel extract
Vitamin A, C, and E preservative (see page 36)
10 to 20 drops lavender essential oil

The day before, make an herbal water infusion (see page 32). Strain. Combine the ingredients in a glass jar and shake to blend. If using grated soap, let set overnight to dissolve. Dab some on your fingers and massage into your skin. Rinse with warm water.

**Makes 1 cup**

*Preparation Time:* About 10 minutes
*Shelf Life:* Up to 1 month refrigerated
*Storage:* Glass jar with a screw top

### SOAP-FREE CLEANSING MILKS AND WATERS
These formulas tend to be emollient and moisturizing. If herbs with saponin (a soapy ingredient) were more available commercially, the recipes here would be as infused with them as possible. If you are lucky enough to have a good supply of saponin-rich weeds in your vicinity, such as bouncing bet, infuse them in the liquid (water, alcohol, or oil) of the following preparations. Or buy soap bark (see Sources and Resources).

### OIL-FREE ANTISEPTIC CLEANSING GEL ✗ 🎁

*A good all-purpose formula, this is emollient enough for dry skin because of the glycerin and aloe* vera gel, and cleansing enough for oily skin because *of the astringent witch hazel extract and lemon juice or organic apple cider vinegar.*

1/4 cup witch hazel extract
1/4 cup aloe vera gel
1 teaspoon vegetable glycerin
1 tablespoon lemon juice or organic apple cider vinegar
10 drops tea tree oil

Combine the ingredients in a glass jar. Shake to blend. Dab some on your fingers and massage into your skin. Rinse with warm water.
**Makes about 1/2 cup**

*Preparation Time:* About 1 minute
*Shelf Life:* About 4 months with vinegar, 1 week refrigerated with lemon juice
*Storage:* Glass jar with a screw top

## OIL-FREE SATINY SMOOTH CLEANSING MILK ✗

*The slight abrasive quality of the cornstarch sloughs off dead skin cells and feels good on the skin.*

1 tablespoon each cornstarch and glycerin
1/4 to 1 teaspoon rum (to "cut" the glycerin)
A few drops essential oil, for fragrance (as desired)

Combine the ingredients in a bowl, and stir to blend. Dab some onto your fingers and massage into your skin. Rinse with warm water.
**Makes 2 tablespoons, enough for a few days**

*Preparation Time:* 1 minute
*Shelf Life:* Make only enough for a few days; it dries out
*Storage:* Glass jar with a screw top

## OIL-FREE ROSE WATER WITH GLYCERIN ✗ 🎁

*Rose water is one of the all-time best and most traditional facial cleansers, because rose is astringent, anti-inflammatory, and antiseptic and has a lovely scent.*

1 cup rose-infused water
2 teaspoons glycerin
5 to 10 drops rose essential oil (optional)

The day before making the rose water with glycerin, place a handful of dried rose petals in a mason jar, cover with boiling water, seal tightly, and let set overnight. Strain carefully. Combine the ingredients in a glass jar, and shake to blend. Dab some on your fingers and massage into your skin. Rinse with warm water.
**Makes about 1 cup**

*Preparation Time:* About 10 minutes
*Shelf Life:* Some rose water lasts a long time, and others turn moldy quickly; discard at first sign of any mold
*Storage:* Glass jar with a screw top
NOTE: It is confusing that sometimes commercial rose water has glycerin in it, and sometimes it is just a rose petal infusion. For clarity, rose water in *Better Basics for the Home* refers to a rose infusion without glycerin.

## Variation

CUCUMBER LAVENDER MILK: Substitute freshly made cucumber juice for the rose water. Cucumber juice is good for the skin as a toner, astringent, and pH restorer. However, products with cucumber juice last only 3 to 4 days in the refrigerator.

## ALOE AND CALENDULA CLEANSING MILK 🎁

4 tablespoons avocado oil
1 tablespoon calendula flowers
2 tablespoons aloe vera gel
25 drops grapefruit seed extract

Heat the oil and calendula in a double boiler over very low heat for 30 minutes. Remove from the heat and let cool. Strain out all the calendula. Stir in the aloe vera gel and grapefruit seed extract. Scoop some onto your fingers and massage into your skin. Rinse well with warm water.
**Makes about ½ cup**

*Preparation Time:* About 40 minutes
*Shelf Life:* 1 to 2 months refrigerated (discard at the first sign of mold)
*Storage:* Glass jar with a screw top

## Variation

WITCH HAZEL EXTRACT AND CALENDULA MILK: Add 2 tablespoons witch hazel extract to the mixture right before stirring in the final ingredients. Witch hazel extract is very astringent and makes this formula better for oily skin.

## SILICON-RICH OATMEAL MILK

2 tablespoons oatmeal flour
1 cup boiling water
1 teaspoon oil of choice, such as avocado (a very emollient oil)

Place the oatmeal in a bowl and cover with the boiling water. Add the oil and stir to blend. Let cool. Scoop some onto your fingers and massage into your skin. Rinse well with warm water.
**Makes 1 cup**

*Preparation Time:* About 10 minutes
*Shelf Life:* A few days refrigerated
*Storage:* Glass jar with a screw top

## Variation

OATMEAL SOLO: I love the way dry oatmeal takes away the grime and relieves itches. Rub plain oatmeal on greasy skin. Wipe off the residue.

## OIL-FREE PEPPERMINT ACNE CLEANSER

*Peppermint is refreshing and stimulating for the skin.*

Peppermint
½ cup water
1 teaspoon sea salt

Make a strong cup of peppermint tea. Let cool. Strain, and stir in the salt. Dab some on a washcloth or cotton ball and massage into your skin. Rinse with warm water.
**Makes ½ cup**

*Preparation Time:* About 5 minutes
*Shelf Life:* A few days refrigerated
*Storage:* Glass jar with a screw top

## ALMOND MILKS

## BASIC ALMOND MILK FORMULA 🎁

*You can't do much better than this cleanser if you have dry or aged skin. Almond oil lubricates and softens the skin, and glycerin helps it retain moisture. The herbal waters are antiseptic and toning.*

½ cup rose, lavender, or distilled water
1 teaspoon glycerin
¼ to 1 teaspoon almond oil
12 drops grapefruit seed extract
5 to 10 drops essential oil, for fragrance
(optional)

Make the rose or lavender water by placing a couple tablespoons of rose or lavender in a pint mason jar and adding boiling water to cover. Let set overnight, then thoroughly strain out the plant matter. Combine the remaining ingredients in a glass jar and shake to blend. Dab some on your fingers or a cotton ball and massage into your skin. Rinse with warm water.
**Makes about ½ cup**

*Preparation Time:* About 10 minutes
*Shelf Life:* 1 to 2 months (discard at the first sign of rotting—a bad smell or mold)
*Storage:* Glass jar with a screw top

### Variations

LANOLIN AND HONEY: If you have very dry or troubled skin (such as eczema or psoriasis), include these extra emollient and moisturizing ingredients: 1 teaspoon each anhydrous lanolin and honey.

CREAM AND HONEY: These AHAs provide extra exfoliation. Add 1 teaspoon honey, 1 teaspoon organic apple cider vinegar, and 1 tablespoon cream to the mixture before shaking to blend. The shelf life is about 1 week.

## EGG CLEANSING LOTIONS

*Caution:* Raw eggs can be contaminated with salmonella, so avoid getting these in your mouth. Some organic farms now test their eggs for salmonella, and it is only from such farms that you should buy eggs for cleansing lotions.

## NUTTIN' HONEY EGG CLEANSING LOTION

*Eggs provide the skin with protein, conditioning, and toning.*

1 egg, beaten
½ teaspoon honey
1 tablespoon ground almonds

Combine the ingredients (almonds are easily ground in a blender) in a bowl, and stir to make a paste. Rub gently onto the face, and rinse thoroughly with warm water.
**Makes about 2 tablespoons**

*Preparation Time:* About 10 minutes
*Shelf Life:* Use immediately; discard leftovers

### Variations

LEMONY LOTION: Lemon juice adds some AHA benefit. Add 1 teaspoon lemon juice.

EGG WHITE AND LEMONS: This formula combines slightly different ingredients in a slightly different way, and leaves out the egg yolk. Whip 2 egg whites, 1 teaspoon nut or vegetable oil of choice, 1 teaspoon lemon juice, and enough flour to make a paste. Up to 4 drops essential oils and ground herbs are also a good addition. Discard any leftovers.

EGG WHITE AND ROSE WATER: Add 2 egg whites, 2 to 3 tablespoons rose water, and 4 drops essential oil of rosemary (optional) to main recipe. Discard any leftovers.

EGG WHITE AND HERB MILK: Combine ¼ cup herbal water (sage and rosemary are good choices—just make a strong tea, steep for a few hours, then strain), ¼ cup milk, ½ cup mashed strawberries, ½ cup mashed cucumber, and 2 egg whites. Whip in a blender or mix with a hand beater. Dab on your face, let dry, then rinse thoroughly. Discard any leftovers.

## FLAX MUCILAGE CLEANSING LOTIONS

I love these lotions. The flax and glycerin ensure that the skin doesn't dry out too much, yet the entire combination is very cleansing.

## BASIC FORMULA FOR FLAX LOTION ✘

*This formula is particularly good for softening the skin.*

1 cup distilled or herbal water
1 tablespoon flax seed
1 tablespoon witch hazel extract

1 teaspoon (or less) vegetable glycerin
⅓ teaspoon grapefruit seed extract
Fragrance, if desired (see page 37)

To make herbal water, make a cup of strong herbal tea (using one or more of the 16 cosmetic herbs listed on page 106). Place the water and flax seed in a small pan and simmer for 15 minutes. Strain out the seeds as much as possible as you pour the mucilage into a bowl. Add the witch hazel extract, glycerin, grapefruit seed extract, and fragrance (if using). Blend with a hand mixer. Dab some onto your fingers and rub into your skin. Rinse well with warm water.

**Makes about 1¼ cups**

*Preparation Time:* About 30 minutes
*Shelf Life:* About 1 week refrigerated
*Storage:* Glass jar with a screw top

## Variations

BAY RUM LOTION: For a more astringent cleanser, add 1 tablespoon bay rum.

FLAX AND ALOE LOTION: For a more emollient and hydrating lotion, add 1 tablespoon aloe vera gel.

LEMON LOTION: For some AHA benefit, substitute lemon juice for the witch hazel.

QUINCE SEED LOTION: Quince is the seed traditionally used in these recipes, but is not easily available. If you can find it, substitute quince seed for the flax seed.

FLAX AND LEMON LOTION: For oily skin, add 2 tablespoons lemon juice in addition to the witch hazel extract.

EMOLLIENT AND CLEANSING LOTION: Glycerin is emollient, and the alcohol and witch hazel are cleansing and astringent. In addition to the main recipe, add 1 teaspoon glycerin; 1 tablespoon rum, vodka, or brandy; and 2 tablespoons witch hazel extract.

# Toners: Astringents, Clarifying Lotions, and Skin Fresheners

A toner makes the skin smooth and firm because it closes pores, adjusts the pH of the skin, removes residual soaps and oils, and nourishes the skin before moisturizing. Sometimes, but not always, toners are antiseptic. Toners remove oil, which may dry out the skin. If using a toner, you need to follow with a moisturizer, especially if you have dry skin.

There are three common types of toners.

**CLARIFYING AND EXFOLIATING LOTIONS.** The fruit acids (AHAs) and enzyme exfoliants fall under this category and do wonderful things for the skin. For more on AHAs, see page 107.

**ASTRINGENTS.** Astringents, which close the pores, include witch hazel, berry leaves, organic apple cider vinegar, or floral waters made with astringent herbs.

**SKIN FRESHENERS.** These are skin tonics, such as a spritzer of astringent herbs—usually menthol essential oils such as peppermint and eucalyptus.

The best approach is to use all three types of toners. Exfoliate the skin with an AHA, close the pores with an astringent, and hydrate the skin before moisturizing. If you wash your face with soap, you need to restore the slightly acidic acid mantle of your skin, so be sure to choose an acidic toner.

Note that many toners are similar to cleansing lotions; in fact, many cleansers and toners are interchangeable.

## EXFOLIATING AND CLARIFYING LOTIONS

### FRUIT ACID (AHA) EXFOLIATING LOTIONS
NOTE: Be sure to avoid the eyes when using acids such as lemon juice, lime juice, organic apple cider vinegar, and pineapple juice.

## MAYAN ZAZIL TONER

See page 115.

## BASIC FRUIT ACID FORMULA ✗

*I can see the difference in people's skin overnight when they start using natural fruit acids. I find lemon juice the easiest to manage—I squeeze the juice of one lemon, put it in a glass jar with a screw top, and refrigerate. It keeps about a week.*

Tomato, lemon, or apple juice (see Fruit Acids on page 108 for a complete list)

Pat the face with the juice. Let rest for 10 minutes before rinsing if possible, then apply a moisturizer. Make only enough to last a few days—about ¼ cup.

*Preparation Time:* About 5 minutes
*Shelf Life:* 1 week or less refrigerated (discard if you see mold)
*Storage:* Glass jar with a screw top

## Variations

AU NATURELLE: Just rub face with slices of fresh fruit. Discard any leftovers.

BLENDED BEAUTY: Combine orange juice, strawberries, apples, grapes, lemon juice, and cherries (or as many of these as you have on hand) in the blender. Add a bit of brandy if desired. Use as an astringent.

WINED AND DINED: This is an antiseptic and emollient exfoliant, thanks to the glycerin combined with AHAs. Combine 1 teaspoon each of the antiseptic herbs rosemary, bay, and thyme in 1 cup white wine. Simmer over very low heat for 15 minutes. Let cool and strain. Add 1 teaspoon vegetable glycerin.

BLOODY MARY: Vodka is an astringent; tomato juice is an AHA. Combine equal amounts of vodka, tomato juice, and water (herbal water is optional).

EMOLLIENT FRUIT ACIDS: For those with dry or aged skin, adding a few drops of oil gives extra lubrication. Combine 3 parts fruit acid juice to 1 part avocado oil or other emollient oil. Avocado oil is particularly rich.

VINEGAR BRACER: In a saucepan combine 2 to 3 teaspoons antiseptic herbs such as rosemary and 1 cup organic apple cider vinegar. Simmer over very low heat for 15 minutes. Let cool.

HOT WEATHER COOLER: Not only does this lotion refresh, it also saves time—make enough juice at a time to last awhile. Freeze fruit acid juice (such as lemon juice) in an ice cube tray, and pop out one at a time as needed. Rub the ice cube on your face, or melt in a bowl and dab on your face.

OF RENOWNED BEAUTIES: This is a softening and anti-inflammatory preparation. Combine 1 part milk to 1 part aloe vera gel.

MILK AND HONEY: Combine 1 tablespoon each honey and rose water with 1 cup milk.

WINE BARREL VINEGAR: Cream of tartar and vinegar are strong AHAs. Combine 1 teaspoon cream of tartar and ½ cup each organic apple cider vinegar and water.

STRAWBERRY VINEGAR: Steep mashed strawberries in enough organic apple cider vinegar to cover. Let rest overnight in the refrigerator. Strain. Combine with equal amounts water or rose water.

pH RESTORING EXFOLIATOR: This is a good formula to use when you have an abundance of vegetables from your garden or a local farmers' market. Process 1 cucumber, 2 or 3 big lettuce leaves, and half a tomato in a blender. Add 1 to 2 tablespoons lemon juice.

## BASIC BIRCH WATER FORMULA

*Birch sap is high in salicylate acids and a potent antibacterial. It was a staple in old-fashioned recipes for contributing to clear complexions.*

2 cups birch infusion or tincture
2 teaspoons glycerin
½ cup vodka
10 to 30 drops fragrance, such as birch bud essential oil, as desired

To make the infusion, pack a quart mason jar with birch twigs and small branches broken to fit. Pour in boiling water, cover, and let set overnight. Strain 3 cups of the birch water into a clean quart mason jar; add the glycerin, vodka, and fragrance (if desired). Shake to blend. Dab some on your fingers, washcloth, or cotton ball and rub into the skin. Rinse with warm water.
**Makes 3 cups**

*Preparation Time:* About 30 minutes
*Shelf Life:* 6 months
*Storage:* Glass jar with a screw top

ENZYME EXFOLIATORS. Green papayas contain papain enzymes; fresh pineapples contain the enzyme bromelain. The enzymes dissolve dead skin cells, leaving the skin soft and unusually supple. For directions on how to use these exfoliators, see page 123.

## ALOE AND SEAWEED GEL

*Irish moss powder, available in health food stores, is rich in minerals.*

1 teaspoon Irish moss powder
Enough aloe vera gel to make a paste

Combine the ingredients in a bowl. Stir to blend. Dab on your face and massage into your skin, then rinse with warm water.
**Makes about 2 teaspoons**

*Preparation Time:* A few minutes
*Shelf Life:* Make only enough to use at a time
*Storage:* Discard leftovers

**EGG WHITE TONER.** A beautiful Swedish woman from the town where I grew up, now in her late sixties and with astonishingly firm and healthy-looking skin, told me her beauty secret: She rubs raw egg whites on her face every day. Egg whites are excellent pore tighteners.

*Caution:* Raw eggs can be contaminated with salmonella. Some organic farms now test their eggs for salmonella, and it is only from such farms that you should buy eggs for egg white toner formulas.

## EGG WHITE TONER ✄

1 or 2 egg whites

Separate the egg whites from the yolks, and whip until stiff but not dry. Scoop some onto a washcloth and pat on your face, avoiding the mouth. Leave on until dry. Wash off well with warm water. Wash your hands with soap and water.

**Makes enough for 1 day**

*Preparation Time:* About 5 minutes
*Shelf Life:* Use immediately
*Storage:* Discard leftovers

Variation

STARCH AND EGGS: This toner is antiseptic and drying. To 1 egg white add ¼ teaspoon cornstarch and a few drops essential oil of lavender. Blend with a whisk.

**ROYAL JELLY TONER.** Like egg white, royal jelly tightens the skin to an astonishing degree. After I put it on and let it dry, I look ten years younger. Too bad it is shiny when it dries. (It dries to less of a shine if you clean your skin with lemon juice first. Also, women who are very thin complain that the royal jelly toner tightens their skin so much that it is uncomfortable.)

Royal jelly is just about the most nourishing and extraordinary of all natural materials for the skin. My favorite way of using it is to put it on my face and let it dry before getting into a sauna. As the royal jelly softens in the heat, I massage it into my face. Buy "active" royal jelly from the refrigerated section of your health food store. Just pat it on and let it dry. Leave it on as long as possible for its face-lifting properties, rinsing it off only if it feels uncomfortable.

### ASTRINGENTS

**NOURISHING HERBAL VINEGAR ASTRINGENTS.** These are very healing and softening for the skin.

*Caution:* Make sure to close the eyes when applying.

## BASIC HERBAL VINEGAR FORMULA

1 ounce herbs (see page 137 for list)
1 cup organic apple cider vinegar, or as needed

Place the herbs in a glass jar and add the vinegar to cover completely. Seal tightly and let set in a dark place for 4 to 6 weeks. Strain thoroughly.

## GOOD ASTRINGENT HERBS

COMFREY, chamomile, aloe vera, calendula, lavender, lemon balm, nettle, rose, rosemary, sage, St. John's wort, witch hazel, bay, yarrow flowers, red raspberry, colt's foot, myrrh

Dab some on your fingers, and massage into your face. Rinse with warm water if desired. (I like to leave it on to reap its full benefit.)
**Makes 1 cup**

*Preparation Time:* About 10 minutes
*Shelf Life:* Indefinite
*Storage:* Glass jar with a screw top
NOTE: It makes a lot of sense to prepare much larger quantities of this, because it stores indefinitely. A quadrupled recipe will make enough astringent for a year with moderate use.

## Variations

pH RESTORER: Cover ½ ounce each rose petals, witch hazel extract, berry leaves, and rosemary with enough organic apple cider vinegar to completely cover.

FRAGRANT VINEGAR: If you are lucky enough to have a source of jasmine flowers, this vinegar will smell exotic and floral. If not, just use rose petals and lavender; they have a lighter floral scent. Cover ½ ounce rose petals, lavender, and jasmine flowers with enough organic apple cider vinegar to cover.

## QUEEN OF HUNGARY WATER

*Gypsies first formulated this wonderful astringent, which they used primarily as a medicinal remedy. I have seen this formula in many places, using a variety of herbs. The Vinegar of the Four Thieves is a version of this formula (see page 71) used as a disinfectant. I have often made a version by herbalist Rosemary Gladstar for Christmas gifts, bottling it in beautifully shaped blue glass. Here is my favorite adaptation of the recipe. Because so many people are allergic to ragweed, I delete the chamomile that she calls for and increase the calendula; feel free to adapt it again to suit your skin type.*

6 small handfuls lemon balm
5 small handfuls calendula flowers
4 small handfuls rose petals
3 small handfuls comfrey
1 small handful each rosemary, lemon peel, and sage
Organic apple cider vinegar, as needed
Rose water or witch hazel, as needed

Place the herbs in a large glass jar that will hold at least a gallon of liquid. Cover the herbs completely with organic apple cider vinegar, leaving about 2 inches to spare in the jar. Screw the lid on tightly. Let it set for 4 to 6 weeks. Strain. Divide the mixture into smaller jars, and dilute to half its strength with rose water or witch hazel extract. Dab some on your fingers, and massage into your face. Rinse with warm water if desired. (I like to leave it on to reap its full benefit.)
**Makes at least 1 gallon**

*Preparation Time:* About 30 minutes
*Shelf Life:* Indefinite
*Storage:* Glass jars with screw tops

**CUCUMBER FORMULAS.** Beauties of times past used cucumber on their skin because they believed that it imparted a clear complexion. We now know that cucumber is conditioning and toning and has the same pH as the skin, so it helps restore its acid balance. Cucumber also contains softening enzymes.

## CUCUMBER VINEGAR ✘

5 cucumbers
Organic apple cider vinegar to cover

Peel the cucumbers and mash them in a bowl. Scoop the pulp into a quart mason jar and pour in vinegar to completely cover. Close the lid tightly and let set for 3 weeks. Strain. Dab some on your fingers, and massage into your face. Rinse with warm water if desired. (I like to leave it on to reap its full benefit.)
**Makes about 4 cups**

*Preparation Time:* About 15 minutes
*Shelf Life:* About 3 months; discard if you detect an odor or see mold
*Storage:* Glass jar with a screw top

Variation
CUCUMBER AND ALCOHOL: For an especially antiseptic formula that is good for oily skin, substitute vodka, rum, or brandy for the vinegar.
**FLORAL WATER ASTRINGENTS.** Most floral water astringents are emollient and hydrating

due to the glycerin and aloe vera gel they contain. In fact, many of these can be used as moisturizers as well as astringents; just be sure to close the pores first by washing with fresh lemon juice or other fruit acid.

## BASIC HERBAL ASTRINGENT FORMULA

*Glycerin is a very sticky but wonderful humectant and moisturizer. I find that the ratio of 1 part glycerin to 4 parts water works for most people. If the mixture feels too sticky on your skin, reduce the amount of glycerin.*

1 cup herbal water made with astringent herbs such as birch, calendula, lavender, and rosemary
2 tablespoons glycerin (or less if this is too sticky)
$\frac{1}{3}$ teaspoon grapefruit seed extract

To make the herbal water, prepare a strong cup of herbal tea and steep for a few hours. Strain. Combine the ingredients in a jar, cover, and shake to blend. Dab some on your fingers, and massage into your skin. Rinse with warm water if desired. (I like to leave it on to reap its full benefit.)
**Makes about 1 cup**

*Preparation Time:* About 10 minutes
*Shelf Life:* 6 months with birch twigs; 1 month with highly antiseptic herbs such as thyme or lavender; a couple of weeks with less antiseptic herbs (discard if you detect an odor or see mold)
*Storage:* Glass jar with a screw top, refrigerated

## Variations

CHAMOMILE AND LAVENDER WATER: Make the herbal water with chamomile (an emollient) and lavender; add 5 to 10 drops lavender essential oil.

LAVENDER AND ROSE: Lavender and rose are astringent, fragrant, and antiseptic, and rose is emollient. Make the herbal water with lavender and rose flowers.

YLANG-YLANG WATER: For a more exotic fragrance, try the essential oil of ylang-ylang (available in health food stores). Combine 3 parts herbal water, 1 part aloe vera gel, and 1 part glycerin. Add 5 or 6 drops each essential oils of lavender, ylang-ylang, and lemongrass (optional).

ALOE WATER: Aloe is a good antiseptic astringent in its own right. Make the herbal water with rose, and add $\frac{1}{4}$ cup aloe vera gel.

HYDRATING TONER: Substitute cucumber juice for the herbal water, and add $\frac{1}{4}$ cup each aloe vera gel and witch hazel extract. The shelf life of this formula is 3 to 4 days.

## BASIC ROSE WATER AND GLYCERIN FORMULA 🎁

$\frac{1}{2}$ cup rose water (see Note)
$\frac{1}{2}$ cup glycerin
$\frac{1}{3}$ cup grapefruit seed extract

Make the rose water by placing a handful of rose petals in a pint mason jar and adding boiling water to cover. Seal tightly and let set overnight. Strain the rose water, and place $\frac{1}{2}$ cup in a clean glass jar. Add the glycerin and grapefruit seed extract, and shake to blend. Dab some on your fingers, and massage into your skin. Rinse with warm water if desired. (I like to leave it on to reap its full benefit.)

**Makes 1 cup**

*Preparation Time:* About 15 minutes
*Shelf Life:* 2 to 4 months
*Storage:* Glass jar with a screw top
NOTE: Do not use store-bought rose water; it usually already contains glycerin.

## Variations

DRY SKIN ROSE WATER: Add up to 1 teaspoon honey, an excellent humectant and moisturizer.

OILY SKIN ROSE WATER: Substitute lemon juice—a good AHA—for a quarter of the rose water. The shelf life is about 1 week.

ALMOND ROSE WATER: Substitute finely ground almonds for the glycerin. This formula was used a lot in the nineteenth century. Almonds are softening and lubricating.

ALMOND ROSE WATER II: Add $\frac{1}{8}$ cup finely ground almonds. Blend well with an electric mixer or blender.

## SIMPLE FLORAL WATER ✂

*This floral water is very easy to make; you just have to open a few bottles.*

20 drops essential oil (such as the astringent herb lavender)
1 cup distilled water

Combine the ingredients and shake to blend. Dab some on your fingers, and massage into your skin. Rinse with warm water if desired. (I like to leave it on to reap its full benefit.)
**Makes 1 cup**

*Preparation Time:* About 1 minute
*Shelf Life:* Indefinite
*Storage:* Glass jar with a screw top

### WITCH HAZEL EXTRACT ASTRINGENTS

## BASIC WITCH HAZEL EXTRACT ASTRINGENT FORMULA

*Witch hazel is an excellent astringent for oily skin.*

½ cup each rose water and witch hazel extract
⅓ teaspoon grapefruit seed extract

To make the rose water, prepare a strong cup of rose petal tea. Let set for a few hours before straining. Combine the ingredients in a glass jar, cover, and shake to blend. Dab some on your fingers, and massage into your skin. Rinse with warm water if desired.
**Makes 1 cup**

*Preparation Time:* 10 minutes
*Shelf Life:* 2 to 4 months; refrigerate
*Storage:* Glass jar with a screw top

### Variations
**LAVENDER WITCH HAZEL:** If you prefer the scent of lavender to that of roses, substitute lavender water (see Simple Floral Water, page 139) for the rose water.

**BRANDY ASTRINGENT:** For a more antiseptic astringent, add ⅛ part brandy (or vodka) to the mixture.

**LEMON ASTRINGENT:** Substitute lemon juice for the rose water. The addition of lemon juice gives some AHA exfoliating benefit. The shelf life is 1 week, refrigerated.

**EMOLLIENT ASTRINGENT:** Instead of rose water, add 1 tablespoon glycerin and ½ cup cucumber or lemon juice. This is one of my favorite formulas, because it is cleansing, astringent, emollient, and toning. The shelf life is 4 to 5 days, refrigerated.

**TEA TONER:** Substitute peppermint and/or chamomile tea for the rose water. Peppermint is stimulating and refreshing for the skin; chamomile is anti-inflammatory, astringent, and antioxidant. The shelf life is about 1 week, refrigerated.

**ALOE ASTRINGENT:** Substitute aloe vera juice for the rose water. Aloe is hydrating and healing for the skin.

**LEMON ALOE:** For added AHA benefit, substitute ¼ cup lemon juice and ¼ cup aloe vera gel for the rose water. The shelf life is about 1 week, refrigerated.

**NOURISHING SEAWEED TONER:** For a toner rich in nourishing minerals, substitute 1 teaspoon dried seaweed infused in ½ cup bottled mineral water for the rose water. The self life is about 4 days, refrigerated.

**EVERYTHING BUT THE KITCHEN SINK ASTRINGENT:** Infuse 1 cup water with 1 teaspoon eucalyptus, calendula, chamomile, lavender, nettle, kelp, or other herbs. Combine with 1 cup witch hazel extract, ½ cup aloe vera gel, and ¼ cup glycerin; add essential oils of sage and lavender to desired strength (no more than 20 drops total per ounce). The shelf life is about 1 week, refrigerated.

OILY SKIN JUICE: Substitute orange juice for half of the rose water. The shelf life is about 1 week.

## SKIN FRESHENERS, HYDRATORS, AND SPRITZERS

Menthol, the common constituent in skin fresheners, is made of the essential oils of peppermint and eucalyptus.

### BASIC SKIN FRESHENER FORMULA ✗ 🎁

*Refreshing and stimulating for the skin because of the menthol herbs, this freshener also hydrates.*

10 drops each peppermint and eucalyptus essential oils
2 cups bottled mineral water

Combine the ingredients in a spray bottle, and shake to blend. Spritz to freshen the skin. Be sure to keep your eyes closed when spraying.
**Makes 2 cups**

*Preparation Time:* About 1 minute
*Shelf Life:* Indefinite
*Storage:* Leave in the spray bottle

### Variation

EXTRA-EMOLLIENT SKIN FRESHENER FORMULA: Add 2 teaspoons glycerin. Glycerin draws moisture to the skin, hydrating it.

### SPRITZER ✗

1 cup bottled mineral water
10 drops essential oil of choice

Combine the ingredients in a spray bottle, shake to blend, and spritz the face for a moisturizing pick-me-up. Be sure to keep your eyes closed when spraying.
**Makes 1 cup**

*Preparation Time:* About 1 minute
*Shelf Life:* Indefinite
*Storage:* Leave in the spray bottle

### Variations

AVOCADO OIL AND WATER: For a softening emollient formula, add a few drops avocado oil (or apricot kernel oil) to the mineral water. The shelf life is about 2 months.

ORANGE HYDRATOR: Infuse the water with orange peels; add a few drops orange flower essential oil to the spray bottle. Orange is a good AHA. The shelf life is 1 week.

# Moisturizing and Nourishing Skin Products

I first learned in *Jeanne Rose's Herbal Body Book* that thick, oily skin creams could suffocate the skin and clog pores. I was astonished; I had slathered moisturizing creams on my skin for as long as I could remember. The book inspired me to abandon my moisturizing cream and preconceived notions and try instead some simple alternatives, such as aloe

## GOOD EMOLLIENT AND MOISTURIZING HERBS

COMFREY, flax, Irish moss, slippery elm, marshmallow, licorice, aloe vera, mint, orange flowers, rosemary, chamomile

vera gel and glycerin. To my surprise, my skin benefited so much and felt so wonderful that I have never gone back to thick creams.

That said, I realize that there are some important uses for these creams, not the least of which is to protect the skin from the elements. Beeswax, a key ingredient in many moisturizers, provides a protective coating on the skin against wind and sun and also helps prevent skin moisture from evaporating. Using a good skin cream on a cold and blustery winter day makes a great deal of sense. During my severe arthritic bouts with Lyme disease, I would add rosemary essential oil (good for stiff joints) to creams and rub it into my joints to soothe them. Making a special eye cream is worthwhile, because the oils in creams are emollient and softening for the wrinkle-prone area around the eyes. The oils in sunscreen creams actually have UV-screening properties and are healing for the skin. Even if, like me, you don't want to use a cream as a moisturizer, it can fill other important roles in body care. Not all of the moisturizers described here are rich creams. My favorite is a combination of aloe vera gel and vegetable glycerin; it drenches the skin, leaving it soft and hydrated.

## HYDRATING THE SKIN

Dampen the skin before moisturizing with a freshener (see Toners, page 133), bottled mineral water, or plain water.

## MOISTURIZING SIMPLES

Vegetable glycerin is a humectant, drawing moisture from the surrounding air to your skin. Because it comes from vegetable oils, it is emollient and moisturizing. It is called for in a large number of moisturizing products you can make yourself. If products using vegetable glycerin feel too sticky on your skin, reduce the amount of glycerin.

## THE BEST BASIC SOFT AND SILKY MOISTURIZER ✂ 🎁

*You may not need to look further for a favorite moisturizer than this favorite of mine. It comes highly praised and prized by me and my friends and family. Aloe vera gel is emollient, hydrating, and a profound healer for the skin. Using it daily for four months made my age spots disappear.*

½ cup aloe vera gel
⅛ cup glycerin

Combine the ingredients in a glass jar. Shake or stir to blend. Dampen your face, then dab the mixture on your fingers and massage into the skin.
**Makes ⅝ cup**

*Preparation Time:* About 1 minute
*Shelf Life:* 4 months
*Storage:* Glass jar with a screw top

## BUYER'S GUIDE

### MOISTURIZING CREAMS

**A**N increasing number of natural plant-based moisturizing creams are on the market. However, many brands that appear to be all plant based can contain petroleum and synthetic fragrance. Just because a product is in a health food store, for example, doesn't ensure that it is pure and natural. Some excellent brands with strict integrity that are found in many health food stores include Aubrey Organics, Weleda, Logona, Lily of Colorado, and Lakon Herbals. Autumn Harp sells Un-Petroleum, a plant-based "petroleum" jelly. The mail order catalog TerrEssentials offers many of these brands as well as their own label on products such as TerrEssentials moisture cream, made with just pure cold-pressed shea butter and vitamin E. Another mail order catalog offering pure skin care products is N.E.E.D.S.; they sell a fragrance-free natural moisturizer manufactured by Granny's Old Fashioned Products. Another catalog is An Ounce of Prevention, offering Real Purity products. You can also find fresh, herbal moisturizing creams from small cottage industries such as Hermana skin care products. See Sources and Resources for addresses.

## GLYCERIN WATER BODY LOTION ✄

1 cup water (ideally rose water)
¼ cup vegetable glycerin
10 to 20 drops essential oil of choice
**Makes 1¼ cups**

*Preparation Time:* About 1 minute
*Shelf Life:* Indefinite
*Storage:* Glass jar with a screw top

### Variation

HONEYED GLYCERIN: Add 1 tablespoon honey. It is a good moisturizer and humectant.

## HONEYED ALMOND OIL ✄

*Try this for dry, winter-chapped skin.*

3 teaspoons almond oil
1 teaspoon honey

Combine the ingredients in a bowl, and stir to blend. Dab some on your fingers and massage into your skin. Don't rinse unless it feels too greasy.
**Makes 4 teaspoons**

*Preparation Time:* A few minutes
*Shelf Life:* 2 to 4 months
*Storage:* Glass jar with a screw top

### Variation

HONEY APPLE OIL: Add 1 teaspoon apple cider. It provides AHA benefits and cuts the oil.

## HYDRATING AND HEALING ALOE VERA GEL ✄

*Feel your skin drink this up. When I first started using it, I couldn't get enough and kept returning to it again and again.*

Aloe vera gel

Simply massage into your face with your fingertips.

*Preparation Time:* None
*Shelf Life:* Several months refrigerated

### Variation

LOVELY LIGHT LOTION: For a more emollient product, for each teaspoon aloe vera gel, add 2 to 3 drops avocado oil or food-grade linseed oil—an essential fatty acid.

## FLAX SEED GEL

*Flax seed gel exfoliates as well as moisturizes, leaving your face feeling astonishingly soft and silky.*

1 to 2 teaspoons flax seed
½ cup water

Combine the flax seeds and water and bring to a boil; reduce the heat to low and simmer until the mixture becomes a thick gel. Let cool, then strain out as many seeds as you can. Dip your fingers into the gel and rub on your face.
**Makes ½ cup**

*Preparation Time:* About 15 minutes
*Shelf Life:* A few days refrigerated
*Storage:* Glass jar with a screw top

## WHEAT GERM OIL ✄

*Rich in vitamin E, wheat germ oil can be massaged into the skin for a healing dose of antioxidants.*

Wheat germ oil

Massage a few drops of the oil into your skin.

*Preparation Time:* None
*Shelf Life:* Make only as much as you need at a time
*Storage:* Seal bottle tightly and store in refrigerator

### Variations

DOUBLE POWER: For an extra antioxidant boost, blend 1 teaspoon oil with 1 teaspoon carrot juice. Refrigerate leftovers, and discard after a few days.
ENZYME E: For an antioxidant and exfoliating moisturizer, combine 1 teaspoon wheat germ oil with 1 mashed green papaya. Discard leftovers.

## SHE'S AS SWEET AS TUPELO HONEY

*Calendula and chamomile flowers are good choices of herbs for this moisturizer.*

1 cup strong herbal tea

1 tablespoon honey

Make the tea with any of the 16 cosmetic herbs discussed on page 106. Add the honey, stir to dissolve, then steep the tea for a few hours. Strain. Dab some of the mixture on your fingers, and massage into your skin.

**Makes 1 cup**

*Preparation Time:* About 10 minutes
*Shelf Life:* 3 to 4 days refrigerated
*Storage:* Glass jar with a screw top

## OLIVE AND OATMEAL ✖

*Oats are softening for the skin.*

2 teaspoons oat flour

1 teaspoon olive oil

1 cup boiling water

Combine the ingredients, steep for a few hours, then strain through cheesecloth. Scoop a bit of the strained mixture on your fingers and massage into your skin.

**Makes 1 cup**

*Preparation Time:* About 10 minutes
*Shelf Life:* About 1 week
*Storage:* Glass jar with a screw top

## MOISTURIZING OIL ✖

*Choose vegetable oils that feel good on your skin. For dry skin try a combination of avocado,*

*almond, apricot kernel, and wheat germ oil; for oily skin try a combination of coconut, jojoba, peanut, and sesame oil.*

¼ cup vegetable oils

10 to 15 drops essential oil, for fragrance (if desired)

Combine the ingredients. Dab some of the mixture on your fingers, and massage into your skin.

**Makes ¼ cup**

*Preparation Time:* 10 minutes
*Shelf Life:* 4 months refrigerated, longer with antiseptic essential oils
*Storage:* Glass jar with a screw top

### Variations

HERBAL OIL: Infuse a handful of herbs such as calendula and lavender flowers and rose petals in 2 cups oil (see suggestions above) in a Crock-Pot for 7 hours. Let cool. Add ⅔ teaspoon grapefruit seed extract as a preservative. Refrigerate leftovers. The shelf life should be a few weeks; discard if you detect an odor or see mold.

JOJOBA JANGLE: Jojoba is a nongreasy wax that is good for oily skin. Use mostly jojoba in your oil blend.

LEMON SESAME: Include sesame oil and lemon oil in the oil blend.

### GLYCERIN LOTIONS

These lotions feel glorious on winter-chapped hands and legs but are too rich for the face. To make a less rich lotion, reduce the oil to just a few drops, or skip it entirely.

## BASIC GLYCERIN LOTION FORMULA 🎁

*Glycerin and oil are the important ingredients in this formula. Being a humectant, glycerin helps the skin retain moisture and in fact pulls moisture from the air to the skin. Oil lubricates and nourishes the skin.*

4 tablespoons bottled mineral water, rose water, or lavender water

¼ to ½ teaspoon each (more for a richer lotion) vegetable glycerin and cold-pressed vegetable oil (avocado for dry or aged skin, peanut or sesame oil for oily skin)

4 or 5 drops essential oil of choice

Combine the ingredients in a bowl, and mix with a hand mixer or whisk. Dab some on your fingers and massage into your skin.

**Makes about ⅓ cup**

*Preparation Time:* About 5 minutes
*Shelf Life:* 2 to 4 months refrigerated
*Storage:* Glass jar with a screw top

### Variations

ALOE MOISTURIZER: Substitute aloe vera gel for 1 to 2 tablespoons of the water.

TRADITIONAL CALENDULA MOISTURIZER: Calendula is excellent for the skin—it is antiseptic, astringent, anti-inflammatory, emollient, moisturizing, and healing. Soak 1 teaspoon finely ground calendula flowers in 3 tablespoons vodka, rum, or brandy overnight. Strain completely. Substitute 1 tablespoon of the alcohol infused with calendula for 1 tablespoon of the water. Add 12 drops grapefruit seed extract.

SOFT AND SILKY MOISTURIZER FOR OILY SKIN: Follow directions for Traditional Calendula Moisturizer, above, but add 1 teaspoon cornstarch to the mixture. Cornstarch draws oil off the skin.

### CREAMY LOTIONS

The word *lotion* can mean a wide range of liquid skin care products. Generally, they are much thinner than creams and do not always contain wax. Many commercial lotions have high amounts of alcohol, which is why they can dry out and sting your skin. Homemade lotions without alcohol can be lovely and light and a nice change from heavy creams.

## BASIC CREAMY LOTION FORMULA 🎁

*Often a folk recipe for a lotion is exactly like that for creams but calls for about twice as much water. This makes a spongy-feeling cream. My friend Josie, an accomplished herbalist, came to my rescue after many failed attempts with that approach, suggesting that I follow my cream recipe but simply halve the beeswax and add a little glycerin. What a great lotion this makes.*

2½ ounces almond, olive, or peanut oil (or a combination)

1½ ounces coconut oil
¼ ounce beeswax
2 ounces aloe vera gel
2 ounces water or rose water
1 tablespoon glycerin
Preservative (1 teaspoon vitamin C powder,
¼ teaspoon vitamin A powder, and 1 tablespoon wheat germ oil, or ⅓ teaspoon grapefruit seed extract)
10 to 25 drops fragrant essential oil, if
desired
1 teaspoon borax (optional)

Melt the oils and beeswax over medium heat in a double boiler. Remove from the heat, pour in the aloe vera gel, water, glycerin, preservative, and fragrance (if using), and mix with a hand or electric mixer until thick and creamy. For a thinner lotion, decrease the amount of beeswax but not so much that the lotion won't emulsify. (You can add 1 teaspoon borax to help this process.)
**Makes 1 cup**

*Preparation Time:* 25 minutes
*Shelf Life:* 4 to 6 months
*Storage:* Glass jar with a screw top

Variation
GREEN TEA AND HERB LOTION: Infuse beneficial skin herbs such as calendula in the oils, and substitute a strong infusion of antioxidant green tea for the rose water. The shelf life is 1 month.

## LANOLIN LOTION ✗

*Anhydrous lanolin—oil from sheep's wool—is found in most pharmacies. It is emollient and naturally water repellent (helpful for sunscreens) and can be removed with no harm to the animal.*

As much anhydrous lanolin as you need to
moisturize your skin at one time (1 teaspoon
or less)
Enough apricot kernel oil to make a lotionlike
consistency
A few drops wheat germ oil (for the vitamin E)

Combine the ingredients in a bowl and stir to blend. Dab some on your fingers and rub into your skin.
**Makes enough for 1 moisturizing**

*Preparation Time:* About 1 minute
*Shelf Life:* Make only enough for one time

## COCOA BUTTER ANTIBACTERIAL MOISTURIZING LOTION

1 tablespoon cocoa butter
2 tablespoons jojoba
1 tablespoon aloe vera gel

Melt the cocoa butter with the jojoba in a double boiler over medium heat. Remove from the heat, let cool for a few minutes, then mix with the aloe vera gel using a whisk or hand mixer. Dab some on your fingers and rub into your skin.
**Makes about ¼ cup**

*Preparation Time:* About 15 minutes
*Shelf Life:* 6 months
*Storage:* Glass jar with a screw top

## MOISTURIZING CREAMS

Learning how to make your own skin cream is empowering, and creams made with pure, natural, wholesome ingredients do wonders for the skin. Creams also make wonderful gifts. Try out the basic moisturizing cream—make it a few times until you feel confident—then experiment with fragrances and oils until you perfect the process. Package the cream in beautiful bottles, and give them to your friends and family.

## BASIC MOISTURIZING CREAM FORMULA

*This cream is all that a cream should be: creamy, spreadable, moisturizing, and hydrating.*

2½ ounces blended oils (such as almond, sesame, and apricot kernel)
1½ ounces coconut oil
½ ounce beeswax
4 ounces distilled water
Preservative (1 teaspoon vitamin C powder, ¼ teaspoon vitamin A powder, and 1 tablespoon wheat germ oil, or ⅓ teaspoon grapefruit seed extract)
10 to 25 drops fragrant essential oil, if desired

Melt the oils and beeswax in a double boiler over medium heat. Remove from the heat, pour in the water, and mix with a hand or electric mixer until thick and creamy. Stir in the preservative and essential oil (if using). Dab some on your fingers and massage into your skin.
**Makes 1 cup**

*Preparation Time:* 25 minutes
*Shelf Life:* 6 months
*Storage:* Glass jar with a screw top

## Variations

LANOLIN CREAM: Anhydrous lanolin (sheep's wool oil) resembles human skin oil (sebum) and does a good job at holding in the skin's moisture while allowing the skin to breath normally. Substitute anyhdrous lanolin (available in pharmacies) for some or all of the blended oils.

SEAWEED SHINE: Infuse the water with the seaweeds Irish moss and/or kelp. They are rich in minerals and nourish the skin. The shelf life is about 1 week refrigerated.

ALOE HYDRATOR: Substitute aloe vera gel for half of the water.

HERBAL CREAM: Infuse herbs appropriate for your skin in both the oil and water. The shelf life is less than plain creams—a week or so refrigerated. Discard if the product smells off or you see mold.

FRAGRANCE CREAM: Add 20 drops or so pure essential oil perfume blends.

ANTISEPTIC CREAM: Add antibacterial essential oils such as tea tree, clove, cinnamon, lavender, or rose.

RICH CREAM: For dry and dehydrated skin, choose emollient avocado oil as the oil, and substitute moisturizing cocoa butter for the coconut oil.

## CELL RENEWAL COMFREY CREAM

*Comfrey is exceptionally healing for injured or aged skin. It is considered a liver poison if ingested, so be sure to use only externally.*

2½ ounces oil infused with comfrey leaf and root
4 ounces comfrey water
1½ ounces coconut oil
⅔ ounce beeswax
Preservative (1 teaspoon vitamin C powder, ¼ teaspoon vitamin A powder, and 1 table-spoon wheat germ oil, or ⅓ teaspoon grape-fruit seed extract)
10 to 25 drops fragrant essential oil, if desired

Prepare the oil and water infusions as described in Chapter One. Melt the oils and beeswax in a double boiler over medium heat. Remove from the heat, pour in the comfrey water, and mix with a hand or electric mixer until thick and creamy. Stir in the preservative and essential oil (if using). Dab some on your fingers and massage into your skin.
**Makes 1 cup**

*Preparation Time:* About 1 hour
*Shelf Life:* Up to 4 weeks (discard if you detect mold or a rancid smell)
*Storage:* Glass jar with a screw top

## EYE CREAMS

Eye creams are designed to be rich and emol-lient, to help reduce wrinkles. The skin right around the eyes doesn't have oil glands and can thus be prone to dehydration, especially as we age. As an experiment, try massaging a drop of avocado oil around your eyes and see how it feels. If it is too thick, try apricot ker-nel oil or even grapeseed oil. Try out a num-ber of oils until you find one or two that feel just right.
NOTE: Be sure to avoid getting any of these oils in the eyes.

## AVOCADO CREAM ✗

¼ cup avocado oil, apricot kernel oil, or sesame oil (or mixture of these)
¼ cup aloe vera gel

Combine the ingredients in a glass jar. Shake to blend. Dab a little on your fingers and mas-sage around your eyes, being careful not to get any in your eyes.
**Makes ½ cup**

*Preparation Time:* About 1 minute
*Shelf Life:* About 4 months refrigerated
*Storage:* Glass jar with a screw top

### Variation
CHANGE OF OIL: Try various combinations of borage, jojoba, almond, and other oils until you find those that feel best on your skin.

### Rx for Tired Eyes

Place cucumber slices over your eyes, or use cooled chamomile or peppermint tea bags. For puffiness, massage rose water around the eyes.

### Winter Winds and Summer Sun Protection Creams

Some skin care experts believe that cocoa butter is too thick and pore clogging to be used regularly. Nonetheless, cocoa butter is in many moisturizing products for just this reason: It isn't absorbed well into the skin, thereby providing the skin with a protective coating, helpful against winter winds and summer sun.

## LANOLIN AND COCOA BUTTER CREAM

Follow the directions for Basic Cream Formula (page 30), substituting cocoa butter for the coconut oil and 1 ounce lanolin for 1 ounce of the blended oils.

**Makes 1 cup**

*Preparation Time:* 25 minutes
*Shelf Life:* About 6 months
*Storage:* Glass jar with a screw top

Variation

Everything Cocoa Butter Cream: Substitute cocoa butter for the coconut oil. Make the blended oils a mixture of emollient and nutritious avocado, wheat germ, and sesame oils. Add 2 teaspoons honey and 2 tablespoons organic apple cider vinegar or lime or lemon juice. If you use lemon or lime, the shelf life is

lessened. Refrigerate. Discard if you detect mold or an odor.

## ALPINE JELLY CHAPPED SKIN LOTION

Follow the directions for Basic Nonpetroleum Jelly on page 31, adding 1 tablespoon each anhydrous lanolin and glycerin after removing the beeswax and oil mixture from the heat.

Variation

Plain: Basic Nonpetroleum Jelly, page 31.

# Natural Facials

### Facial Steams and Body Steams

Steam opens the pores and deeply cleanses the skin, hydrating it at the same time. Once you have experienced a facial steam, you will have a strong urge to steam your whole body because your face feels so refreshed and c-l-e-a-n. A hilarious technique for body steams, found in a nineteenth-century formula book, describes how you position sturdy boards across a tub of hot water and sit on them cautiously, making sure not to fall or scald delicate skin. Yeow! I don't think I could recommend going to this extreme, but the story certainly illustrates the lengths to which one is inspired to go to experience the feeling of steam-cleaned skin. (If you like the idea of a body steam, join a gym that offers steam baths—rooms that pipe in hot steam—or you can install one in your bathroom for about $3,000.)

## GENERAL DIRECTIONS FOR FACIAL STEAMS

Be sure to use spring water, well water, or bottled mineral water to make steam; avoid chlorinated water.

1. Place a handful of herbs in a pot of water. Bring to a boil, then reduce the heat and let simmer.

2. Secure your hair back from your face with a headband, hair wrap, or whatever feels comfortable.

3. Wash your face as usual.

4. Place the pot of steaming water on a trivet or potholder on a table or countertop. Make a tent over your head with a towel, and hang your head over the steaming pot. Do not lean close enough to the pot to scald yourself.

5. Keep your face in the steam tent for about 5 minutes.

6. Rinse your face with cold water.

7. Follow with an astringent to close the pores.

Combine 4 cups or so of herbs that are good for your skin type (see page 107) in a glass jar, so they are ready for use. Although licorice root isn't one of the sixteen top cosmetic herbs listed, for steaming it is the number one herb, because it helps open the pores, soothes, cleanses, and lubricates. Break a piece of root into your steam pot.

Instead of steaming your face with herb-infused water, you can use the hot-towel method. Saturate a towel with steaming hot water. Let cool enough to touch the skin, then wrap your clean face with it, and leave it on for two minutes or so.

## SAUNAS

Profuse sweating is another way to deeply cleanse your skin, and saunas provide the high heat conducive to this. Regular use of the sauna will improve the tone and texture of your skin, relieving it of a layer of dead skin cells and allowing the skin's natural oils to rise to the surface. Saunas are also a good place to do hot-oil hair treatments; for instance, you can massage warmed oil into your hair and sit in the sauna with it on. Royal jelly facial masks are also excellent in saunas: Cover your face with royal jelly and, as it softens in the heat of the sauna, gently massage the jelly into your skin.

## EXFOLIATING SCRUBS

The purpose of a skin scrub is to exfoliate the top layer of dead skin cells. Scrubs can be gentle and soft, suited to sensitive skin (such as a paste of finely ground brown rice flour and cold-pressed vegetable oil or yogurt) or more aggressive (such as baking soda and soap that sometimes even includes pumice stone powder). A scrub is both stimulating and soothing, and your skin gets a massage as you apply it. I particularly like the softness of brown rice flour or oatmeal (and the way the flours absorb all excess oil from the skin) and the emollient quality of finely ground almonds or flax seeds.

If you are using natural fruit acid or enzyme exfoliants regularly on your face, scrubs will be too harsh and, in fact, unnecessary, because the fruit acids remove the layer of dead skin on the surface and expose tender, new cells that scrubs could damage. You should skip scrubs and look for a recipe for a soft, nutritive mask to use instead. People with sensitive skin or acne can also find scrubs to be too rough.

Body scrubs are a whole different story, however, and can even be a way to get fruit acids onto your whole body for a deep cleansing. Besides that, body scrubs feel wonderful, relieving itches you never knew you had. I like to call body scrubs scratch scrubs for this reason. Although body scrubs are beneficial at any time of year, it is helpful to do one at the end of summer or in early fall when your tan is flaking off.

**EQUIPMENT FOR SCRUBS.** I have a hand grain grinder, which works beautifully for making grain and bean flours for face and body scrubs. A blender or coffee grinder works well for grinding nuts, herbs, and most flours. If you do not have equipment suitable for grinding, you'll find a wide range of ground flours in most health food stores.

## SCRUB FORMULAS

Although the basic scrub formula calls for ground nuts, grains, liquids, herbs, and essential oils, just about anything goes as long as it isn't too harsh on the skin. For example, sometimes I like to use just oatmeal flour as a scrub (it removes oils and relieves itching); at other times I want something more elaborate, such as when my skin is dry in winter and I want a moisturizing scrub. Then I might include an oil or a mixture of aloe vera gel and glycerin as a binder.

## GOOD INGREDIENTS FOR SCRUBS

**GRAINS:** Flour made of brown rice, oatmeal, wheat, orris root powder
**NUTS OR SEEDS:** Ground almonds, flax seed, sunflower seeds
**LEGUMES:** Flour made of chickpeas, black beans, lentils, and other beans
**HERBS:** Ground rosemary, sage, lavender
**CITRUS FRUIT PEELS:** Ground peels—fresh or dried—of oranges, lemons, limes
**BINDERS:** Glycerin, aloe vera gel, egg whites, yogurt, cold-pressed vegetable and nut oils, fruit juices, milk, mineral water

## BASIC BODY SCRUB FORMULA 🎁

*The variations of this formula are endless, but here are some ideas for a start.*

⅔ cup finely ground nuts or seeds
⅓ cup grain or legume flour
½ to 1 teaspoon ground herbs such as the antiseptic herbs rosemary and sage (optional)
20 drops or so essential oils (optional)
Enough water (bottled mineral water is good) to make a paste

In a blender grind the dry ingredients to a medium-fine powder. Stir in the essential oils (if using). and store in a glass jar with a screw top. When you are ready to make a scrub, pour about $\frac{1}{3}$ cup of the mixture into a bowl, and stir in enough water to make a paste. After you get your body wet, scoop some of the paste on your hand and rub and scrub it all over your body, avoiding your eyes. Take your time and really exfoliate the dead skin cells. Rinse thoroughly. **Makes 1 cup**

*Preparation Time:* 15 minutes

*Shelf Life:* The dry ingredients will store indefinitely in the freezer, a few months in the refrigerator, a month or so at room temperature. For all of these scrubs, once liquid has been added, discard leftovers.

*Storage:* Glass jar with a screw top

## Variations

ALMOND SCRUB: For the dry ingredients, choose ground almonds, rice flour, and orris root powder. For the liquids, add a dab of castile soap, and use rose water.

ENZYME SCRUB: Place $\frac{1}{3}$ cup sunflower seeds, half a papaya (as green as possible—these are rich in exfoliating enzymes), 1 teaspoon molasses (rich in minerals), 1 egg white, and $\frac{1}{4}$ cup whipped cream in a blender and blend thoroughly. Use instead of the basic formula.

VERY GENTLE CLEANSER: For the liquid component, blend $\frac{1}{4}$ cup plain yogurt, 1 teaspoon honey, $\frac{1}{2}$ teaspoon vegetable oil, and 1 tablespoon lemon juice. Softening and emollient, this formula is also rich in exfoliating AHAs.

LEMON SCRUB: Include 2 teaspoons grated lemon peel and $\frac{1}{4}$ cup powdered milk with the rest of the dry ingredients.

REFRESHING CITRUS SCRUB: Make $\frac{1}{3}$ cup dry ingredients by grinding lemon, orange, and lime peels. Substitute yogurt for the water, and add enough yogurt to make a paste.

SOFT SCRATCH SCRUB: For the dry ingredients, combine flax-seed meal and brown rice flour. Moisten $\frac{1}{3}$ cup with canola oil or aloe vera gel instead of water at the time of use. Flax seeds are wonderfully emollient when they are ground.

SEA SALT SCRUB: Substitute sea salt for the grain. Sea salt is antibacterial and rich in nourishing minerals. Or simply moisten $\frac{1}{3}$ cup salt with vegetable oil.

RED LENTIL SCRUB: Soak $\frac{1}{2}$ cup red lentils in milk to cover overnight in the refrigerator. Grind to a paste. Use instead of the basic formula.

ORRIS ROOT SIMPLE: Use just orris root powder; it has a lovely violet scent and is very antiseptic.

ANTIBACTERIAL SCRUB: Substitute these ingredients. Grind $\frac{1}{2}$ teaspoon each antibacterial herbs such as rosemary, sage, and calendula. Add to $\frac{1}{2}$ cup sea salt. Moisten with enough aloe vera gel to make a paste, and add a few drops tea tree oil.

SOAP AND SODA: For an abrasive and cleansing substitute scrub, combine $\frac{1}{3}$ cup baking soda and enough liquid castile soap to make a paste.

HONEY SCRUB: For the dry ingredients, use almonds, coconut, and oatmeal. For the liquid ingredients, combine 1 teaspoon honey and enough rose water to make a paste.

OATMEAL AND ALOE: In a bowl, moisten oat flour with aloe vera gel until it reaches a pastelike consistency. Use instead of the basic formula.

ACNE SCRUB: Instead of the basic formula, combine ½ cup sea salt and 2 teaspoons ground calendula flowers (an antibacterial and anti-inflammatory herb). Scoop some into your hand and rub over your body. Rinse well.

SUGAR SIMPLE: Simply rub your skin with sugar. Sugarcane is a famous AHA, and sugar is mildly abrasive.

COFFEE GROUNDS SIMPLE: Rub your skin with coffee grounds, which are very astringent.

FRUIT ACID SCRUB: Substitute ½ cup paste of ground nuts and mashed fruit, such as applesauce, for the basic formula.

NUTRITIOUS SCRUB SIMPLES: Use any vegetables and fruit you have on hand, such as carrots, spinach leaves, peas and pea pods, lettuce, pumpkin, and avocado. Puree in a blender. Freeze any leftovers.

## MASKS

*Every vegetable, fruit, seed, or nut has a place in a facial or body mask. Indeed, masks can be used by any sex and any age of human being and on any part of the body. They are used to clear up pimples or blackheads, exfoliate the outer scaly surface of the skin, refine the pores, nourish, heal and soothe, absorb excess oil, texture the skin's surface, moisturize, hydrate, lubricate, or smooth.*

—JEANNE ROSE'S HERBAL BODY BOOK

Masks are good to do as often as you can. Ideally try to do one every week, or at least every month, after a facial steam. Masks absorb oils, draw out impurities, and deeply nourish the skin.

### BASIC DIRECTIONS FOR MASKS

1. It is very important to steam-clean the face before covering the skin with a mask. If you are traveling and can't make an herbal steam, use the hot-towel method described on page 151.

2. Apply a mask to damp skin.

3. Leave a mask on from 10 to 20 minutes, or until it has dried. Soften the mask with a wet washcloth, then wash it off.

4. Follow the mask with a cold water rinse, an astringent, and your choice of moisturizer.

*Caution:* Many masks specify raw egg: either the white, the yolk, or the entire egg. Raw eggs can be contaminated with salmonella. Some organic farms now test their eggs for salmonella, and it is only from such farms that you should buy eggs for egg masks.

**CLAY MASKS.** Traditionally, masks are made of clay. Clay absorbs up to two hundred times its weight in water. When clay is made into a paste with water or other liquid and patted over the face and left to dry, it pulls not only impurities from the skin but also moisturizes it. Because clay can dehydrate the skin, people with dry skin may want to choose an alternative to a clay mask, and even those with oily skin should not use a clay mask for more than fifteen minutes. Those with dry skin should use white clay (see below) and combine it with a hydrating material, such as aloe vera gel and/or glycerin. When possible, use bottled mineral water instead of distilled water, to add extra nourishment.

## BASIC CLAY MASK FORMULA

Clay (for just the face you will need ⅛ to ¼ cup)
Enough bottled mineral water or distilled water to make a paste (the less water, the more drying the mask)

Follow the Basic Directions for Masks on page 154.

*Preparation Time:* None
*Shelf Life:* Discard any leftovers

## GOOD CLAYS FOR DIFFERENT SKIN TYPES

**FOR DRY SKIN:** If you choose to use a clay, use a white clay such as French white, or use kaolin or bentonite (light gray); these are the least drying.

**FOR OILY SKIN:** Use green or red clay.

**TO NOURISH THE SKIN:** Use a mineral-rich black clay from the Dead Sea.

## Variations

*Liquids to Use in Addition to or as a Substitute for Water:* Witch hazel extract; yogurt; heavy cream; strawberry or lemon juice; aloe vera gel; honey; avocado oil; flax mucilage (make the mucilage with 1 tablespoon flax seed simmered over low heat in 1 cup water until gel-like, about 10 minutes); egg white; mashed fruit, such as bananas or strawberries, for their enzymes; or carrot juice.

*Dry Ingredients to Use in Addition to the Clay:* ½ teaspoon ground herbs such as mineral-rich Irish moss or antiseptic lavender, or a few teaspoons of skin-softening oat flour or cooked oatmeal.

**CLAY-FREE MOISTURIZING AND ANTIOXIDANT MASKS.** One purpose of masks *without* clay is to replenish moisture and oil to the skin. These masks are best for dry and problem skin. Make the masks more nourishing with floral and herbal extracts, essential oils, seaweed, vitamins, minerals, antioxidants, and other nourishing ingredients.

**GENERAL DIRECTIONS:** The ingredients listed below are just suggestions. How do you combine the ingredients? In any way that works so that they aren't too thin to hold together as a mask. Start with the more solid ingredients, then add the liquid, using just enough to produce a soft paste..

## ROSEMARY AND SAGE STRAWBERRY MASK

4 or 5 strawberries
2 cucumbers, peeled

2 egg whites
½ teaspoon each ground rosemary and sage
Enough yogurt to bind everything together
(about ¼ cup)

Mash the berries and cucumber; place in a blender with the egg whites and herbs and puree, adding yogurt bit by bit. Scrape into a bowl. Scoop the mixture onto your fingers and spread over your clean, damp face. Leave the mixture on until dry (10 to 20 minutes). Rinse well with cold water and follow with a moisturizer.
**Makes about 1 cup**

*Preparation Time:* 15 minutes
*Shelf Life:* Discard leftovers

Variations

*Mashed Fruit and Vegetable Substitute Suggestions:* Avocado, banana, applesauce, peach, green papaya, fresh pineapple, watermelon, or cooked carrot.

*Yogurt and Egg White Substitute Suggestions:* Buttermilk, lemon juice, heavy cream, pineapple juice, glycerin, herb-infused water such as mint tea, aloe vera gel, and vegetable or nut oil such as almond or wheat germ.

*Ground Herb Substitute Suggestions:* Kelp, Irish moss, comfrey, or calendula.

*Mask for Dry Skin:* Add a dab of glycerin, aloe vera gel, honey, molasses, wheat germ oil, and/or jojoba.

## MASK SIMPLES

MASHED FRUIT MASK: Just use about ½ cup mashed fruit.

ROYAL JELLY MASK: Massage ¼ teaspoon royal jelly into the skin.

APPLESAUCE VITAMIN E MASK: Combine ½ cup applesauce (an AHA) with ½ teaspoon wheat germ oil (high in vitamin E).

ENLARGED PORE MASK: Make ½ cup cooked oatmeal. Let cool, then add ¼ cup buttermilk.

AVOCADO MASK: Mash 1 avocado (nourishing and emollient), and add 1 tablespoon lemon juice, an AHA.

ALMOND MASK: Grind a handful of almonds with milk in the blender. This is softening and exfoliating.

ENZYME EXFOLIANT PAPAYA AND/OR PINE-APPLE MASK: Mash a green papaya and/or about a 4-inch-square chunk of fresh pineapple.

HONEY MASK: Stir together ¼ cup cornstarch and 1 tablespoon honey. Cornstarch draws moisture and oils off the face, and honey is emollient.

TIGHTENING AND FACE-LIFTING MASKS. Sometimes face-lifting masks contain clay, but usually their base is protein, primarily egg whites. A face-lift mask tightens the skin; the longer you keep it on, the more your skin will benefit.

NOTE: Raw eggs can be contaminated with salmonella. Some organic farms now test their eggs for salmonella, and it is only from such farms that you should buy eggs for egg masks.

GENERAL DIRECTIONS: Using egg white as a base, gradually add other ingredients, making sure that the mask doesn't become too liquid.

## EGG WHITE TIGHTENER

1 or 2 egg whites

Beat the egg whites until slightly stiff. Rub onto your face and let dry. Leave on as long as possible before rinsing.
**Makes about ¼ cup**

*Preparation Time:* About 10 minutes
*Shelf Life:* Discard leftovers

### Variations
Add 1 tablespoon beneficial liquid such as: witch hazel extract, lemon juice, aloe vera gel, honey, mineral water, milk, heavy cream, or rose water.
Add 1 tablespoon almond meal.
Add ¼ teaspoon royal jelly.

## PEACHES AND CREAM

*Have you ever heard of a "peaches and cream complexion"? Cream is an AHA, and peaches have skin softening enzymes.*

2 peaches, peeled and mashed
½ teaspoon almond oil
1 tablespoon heavy cream

Combine the ingredients in a bowl, mash with a spoon or pestle, then stir to blend. Dab on your face. Rinse with warm water.

**Makes about ½ cup**

*Preparation Time:* About 5 minutes
*Shelf Life:* Discard leftovers

### Variations
APPLES AND CREAM: Substitute applesauce for the peaches.
CUCUMBERS AND CREAM: Substitute 1 cucumber for the peaches, omit the almond oil, and combine with heavy cream (or yogurt). Stir to blend.

# Skin Problems

### AGED AND WRINKLED SKIN
The best way to care for older skin is to hydrate it; help it retain moisture; exfoliate it with fruit acids; nourish it deeply with antioxidant-rich bioflavonoids, which are found in most fresh fruits and vegetables; tighten it with a protein-based natural face-lift; and provide it with herbs such as comfrey that aid cell renewal.

### Hydrating and Moisturizing
TIPS
* Humidify rooms during the heating season.
* Make a mineral water spritzer (see Toners, page 141) and use it to freshen the skin throughout the day.
* Use aloe vera gel on your face and body as much as possible (see the Aloe and Glycerin Moisturizer, page 142).
* Use a honey mask to help aging skin retain moisture; add the contents of a vitamin E capsule (200 i.u.) to the mask.

## GOOD AGING SKIN HERBS

Nettle, kelp, calendula, comfrey, licorice, lavender, rose

* When making moisturizing creams, use olive oil, lanolin, coconut oil, avocado oil, and cocoa butter, to help remove wrinkles.
* Add carrot juice and other bioflavonoid-rich fruit and vegetable juices as the liquid ingredient in moisturizing creams, lotions, and masks.
* Add wheat germ oil, rich in vitamin E, to any cream or lotion, or rub it straight onto wrinkles. Vitamin E oil is particularly good for lines above the mouth.
* Be aware that witch hazel is a powerful antioxidant, something we need more and more as we age because of a lifetime of exposure to pollutants.
* Be sure to use the vitamin A, E, and C preservative blend in your moisturizers and lotions.

### Cell Renewal
TIPS

* Comfrey heals wounds quickly because it is rich in allantoin, which speeds up the process of cell renewal. But it is a controversial herb because it has been found to cause liver cancer if taken internally. External use appears to be safe, but don't overuse.

* Herbs for wrinkles and cell renewal include St. John's wort, ginseng, sage, and cowslip.
* Egg whites are also rich in allantoin.

**IF ALL ELSE FAILS.** There is always the "Brownies and Wrinkles" tape approach, used since the nineteenth century. Apply special adhesive paper patches to the forehead or the corners of the eyes or mouth; leave in place overnight or at least three hours. Users claim a distinct reduction of sagging skin and wrinkles after two to three weeks. A year's supply of tape is available for eighteen dollars from the Vermont Country Store (see Sources and Resources).

### BROWN SPOTS, AGE SPOTS, OR LIVER SPOTS

There are certain ingredients I've seen used over and over again for the brownish spots that are the result of sun exposure—called brown spots, age spots, or liver spots. The ingredients include vitamin E, aloe vera gel, fruit acids such as lemon juice and organic apple cider vinegar, enzymes such as papaya and pineapple, witch hazel extract, and horseradish mixed with lemon juice, organic apple cider vinegar, or milk (horseradish is very strong, so use only a little at a time). I've seen my age spots significantly diminish over a number of months using lemon juice as an astringent and an aloe vera gel and glycerin moisturizer.

### FRECKLES

The ingredients that show up in folk formulas for removing freckles are similar to those for age spots. These include lemon juice, lavender oil, rose water, organic apple cider vinegar, buttermilk, and horseradish.

## INJURED SKIN

Healing herbs and other ingredients for salves, creams, and lotions include calendula, comfrey, chamomile, aloe vera, mallow, wheat germ oil (for the vitamin E), burdock, St. John's wort, sage, and rosemary. For more, see the Glossary of Ingredients in Chapter One.

## ECZEMA AND PSORIASIS

Healing eczema and psoriasis is complex and beyond the scope of this book, because the cause can be a myriad of factors including food and mold allergies and inadequate essential fatty acid intake. However, there are herbal salves than can help heal the rashes, and oils that are particularly soothing. Many doctors now believe that eczema is a fungus. Try tea tree salves; I've used them with good success. See page 31 for recipes to make your own salves, and experiment with the following ingredients. Or make herbal-infused baths and oils.

## BROKEN CAPILLARIES

Although usually associated with alcohol consumption, broken capillaries can also be caused by saunas and other factors. The best treatment is a salve with St. John's wort, calendula, and aloe vera gel. Other good herbs to include are rose, chamomile, and lavender.

## PIMPLES AND BLACKHEADS

Most everyone has pimples and blackheads at one time or another; there are numerous

## GOOD THINGS FOR ECZEMA AND PSORIASIS

### HERBS
Nettle, chickweed (commonly used infused in oil, or in baths), cleavers, horsetail, red clover, burdock, thyme, calendula, chamomile, St. John's wort

### ESSENTIAL OILS
Antifungal oils such as tea tree

### OILS
Avocado oil, olive oil, and apricot kernel oil

### GOOD BATHS
Herbal baths using chickweed, Dead Sea salt (soak for forty-five minutes daily for three weeks or more), Epsom salts

causes including food allergies and hormonal fluctuations. To reduce the risk of outbreaks, keep the skin clean. Antibacterial herbs and essential oils help do this. After cleansing, use astringents, and at least once a month do a full facial including a facial steam and mask (see pages 151 and 154). Choose a diet rich in antioxidant bioflavonoids (found in fruits and vegetables), and avoid fatty foods except those containing omega-3 essential fatty acids. Eat natural antibiotic-rich foods such as garlic, and drink purifying herbal teas such as nettle, dandelion, and burdock root. And spend a bit of time in the sun—not enough to burn yourself but enough to help your body produce its own vitamin D—about twenty minutes a day.

### DRYING LOTIONS

For more suggestions, see Astringents, page 133.

## HORSERADISH VINEGAR

4 tablespoons horseradish
Enough organic apple cider vinegar to cover
Water

Steep the horseradish in the vinegar for 2 weeks. Strain. Add half again as much water. Shake to blend. Dab on problem areas with a cotton ball; leave on for 10 to 15 minutes before rinsing.
**Makes about ½ cup**

*Preparation Time:* 15 minutes
*Shelf Life:* Indefinite
*Storage:* Glass jar with a screw top

Variation
LAVENDER VINEGAR: Infuse a small handful of lavender flowers in organic apple cider vinegar.

## GOOD THINGS FOR THE CARE OF ACNE AND BLACKHEADS

### HERBS AND ESSENTIAL OILS

Horseradish, witch hazel extract, lemon balm, lavender, tea tree oil, eucalyptus, rosemary, sage, rose, chamomile, nettle, licorice, thyme, calendula
NOTE: Do not use more than a drop or two of diluted essential oils on the face.

### NOURISHMENT

Include vitamins A, C, and E in lotions and salves.

### OTHER HELPFUL INGREDIENTS

Baking soda, Epsom salts, lemon juice, organic apple cider vinegar
**FOR STEAMS:** Follow the General Directions for Facial Steams (page 150), but use herbs such as witch hazel, lemon balm, lavender, and eucalyptus. (Don't use horseradish in a steam.)
**FOR FRUIT ACIDS:** Substitute lemon juice or buttermilk for the liquid in lotions.
**FOR FACIAL SCRUBS:** Include witch hazel extract.
**FOR MASKS:** Include ground rosemary and sage and a few drops of tea tree oil.

## EPSOM SALTS AND WITCH HAZEL EXTRACT

¼ cup Epsom salts
Witch hazel extract
Lavender water

Pour the Epsom salts in a bowl. Add equal amounts witch hazel extract and lavender water (make a cup of strong lavender-flower tea, steep for a few hours, and strain) until the mixture is a paste. Scoop some onto your fingers and massage into problem areas. Leave on for a few minutes before rinsing.
**Makes ¼ cup**

*Preparation Time:* About 10 minutes.
*Shelf Life:* Indefinite
*Storage:* Glass jar with a screw top

## TEA TREE OIL ✗

*Tea tree oil is highly antiseptic and antifungal.*

10 drops tea tree oil
1 cup water

Add tea tree oil to the water. Dab the liquid on the face gently with a cotton ball, avoiding the eyes. Rinse with warm water.
**Makes 1 cup**

*Preparation Time:* About 1 minute
*Shelf Life:* Indefinite
*Storage:* Glass jar with a screw top

### Variation

TEA TREE OIL AND ALOE: For a more emollient, slightly abrasive antiseptic cleanser, combine ¼ cup salt, enough aloe vera gel to make a paste, and 5 drops tea tree oil.

## BAKING SODA RUB ✗

*Baking soda is softly abrasive to the skin.*

¼ cup baking soda
Enough water to make a paste

In a small bowl make a baking soda paste. Gently massage the paste onto blackheads. Rinse with warm water.
**Makes ¼ cup**

*Preparation Time:* About 1 minute
*Shelf Life:* Add more water if it dries out
*Storage:* Glass jar with a screw top

## SALT AND LEMON JUICE ✗

*Salt is one of the best antibacterial ingredients, and it is slightly abrasive. Lemon juice exfoliates as it cleans.*

¼ cup sea salt
Enough lemon juice to make a paste

Combine the ingredients in a bowl. Dab on the face with a cotton ball. Massage into the skin, being careful to avoid your eyes. Rinse thoroughly with warm water.
**Makes ¼ cup**

*Preparation Time:* About 1 minute
*Shelf Life:* Discard leftovers

## OLD-FASHIONED CAMPHOR TREATMENT

Camphor-infused olive oil (see page 33)

Dab the oil on blackheads with a cotton ball. Leave in place overnight or as long as possible. Rinse thoroughly.

*Preparation Time:* About 10 minutes
*Shelf Life:* Up to 2 months refrigerated
*Storage:* Glass jar with screw top

## ANTIBACTERIAL HERBAL BLEND

¼ cup aloe vera gel
5 drops antibacterial essential oils, such as sage, rosemary, lavender, cinnamon, or clove

Combine the ingredients in a jar. Shake or stir to blend. Dab on your face with a cotton ball. Rinse thoroughly with warm water.
**Makes ¼ cup**

*Preparation Time:* A few minutes
*Shelf Life:* 6 months
*Storage:* Glass jar with a screw top

CHAPTER 4

# Whole Body Care

**N**ATURAL, botanical ingredients soothe, heal, and nourish, whether you are dyeing your hair, filing your nails, brushing your teeth, or washing a baby. Please read the introduction to the previous chapter on skin care. All the same principles apply to whole body care.

## Baby Care

A newborn baby's skin and hair present one of the rarest of circumstances—they have never been touched by a cream, lotion, or bar of soap. They are soft, pure, and unsullied. Let's try to keep them this way as long as possible. Use ingredients that have stood the test of time, eschewing anything synthetic or petroleum based and choosing instead products that are natural and nourishing.

*A Word of Caution About Ingredients*

* Your baby may have unrevealed allergies to herbs and oils. Pay close attention when using new substances. Note that chamomile is in the ragweed family and should be avoided if there is a family history of hay fever.

* Because essential oils are potentially dangerous if used in too strong a dosage, they are not recommended for use on babies.

✳ Traditionally, comfrey root or leaf is often used in herbal diaper rash and cradle cap creams because of its cell renewal constituent (allantoin). I have risked erring on the side of caution and have omitted comfrey for use on babies, because the herb contains pyrrolizidine alkaloids, which are serious liver irritants and can be harmful if taken internally. Besides, cell renewal happens practically before your eyes with babies.

### DIAPER-RELATED CONCERNS

The purest, cheapest, and easiest way to clean a baby's bottom is with warm water and soft paper towels. This will reduce a baby's exposure to synthetic fragrances and other chemicals. My sisters and I—all four of us—did this successfully with our children, and we saved a lot of money, too. Simply place a bowl of warm water on the changing table, and dip paper towels into the water to moisten. My friend Pat, who runs a day care center, often places the warm water in a spray bottle to spray a baby's bottom clean with minimal wiping. This technique is especially good if the baby's skin is irritated.

A good way to avoid diaper rash is to change a diaper when it is soiled. Also, when washing diapers, add white distilled vinegar to the rinse water to neutralize the alkalinity of detergents.

## ALOE VERA GEL SIMPLE ✄ 🎁

*Aloe vera is such a powerful healing plant for the skin that it deserves a place in every home.*

Aloe vera gel

Massage aloe vera gel on the affected area.

## ZINC OXIDE CREAM

*This is a petroleum-free version of the cream recommended by pediatricians.*

2 tablespoons zinc oxide powder
Basic Cream Formula (page 30)

Combine the ingredients and spread on the affected area.
**Makes 1 cup**

*Preparation Time:* 25 minutes
*Shelf Life:* 6 months
*Storage:* Glass jar with a screw top

## DIAPER RASH SALVE

*The herbs in this balm are healing and antibacterial.*

4 ounces oil infused with calendula
and chamomile
1 ounce beeswax
¼ teaspoon grapefruit seed extract

Prepare the infused oil as described on page 33. Combine the oil and beeswax in a double boiler and place over medium heat until the wax is melted. Remove from the heat, add the grapefruit seed extract, and mix with a hand or electric mixer until creamy. Rub a dab into the rash.

**Makes ½ cup**

*Preparation Time:* 25 minutes
*Shelf Life:* 2 to 4 months; discard if you see mold
*Storage:* Glass jar with a screw top

## NONPETROLEUM JELLY 🎁

2 ounces olive oil (more oil to make it less thick)
½ ounce beeswax
12 drops grapefruit seed extract

Combine the oil and beeswax in a double boiler and place over medium heat until the wax is melted. Remove from the heat, add the grapefruit seed extract, and mix with a hand or electric mixer until creamy.

**Makes ¼ cup**

*Preparation Time:* 25 minutes
*Shelf Life:* 1 year
*Storage:* Glass jar with a screw top

### SOAP

Because a main ingredient of soap is lye, a caustic chemical, it is best to use soap sparingly if at all on babies. It's also very drying to the skin. When you do use soap, choose a pure olive oil castile soap without antibacterial or deodorizing additives.

### Soap-Free Cleansers

## ANTISEPTIC CLEANSING GEL ✗ 🎁

*A good all-purpose formula, this is an emollient cleanser.*

¼ cup aloe vera gel
1 teaspoon vegetable glycerin
1 tablespoon lemon juice or organic apple cider vinegar

Combine the ingredients in a glass jar. Shake to blend. Dab some on your fingers and massage into the skin, avoiding the eyes. Rinse with warm water.

**Makes about ¼ cup**

*Preparation Time:* About 1 minute
*Shelf Life:* About 4 months with vinegar; 1 week with lemon juice, refrigerated
*Storage:* Glass jar with a screw top

### BABY OILS AND MOISTURIZERS

If your baby's skin is dry enough to need frequent moisturizing, check with your pediatrician to make sure that the child's diet is rich enough in essential fatty acids. Another possible cause of dry skin is the use of too much soap. If occasional moisturizing is needed, use one of the following preparations.

## A LITTLE DAB'L DO YA BABY LOTION ✗ 🎁

*The aloe vera gel in this product will help heal skin problems as well as provide deep moisturizing.*

*Glycerin's humectant properties help to draw and retain moisture.*

¼ cup aloe vera gel
½ tablespoon glycerin

Pour ingredients into a small, clean jar. Cover and shake to blend. A little of this lotion goes a long way—just dab some on a finger and rub into the skin.
**Makes about ¼ cup**

*Preparation Time:* A few minutes
*Shelf Life:* 6 months refrigerated
*Storage:* Glass jar with a screw top

## SOFT AND SILKY BABY LOTION

*This is a simple, wholesome, fragrance-free lotion.*

2½ ounces olive oil
1½ ounces coconut oil
¼ ounce beeswax
4 ounces distilled water
1 tablespoon glycerin

Melt the oil and beeswax in a double boiler over medium heat. Remove from heat, add the water and glycerin, and blend with an electric hand mixer.
**Makes ½ cup**

*Preparation Time:* 25 minutes
*Shelf Life:* 2 months
*Storage:* Glass jar with a screw top

## BABY-OIL LOOK-ALIKE ✂ 🎁

*This is a commercial baby-oil look-alike with a big difference: It contains no petroleum mineral oil. For a healing oil, infuse it with calendula.*

1 tablespoon each wheat germ, almond, and avocado oil
¼ teaspoon grapefruit seed extract

Combine the ingredients in a small glass jar. Stir to blend. Dab some on your fingers and rub into the skin.
**Makes ¼ cup**

*Preparation Time:* A few minutes
*Shelf Life:* 4 months refrigerated; discard if the oils smell rancid
*Storage:* Glass jar with a screw top

### BABY MASSAGE OILS

Herbalists have always used herb-infused oils as a way of transmitting the nourishing and medicinal attributes of plants to the skin. Use just a dab of oil, so as not to clog the baby's tiny pores.

A NOTE ABOUT OILS: Jojoba is the first choice for infusing an oil for massage, because it is a liquid wax and doesn't go rancid. Olive oil holds up to time without going rancid better than most oils and therefore is a good choice for massage oil. If you don't plan to infuse herbs in the oil, the best choice is coconut oil: It lathers well and washes out of towels.

## PETER PAN AND TINKERBELL OIL 🎁

*The gentle, antibacterial, and antiseptic qualities of calendula add value to this oil blend. Calendula oil is a rich yellow color. Mothers who developed varicose veins while pregnant should rub some of this healing oil on their legs.*

½ cup each jojoba and olive oil
infused with calendula
⅓ teaspoon grapefruit seed extract

Infuse the calendula in the jojoba and olive oil as described on page 33. Combine the ingredients. Dab some on your finger and rub into the skin.
**Makes 1 cup**

*Preparation Time:* About 15 minutes plus infusing time
*Shelf Life:* 2 months; discard if you see mold
*Storage:* Glass jar with a screw top

### BABY BATHS

Safety is the number-one priority when bathing a baby. Babies are incredibly slippery when they are wet. A helpful invention for washing newborns is a sloped portable bath, available in most department stores; it keeps the baby's head above water if your hands slip. A friend told me that she once rubbed olive oil onto her baby before placing it in the bath, resulting in such a slippery baby that she couldn't hold on to it, so skip the oil.

The bath temperature should be between 98°F and 100°F. Be sure to test the water before placing the baby into the tub to avoid all danger of scalding. Metal spouts in tubs and sinks should be covered with something soft to prevent injury if bumped against, and the water should be only a few inches deep.

### BABY POWDERS

Powders are a thing of the past for babies: Pediatricians now believe you shouldn't use them at all. The foremost reason for this is that they promote bacterial growth and they irritate the lungs and can cause choking—not just talc, which can be contaminated with asbestos, but also talc's common substitute, cornstarch. In lieu of powders, dry a baby well with a towel.

### CRADLE CAP

Cradle cap—most commonly a skin disease called seborrhea but sometimes a fungus—leaves crusty yellowish flakes on the top of the baby's head. Wash the scalp once a day and rub it with a towel to remove as much of the flaking skin as possible by simple friction.

## OLD-FASHIONED SIMPLE ✂ 🎁

Cocoa butter

Rub the cocoa butter on top of the head as if the butter was a crayon (it is about the same hardness). Avoid the baby's "soft spot," the place on the skull that hasn't fully closed at birth.

## CRADLE CAP CREAM

*Follow the directions for Basic Cream Formula on page 30, using almond oil infused with burdock and chamomile and using a strong slippery elm bark tea for the water.*

*Shelf Life:* 2 weeks

## SLIPPERY ELM BALM

*Slippery elm is full of mucilage, which coats and soothes the skin.*

½ cup almond oil
1 ounce cocoa butter (or more for
a thicker balm)
3 tablespoons powdered slippery elm bark
¼ teaspoon grapefruit seed extract

Combine the oil and cocoa butter in a double boiler and place over medium heat until the cocoa butter is melted. Remove from the heat and add the slippery elm bark and grapefruit seed extract. Whip with an electric handheld mixer until creamy.
**Makes ½ cup**

*Preparation Time:* 25 minutes
*Shelf Life:* 2 weeks to 1 month
*Storage:* Glass jar with a screw top

### BABIES AND THE SUN

The fair and tender skin of babies should always be protected from sunburn with suitable clothing, equipment such as an umbrella, and sunblock. See page 210 for sunblocks that contain UVB and UVA blocking ingredients.

# Baths

Soaking in hot water (or sitting in a sauna) relaxes the body and stimulates the immune system to fight off viruses and bacterial infections. Cold water, on the other hand, stimulates circulation and reduces inflammation. The Swedes are famous for going from hot saunas to cold showers (or rolling in the snow) to give the body the benefits of both. You can achieve the same effect by soaking in a hot bath followed by taking a cool shower. Baths are also a means of deeply cleansing the body and helping the skin absorb the benefits of herbs and salts. Last but not least, baths can be calming, relaxing, and rejuvenating after a long, stressful day.

*Caution About Water Temperature:* Very hot baths are not good for those with high blood pressure, and they can be draining for anyone.

### TIPS

* To increase your relaxation, place a full hot water bottle under your neck to relax against while in the bath.
* Clean the bathtub with a baking soda and detergent soft scrub (see page 96) so you don't breath toxic fumes while bathing.
* Many like to bathe by candlelight. Most candles are made with petroleum waxes and are often scented with synthetic fragrances that will pollute the air in your bathroom. Look instead for pure beeswax candles; the smell is rich with a touch of honey.
* Salts and soaps are alkaline. If these ingredients are in your bath, you should return your skin to a more acidic state before you

leave the tub. Add $\frac{1}{4}$ cup organic apple cider vinegar to the bath before you step out. If you've used baking soda in the bath, the addition of vinegar will result in some foaming and fizzing, but think of it as a bubble bath.

## MINERALS AND SALTS

Minerals and salts make the bathwater feel silky and leave your skin cleansed and soft. Salts used in baths include sea salt, baking soda, clay, Epsom salts, and Dead Sea salts. See Chapter One for a detailed Glossary of Ingredients.

## BASIC SALT SOAK BATH FORMULA ✂ 🎁

*Minerals nourish the skin and neutralize odors.*

1 cup sea salts
2 cups baking soda
1 cup Epsom salts
1 to 2 tablespoons glycerin per bath
Essential oils of choice

Combine the sea salts, baking soda, and Epsom salts in a bowl. Stir to blend. Pour $\frac{1}{4}$ cup or so into the bath while the tub is filling. Add 1 to 2 tablespoons glycerin to keep your skin from drying out (more for dry skin, less for oily skin) and essential oils of choice.
**Makes 4 cups**

*Preparation Time:* 2 to 3 minutes
*Shelf Life:* Indefinite
*Storage:* Glass jar with a screw top

## Variations

BATH WITH MINERAL-RICH CLAY: Substitute 1 cup baking soda, $\frac{1}{8}$ cup sea salt, and $\frac{1}{8}$ cup cosmetic clay for the first 3 ingredients.

BAKING SODA SPORTS BATH: Use an additional $\frac{1}{2}$ cup baking soda in the bath to neutralize perspiration odors after sports.

SEA SALT SOAK: Use an additional 1 cup sea salt in the bath. Salt is very antiseptic.

DEAD SEA SALTS SOAK: Use Dead Sea salts (available from health food stores) in the bath instead of plain sea salt. They are particularly healing for psoriasis. Bathe in Dead Sea salts every day for 3 weeks.

SEA SALT GLOW: Soak in a warm bath for a few minutes, then stand up and stimulate circulation by massaging Basic Salt Soak Bath Formula into the skin over the whole body. Sit back down in the bath or take a shower to rinse off.

## HERBAL BATHS

Herbal baths—a wonderful way to absorb the emollient, astringent, or healing qualities of herbs—are a luxury worth integrating into your life. Try to have an herbal bath every week, or more often if possible, especially during times of stress or physical injury.

## BASIC HERBAL BATH FORMULA 🎁

$\frac{1}{2}$ to 1 gallon organic apple cider vinegar herbal infusion

## GOOD BATH HERBS FOR DIFFERENT NEEDS

**RELAXING AND CALMING BATHS:** Chamomile, hops, valerian, skullcap, rose, orange blossom, lavender

**REJUVENATING AND STIMULATING BATHS:** Rosemary, nettle, mint, lemon balm, bay leaf, eucalyptus, lavender

**DRY SKIN BATHS:** Chamomile, lavender, rose, St. John's wort, comfrey root, orris root

**OILY SKIN BATHS:** Rosemary, calendula, thyme, lemongrass, witch hazel

**HOT DAY BATHS:** Mint, lemon balm

**WINTER BATHS:** Cloves, cinnamon, orange peel, ginger

**ANTISEPTIC BATHS:** Thyme, sweet orange, lemongrass, rose, clove, eucalyptus, orris root, cinnamon, rosemary, birch, lavender, tea tree oil

*Preparation Time:* About 30 minutes
*Shelf Life:* Indefinite
*Storage:* Glass jar with a screw top

Variations

EMOLLIENT HERB BATH: Add a few tablespoons glycerin to the bathwater.

MINERAL-RICH SEAWEED BATH: Make an infusion of kelp or other seaweed to add to the bathwater. The shelf life is 1 week.

NUTRIENT-RICH BATH: Make an infusion of nettle, burdock, and seaweed to add to the bathwater. The shelf life is 1 week.

ARTHRITIS BATH: Make a strong infusion of fresh grated ginger root and add 10 drops rosemary essential oil. The shelf life is 1 week.

TINCTURED HERB BATH: Infuse herbs in vodka, rum, or brandy instead of vinegar. Add ¼ cup to the bathwater.

## BASIC SALT AND HERB SOAK BATH FORMULAS

*Combine the Basic Salt Soak Bath Formula (page 169) and the Basic Herbal Bath Formula, above.*

## ACHING MUSCLE BATH

Handful each rosemary and sage
A few sticks cinnamon
1 teaspoon grated ginger root
A few leaves eucalyptus
Boiling water, to cover

To make the infusion, choose herbs suited to your skin or special needs, and infuse them in vinegar as described on page 32. Strain well, then pour 1 to 2 cups into the bath just before getting in. You can also infuse herbs in water, but these infusions don't have a shelf life, so make only as much as you can use in a few days.
**Makes ½ to 1 gallon**

Place the herbs and spices in a quart mason jar. Cover with boiling water and let set overnight. Strain. Pour into the bathwater.

**Makes 4 cups**

*Preparation Time:* About 15 minutes
*Shelf Life:* A few days refrigerated
*Storage:* Glass jar with a screw top

Variation

DETOX BATH: Use rosemary, echinacea, burdock root, and lemon balm.

## SOAPY SALTS WITH LEMON AND CLOVE 🎁

*The salts will soften your skin, the soap will cleanse it, the orris root is antibacterial and smells of violets, and the almond meal and glycerin are emollient and softening. The soap and baking soda are the key ingredients; if you don't have some of the other ingredients, make this formula with what you have.*

⅛ cup grated or liquid soap
1 cup baking soda
¼ cup orris root powder
¼ cup almond meal
1 tablespoon vegetable glycerin
A few drops essential oils of lemon and clove

Combine the ingredients in a quart mason jar. Shake to blend. Add ½ cup to the tub while it is filling.

**Makes 1½ cups**

*Preparation Time:* About 15 minutes
*Shelf Life:* A few months refrigerated
*Storage:* Glass jar with a screw top

## SOFTENING ROSE WATER BATH 🎁

2 cups rose petal infusion
2 tablespoons vegetable glycerin or honey
1 cup hot water

Strain the rose petal infusion, and pour it into the bath. Blend the glycerin with the hot water to dissolve, and add to the tub.

**Makes 2 cups, enough for one bath**

*Preparation Time:* 15 minutes
*Shelf Life:* None

## BASIC FRUIT ACID (AHA) SOFTENING AND CLEANSING BATH 🗡

*Baths are a good way to utilize fruit acids for a thorough cleansing, because the fruit acids help dissolve dead skin cells. See page 108 for a list of AHAs. Add the AHA while the tub is filling. Rinse your body after soaking.*

Variations

FAMED CLEOPATRA MILK BATH: Add 2 cups milk to the bathwater.

QUEEN OF HUNGARY WATER BATH: Add 1 to 2 cups Queen of Hungary Water (see page 137 for the recipe) to the bathwater.

LEMON AND LIME JUICE BATH: Add 1 cup freshly squeezed juice to the bathwater.

CLEOPATRA'S CALENDULA MILK CLEANSER : Add 2 cups milk and 1 tablespoon ground calendula flowers to the bathwater. If you are traveling and it is awkward to carry fresh milk, substitute ¼ cup powdered milk.

## EMOLLIENT BATH

*Midwinter, when so many of us have dry skin, is an excellent time to treat your skin to these moisturizing, softening, and hydrating ingredients.*

1 to 2 ounces apricot kernel, avocado, or flax seed oil
1 ounce glycerin
2 ounces aloe vera gel
A few drops essential oils of choice

Add the ingredients to the tub while it is filling.
**Makes about ¼ cup, enough for one bath**

*Preparation Time:* A few minutes

## BASIC HONEY BATH

*Herbalists have touted honey for centuries because it helps skin retain moisture and thereby rejuvenates and softens it. Honey is a humectant and is very softening.*

2 tablespoons honey
About 1 cup very hot water
A few drops essential oils, if desired

Dissolve the honey in the water. Add essential oils, if using. Pour into the bathwater.
**Makes 1 cup, enough for one bath**

*Preparation Time:* A few minutes

## BUBBLE BATHS

Most of us don't think of bubble baths much more than for the fun and luxury of them, but natural bubble baths made with minerals and pure essential oils are extra-special. The minerals cleanse the skin of odors, and the essential oils provide some antibacterial protection and relaxation via aromatherapy, such as with rosemary and lavender.

## BASIC BUBBLE BATH FORMULA

*Cream of tartar is an AHA and softens the skin; baking soda cleanses it of odors.*

1 cup each baking soda and cream of tartar
¼ cup cornstarch
Up to 5 drops essential oil per bath, if desired

Combine the baking soda, cream of tartar, and cornstarch in a jar. Use a few tablespoons per bath. Add the essential oil at the time of the bath; otherwise, the baking soda will neutralize the scent during storage.
**Makes 2¼ cups**

*Preparation Time:* A few minutes
*Shelf Life:* Indefinite
*Storage:* Glass jar with a screw top

## FOAM SIZZLER ✘

*A common science project for a child is to make a volcano with baking soda and vinegar, because they cause a lot of bubbling when they combine. You can make a fun and fizzing bath with these same ingredients.*

¼ cup baking soda
¼ cup organic apple cider vinegar

Add the baking soda to the bathwater while the tub is filling. Pour in the vinegar before you get in, and watch the foaming and sizzling.
**Makes ½ cup**

*Preparation Time:* A minute or so
*Shelf Life:* None

### BATH OILS

I remember loving to play with bath beads in the tub as a girl, particularly pressing out the oil. But until someone makes bath beads without synthetic fragrance, making our own bath oils will have to do instead; we just miss the squashing-the-oil-out part. Choose oils that feel good on your skin, and add a few drops of essential oils with fragrances that appeal to you. Jasmine is expensive, but what a luxurious scent.

## BASIC BATH OIL ✘

*Avocado oil is ideal for dry skin, and jojoba is good for normal and oily skin. Castor oil leaves*

*less of an oily film on the body and tub. (See page 21 for more on oils.)*

1 to 2 teaspoons oil of choice
A few drops fragrant essential oil of choice

Add the oils to the bathwater while the tub is filling.
**Makes enough for 1 bath**

*Preparation Time:* Less than 1 minute

# Body Powders

Powders effectively absorb moisture (cornstarch is excellent for this); many, such as those based on baking soda, neutralize odors. Other ingredients, such as zinc oxide and orris root, are antibacterial. Choose among the following natural powders: arrowroot, baking soda, cornstarch, flours (such as brown rice, wheat, and oat), kaolin and other clays, orris root powder, potato starch, zinc oxide powder, or ground herbs such as calendula and chamomile. Talc is known to be contaminated with asbestos and should be avoided.

A powder puff is a useful accessory for dusting powders onto your body. Look for natural puffs at cosmetic counters and health food stores. Cotton balls can be substituted.

## BASIC BODY POWDER FORMULA ✘ 🎁

4 ounces powder material
4 drops essential oil of choice

½ teaspoon oil or vegetable glycerin
(for those with dry skin)

Combine the ingredients in a widemouthed glass jar, and shake to blend. Dab a puff into the powder and dust onto your body as desired. **Makes ½ cup**

*Preparation Time:* A few minutes
*Shelf Life:* Indefinite
*Storage:* Glass jar with a screw top

### Variations

ORRIS ROOT AND CORNSTARCH: Use 2 ounces orris root and 2 ounces cornstarch for the powder material. Cornstarch absorbs moisture, and orris root has a lovely violet scent and is antibacterial.

BASIC FLOWER POWER POWDER FORMULA: Flower petals and herbs add their aromatic, emollient, and antibacterial qualities to the powder. Combine 4 ounces powder material, 2 tablespoons ground dried flowers (such as lavender and roses) or herbs (such as rosemary and sage), and 4 drops essential oil of choice. (Once dry enough, herbs and flowers can be crumbled or easily ground in a mortar and pestle.)

# Deodorants

Most people think that antiperspirants and deodorants are the same thing. Antiperspirants work by clogging, closing, or blocking the pores with powerful astringents such as aluminum salts so they can't release sweat. Deodorants work by neutralizing the smell of the sweat and by antiseptic action against bacteria. Health concerns about antiperspirants include the use of aluminum salts (they may or may not contribute to Alzheimer's disease—the science isn't clear yet—but better safe than sorry), and they interfere with sweating, a natural cooling process. For these reasons, this section provides recipes only for deodorants.

Use a powder puff, sea sponge, washcloth, or cotton balls to apply powders.

## DEODORANT POWDER SIMPLES

### BAKING SODA SIMPLE

*Nothing is as good as baking soda for eliminating perspiration odors; it literally neutralizes them.*

Sprinkle a light covering of baking soda onto a powder puff or damp washcloth. Pat on the body where needed. Don't rinse. You can also dust baking soda inside your shoes if odor is a problem.

*Preparation Time:* None
*Shelf Life:* Indefinite
*Storage:* Leave in original box

### Variations

BAKING SODA SPRAY: For a more convenient way of applying baking soda, add 3 teaspoons baking soda to 1 cup water in a spray bottle; use less baking soda if the sprayer gets clogged.

SODA AND SCENTS: Baking soda can be scented with a few drops of essential oil per ounce of baking soda. Place baking soda in a glass jar and add a few drops of antibacterial essential oil (lavender); cover and shake to blend. This preparation can also be made into a spray, as described above.

WITCH HAZEL EXTRACT: Sprinkle antibacterial and astringent witch hazel extract onto a cotton ball or washcloth, and dab onto the body where needed. Or place in a spray bottle. Use instead of baking soda.

VINEGAR WATER: See Astringents (page 133) for vinegar waters. I particularly recommend Queen of Hungary Water, because it is rich with antibacterial herbs. Dab on with a cotton ball or place in a spray bottle. Use instead of baking soda.

ESSENTIAL OILS AND WATER: Simply add 5 to 10 drops antibacterial essential oils to a cup or so of water in a spray bottle. Don't add too much essential oil or you will overpower everyone in your vicinity. Lavender oil is a good choice, because it is antiseptic and smells lovely. Use instead of baking soda.

## DEODORANT POWDERS

### BASIC DEODORANT POWDER FORMULA ✘

*Cornstarch absorbs moisture, and baking soda neutralizes odors.*

½ cup baking soda
½ cup cornstarch
Antibacterial essential oils such as cinnamon, rose, birch, or lavender, as preferred

Place the baking soda and cornstarch in a glass jar. Add the essential oils; stir and cover.

Dampen a powder puff, cotton ball, or sea sponge and dab into the mixture (or sprinkle the mixture on the sponge); pat underarms.
**Makes 1 cup**

*Preparation Time:* A few minutes
*Shelf Life:* Indefinite
*Storage:* Glass jar with a screw top

### Variations

BIRCH BUD POWDER: Use the antibacterial essential oil of birch bud, which smells like wintergreen.

REFRESHING BLEND: Use essential oil of eucalyptus or wintergreen.

PARSLEY, SAGE, ROSEMARY, AND THYME: Grind the dried herbs to a powder and add to the blend. This herbal combination has a woodsy aroma.

## LIQUID DEODORANT SPRAYS

Liquid deodorants are a good place to experiment with essential oils for scents. See Fragrances (page 180) for more ideas about scents.

### BASIC LIQUID DEODORANT FORMULA ✘

*This astringent yet soothing balm contains witch hazel extract and aloe vera gel, which are both antibacterial.*

¼ cup witch hazel extract
¼ cup aloe vera gel
¼ cup bottled mineral water (or herbal water)

1 tablespoon vegetable glycerin (less if it feels too sticky on your skin)

⅓ teaspoon grapefruit seed extract (as a natural preservative if you use herbal water)

Antibacterial essential oils, as preferred

Combine the ingredients in a spray bottle. Shake to blend.

**Makes ¾ cup**

*Preparation Time:* A few minutes (15 minutes if you need to make herbal water)
*Shelf Life:* Indefinite with mineral water, 1 to 4 months refrigerated with herbal water
*Storage:* Spray bottle

## Variations

ROSE WATER DEODORANT: Use equal amounts rose water, organic apple cider vinegar, and witch hazel extract; choose essential oils and preservatives as above.

EMOLLIENT ROSE WATER DEODORANT: Use ½ cup rose water for the herbal water and add ½ cup rum, vodka, or brandy. Alcohol has strong antibacterial action.

WITCH HAZEL EXTRACT WHIMSY: Straight witch hazel extract, with the addition of a few drops of antibacterial essential oils per ounce, is a good, quick-to-make liquid deodorant that will give hours of antibacterial protection.

RUM AND SPICE: For a spicy, bay rum kind of scent, substitute rum for the aloe vera gel, and add essential oils of spices such as cinnamon and clove or other oils and herbs used in aftershave lotions (page 208).

# Foot Care

"The true man breathes with his heels; the mass of men breath with their throats." So says Chuang Tzu, an ancient Taoist teacher. It does seem sometimes that we are so cerebral that our feet are the last part of our bodies we pay attention to. Yet if we think of our feet, we suddenly realize how important they are. Our feet have to support all our weight every day, and that takes its toll.

When my Lyme disease was bad and I had terrible arthritis in my feet, nothing felt as wonderful as a foot rub of sand and rosemary oil. The rosemary numbed the pain, and the sand exfoliated dead skin and seemed to penetrate into my feet and sooth the aches and pains. Soaking feet in warm water with antiseptic essential oils will kill bacteria and deeply cleanse. Anyone with nail fungus or athlete's foot should soak their feet in a tea tree oil foot bath. Diabetics in particular need to take good care of their feet, and a footbath with an oil such as lavender or tea tree oil is very protective.

## THE NATURAL PEDICURE

**ACCESSORIES.** Toenail clippers, pumice stone or pumice stone sand stick, nail cleansing brush, large basin, antibacterial essential oils such as thyme, rosemary, lavender, and orange flower oil.

**1. FOOTBATH OR SOAK.** Add 10 drops or so antibacterial essential oils to warm water. Soak feet for 15 minutes or more.

**2. CLEAN AND CUT TOENAILS.** Wash feet in liquid castile soap with up to 10 drops antibacterial clove or rosemary essential oil per ounce of soap; use a toenail brush. Dry thoroughly. Clip toenails or file with an emery board to desired length.

**3. EXFOLIATE.** Remove dead skin cells with fruit acids, enzymes, or a cleansing scrub (see below for recipes) or by gently massaging the skin with pumice stone. Apply the fruit acid, enzyme, or scrub; let set for a few minutes, then wash with warm water.

**4. FOOT RUB.** Massage feet with a massage or body oil. Or fill a basin with marbles and water and "walk" over the marbles.

**5. CUTICLE CARE.** Massage cuticle cream into toenails (see Cuticle Creams on page 201 for recipes).

**6. MOISTURIZE.** Choose a moisturizer such as The Best Basic Soft and Silky Moisturizer (page 142) and massage into feet.

**7. SAND AND BUFF NAILS.** Dry feet. Sand and buff the nails with a pumice stone sand stick and smoothing files.

FOOTBATHS

## BIRCH WATER SOAK

*The salicylic acid in birch is excellent for helping to remove dead tissue from the feet, and it is very antiseptic.*

1 quart birch infusion
Essential oil of birch bud (optional)

Fill a quart mason jar with birch twigs and cover with boiling water. Cover and let set overnight. Strain and pour into a basin. Add a few drops birch bud oil if desired. Fill with warm water. Soak feet.
**Makes enough for 1 soak**

*Preparation Time:* About 25 minutes
*Shelf Life:* Discard

## ARTHRITIS FOOT SOAK

*Ginger provides soothing heat for arthritic aches and pains.*

1 quart strong ginger infusion
10 to 15 drops rosemary essential oil

Cover the infusion and let set overnight. Strain into a basin and add enough warm water to cover your feet. Add the rosemary essential oil, and soak.
**Makes enough for 1 soak**

*Preparation Time:* 30 minutes
*Shelf Life:* Discard

## ANTIFUNGAL FOOT SOAK ✗

*Tea tree oil has been used for centuries in Australia to treat fungal diseases of all kinds. Soak your feet in this powerful essential oil for help with nail fungus or athlete's foot.*

10 drops tea tree oil
About 1 gallon warm water

In a basin, combine the tea tree oil and enough warm water to cover your feet. Soak.
**Makes enough for 1 soak**

*Preparation Time:* A few minutes
*Shelf Life:* Discard

## SOFTENING SOAK ✄

*Alpha-hydroxy acids exfoliate, removing old, dead skin cells.*

1 to 2 cups fruit acids, such as buttermilk, organic apple cider vinegar, or lemon juice
About 1 gallon warm water

In a basin, combine the fruit acids with enough warm water to cover your feet. Soak.
**Makes enough for 1 soak**

*Preparation Time:* A few minutes
*Shelf Life:* Discard

## SALT AND SODA SOAK ✄

*Sea salt is antibacterial, and baking soda takes away odors. The combination helps smelly feet.*

½ cup sea salt
½ cup baking soda

Combine the salt and baking soda in a glass jar; shake or stir to blend. Place 2 to 3 tablespoons in a basin with enough warm water to cover your feet.
**Makes 1 cup**

*Preparation Time:* About 1 minute
*Shelf Life:* Indefinite
*Storage:* Glass jar with a screw top

## FOOT RUBS AND EXFOLIATING SCRUBS

## SAND SCRUB ✄ 🎁

*The next time you are at the beach, collect a bucket of sand to take home for fabulous foot rubs.*

1 cup beach sand
1 to 2 teaspoons oil
10 to 20 drops essential oil of choice

Combine the sand, oil, and essential oil in a bowl. Stir well. Holding your feet over a basin or old newspapers to catch falling sand, scoop out a small handful at a time, and massage into your feet. Rinse well.
**Makes 1 cup**

*Preparation Time:* About 2 minutes
*Shelf Life:* Indefinite
*Storage:* Glass jar with a screw top

### Variation
ROSEMARY ARTHRITIS RUB: Use rosemary as the essential oil if you have arthritis. It is soothing beyond belief.

## ANTIFUNGUS FOOT RUB ✄

2 tablespoons oil (jojoba is good)
10 to 20 drops antibacterial essential oils such as clove or tea tree oil

Combine the ingredients in a bowl or jar.
**Makes 2 tablespoons**

*Preparation Time:* About 1 minute
*Shelf Life:* Indefinite with jojoba; up to 6 months refrigerated with other oils
*Storage:* Glass jar with a screw top

## FRAGRANT FOOT SCRUB ✗

*Baking soda is slightly abrasive as well as an odor remover.*

½ cup baking soda
10 drops antibacterial essential oil
such as lavender

Combine the ingredients. Scoop some into your hand, and rub onto your feet.
**Makes ½ cup**

*Preparation Time:* A few minutes
*Shelf Life:* Indefinite
*Storage:* Glass jar with a screw top

## NONPETROLEUM JELLY WITH ESSENTIAL OILS 🎁

*This is a good preparation for dry, flaking skin or callused feet.*

Basic Nonpetroleum Jelly Formula (page 31)
6 drops essential oil of choice

Combine the ingredients. Before you go to bed at night, massage the jelly into your feet. Wear 100 percent cotton or silk socks to sleep in so the lubricating oils won't dry out.
**Makes ¼ cup**

*Preparation Time:* About 25 minutes
*Shelf Life:* 6 months
*Storage:* Glass jar with a screw top

## DEAD SKIN FOOT RUB

*Pumice stone is excellent for exfoliating because it is soft and abrasive; it has been used to rub off dead skin for centuries.*

Pumice stone

Gently massage the feet with the stone. Rinse well.

*Preparation Time:* None
*Shelf Life:* Indefinite

## TIRED FEET PICK-ME-UP ✗ 🎁

*Aloe is moisturizing and anti-inflammatory; peppermint is refreshing and rejuvenating.*

¼ cup aloe vera gel
10 drops peppermint essential oil

Combine the ingredients, and massage into the feet.
**Makes ¼ cup**

*Preparation Time:* A few minutes
*Shelf Life:* 6 months refrigerated
*Storage:* Glass jar with a screw top

## VIM AND VINEGAR ✗

*The vinegar will exfoliate dead skin cells, and the glycerin will moisturize.*

¾ cup organic apple cider vinegar
¼ cup vegetable glycerin

Combine the ingredients in a jar. Shake to blend. Pour some into your hand and massage into the feet; do not rinse. Repeat a few times.
**Makes 1 cup**

*Preparation Time:* About 1 minute
*Shelf Life:* Indefinite
*Storage:* Glass jar with a screw top

## FANCY FOOT RUB

*Sometimes it's nice to treat your feet to a softening rub with a lovely fragrance. This formula is for just such a time.*

½ cup rose water
2 tablespoons vegetable glycerin
2 tablespoons almond oil
Essential oil of jasmine, as desired

Combine the ingredients in a jar and shake to blend. Massage into the feet.
**Makes about ¾ cup**

*Preparation Time:* A few minutes
*Shelf Life:* 2 to 4 months; discard if moldy
*Storage:* Glass jar with a screw top

## FOOT POWDERS

Borax is a good choice for feet because it has antifungal properties. It is also alkaline and does a good job at deodorizing. Zinc oxide powder is also antibacterial. Baking soda absorbs odors.

Cornstarch is in a lot of foot powders, because it is excellent for absorbing moisture.

## BASIC ANTIBACTERIAL FOOT POWDER FORMULA

3 tablespoons cornstarch
1 tablespoon zinc oxide or borax
10 drops antibacterial essential oil such as tea tree, clove, or rosemary

Combine the ingredients in a glass jar. Shake or stir to blend. Dab some of the mixture on a cotton ball and powder the feet.
**Makes about ¼ cup**

*Preparation Time:* A few minutes
*Shelf Life:* Indefinite
*Storage:* Glass jar with a screw top

Variations
BORAX POWDER: Make the powder with 3 tablespoons borax and 1 tablespoon zinc oxide or cornstarch.
BAKING SODA POWDER: Make the powder with 3 tablespoons baking soda and 1 tablespoon borax.
ORRIS ROOT AND BIRCH POWDER: Make the powder with 1 tablespoon orris root powder and 10 drops essential oil of birch bud (for its salicylic acid and antibacterial properties).

# Fragrances

Everybody likes to smell good, but many people are allergic to commercial perfume products. One can escape the discomfort of synthetic fragrances by making scents using essential oils. Essential oils should never be placed directly on the skin; they are so strong they can burn. For perfumes and colognes, the oils are blended with alcohol and water. The ratio of essential oils to alcohol and water in fragrances varies considerably; perfume is the strongest aroma, containing the most essential oils to the least alcohol-water mixture.

The following figures are adapted from *The Complete Book of Essential Oils and Aromatherapy,* by Valerie Ann Wormwood.

Perfume (as much as 30 percent essential oil)

Eau de Perfume (up to 15 percent)

Eau de Toilette (up to 8 percent)

Eau de Cologne (up to 5 percent)

Splash Cologne (as little as 1 percent)

NATURAL MATERIALS FOR MAKING PERFUMES, WATERS, AND COLOGNES

### Fragrance Materials

*Flowers:* Cassia, carnation, clove, hyacinth, heliotrope, mimosa, jasmine, jonquil, orange blossom, rose, violet, ylang-ylang

*Flowers and Leaves:* Lavender, rosemary, peppermint, violet

*Leaves and Stems:* Geranium, cinnamon, patchouli

*Bark:* Cinnamon, cassia

*Wood:* Cedar, sandalwood

*Roots:* Angelica, sassafras, vetivert

*Rhizomes:* Calamus, ginger, orris root

*Fruits:* Bergamot, lemon, lime, orange

*Seeds:* Bitter almond, anise, nutmeg

## THE PURE ESSENTIAL OIL PAPER TEST

IT is important to buy pure, solvent-free essential oils. Do a blotting paper test to see if your oils are pure. Pure essential oils will not leave any residue once evaporated, whereas petroleum will.

*Gums or Oleoresinous Materials:* Myrrh, Peru balsam, and storax.

### Balsams, Gums, and Oleoresins

Consisting of essential oils and soluble resins and considered to have soft and persistent odors, these plant materials are also important in perfumes as fixatives. The plant matter is extracted from the plant with alcohol or a chemical solvent. Some examples are benzoin (considered the best fixative; trees are found in Thailand, Sumatra, and Java), labdanum (from the leaves of the rockrose family), and storax (a balsam tree).

*Essential Oil Fixatives:* Commonly used examples are patchouli, clary sage, sandalwood, orris root (smells like violets), and vetiver.

*Alcohol:* Essential oils are 80 to 90 percent alcohol; the rest is water. The recipes in *Better Basics* use vodka, brandy, or rum.

*Glycerin:* Often used as a fixative.

*Water:* Use distilled water or rose water.

*Caution:* When buying materials, specifically

ask for those that are naturally derived. Examples of chemical duplicates of natural materials include musk ambrette, heliotropin, vanillin, coumarin, ethyl phthalate, and benzyl cinnamate.

## ESSENTIAL OIL BLENDS

One of the best things about making your own fragrances is that you can experiment. Perfumers try out essential oils by placing a few combinations of drops on blotting paper. You can test your own by using a number of different small squares of blotting paper, each with only one essential oil. Smell one after the other, or at the same time, to see which ones you'd like in combination and which aroma should be stronger than others. Once you have created a blend you like, use it as the essential oil in the Basic Formula for Perfume, page 183.

## ESSENTIAL OIL RATIOS

I have not given exact ratios for combining essential oils, because your nose is the only correct criterion for determining what feels balanced for you. But, to give you a starting point, here are examples of commonly combined essential oils. Essential oils are strong, so work in a well-ventilated area, or outside, and make absolutely sure that your oils are pure by doing the paper test described on page 181.

### COMMONLY USED ESSENTIAL OIL PERFUME BLENDS

**Violet:** Violet, cassia, rose, tuberose, orris root, bitter almond

**Violet II:** Orris root, rose geranium

**Wood Violet:** Bitter almond, lavender, verbena, coriander, bergamot, jasmine, orange

**Carnation:** Rose, orange, cassia, vanilla, clove

## ANIMAL EXTRACTS USED IN COMMERCIAL PERFUME

EXTRACTS of animal origin, such as musk, are considered an important component by perfumers and are used to impart "life" and "diffusiveness." Musk is a dried secretion from the male musk deer found in the Himalaya and Atlas Mountains. The deer are killed to obtain the secretions. Ambergris is formed in the intestines of the sperm whale. Sometimes discarded by the whale, it is found floating by sailors, but usually it is removed from dead whales. Civet is a glandular secretion derived from civet cats, which are stimulated (usually through torture) to produce the secretions. Castor oil is derived from the genitals of Russian or Canadian beavers, and the animals have to be killed for the oil. Castor oil is also derived from seeds, but that is not the oil used for perfume. I don't call for any animal extracts in the fragrance recipes in *Better Basics for the Home.*

**Rose:** Rose, neroli, iris, tonka bean, rose essence, jasmine, violet, cassia, vanilla, clove, bergamot, rose geranium

**Rose II:** Rose, bergamot

**Mayflower:** Rose, jasmine, orange, cassia, vanilla, bitter almond

**Narcissus:** Tuberose, jasmine, neroli, ylang-ylang, clove

**Almond Blossom:** Heliotrope, orange, jasmine, rose, lemon, bitter almond

**White Rose:** Tuberose, orange, jasmine, rose, patchouli, orris root

**White Heliotrope:** Vanilla, rose, bitter almond

**White Lilac:** Tuberose, orange, bitter almond

OTHER COMMONLY USED BLENDS

Rose, ylang-ylang

Rose, violet, jasmine, patchouli

Rose, jasmine, rose geranium, clove

Rose, lavender, lemon verbena, mint

Lemon balm, thyme, nutmeg, orris root

Thyme, rosemary, lavender, mint, tansy, clove, orris root

Clove, cinnamon, orris root

Lemon, citronella, lemon verbena, sandalwood

Basil, sage, dill, sandalwood

Rosemary, rose

Geranium, patchouli, clove, lavender

Bergamot, sandalwood

Sandalwood, orange flower, sassafras, white thyme, cassia, clove

Citronella, clove, bitter almond

Neroli, bergamot, rose

Clove, bergamot

Orange flower, sandalwood, geranium, clove

Cinnamon, eucalyptus

Rose, rose geranium, clove, sandalwood

Thyme, bergamot, clove, geranium

Lavender or rose geranium

Neroli, orange, jasmine

White rose, jasmine, orange flower, cassia, myrrh

Jasmine, neroli, vanilla

Orris root, cassia, jasmine

Rose, wintergreen, jasmine

Rose, jasmine

Bergamot, rose geranium

Rose, patchouli, rose geranium, sandalwood, lavender, clove, neroli, bergamot, vanilla

Lavender, bergamot, rose, cinnamon, clove

Rose, orange

Clove, bergamot, lavender, sandalwood, rose and orange flower waters, honey

Violet, rose

Rose, jasmine, ylang-ylang

Bay, rosemary, verbena

Violet, cassia, jasmine, benzoin, orris root, rose, rose geranium, bergamot, orris root, vervain, rose water

Rose water, orange flower water, violet, jasmine, lemon verbena, rosemary, bergamot

Bitter almond, orange flower extract, tuberose, orris root

PERFUMES

## BASIC FORMULA FOR PERFUME 🎁

3 parts pure essential oil blend (page 182)
7 parts vodka, rum, or brandy
20 drops per ounce of orris root tincture

Combine the ingredients and let set for 1 to 2 months

*Preparation Time:* 10 minutes
*Shelf Life:* Indefinite
*Storage:* Glass jar (preferably dark) with a screw top, away from light

### Examples

LILY PERFUME: For the essential oil blend, combine 8 parts tuberose, 2 parts each rose and cassia, and 1 part each jasmine, orange flower, rose, and vanilla.

WHITE LILAC: For the essential oil blend, combine 11 parts tuberose, 6 parts orange flower, and 1/4 part bitter almond.

WOOD VIOLET: For the essential oil blend, combine 20 parts orange flower tincture, 4 parts jasmine oil, 1/4 part lavender oil, 1/16 part each verbena and coriander oil, 3/4 part bergamot oil.

### Variation

PERFUME II: 3 parts essential oils, 7 to 8 parts vodka, 1 to 3 parts rose water, 1/4 part orris root and/or benzoin tincture.

### PERFUME SIMPLES

Use only one or two essential oils, such as lavender and rose, in the Basic Formula for Perfume (page 183).

## BASIC FORMULA FOR PERFUME OILS (ALCOHOL FREE)

1 ounce oil
25 drops essential oils

Combine ingredients in a glass bottle. Shake to blend.
**Makes about 1 ounce**

*Preparation Time:* 1 or 2 minutes
*Shelf Life:* Indefinite
*Storage:* Amber or blue glass bottles
NOTE: Grapeseed and jojoba are excellent oils for perfume bases because they won't alter the essential oil's aroma. Jojoba is a natural preservative and will never go rancid.

## BASIC FORMULA FOR SOLID PERFUMES

2 ounces beeswax
1/8 ounce oil
1/4 ounce essential oil blend

Melt the beeswax and oil in a double boiler over medium heat. Remove from the heat and let cool. Just before the mixture hardens completely, stir in the essential oils.
**Makes about 2 ounces**

*Preparation Time:* 25 minutes
*Shelf Life:* Indefinite
*Storage:* Amber or blue glass bottles

### EAU DE PERFUME AND EAU DE TOILETTE

## BASIC FORMULA FOR EAU DE PERFUME

1 1/2 parts each essential oil blend and water or rose water
7 parts vodka, rum, or brandy

Combine the ingredients and let set for 3 to 6 weeks.

*Preparation Time:* 10 minutes
*Shelf Life:* Indefinite
*Storage:* Amber or blue glass bottles

### Examples

YLANG-YLANG: For the essential oil blend, combine 10 parts ylang-ylang, 5 parts each neroli and rose, and 3 parts bergamot.

HONEYSUCKLE: For the essential oil blend, combine 15 parts cassia, rose, tuberose, and violet, and $\frac{1}{2}$ part neroli and bitter almond.

VERBENA: For the essential oil blend, combine 6 parts lemongrass and $\frac{1}{2}$ parts bergamot and orange.

## BASIC FORMULA FOR EAU DE TOILETTE 🎁

1 part essential oils
1.2 parts water or floral water
8 parts vodka, rum, or brandy

Combine the ingredients and let set for 3 to 6 weeks.

*Preparation Time:* 10 minutes
*Shelf Life:* Indefinite
*Storage:* Amber or blue glass bottles

### Examples

EAU DE LAVENDER: For the essential oil blend, use 15 parts lavender and 1 part bergamot.

EAU DE SPICE: For the essential oil blend, use 3 parts bergamot, 1 part lemon, $\frac{1}{2}$ part sandalwood, and $\frac{1}{4}$ part each lavender and clove.

EAU DE ELDER FLOWER: For the essential oil blend, use 2 parts each jasmine and bergamot and 1 part palmerosa.

### COLOGNES

**COMMONLY USED ESSENTIAL OILS IN COLOGNES.** Rosemary, lemon, orange flower, lavender, cinnamon, clove, rose, neroli, vanilla, bergamot, orange, rose, ylang-ylang

**NOT QUITE SO COMMONLY USED ESSENTIAL OILS IN COLOGNES.** Cardamom, ginger, geranium, sandalwood, patchouli, honeysuckle, grapefruit

## BASIC FORMULA FOR COLOGNES 🎁

$\frac{1}{2}$ part essential oil blend
$1\frac{1}{2}$ parts water or floral water
8 parts vodka, rum, or brandy

Combine the ingredients and let set for 3 to 6 weeks.

*Preparation Time:* 10 minutes
*Shelf Life:* Indefinite
*Storage:* Amber or blue glass bottles

### Examples

COLOGNE I: For the essential oil blend, use 15 parts neroli, 10 parts bergamot, 5 parts lemon, and 1 part rosemary.

COLOGNE II: For the essential oil blend, use 10 parts each lemon and rosemary, 5 parts each lavender and bergamot, and $\frac{1}{4}$ part each cinnamon and clove.

COLOGNE III: For the essential oil blend, use 10 parts bergamot, 4 parts lavender, 2 parts rose geranium, and 1 part each patchouli and neroli.

## FRESH INGREDIENT COLOGNE

### Examples

INFUSION OF SCENTS: Combine 1 to 2 tablespoons lemon balm, lemon peel, nutmeg, coriander seeds, cloves, cinnamon, and angelica root in a quart jar. Cover with rum, vodka, or brandy. Let set for a month or more. Strain and bottle.

EXAMPLE II: Combine a small handful each of rose petals, lavender flowers, and lemon and orange peel. Cover with rum, vodka, or brandy. Cover and let set for up to a month. Strain and bottle.

# Hair Care

Look to more than your shampoo and conditioner to establish a beautiful, bouncy head of hair. Healthy hair is a sign of a healthy body. Just as you can quickly tell the health of a dog by its coat, so too with humans and their hair. If a dog has a less than lustrous coat, the first thing to do is give it oils rich in omega-3 essential fatty acids such as flax seed oil. The same for humans, although there are other reasons for dull, lifeless, or falling hair, such as chronic illness.

## SOAP SHAMPOOS VERSUS DETERGENT SHAMPOOS

Choosing between soap and detergent for shampoo is an important decision and one that affects how you make shampoo at home. Soap and detergent shampoos are not the same thing, and there are advantages and disadvantages to both for your hair. Soap is the purest choice next to using soapy herbs such as soap bark. However—and this is a big *however*—if you have hard water, soap can cause soap scum, which will dull your hair. Whatever the disadvantages of detergent shampoos, they leave the hair shiny and far from dull. What to do? Herbal body care books are about evenly split on this issue: Many books recommend buying a detergent shampoo and adding herbs to it; others call for herbs and liquid castile soap. You are the only person who can decide what compromises you will tolerate for your hair. I alternate between soap- and detergent-based products. If my hair seems dull from using soap, I switch back to a detergent for a while.

Because hair should be slightly acidic, if you use soap shampoo (which is alkaline), you will need to rinse the hair with an acid such as lemon juice or organic apple cider vinegar, to restore its acid mantle.

## HAIR TREATMENTS

**Hair Loss Tips and Treatments.** It is particularly hard on women when they lose their hair. There are many different reasons for hair loss—pregnancy and other hormonal fluctuations, chronic illness, nutritional or protein deficiencies, even too-tight ponytails—so there is no one magic bullet for helping it grow back. I lost a lot of hair during my bout with Lyme disease, and I tried many of the following treatments with success.

HERBS FOR HAIR GROWTH AND PREVENTING HAIR LOSS. Nettle, rosemary, lavender, yarrow, jaborandi (this herb is in a lot of folk recipes), maidenhair fern, burdock root, oat straw, and wild cherry bark.

ACUPUNCTURE. Hair loss has been attributed to a weakness in the kidney meridian, and treatment can significantly help the regrowth of hair. I can personally attest to this, having had my hair grow back profusely during an intensive twice-a-week acupunc-

ture treatment for the kidney and immune system.

OMEGA-3 OILS. Take 1 tablespoon omega-3 oils every day for a few months. You will know you have enough omega-3 oils if your skin does not need a moisturizer.

NETTLE AND BURDOCK ROOT TEA. Nettle is the most universally recommended herb for hair loss.

## BUYER'S GUIDE
### DETERGENT SHAMPOO

SODIUM lauryl sulfate, the detergent usually found in commercial shampoos, is a synthetic substance that can be drying and harsh for the hair and cause eye irritation, allergic reactions, and hair loss. Sodium lauryl sulfate is frequently combined with TEA (triethanolamine), DEA (diethanolamine), or MEA (mono-ethanolamine), which can cause the formation of the carcinogenic substances nitrosamines. To be on the safe side, add the antioxidant vitamins A, C, and E combination of preservatives, described on page 36, to any product that contains TEA, DEA, or MEA. The addition of antioxidants will help protect against nitrosamine contamination.

Also be on the lookout for toxic antibacterial agents in shampoos, such as Germall (imadazolidinyl urea) and quaternium-15. These are registered with the Environmental Protection Agency as pesticides. And some shampoos have solvents (VOCs) such as butyl alcohol.

Aubrey Organics does not use detergents or synthetic chemicals in its shampoos; instead it uses coconut oil soap and herbal blends. I have used these shampoos for years because I feel they are as pure as anything I could make at home. The only drawback is for those who don't like to wash their hair every couple of days: Without drying detergents, the scalp's natural oils are more present.

Logona also has a line of pure shampoos, as does Real Purity Inc.; both lines are available by mail order (see Sources and Resources). Aubrey products are available in most health food stores.

## GOOD PLANTS FOR HEALTHY HAIR

SILICON and sulfur are excellent for hair. Herbs rich in these are nasturtium, watercress, nettle, rosemary, sage, seaweed, burdock root, horsetail, and lavender.

## NETTLE AND BURDOCK ROOT SCALP WASH

½ cup chopped nettle leaves
or chopped burdock root
2 cups water
2 cups organic apple cider vinegar

Combine the ingredients in a pan and bring to a boil, then reduce the heat and simmer for 5 minutes. Strain thoroughly and let cool. Rinse through the hair.

**Makes 4 cups**

*Preparation Time:* 15 minutes
*Shelf Life:* Enough for 1 treatment

CAYENNE PEPPER. Cayenne is a circulatory system stimulant, and circulation is important for hair growth. Look in health food stores for a cayenne tincture (rub some directly on bald spots every day) or capsicum, cayenne's essential oil (dilute 20 drops per cup water and rub on bald spots every day).

INFUSED OILS. Rub oils such as jojoba into your hair an hour or so before shampooing.

ROSEMARY AND LAVENDER. Infuse herbs in olive oil in a Crock-Pot, strain, and store in the refrigerator in a covered glass jar. Or add essential oils of rosemary and lavender to olive oil or jojoba in a glass jar; shake to blend.

HAIR BRUSHING. Brushing your hair promotes circulation in the scalp. Thorough brushing also helps distribute your hair's natural oils evenly.

### OILY HAIR TREATMENTS

EPSOM SALTS. Add 1 teaspoon Epsom salts to ½ cup shampoo; increase the amount of Epsom salts bit by bit as needed.

LEMON RINSE. Use lemon juice to rinse hair.

NEUTRAL HENNA HAIR TREATMENT. Mix ½ cup neutral henna with 1 cup boiling water and 1 teaspoon organic apple cider vinegar or lemon juice. Massage into damp hair and let set overnight, if possible.

### DRY HAIR TREATMENTS

HOT OIL TREATMENTS. See below. Avocado is particularly good for dry hair.

### DAMAGED HAIR TREATMENTS

BLACKSTRAP MOLASSES. Massage blackstrap molasses into the hair. Cover. Let set for as many hours as possible; rinse.

ACIDIC SHAMPOO AND RINSE. Avoiding the eyes, add lemon juice or organic apple cider vinegar to your shampoo and rinse water.

### DANDRUFF TREATMENTS

HERBS FOR DANDRUFF. Sage; birch; peppermint; comfrey; high-sulfur herbs such as nasturtium, watercress, nettle, rosemary, seaweed, and lemongrass.

EGG YOLK. Add egg yolks (high in sulfur) to shampoo. Discard leftovers.

DANDRUFF BRUSH. Infuse nettle in water or organic apple cider vinegar. Soak your hairbrush in the infusion for a minute or two, then brush your hair for a few minutes.

GLYCERIN EMOLLIENT. Add an extra teaspoon of vegetable glycerin to shampoo.

FRUIT ACIDS FOR DANDRUFF. Add fruit acids (see list on page 108) to shampoos; they will help remove the dead cells.

ALOE SCALP MASSAGE. Massage aloe vera gel into the scalp before washing.

HOT OIL TREATMENTS. See below.

NEUTRAL HENNA TREATMENT. See Oily Hair Treatments on page 188.

### PRESHAMPOO HAIR LOTIONS

## PREWASH SIMPLES

*Massage any of these simple ingredients into your hair. Let set for an hour before washing your hair as usual.*

Mashed avocado, egg yolk (add yogurt, lemon peel, and/or kelp, if desired), honey (soften with lemon juice, if desired), mayonnaise, yogurt, molasses, oils and essential oils

### HAIR OILS AND HOT OIL TREATMENTS

Oils (such as jojoba or avocado) are good emollients for your hair. Warm the oil, then remove from the heat. Add up to 3 drops essential oils (such as rosemary and lavender) per ounce, and massage deeply into the scalp. Cover the head with a towel.

### HAIR TONICS AND TREATMENTS

## ALOE VERA GEL ✘

Aloe vera gel

Massage into the hair. Let rest for 30 minutes or so, then wash and rinse as usual.

## OIL-RICH CONDITIONER ✘

2 ounces aloe vera gel
½ teaspoon oil (such as avocado or jojoba)
2 ounces organic apple cider vinegar
1 ounce powdered milk

Combine the ingredients in a glass jar and stir to blend.
**Makes about ½ cup**

*Preparation Time:* 2 minutes
*Shelf Life:* Discard leftovers

### Variation

OIL AND OIL: Use just fruit or nut oil, and add 10 drops per ounce essential oil of choice.

#### SHAMPOO

*A good shampoo should contain a medicinal or cleansing herb, an emollient, an herb for color, an herb for conditioning, scents if you like. . . .*
—*JEANNE ROSE*

## BASIC SOAP SHAMPOO FORMULA 🎁

10 ounces water (herbal water preferred)
1 to 2 ounces liquid castile soap
(the less the better)

1 teaspoon glycerin or ¼ teaspoon oil
20 to 35 drops essential oil (optional)

Make the herbal water infusion by putting a handful of herbs in a pint mason jar and covering with boiling water. Cover tightly, let set overnight, then strain. Add the soap, glycerin, and essential oil (if using); cover and shake to blend. Shampoo as usual.
**Makes 1½ cups**

*Preparation Time:* 15 minutes with herbal water, otherwise just a few minutes
*Shelf Life:* Indefinite with water; a few weeks refrigerated with herbal water
*Storage:* Glass jar with a screw top
*Caution:* Essential oils can harm the eyes, so be sure not to get shampoos, rinses, or conditioners in the eyes. Don't add more than 3 drops essential oil per ounce of base preparation.

Variations

PROTEIN SHAMPOO: Add 3 egg whites with the soap; rinse the hair with organic apple cider vinegar after shampooing. Discard leftovers.

ROSEMARY LAVENDER SHAMPOO: Use a strong rosemary infusion for the herbal water, and use lavender essential oil. Lavender and rosemary are renowned for the hair and very antiseptic.

BAY RUM OILY HAIR SHAMPOO: Substitute 2 ounces bay rum (see page 208 for recipe) for 2 ounces of the herbal water, and 1 ounce witch hazel extract for 1 ounce of the herbal water. Skip the glycerin and essential oil.

BAY RUM FOR DRY HAIR: Substitute bay rum (see page 208 for recipe) for 2 ounces of the herbal water.

ALOE SHAMPOO: Substitute 2 ounces aloe vera gel for the herbal water.

BODY BUILDING SHAMPOO: Add 1 mashed avocado. Avocado is rich in nutrients and emollient oil. Discard leftovers.

ANTISEPTIC CLOVE DANDRUFF SHAMPOO: Add 10 to 20 drops essential oil of clove and an extra teaspoon vegetable glycerin.

## BASIC BIRCH SOAP SHAMPOO FORMULA 🎁

*You may be surprised to learn that birch was a major component of nineteenth-century shampoos. It was considered an excellent hair conditioner. I like to use black birch, sometimes known as sweet birch, for its wintergreenlike fragrance.*

6 ounces birch water
4 ounces organic apple cider vinegar
1 ounce castile soap
1 teaspoon vegetable glycerin
Natural preservatives and essential oils,
as desired.

Make the birch infusion by packing a quart jar with thin, pliable birch branches about 6 inches long and covering with boiling water; cover tightly, let set for 8 hours or so, then strain. Combine the infusion and the rest of the ingredients in a glass jar and shake well.
**Makes 1½ cups**

*Preparation Time:* About 20 minutes
*Shelf Life:* 6 months
*Storage:* Glass jar with a screw top

## Variations

RUM BIRCH SHAMPOO: Substitute rum for the vinegar; add up to 3 drops essential oil of birch bud per ounce.

BIRCH DANDRUFF SHAMPOO: The high salicylic content of birch is beneficial for dandruff. Increase the vegetable glycerin by 1 teaspoon, and add 1 ounce aloe vera gel.

## BASIC DETERGENT SHAMPOO FORMULA

*For the detergent base for your shampoo, choose a basic shampoo without artificial fragrance and dyes. The Weleda brand has a good, simple detergent with rosemary that I recommend for this base. It is available in health food stores.*

10 ounces water (herbal water
infusion preferred)
2 to 4 ounces detergent shampoo base
1 teaspoon each glycerin and avocado oil
20 drops essential oils, if desired

To make the herbal water, place a handful of herbs in a quart mason jar and cover with boiling water; cover tightly, let set overnight, then strain. Combine the herbal water, shampoo base, glycerin, and essential oils if using in a glass jar, and shake to blend. Wash your hair as usual.

**Makes 1½ cups**

*Preparation Time:* 15 minutes with herbal water, otherwise just a few minutes
*Shelf Life:* Indefinite with water; a few weeks refrigerated with herbal water
*Storage:* Glass jar with a screw top

## Variation

OILY HAIR DETERGENT SHAMPOO: Substitute lemon juice or organic apple cider vinegar for the glycerin and oil. Lemon juice reduces the shelf life to 1 week.

## BASIC SOAP- AND DETERGENT-FREE SHAMPOO FORMULA 🎁

3 ounces soap bark
Water
5 ounces vodka, rum, or brandy
1 ounce glycerin
20 drops essential oils, if desired
(lavender is a good choice)

Place the soap bark in a pan and cover with water. Bring to a boil, then reduce the heat and simmer for 2 hours. Add more water as it evaporates. Strain thoroughly. Pour the mixture into a quart mason jar, adding water if necessary to make 10 ounces of liquid. Add the alcohol, glycerin, and essential oils (if using). Shake to blend. Shampoo as usual.

**Makes 2 cups**

*Preparation Time:* About 20 minutes
*Shelf Life:* 1 to 2 weeks
*Storage:* Glass jar with a screw top

## BASIC DRY SHAMPOO FORMULA

*I remember using dry shampoo in the old days when I had to stay in the hospital for two weeks having my appendix out. Fortunately, most operations require much less bed rest these days, but for those who can't wash their hair with water, here is a dry rescue remedy for dirty hair. Orris root has a lovely, mild smell of violets. Almond meal is easy to make from whole almonds in a blender.*

Equal parts cornmeal or other flour, almond
meal, and orris root powder

Combine the ingredients in a bowl. Dust into the hair and leave on for 10 minutes before brushing it out.

*Preparation Time:* 10 minutes
*Shelf Life:* 1 year frozen
*Storage:* Plastic container

## BASIC CLAY SHAMPOO FORMULA ✗

*For millennia people in the Middle East and Africa have washed their hair and bodies with Rhassoul clay, found in the Atlas Mountains of North Africa. The clay binds oil and dirt particles and washes them away. There are no suds.*

Rhassoul clay (commonly available in health
food stores or through Logona's mail order
catalog; see Sources and Resources)

Wet the hair. Massage in a few tablespoons clay. Let the clay set for a few minutes before rinsing thoroughly with warm water.

*Preparation Time:* None
*Shelf Life:* Indefinite
*Storage:* Glass jar with a screw top

### HAIR RINSES AND CONDITIONERS

Hair rinses and conditioners are meant to soften and nourish the hair, help in detangling, and return the hair to its naturally acidic pH. Use conditioners and rinses after you have rinsed out the shampoo, and leave them in your hair for 10 minutes or so before rinsing.

Organic apple cider vinegar is a good rinse for the hair and scalp; it not only returns them to their naturally acidic pH, it is an AHA and removes dead skin cells from the scalp and residue from the hair.

### RINSES FOR DANDRUFF

## VINEGAR AND NETTLE DANDRUFF RINSE

*Nettle is rich in nutrients, silica, and flavonoids. It is one of the top herbs used by herbalists for strengthening and repairing hair.*

Large handful nettle leaves
4 cups organic apple cider vinegar
1 tablespoon vegetable glycerin
Up to 40 drops essential oil such as
birch bud oil (rich in sulfur)

Place the nettle leaves in a quart mason jar. Add the vinegar, cover tightly, and let set for 3 to 6 weeks. Strain thoroughly. Combine the infusion with the glycerin and essential oil. Use as a rinse, or dip a hairbrush into the mixture before brushing the hair each morning.
**Makes 4 cups**

*Preparation Time:* About 15 minutes (plus 3 to 6 weeks for the infusion)
*Shelf Life:* Indefinite; discard if you see mold
*Storage:* Glass jar with a screw top

## ALL-PURPOSE ANTISEPTIC RINSE FOR DANDRUFF ✂

*Vinegar, rum, and cloves are combined in this easy-to-make and powerfully antifungal and antibacterial hair rinse. Clove oil is slightly numbing.*

8 ounces organic apple cider vinegar
2 ounces bay rum
10 drops essential oil of clove

Combine the ingredients in a pint mason jar. Shake to blend. Pour out about ¼ cup and use to rinse the hair after washing. Let the rinse sit on the hair for a few minutes before rinsing thoroughly with warm water.
**Makes 1¼ cups**

*Preparation Time:* A few minutes
*Shelf Life:* Indefinite
*Storage:* Glass jar with a screw top

**EMOLLIENT CONDITIONERS**

## GLYCERIN CONDITIONER

*Glycerin will help the hair retain moisture, and lemon juice will cleanse the scalp.*

5 ounces herbal water (such as rose, lavender, chamomile, calendula, or nettle)
2 ounces glycerin
1 ounce lemon juice

To make the herbal water, place a small handful of herb in a pint mason jar. Cover with boiling water, cover tightly, and let set overnight. Strain. Place the herbal water, glycerin, and lemon juice in a glass jar. Shake to blend. Use ¼ cup as a rinse after rinsing out your shampoo. Rinse with warm water.
**Makes 1 cup**

*Preparation Time:* About 15 minutes
*Shelf Life:* 1 week or so
*Storage:* Glass jar with a screw top

## LICORICE ROOT RINSE

*Licorice is emollient and cleansing and an excellent herb for dry or damaged hair.*

16 ounces licorice water (made by decoction)
2 ounces vegetable glycerin

Make the licorice decoction by placing 4 or 5 pieces of licorice stick in a pan and covering with about 4 cups water. Simmer over low heat for about 1 hour. Cool, then strain. Combine the licorice water and glycerin in a jar, and shake to blend. Use ¼ to ½ cup at a time as a hair rinse.
**Makes about 2 cups**

*Preparation Time:* About 5 minutes
*Shelf Life:* About 1 week refrigerated
*Storage:* Glass jar with a screw top

Variations
ROSEMARY CREAM CONDITIONER: Infuse rosemary in water for the herbal water (see page 32 for directions on making infusions).

PROTEIN CONDITIONER: Halve the recipe; substitute organic apple cider vinegar for the licorice water, and add 2 egg whites and ½ ounce wheat germ oil when you add the glycerin. Discard leftovers.

GREEN TEA RINSE: Substitute steeped, cooled, and strained green tea for the licorice water.

## FRUIT ACID RINSE FOR HAIR ✄

*Alpha-hydroxy acids are good for the hair as well as the skin, sloughing off damaged hair particles and residue. Queen of Hungary Water is full of herbs that are excellent for hair care because they are nourishing, emollient, and antiseptic.*

¼ cup Queen of Hungary Water (see page 137), lemon juice, or organic apple cider vinegar

Pour the liquid through the hair. Leave on for a few minutes before rinsing with warm water.
**Makes enough for 1 rinse**

*Preparation Time:* None

## CHLORINE-GREEN RECOVERY RINSE ✄

*Those who swim in chlorinated pools know that the chemical can cause hair to become an ugly greenish color. Tomato juice can stop this chemical reaction.*

¼ cup tomato juice

Massage tomato juice into wet hair. Let set for a few minutes before washing as usual.
**Makes enough for 1 rinse**

*Preparation Time:* None

## ESSENTIAL OIL DETANGLERS ✄

*Besides helping the hair detangle, rosemary and lavender help reduce hair loss.*

5 drops essential oil of rosemary or lavender

Sprinkle the drops directly onto your hair, and rub in with your fingertips.

*Preparation Time:* None

HAIR STYLING

## FLAX HAIR SET

*Besides helping hair to set, flax gel is softening for the hair and scalp.*

1 tablespoon flax seed
¾ cup water, or to cover

Place the seeds in a small pan, and cover with water. Bring to a boil, then reduce the heat and simmer until gelatinous (about 10 minutes). The consistency should be that of a gel. Strain out the seeds; you may need to remove some with a spoon. Dilute the mixture with more water if too thick. Dip your comb into the gel and comb through the hair before setting.
**Makes ¾ cup**

*Preparation Time:* About 20 minutes
*Shelf Life:* 1 week refrigerated
*Storage:* Glass jar with a screw top

## LIGHT AND LEMON HAIR SPRAY

3 or 4 lemons
Water

Slice the lemons and cover with water in a pan. Simmer for 1 hour, adding more water as it evaporates. Let cool, then strain. Pour the lemon liquid into a pump spray bottle.
**Makes 2 to 3 cups**

*Preparation Time:* About 10 minutes plus simmering time
*Shelf Life:* About 1 week refrigerated
*Storage:* Pump spray bottle or glass jar with a screw top

## EGG WHITE STYLING MOUSSE ✘

2 egg whites

Beat the egg whites until stiff. Rub into the hair and let dry.
**Makes enough for 1 use**

*Preparation Time:* 10 minutes
*Shelf Life:* None

## ROSEMARY HAIR SPRAY FOR FLYAWAY HAIR

1 cup strong rosemary infusion

To make the infusion, place 2 teaspoons rosemary in a coffee mug, and cover with boiling water. Cover and let set for a few hours. Strain and pour into a spray bottle.
**Makes 1 cup**

*Preparation Time:* 5 minutes
*Shelf Life:* 1 week refrigerated
*Storage:* Glass jar with a screw top

## HAIR VOLUMIZER ✘

½ cup coconut milk

Place the coconut milk in a spray bottle, and spray your wet hair. Blow dry.
**Makes ½ cup**

*Preparation Time:* None
*Shelf Life:* About 1 week refrigerated
*Storage:* Glass jar with a screw top

### HAIR DYES

Natural dyes look much more natural than synthetic ones, and they are free of coal tar dyes. But use these homemade dyes at your own risk. Test them first on an inconspicuous spot.

### TIPS FOR DYING HAIR WITH NATURAL MATERIALS

* Don't use metal for mixing hair dyes.
* Always test hair dye on a few strands or a small patch of your hair before you dye the whole head.
* Remove dye stains from the skin with acids such as lemon juice or organic apple cider vinegar, soap and water, or oil.
* Wear gloves when mixing and applying the dyes.

* Dyes can stain clothing, so wear old clothing or an apron.
* Herbal rinses are not long-lasting, so they will need to be repeated at every shampoo.

### FIXATIVES

* Use organic apple cider vinegar or lemon juice as a fixative for henna.

## BUYER'S GUIDE

### HAIR DYES

IF you choose to have your hair dyed using commercial synthetic dyes (most so-called natural dyes are actually synthetic; they just don't contain as many chemicals), ask your hairdresser to highlight instead of dye the hair. In the highlighting process, the dyes do not reach your scalp. Aveda in particular has a line of dyes that contain fewer chemicals.

If you choose to dye your hair yourself, Logona has the purest line of hair dyes I have seen—no FD&C (Food, Drug, and Cosmetic; certified by the FDA) dyes—and the result looks natural. Another good brand is Herbaltint, available in health food stores. A good source of henna is Rainbow Henna, also found in health food stores. See Sources and Resources.

* Use neutral henna as a fixative for herbal and vegetable dyes. The traditional recipes call for alum, but that is an aluminum salt and is best avoided.

Henna, a strong dye, available in health food stores, is derived from the leaves of a Middle Eastern plant. Be aware that white hair will take henna differently than nonwhite hair, so if you have some "salt and pepper" hair, using a henna dye will result in two hair colors. You may also be surprised at how red hair can become when dyed with henna, although now you can buy henna appropriate for a variety of different hair colors (Rainbow Henna; see Sources and Resources). I once dyed my hair with henna, and the white became bright red. Adding black tea, sage, and vegetable dyes helps tone down the carrot-top look. If you use a henna dye and the result is too red for your liking, rub olive oil into your hair and leave it in for an hour, then wash as usual. This will tone down the color a little. Henna is also drying to the hair, which is why a neutral henna rinse is good for oily hair and dandruff. Add a bit of oil to henna mixes if you have dry hair.

## BASIC HENNA PASTE FORMULA

Enough boiling water to make a paste
1 cup henna

In a glass or plastic bowl, add enough water to the henna to make a paste. Mix until creamy. Wearing gloves, apply to the hair, working in small sections at a time. With a brush, first work the henna into the roots, and then the ends. Cover the hair with a hot towel that has been wrung out. Leave it on for a few minutes for a light dye, 30 to 45 minutes for a darker dye. Rinse thoroughly. Rinse once with 2 tablespoons organic apple cider vinegar to help the dye hold. Wash as usual.

**Makes enough for 1 dye**

*Preparation Time:* 5 minutes
*Shelf Life:* None

Variations

BROWN-RED: Make the paste with strong black tea instead of water.

TO TONE DOWN RED: Make the paste with black coffee instead of water.

DEEP RED: Substitute a logwood chips decoction for the water. Make a decoction by simmering the chips in enough water to cover.

DARKER RED: Add 2 tablespoons ground cloves, or substitute red wine for the water.

SAGE FOR BROWN: Substitute a strong sage infusion for the water; add 2 tablespoons ground cloves.

WALNUT BROWN: Boil walnut hulls in water until the water is a rich, dark brown. Strain. Use the walnut hull infusion to make the henna paste.

AUBURN: Substitute a strong chamomile flower infusion for the water.

RINSES, HIGHLIGHTS, AND LIGHTENERS

## CHAMOMILE BLOND RINSE

4 cups strong chamomile flower infusion

Make the infusion according to the directions on page 32. Let cool, then strain. Rinse into the hair. Let dry.

**Makes 4 cups**

*Preparation Time:* 15 minutes
*Shelf Life:* 1 week; refrigerate
*Storage:* Glass jar with a screw top

Variations

RHUBARB ROOT: Substitute a rhubarb decoction for the chamomile.

CALENDULA INFUSION: Substitute calendula for the chamomile.

CITRUS JUICE: Substitute $\frac{1}{4}$ cup citrus juice for the herb infusion.

## SAGE BROWN RINSE

4 cups strong sage infusion

Make the infusion according to the directions on page 32. Let cool, then strain. Rinse into the hair. Let dry.

**Makes 4 cups**

*Preparation Time:* 15 minutes
*Shelf Life:* 1 week
*Storage:* Glass jar with a screw top

Variations

WALNUT WASH: Make 4 cups strong walnut hull decoction (boil until dark brown); strain, then let cool. Rinse the hair with this every time you shampoo.

GRAY RINSE II: Combine 2 cups each strong sage and black tea infusions. Rinse into the hair and let dry.

WALNUT AND SAGE GRAY RINSE III: Combine 2 cups each walnut hull decoction (see above) and strong black tea.

ONION SKIN AND WALNUT RINSE: Prepare 2 cups each strong infusion of onion skins and walnut hull decoction. The onions will give the rinse a slightly reddish cast and the walnuts a brown cast, so combine according to your preference.

ROSEMARY RINSE: Substitute rosemary for the sage.

OREGANO RINSE: Substitute oregano for the sage.

# Hand and Nail Care

## THE NATURAL MANICURE

**ACCESSORIES.** Cardboard emery board, manicure sticks (sometimes called orangewood sticks), fine pumice-stone sand stick, fine-grit block, smoothing files, and buffing chamois.

**1. FILE NAILS.** Always do this when your nails are dry, so as not to fray the edges. Place an emery board under the nail edge at a slant and file in one direction only. File into oval or square shapes, not points, which can weaken the nail. Replace emery boards every eight uses; an uneven grain can cause uneven filing.

**2. WASH AND SOAK NAILS.** Wash your hands, and soak your nails in warm, sudsy water or a fruit acid solution such as buttermilk or organic apple cider vinegar (see list of fruit acids, page 108) to soften the cuticles.

**3. APPLY A CUTICLE SOFTENER.** The cuticle is the tough skin that overlaps the nail near the half-moon at the base of the nail. Cold-pressed fruit and nut oils such as sesame or avocado oil, or the liquid wax jojoba, work well to soften this area (see below for other recipes). Try to do this every day.

**4. CLEAN AND SHAPE CUTICLES.** Use the blunt end of an orangewood manicure stick to gently push the cuticles back from the nails. Use the pointed side of the stick to clean under the nails. Avoid cutting your cuticles; they are there to protect the nail and will only grow back thicker, and cutting them increases the risk of infection. Put a drop of oil on the cuticle, and massage it in.

**5. SAND AND BUFF NAILS.** Dry your hands completely. Sand and polish the top of each nail with a fine pumice-stone sand stick to remove any ridges. Do the same thing with a fine-grit block. Once the ridges are removed, smooth the top of the nail with a smoothing file and a buffing chamois. You'd be amazed at how shiny your nails will look following these steps, almost as if you were wearing a clear polish. You can choose a more natural, less-shiny matte finish if preferred, by not using the finest grade buffing files.

**6. HAND MASK (OPTIONAL).** If you have the time, cover your hands with a nourishing fruit acid mask (see page 154 for ideas and recipes); let set for 15 minutes or so, then rinse.

**7. MASSAGE WITH MOISTURIZER.** Massage your hands with a healing and moisturizing

## TOXIC NAIL POLISHES

HAVE you ever sat on a train—or worse, an airplane—near someone polishing their nails? The smell of the solvents can be overwhelming. There are no environmentally safe nail polishes or nail polish removers on the market. Almost all contain toluene (toxic) and formaldehyde (a known carcinogen). There are some toluene- and formaldehyde-free varieties, but there are none without petroleum solvents of some sort. Petroleum solvents are long-lasting in the environment; they are stored in body fat and passed on in breast milk. Nails can be beautiful without nail polish. I once had my nails "done" in a natural way at a salon for a television show where my hands would be very visible. Friends who saw the show still compliment me on how beautiful my nails looked.

cream or lotion (see page 141) or hand softener (see page 202).

### NATURAL NAIL COLORS

There are times when color on nails is nice. At the very least, young girls love coloring their nails when they play dress-up. Unfortunately, there are no nail polishes without toxic solvents. Alkanet root makes a red color that you can put on a child's nails, but it will quickly wash off. To make an alkanet paint, prepare a small batch of oil and alkanet infusion (3 tablespoons oil to 1 tablespoon alkanet) by heating them together in a small pan for 10 minutes. Let cool, strain, and paint onto the nails.

### NAIL WHITENER AND STAIN REMOVER

*Three percent hydrogen peroxide is a natural nail whitener and stain remover.*

3 percent hydrogen peroxide

Dab the hydrogen peroxide on a cotton ball and rub onto your nails.

### NAIL POLISHING PASTE

*Ridges and grooves can be sanded off by mild abrasion with these minerals.*

4 ounces pulverized chalk (also called calcium carbonate or whiting)
2 ounces baking soda
Enough glycerin to make a paste

Combine the ingredients in a bowl. Scoop some of the paste onto a soft cloth and gently rub back and forth over your nails.
**Makes ¾ cup**

*Preparation Time:* A few minutes
*Shelf Life:* Indefinite
*Storage:* Glass jar with a screw top

NAIL SOAKS

## BASIC BENEFICIAL NAIL SOAK FORMULA

*The herb horsetail has a high silica content, which will help build healthy nails.*

Small handful horsetail
Organic apple cider vinegar, to cover

Place the horsetail in a pint mason jar, and cover with the vinegar. Cover and let set for 3 to 6 weeks. Strain completely. Dab a cotton ball into the infusion, and dab on your nails.
**Makes 2 cups**

*Preparation Time:* About 15 minutes
*Shelf Life:* Indefinite; discard if mold grows
*Storage:* Glass jar with a screw top

## OIL E ✘

*Choose the oil according to your skin type. Those with dry skin and damaged cuticles should consider avocado or apricot kernel oil; those with oily skin should try a nongreasy oil, such as coconut.*

2 to 3 vitamin E capsules (200 i.u.) or
1 teaspoon wheat germ oil
¼ cup oil

Cut the vitamin E capsules and empty their contents into a bowl. Add the oil. Stir to blend. Soak your nails in this mixture for 5 to 10 minutes, or massage it into your nails daily.
**Makes ¼ cup**

*Preparation Time:* A few minutes
*Shelf Life:* 6 months refrigerated
*Storage:* Glass jar with a screw top

Variation
FOR STRONG NAILS: Combine 1 teaspoon each olive oil, aloe vera gel, and wheat germ oil; massage into your nails daily.

## OLD-FASHIONED POTATO WATER SOAK

*Potatoes show up again and again in the old folk recipes for nail care.*

1 potato
Enough water to cover

Cut up the potato into a pan and cover with water. Bring to a boil, then reduce the heat and simmer until the potato is soft. Strain and let cool. Soak your hands in the water.
**Makes about 1 cup**

*Preparation Time:* 15 minutes
*Shelf Life:* Discard

## FRUIT ACID CLEANSING SOAK ✘

*Alpha-hydroxy acids exfoliate and cleanse the skin.*

1 cup milk or other fruit acid, such as organic apple cider vinegar or lemon juice
(see page 108)

Place the milk in a bowl, and soak your hands for 5 to 10 minutes. Rinse and pat dry.
**Makes 1 cup**

*Preparation Time:* None
*Shelf Life:* Discard

## CUTICLE CREAMS

## LANOLIN CREAM SIMPLE ✖

*Lanolin is not only lubricating, it helps the cuticles retain moisture.*

Anhydrous lanolin

Squirt a dab out of the tube onto the nail area and massage into your cuticles.

## VITAMIN E SIMPLE ✖

*Wheat germ oil contains large quantities of vitamin E as well as other antioxidants.*

½ teaspoon wheat germ oil

Dab some on your finger and massage around your nails. Wash away the residue.

## CUTICLE ICE

*Menthol herbs are stimulating and antiseptic.*

1½ tablespoons oil
5 drops each essential oils of peppermint and eucalyptus

Combine the ingredients. Dab some on your finger and massage around your cuticles. Let

set for 5 minutes before washing the residue from your hands.
**Makes 1½ tablespoons**

*Preparation Time:* 1 or 2 minutes
*Shelf Life:* 6 months refrigerated
*Storage:* Glass jar with a screw top

## CUTICLE CREAM

*Vinegar softens cuticles; oil moisturizes and lubricates.*

3 tablespoons each olive oil and organic apple cider vinegar
1 egg yolk

Whip the ingredients together in a bowl. Dab some onto your fingers and massage into your cuticles. Let set for 5 minutes before washing the residue from your hands. Buy eggs from organic farms that test for salmonella contamination.
**Makes about ¼ cup**

*Preparation Time:* A few minutes
*Shelf Life:* Discard leftovers

## HAND WASHING

Soap is alkaline and the skin is naturally slightly acidic. After washing your hands, it is important to restore the skin's acid mantle. You can do this by adding 1 tablespoon lemon or organic apple cider vinegar to the rinse water. Use warm water when you wash your hands with soap to promote lathering.

## HAND CLEANSERS AND SOFTENERS

### FAMOUS SOFT HANDS FORMULA

2 beaten eggs
1 tablespoon honey
¼ cup almond meal

Whip together the eggs and honey in a bowl. Stir in the almond meal (you can easily grind almonds in a blender). Scoop some of the mixture into your hands and scrub. Rinse.
*Caution:* Raw eggs can be contaminated with salmonella. Buy eggs from organic farms that test for salmonella.
**Makes enough for 1 washing**

*Preparation Time:* About 5 minutes
*Shelf Life:* Discard leftovers

### Variations

COMFREY SOFTENER: For hands that are cut, scraped, or otherwise injured, add ½ ounce ground comfrey root when you add the almond meal. Comfrey root helps repair damaged tissue.

ALMOND AID: To make a more lubricating softener, add 1 teaspoon almond oil with the honey.

### ALMOND MEAL "SOAP" 🎁

*Abrasive and cleansing yet not rough on the hands due to the softening effect of almond meal, this is a good cleanser to use after gardening.*

½ cup almond meal
⅛ cup orris root, rice flour, or oatmeal
⅛ cup liquid castile soap
Essential oils of choice (oil of clove, bergamot, and neroli are traditionally used in this formula); about 10 drops per ounce

Mix the ingredients together in a bowl and scrub onto your dampened hands, adding warm water as needed for a good lather.
**Makes ¾ cup**

*Preparation Time:* About 5 minutes
*Shelf Life:* About 1 week
*Storage:* Glass jar with a screw top

### Variations

MILK AND HONEY: For a more softening effect, add ¼ cup powdered milk and 2 tablespoons lemon juice. Both are AHAs. Shelf life is 2 to 3 days refrigerated.

VIVA LA VINEGAR: For another AHA alternative, add 1 teaspoon organic apple cider vinegar.

### HEAVY-DUTY HAND CLEANER ✖

*Sand is the old-timer's hand cleanser—good to get off all sorts of gunk, such as engine oil and grime. Beach sand is the best; the next time you're at the shore, bring home a bucketful.*

4 ounces beach sand
1 ounce pumice powder
Enough glycerin to moisten

Combine the ingredients in a glass jar and stir to blend. Use about 1 tablespoon at a time, rubbing into the hands thoroughly. Rinse well.
**Makes about ½ cup**

*Preparation Time:* A few minutes
*Shelf Life:* Indefinite
*Storage:* Glass jar with a screw top

### HAND CREAMS AND LOTIONS

## CLASSIC HAND LOTION 🎁

*Among rose's attributes is that it is anti-inflammatory. Glycerin is lubricating and helps the skin retain moisture.*

¾ cup rose water (see page 139)
¼ cup glycerin
⅓ teaspoon grapefruit seed extract

Combine the rose water and glycerin in a glass jar, add the grapefruit seed extract, and shake or stir to blend.
**Makes 1 cup**

*Preparation Time:* 20 minutes
*Shelf Life:* Up to 6 months refrigerated; discard if you see mold
*Storage:* Glass jar with a screw top

Variations
BAY LOTION: Add 2 to 3 tablespoons bay rum, which will extend the shelf life.
WITCH HAZEL EXTRACT DELUXE: Add 2 to 3

tablespoons witch hazel extract for a more astringent and antiseptic cleanser.
HONEY HANDS: Add 1 tablespoon honey for increased softening of the skin.

## QUEEN VICTORIA'S HAND CREAM

*Follow the Basic Cream Formula (see page 30), using camphor oil (not synthetic camphor) for the 2½ ounces blended oil.*

## LANOLIN LOTION

*If the skin on your hands is dry and cracked, this is the lotion for you.*

¼ cup anhydrous lanolin
⅛ cup honey
⅛ cup almond oil
About 30 drops essential oil of lavender

Mix the ingredients vigorously with a whisk until well blended. Dab some on your fingers and massage into your hands.
**Makes ½ cup**

*Preparation Time:* About 5 minutes
*Shelf Life:* 6 months refrigerated
*Storage:* Glass jar with a screw top

## RICH LOTION FOR CHAPPED HANDS

*Rich, nutritious, lubricating oils characterize this formula.*

2½ ounces apricot kernel and avocado oil

1½ ounces shea butter

¼ ounce beeswax

4 ounces rose water

1 tablespoon pure vegetable glycerin

⅓ teaspoon grapefruit seed extract

20 or so drops essential oil, as desired

Combine the oils, shea butter, and beeswax in a double boiler over medium heat and cook until the wax is melted. Remove from the heat and add the rose water, glycerin, grapefruit seed extract, and essential oil. Blend with an electric mixer until creamy.

**Makes 1 cup**

*Preparation Time:* About 25 minutes
*Shelf Life:* 6 months, discard if you see mold
*Storage:* Glass jar with a screw top

Variation

COCONUT CREAM: Substitute coconut oil (for lathering) for the shea butter.

# Lip Care

Smooth, soft lips take years off your looks. Lips don't have oil glands; without the natural lubricating benefit of body oils, lips become easily chapped and have difficulty retaining moisture. They are particularly vulnerable to the sun and to the drying winds and heated rooms of winter. Lip balm is easy to make, and different variations will suit different needs. You can even make rosy red lip balm by adding alkanet root. If you have badly chapped lips, try drinking more water in addition to using a balm.

My nine-year-old daughter wouldn't even consider using my homemade lip balm until I made it tasty with peppermint flavoring oil; now she uses it daily in winter. As for selecting oils for your lip balm, I highly recommend trying different oils on your lips to choose the best one for you. I tried a drop of apricot kernel oil on my lips and never had to look further—it felt perfect. Other oils used in lip balms include sesame, almond, grapeseed, and pumpkin. It is important to include honey or glycerin in the balm; they are humectants and draw moisture from the air to hydrate the lips.

## BASIC LIP BALM FORMULA

*Stiff and waxy yet creamy enough to apply easily, this formula is perfect to put in little plastic jars with screw tops (available from herbalist supply catalogs) and carry with you.*

2 ounces oil

¼ ounce beeswax

1 teaspoon honey or glycerin

Natural flavoring oil such as vanilla, cherry, peppermint, lemon, or orange (optional)

Combine the oil and beeswax in a double boiler over medium heat and cook until the beeswax has melted. Remove from the heat, and stir in the honey. Blend with an electric handheld mixer until creamy. Add the flavoring oil to taste (if using), and stir to combine.

**Makes ¼ cup**

*Preparation Time:* 25 minutes

*Shelf Life:* 6 months
*Storage:* Plastic jar with a screw top

## Variations

HEALING HELP: Right before you stop beating the cream, add 1 teaspoon wheat germ oil for extra vitamin E.

THE THREE C'S BALM: Infuse camomile flowers, calendula flowers, and/or comfrey leaf or root in oil (see directions on page 32). Use 2 ounces of the infused oil in the lip balm. Discard after a week or so. A healing salve, this is perfect after a dehydrating illness when a person's lips can be exceedingly chapped and even cracked.

ALOE LIP BALM: Increase the beeswax by $\frac{1}{4}$ ounce, and add 2 tablespoons aloe vera gel to the balm while it is cooling.

ROSY RED BEAUTY BALM: Infuse 1 tablespoon alkanet root in the oil in a double boiler over low heat until the oil is deep red (about 15 minutes).

COCONUT CREAM: Substitute coconut oil for half of the oil as an increased protective barrier for the lips.

LILY'S FAVORITE: Use apricot kernel oil, and add peppermint oil to taste.

COCOA BUTTER LIPS: Substitute cocoa butter for half of the oil.

SUNBLOCK LIP BALM: Add 2 teaspoons zinc oxide powder when you add the honey.

LANOLIN LIPS: Substitute lanolin for the honey.

# Massage and Body Oils

Infusing oils with healing and soothing herbs takes massage to new heights. The Crock-Pot is an excellent utensil for infusing oils, because the process is quick (a few hours) and lessens the chance of the oils going rancid. Many herbalists use canola oil for this process. For directions, see page 33.

## BASIC MASSAGE OIL FORMULA ✗

*Massage therapists I have talked to love coconut oil for massage, because it melts on contact with the skin, leaves a protective barrier on the skin, has a slight lathering ability, and easily washes out of towels. Other oils stain, and towels become odorous after a while.*

Coconut oil

Scoop some coconut oil on your hand, taking only as much as you need at a time, and massage as usual.

*Preparation Time:* None
*Shelf Life:* Several months refrigerated

## Variations

BASIC INFUSED-OIL FORMULA: Infuse 1 cup canola oil (or other oil) with emollient and anti-inflammatory herbs such as calendula and chamomile.

BASIC ESSENTIAL OIL FORMULA: Use 5 drops essential oil per ounce of coconut oil.

THERAPEUTIC OIL: Infuse the oil with herbs having attributes for special needs (such as comfrey for psoriasis and eczema).

FRAGRANT BODY OIL: Use 4 drops jasmine, lavender, or ylang-ylang essential oil per ounce of coconut oil.

GOLDEN BODY OIL: So-called golden oil is sold by herbalists throughout the world for massage. Combine equal portions of almond, olive, and peanut oils.

## BODY BUTTER 🎁

*A semihard massage "oil," cocoa butter provides its distinctive aroma, which always seems to remind me of fun in the sun.*

½ cup coconut oil
¼ cup cocoa butter
5 to 10 drops essential oils of choice
(optional)

Soften the coconut oil and cocoa butter in a double boiler over medium heat. Remove from the heat and blend, adding essential oils (if using). **Makes ¾ cup**

*Preparation Time:* About 15 minutes
*Shelf Life:* About 6 months
*Storage:* Glass jar with a screw top

## OLD-FASHIONED GERMAN MASSAGE SOAP 🎁

*Slightly soapy and sticky yet softening, this soap definitely necessitates a shower or bath after using for a massage.*

3 parts glycerin
3 parts water
1 part soap shavings
1 part vodka, rum, or bourbon

Combine the ingredients in a jar. Let set overnight to dissolve the soap, then shake or stir to blend. Scoop some of the liquid on your fingers and massage as usual.

*Preparation Time:* 10 minutes
*Shelf Life:* Indefinite
*Storage:* Glass jar with a screw top

# Shaving

Using infused herbs in shaving lotions and creams can be healing and therapeutic for numerous skin problems. Many of the herbs and essential oils traditionally used for men's products because of their so-called masculine or woodsy scent are highly antiseptic, such as thyme, lemongrass, clove, eucalyptus, cinnamon, rosemary, lavender, and birch bud.

For women's shaving, see Soapy Shaving Lotion, page 207.

### SHAVING CREAM

## BASIC SHAVING CREAM FORMULA 🎁

2 ounces almond oil
½ ounce beeswax
4 ounces water
2 ounces liquid castile soap
1 ounce glycerin
1 teaspoon borax
⅓ teaspoon grapefruit seed extract
20 drops essential oils

Combine the oil and beeswax in a double boiler over medium heat. When the beeswax is melted, remove from the heat and stir in the water, soap, glycerin, and borax. Blend with an electric handheld beater until creamy. Add the grapefruit seed extract and essential oils and stir to blend.

**Makes 1 cup**

*Preparation Time:* 30 minutes
*Shelf Life:* 6 months
*Storage:* Glass jar with a screw top

## SOAPY SHAVING CREAM 🎁

1 ounce jojoba
1 ounce grapeseed oil
½ to 1 ounce beeswax (less for a thinner cream)
2 ounces rose water
1 teaspoon vegetable glycerin
1 teaspoon borax
1 ounce liquid castile soap
⅓ teaspoon grapefruit seed extract
20 drops essential oils

Combine the jojoba, grapeseed oil, and beeswax in a double boiler over low heat. When the beeswax is melted, remove from the heat and stir in the rose water, glycerin, and borax. Blend with an electric handheld mixer until creamy. Add the soap, grapefruit seed extract, and essential oils, and stir to blend.

**Makes 1 cup**

*Preparation Time:* 30 minutes
*Shelf Life:* 6 months; discard if you see mold
*Storage:* Glass jar with a screw top

## GOOD HERBS FOR SHAVING

**FOR SKIN IRRITATION:** Comfrey, chamomile, calendula, nettle, witch hazel

**FOR SCENT:** Sage, rosemary, lemon balm, lemon, peppermint, thyme, bay, clove, cinnamon, lavender, sweet orange, eucalyptus, birch bud oil, ginger

**FOR MENTHOL (STIMULATING FOR THE SKIN):** Mint oil, or equal parts eucalyptus and peppermint leaves

## SOAPY SHAVING LOTION 🎁

Follow directions for Soapy Shaving Cream, above, but halve the beeswax.

## SHAVING BRUSH-AND-MUG SOAP 🎁

Follow the directions for making superfatted soap (see page 119), but cut back the recipe—quarter it at least—or you'll have enough brush-and-mug soap to last your lifetime. Pour into bowls or mugs to cure.

## EMOLLIENT COCOA BUTTER MUG SOAP 🎁

8 ounces grated castile soap
8 ounces rose water

2 ounces cocoa butter

4 ounces vegetable glycerin

Equal parts essential oils of peppermint and eucalyptus (about 25 drops)

Soak the soap in the rose water overnight. Heat the cocoa butter and glycerin in a double boiler over low heat. Remove from the heat once the cocoa butter is melted, and add the soap mixture. Blend with an electric handheld mixer until creamy. Blend in the essential oils, and pour into a cereal-sized bowl or large mug.

**Makes 1½ cups**

*Preparation Time:* 35 minutes

*Shelf Life:* 6 months; discard if you see mold

*Storage:* Bowl or large mug

### Variation

COCOA BUTTER CREAM: Heat 4 ounces cocoa butter and 1 ounce rose water in a double boiler over low heat. Once the cocoa butter has softened, stir vigorously while cooling, then add the soap mixture, and essential oils of peppermint and eucalyptus. Scoop into a cereal-sized bowl or large mug.

### AFTERSHAVE

Aftershaves double as astringents and toners (see Toners on page 133) for the skin. Astringents help return the skin to a slightly acidic state after using alkaline soaps. Commercial aftershave lotions usually contain synthetic alcohols (see page 134).

## WITCH HAZEL EXTRACT AND GLYCERIN AFTERSHAVE LOTION

8 ounces witch hazel extract

4 ounces vodka, rum, or brandy

1 to 2 ounces vegetable glycerin

10 to 20 drops each essential oils of peppermint and eucalyptus, or as desired

Combine the ingredients in a glass jar and shake or stir to blend. Pat on the face after shaving.

**Makes 1½ cups**

*Preparation Time:* A few minutes

*Shelf Life:* Indefinite

*Storage:* Glass jar with a screw top

## BASIC BAY RUM AFTERSHAVE FORMULA

*This smells good enough to, well, drink!*

1 quart bay leaves

Rosemary

Rum, to cover

If you live in an area where bay leaves are abundant, fill a quart jar with the leaves (otherwise, use as many leaves as you can afford) along with some rosemary. Add enough rum to come a good 2 inches above the leaves. Seal. Let set for 1 month; strain.

**Makes 1 quart**

*Preparation Time:* About 20 minutes

*Shelf Life:* Indefinite; discard if you see mold

*Storage:* Glass jar with a screw top

## Variations

Use any combination of bay leaves, orange peel, cloves, allspice, ginger, or orris root powder. Some recipes call for equal parts rum and water.

ALCOHOL-FREE AFTERSHAVE

## SOFTENING AFTERSHAVE LOTION 🎁

*The ingredients in this aftershave are antiseptic, astringent, hydrating, anti-inflammatory, and emollient.*

2 cups witch hazel extract
2 ounces rose water
2 ounces aloe vera gel
½ to 1 ounce glycerin
Essential oils, as desired (such as equal parts essential oils of peppermint and eucalyptus)
1 drop myrrh tincture

Combine the ingredients in a jar, and shake to blend. Pat on the face after shaving.
**Makes 2½ cups**

*Preparation Time:* About 5 minutes
*Shelf Life:* 6 months; discard if you see mold
*Storage:* Glass jar with a screw top

## Variations

SIMPLE STANDARD AFTERSHAVE: Combine equal parts witch hazel extract and rose water and essential oils, if desired. If you have oily skin, this will be a fine aftershave, but it could be too drying for those with dry or aged skin.

SKIN SOOTHER AFTERSHAVE: Add ½ teaspoon or more apricot kernel oil and wheat germ oil to make a lubricating aftershave.

## HERBAL WATER AFTERSHAVE 🎁

About 2 cups astringent herbs
Boiling water or organic apple cider vinegar, to cover
2 tablespoons or less glycerin, as desired
1 drop myrrh tincture

Put the herbs in a pint mason jar. Cover with boiling water or vinegar. If using vinegar, let the infusion set for 3 weeks. Strain, and add the glycerin and myrrh. Stir or shake to blend. Scoop some onto your hand and dash on face.
**Makes 2 cups**

*Preparation Time:* About 20 minutes
*Shelf Life:* Indefinitely with vinegar; 1 week refrigerated with water
*Storage:* Glass jar with a screw top

## Variation

SAGE, ROSEMARY, AND THYME AFTERSHAVE: Infuse herbs in 2 cups organic apple cider vinegar; let set for 3 weeks. Strain, then combine with 2 cups witch hazel extract. Add 20 to 30 drops each essential oils of peppermint and eucalyptus, if desired.

## AFTERSHAVE GEL

*Flax seed gel, rich in omega-3 essential fatty acids, leaves skin smooth and soft.*

1 tablespoon flax seed
1 cup water
Rose water, if needed

Combine the flax seed and water in a pan. Bring to a boil, then reduce the heat and simmer until the mixture is a thick mucilage (about 10 minutes). Strain to remove the seeds. If the mixture is too thick, add rose water until the desired consistency is achieved.

**Makes 1 cup**

*Preparation Time:* About 20 minutes
*Shelf Life:* About 1 week refrigerated
*Storage:* Glass jar with a screw top

# Sunscreens, Sunblocks, and Sunburns

Many of us love the healthy glow of a tan, but in no other arena do our habits have to change more because of pollution than in our sunbathing practices. As the ozone layer thins, we are more vulnerable to ultraviolet (UV) rays that can cause skin cancer, especially those who live in parts of the world under ozone holes, such as in Australia. But are sunscreens themselves also contributing to the worldwide epidemic of skin cancer? Possibly. Until recently, sunscreens have protected only against UVB rays, not UVA rays. UVB rays cause sunburn, and if you screen them you might stay in the sun longer, overexposing yourself unprotected to UVA rays. UVA rays make up 90 to 95 percent of total UV ray exposure, and overexposure is thought to be one cause of the skin cancer epidemic. UVA rays can pass through glass and clouds.

## TIPS

* For sunburn there is nothing better than aloe vera gel; it is antibacterial and deeply healing for burns in part because of aloectin B, which stimulates the immune system.

* Our bodies need fifteen to twenty minutes of exposure to the sun without sunscreens every day for the skin to manufacture vitamin D. Vitamin D is essential for the assimilation of calcium and other minerals. Deficiency of vitamin D can cause osteoporosis.

* UV rays are the most intense from 10 A.M. to 2 P.M. We need to wear sunblock effective against UVA and UVB rays, with an SPF of at least 15, year-round.

* If you plan to be in the sun, don't use mineral oil (or baby oil, which is mineral oil and fragrance). They are phototoxic, so they increase the chance of the sun's rays burning your skin.

## NATURALLY PROTECTIVE MATERIALS

* Zinc oxide and titanium dioxide protect against UVA and UVB rays. The Better Basic Sunblock Formula (page 211) contains zinc oxide.

* Sesame oil has natural sunscreen elements, as does shea butter.

* Green tea's antioxidant qualities help protect against skin cell damage from UV rays.

* Eating a diet rich in antioxidants, and in particular beta-carotene, helps protect against skin cancer.

* Herbs that are healing for sunburn include aloe vera, St. John's wort, green tea, comfrey, witch hazel (antioxidant), and milk thistle.

* To remove brown spots (also known as liver spots or age spots), cover them daily with mashed green papaya or ripe pineapple. Aloe vera gel removes the spots in three to four months if used daily.

* Should you avoid PABA? Para-amino-benzoic acid (PABA), a member of the vitamin B complex, is the only natural UV absorber accepted by the FDA for use in sunscreen products. PABA is known to cause allergic reactions in many people. Some skin care companies argue that food-grade PABA in vegetable glycerin is tolerated well. Many PABA-free brands of sunscreen are available. The FDA doesn't recognize any protection from PABA higher than SPF 15.

## BETTER BASIC SUNBLOCK FORMULA 🎁

*Sesame oil is a natural sunscreen, and zinc oxide protects against UVA and UVB radiation. Apply this block every hour or so, and reapply after swimming. If you want a thinner cream, add less beeswax; for a stiffer cream, add more. Aloe vera gel and herbal tinctures can be used as part of the water measurement.*

2½ ounces sesame oil
1½ ounces coconut oil or cocoa butter
½ ounce beeswax
4 ounces water or strong green tea
made with distilled water

2 tablespoons zinc oxide
Natural preservatives (1 tablespoon wheat germ oil, 1 teaspoon vitamin C powder equaling 1 gram, and 200 i.u. vitamin A)
10 to 20 drops antiseptic essential oil (optional)

Melt the oils and beeswax in a double boiler over medium heat. Remove from the heat, add the water, and mix with an electric handheld mixer until thick and creamy. Add the zinc oxide and preservatives, followed by the essential oil (if used). Blend.
**Makes 1 cup**

*Preparation Time:* 30 minutes
*Shelf Life:* 6 months with water; about 2 weeks with green tea
*Storage:* Glass jar with a screw top

Variation

PABA SUNSCREEN: To make sunscreen instead of sunblock, use the same recipe, but instead of zinc oxide, substitute 1 teaspoon PABA. The cream will have an SPF of around 15. To be really safe, use zinc oxide and PABA.

There is nothing better for the skin after too much sun than pure, straight aloe vera gel. Other suggestions include vitamin E, glycerin, witch hazel extract, mint tea, lavender or orange flower water, watermelon, cucumber or honeydew melon (mash and put on the burn), honey, black or green tea, chamomile or calendula infusion, baking soda bath, herbal vinegar spritzer, or comfrey poultice.

# Tooth and Mouth Care

In addition to daily brushing and flossing, eating foods rich in vitamins and minerals is important for healthy teeth and gums. Drink nutritional herb teas, add mineral-rich seaweeds to soups and stews, and eat five servings of fresh fruits and vegetables every day. In particular, be sure your diet has adequate calcium, fluoride, magnesium, and vitamin C.

Herbs have been used for hundreds of years for mouth care because many of them have antibacterial properties. For this reason, rosemary, sage, myrrh, tea tree, bloodroot, and aloe vera are all good for toothpastes and mouthwashes. Clove and St. John's wort are often used for toothache pain, and chamomile helps calm teething babies. The herb stevia helps make homemade toothpastes and powders sweet without calories or sugar. Calcium carbonate and baking soda remove plaque with mild abrasion and make an odor-removing base to which herbs and essential oils can be added. The only thing missing from homemade toothpaste is the tube, but who needs that?

### TWIG TOOTHBRUSHES

Twig toothbrushes are also known as tooth twigs, chew sticks, root sticks, or herbal toothbrushes. A five- to six-inch piece of branch about a quarter inch thick is broken from a tree, with care taken to harm the tree as little as possible. Good trees to choose are those with antibacterial properties such as dogwood, birch, willow, poplar, butternut, sassafras, or red sumac (make certain that the sumac has red berries and is not the poisonous variety with white berries). Peelu powder (available in health food stores), which is often recommended for teeth, is the sawdust of the peelu tree instead of a whole twig. Twig toothbrushes are not recommended to replace a regular brushing routine, but they are a plausible way to augment your routine and are good on a camping trip if you forget your toothbrush.

There are different techniques for using twig toothbrushes. Some herbalists recommend simply chewing on the end of the stick until it has softened, then massaging the gums and teeth. I particularly like this method because it is simple. I use black birch, which has a refreshing spearmintlike flavor, and chew

## GOOD HERBS AND ESSENTIAL OILS FOR TOOTH CARE

**HERBS:** Cinnamon, peppermint, echinacea, chamomile, myrrh, witch hazel, rosemary, sage, thyme, licorice root, clove, eucalyptus, seaweed, horsetail

**FLAVORING OILS:** Peppermint, lemon, lime

**ESSENTIAL OILS:** Tea tree, clove, rose geranium, mint, wintergreen, birch (use 1 drop to 1 ounce powder or paste)

on it for an hour or so. Others suggest boiling the stick a long time until the ends split, then drying the stick and dipping it into tooth powder. Still others follow the tradition of soaking the stick in bloodroot—an herb used by the American Indians for cleaning teeth and gums, letting it dry completely, bruising half an inch at the ends (with a mallet or hammer) until they are frayed like a brush, and dipping an end into a powder to rub against the teeth. Or you can soak the stick in an antibacterial essential oil solution, such as a few drops of tea tree oil to 1 cup water, let dry, bruise with a hammer, like above, and massage the gums with the softened, brushlike ends.

## TOOTHPASTES

### BASIC TOOTHPASTE FORMULA

4 ounces calcium carbonate (chalk)
2 ounces baking soda
Enough glycerin to make a paste
⅛ teaspoon refined (white) stevia or
1 teaspoon honey
10 drops essential oils, such as oil of
wintergreen or peppermint

## BUYER'S GUIDE

### TOOTHPASTE

TOM'S of Maine has one of the best formulations of natural toothpaste on the market—similar to toothpaste recipes found in *Better Basics for the Home* except that Tom's toothpaste has the synthetic detergent sodium lauryl sulfate, although it is derived from coconut, not petroleum. (Yes, most toothpastes contain detergents or soaps.) The Natural Dentist toothpaste and the Weleda brand are made with herbs but no sodium lauryl sulfate. Read about how to choose between soaps or detergents in the Buyer's Guide on page 42.

What about fluoride? There is a growing prevalence in the United States of mottled teeth (fluorosis) caused by overexposure to fluoride. Fluoride is found in most toothpastes as well as in half the country's municipal water systems and in food and beverages made from fluorinated water. It is also given to infants and children by pediatricians and dentists. The reason fluoride is such a prevalent additive is because researchers and dental professionals found that it cuts the incidence of dental cavities. But critics fear that the additive is perhaps being ingested in too high quantities. Fluoride is linked to health problems including kidney damage and cancer. Tom's of Maine, as well as other toothpastes available in health food stores, offer both fluoride free and fluoride toothpaste.

Combine the ingredients in a bowl, stirring vigorously until well blended. Scoop the paste onto a toothbrush with a knife or spoon.
**Makes ¾ cup**

*Preparation Time:* A few minutes
*Shelf Life:* 1 year
*Storage:* Glass jar with a screw top

## Variations

ORRIS ROOT TOOTHPASTE: Replace half the baking soda or calcium carbonate with orris root powder, a strongly antibacterial ingredient.

SOAPY TOOTHPASTE: Replace half the baking soda or calcium carbonate with orris root powder (it masks the taste of soap), and add 1 teaspoon liquid castile soap. This recipe was used in many different products in the nineteenth century.

MYRRH AND SPICE TOOTHPASTE: Add 1 teaspoon myrrh powder and 10 drops essential oils of cinnamon, clove, or peppermint. Myrrh is exceptionally antibacterial, as are cinnamon and clove. Peppermint is refreshing.

## TOOTH POWDERS

## BAKING SODA ✂

Baking soda

Place baking soda in a bowl; scoop onto a dampened toothbrush.
*Preparation Time:* None
*Shelf Life:* Indefinite

## SWEET SODA ✂ 🎁

*Stevia, a sweet herb available in health food stores, makes baking soda palatable. This tooth powder actually tastes good.*

2 tablespoons baking soda
⅛ teaspoon white stevia powder

Blend the ingredients in a small glass jar. Scoop onto a dampened toothbrush and brush as usual.
**Makes 2 tablespoons**

*Preparation Time:* Less than 1 minute
*Shelf Life:* Indefinite
*Storage:* Glass jar with a screw top

## Variations

SODA AND SPICE: Add ½ teaspoon ground cinnamon. This formula takes away garlic breath.

BAKING SODA AND HYDROGEN PEROXIDE: Add enough hydrogen peroxide to baking soda to make a paste. Hydrogen peroxide is antibacterial and is often used to cleanse gums for periodontal disease. Be sure to spit out the toothpaste; hydrogen peroxide is an oxidant and shouldn't be ingested. Make only enough for one brushing, and discard leftovers.

SALT AND SODA ANTIBACTERIAL TOOTH-POWDER: Combine equal parts baking soda and salt (salt is antibacterial). If desired, add a few drops antiseptic essential oil such as myrrh, or flavoring oil such as peppermint.

Store in a glass jar with a screw top; the shelf life is indefinite.

SALT AND SODA II: Add 1 teaspoon glycerin and 1 teaspoon water for every $\frac{1}{4}$ cup salt and soda mixture. Add more water as needed to make a creamy paste. Scoop some onto your toothbrush and brush. Rinse thoroughly. Store in a glass jar with a screw top; the shelf life is indefinite.

TOOTH POWDER: Combine equal parts calcium carbonate, myrrh powder, and orris root. Calcium carbonate is a mild abrasive, and myrrh and orris root are highly antibacterial. Sprinkle the powder onto your toothbrush and brush. Rinse thoroughly.

OLD-FASHIONED MYRRH POWDER: Combine $\frac{1}{2}$ teaspoon each powdered myrrh and sage with enough honey to make a paste. Stir to blend. Scoop some onto your toothbrush and brush. Rinse thoroughly. Makes enough for 1 brushing.

## TOOTHACHE POWDER

*Clove oil works wonders to numb the pain of a toothache. Orris root powder works to kill the bacterial infection that could be causing the ache.*

1 tablespoon orris root powder
6 drops essential oil of clove

Combine the ingredients in a bowl and stir to blend. Sprinkle the mixture onto a toothbrush and apply to the aching tooth. Let set for as long as possible before rinsing.
**Makes 1 tablespoon**

*Preparation Time:* Less than 1 minute
*Shelf Life:* 4 months
*Storage:* Glass jar with a screw top

### MOUTHWASH

Mouthwash is a great help for people who have periodontal disease—that is, if they use products made with antibacterial and healing materials rather than synthetic chemicals of little value.

## BASIC MOUTHWASH FORMULA
### (Alcohol Based)

*Myrrh is a tree resin that has been widely used by herbalists around the world for centuries to treat gum and mouth problems. It is highly antiseptic and anti-inflammatory. The alcohol kills bacteria.*

10 ounces vodka, rum, or brandy
8 ounces distilled water
1 ounce liquid castile soap
1 ounce vegetable glycerin
1 ounce powdered myrrh
10 to 15 drops essential oils such as wintergreen (refreshing) and cinnamon, clove, or orange flower (antibacterial)

Combine the ingredients in a quart mason jar. Shake to blend. Swish 1 tablespoonful around the mouth. Spit out; don't swallow.
**Makes 2½ cups**

*Preparation Time:* A few minutes
*Shelf Life:* Indefinite
*Storage:* Glass jar with a screw top

Variation
SKIP THE SOAP MOUTHWASH: Eliminate the soap.

## LEMON SAGE BRANDY

1 cup brandy infused with sage, myrrh,
and thyme
1 cup distilled water
1 teaspoon lemon juice

To make the infusion, place 1 teaspoon each dried sage and thyme and myrrh powder in 1 cup brandy. Cover tightly and let set for 2 weeks. Strain, add the water, and shake to blend. Pour a few tablespoons into a glass, and add the lemon juice. Swirl to blend, swish around the mouth, and spit out.
**Makes 2 cups**

*Preparation Time:* About 15 minutes
*Shelf Life:* Indefinite for brandy infusion; discard leftover lemon juice–brandy blend
*Storage:* Glass jar with a screw top

## BASIC ALCOHOL-FREE HERBAL MOUTHWASH FORMULA

*Make this strong antibacterial infusion using antiseptic plant materials such as cloves, rosemary, and myrrh.*

1 ounce cloves or myrrh; or 2 to 4 ounces
goldenseal or rosemary
2 cups boiling water

Place the plant material in a pint mason jar, cover with the boiling water, and let steep overnight. Strain. Swish around the mouth, then spit out.
**Makes 2 cups**

*Preparation Time:* About 10 minutes
*Shelf Life:* About 1 week refrigerated
*Storage:* Glass jar with a screw top

Variation
SALT AND PEPPERMINT: Add ¼ cup salt to the water and 10 to 15 drops essential oil of peppermint to the cooled infusion.

## GRAPEFRUIT SEED WASH

*Grapefruit seed extract is so antibacterial that it is used as a preservative. Swishing some in your mouth will help eliminate bad breath.*

½ cup water
25 drops grapefruit seed extract
15 to 20 drops essential oils (peppermint is
refreshing), if desired

Combine the ingredients in a glass jar, and shake to blend. Swish around the mouth, then spit out.
**Makes ½ cup**

*Preparation Time:* About 1 minute
*Shelf Life:* Indefinite
*Storage:* Glass jar with a screw top

## WATER AND ESSENTIAL OILS

*Some essential oils are particularly good for killing bacteria. See page 20 for suggested antibacterial herbs.*

1 cup water
10 to 20 drops essential oils such as
cinnamon and clove

Combine the ingredients in a glass jar, and shake to blend. Swish around the mouth, then spit out.
**Makes 1 cup**

*Preparation Time:* About 1 minute
*Shelf Life:* Indefinite
*Storage:* Glass jar with a screw top

## BREATH FRESHENER CHEWS

*An herbalist friend is always chewing on cardamom seeds, and it smells wonderful to be near her. All three of these plant materials kill bad breath.*

Clove buds, cinnamon sticks,
and/or cardamom seeds

Chew, taking care not to swallow.

### GUM CARE

Many plant materials are extraordinary at killing bacteria, and they can help combat gum disease.

## TEA TREE OIL DENTAL FLOSS

¼ cup water
Up to 40 drops antibacterial essential oil
such as tea tree or clove
Dental floss

Combine the water and essential oil. Soak the floss in it for 4 hours; remove and let dry. Use the floss as usual.
**Makes ¼ cup soaking liquid**

*Preparation Time:* About 1 minute
*Shelf Life:* Indefinite
*Storage:* Glass jar with a screw top

## TINCTURE TEETH ✗

*I learned this idea from herbalist Susan Weed. Her friend cured his severe periodontal disease by treating his gums every day with tinctures of antibacterial herbs such as goldenseal and echinacea.*

Tinctures of antibacterial herbs such
as goldenseal and echinacea
½ cup water (optional)

Add drops from a tincture bottle directly to the gums with a dropper. Alternate tinctures throughout a week (but herbalists suggest you use goldenseal for only a few weeks; it is a powerful antibacterial herb). A milder method is to add 10 drops tincture to ½ cup water, swish throughout the mouth, then spit out.

*Preparation Time:* None
*Shelf Life:* Indefinite
*Storage:* Tincture bottle

## OLD-FASHIONED GUM AID ✘

*Vinegar is an old-time disinfectant.*

1 cup water
2 tablespoons organic apple cider vinegar

Combine the ingredients in a glass jar. Swish around the mouth, then spit out.
**Makes about 1 cup**

*Preparation Time:* Less than 1 minute
*Shelf Life:* Indefinite
*Storage:* Glass jar with a screw top

## ALOE VERA SWISH ✘

*Aloe vera gel is not only antibacterial, it is anti-inflammatory and astringent.*

1 tablespoon aloe vera gel

Swish the gel around the mouth, then spit out.
**Makes 1 tablespoon**

*Preparation Time:* None
*Shelf Life:* 6 months refrigerated
*Storage:* Store in its original container

### TOOTH WHITENERS

## HYDROGEN PEROXIDE AND/OR BAKING SODA WHITENER ✘

*Baking soda can work well as a mild abrasive for the teeth; hydrogen peroxide actually bleaches.*

About ½ teaspoon each baking soda and
3 percent hydrogen peroxide solution

Use either material alone on your toothbrush, or combine the ingredients to make a paste. Vigorously brush up and down over the stained teeth. Rinse thoroughly.
**Makes enough for 1 treatment**

*Preparation Time:* About 1 minute
*Shelf Life:* Discard leftovers

## SAGE AND SEA SALT LIGHTENER

*Sage and sea salt are both antibacterial. This powder is gently abrasive.*

2 tablespoons each dried sage leaves
and sea salt

Grind the ingredients together with a mortar and pestle. Spread the mixture evenly on a baking sheet and bake at 250°F for 30 minutes. Let cool, then stir to blend. Scoop the mixture onto a toothbrush, and vigorously brush up and down over the stained teeth. Rinse thoroughly.
**Makes about ¼ cup**

*Preparation Time:* About 4 minutes
*Shelf Life:* The ground sage will lose its potency in a few weeks
*Storage:* Glass jar with a screw top

## LEMON LIGHTENER ✘

*Lemon is a mild bleach.*

1 piece lemon peel

Rub the lemon peel up and down over the stained teeth.
**Makes enough for 1 treatment**

*Preparation Time:* About 1 minute
*Shelf Life:* Discard after using

CHAPTER 5

# Gardening, Pets, and Pest Control

I T IS SAID that spring moves up the East Coast at the rate of fifteen

miles a day. With it come the songbirds and geese, blooming bushes,

the smell of warming earth, and plans for summer gardens. Freed from

the restraint of winter clothing, children joyfully get outside more. After all,

as poet E. E. Cummings said, the world is "mud-luscious," and all of us drink up the sun as winter falls away and the days get warmer.

Clouds of pesticides, herbicides, and fungicides from commercial and private spraying follow the warming, and they drift for miles. Residents spray their homes for wasps, towns aerial-spray for mosquitoes, and farmers spray their crops. Neighborhoods turn toxic from lawn care, and even roadside weeds are sprayed with herbicides. Going for a walk in the woods usually involves using toxic synthetic poisons

to repel ticks and blackflies. Being outside on a beautiful, sunny spring day doing yard work invariably means breathing drifting chemicals. Nobody can attest to the prevalence of pesticides and herbicides more than people who are chemically sensitive, like myself. There is almost no place on earth to go to escape them.

You can make do without pesticides. Thousands—millions—of us do, and we're not overrun by bugs and weeds or burdened with dying lawns and gardens. Quite the contrary. There are natural, commonsense solutions for everything. And one person can change the pesticide load of an entire community. A mother in my town single-handedly established integrated pest management in our school district. A pesticide hasn't been used in or near the school for three years. Three years! Our gardens and lawns are our interface with the natural world. Here we put our hands in the earth, peer at the North Star, drink the water, see the sunlight, and feel the air. Why would we want to poison our homes? We can rebuild poisoned places into thriving ecosystems and habitats for native species of flowers, butterflies, berries, birds, toads, and dragonflies. Even in the city, bird feeders can be hung, "weeds" protected, and trees planted.

Native species are making a comeback in areas where efforts have been made. In the Great Lakes—among the most polluted waterways in the world—there had been massive destruction of habitat from acid rain and chemicals such as PCBs, which decimated native fish populations. Now, thanks to decreased pollution, even fish that no one has seen for years are making a comeback, along with the steadily reviving population of native trout, burbot, and lake sturgeon.

# Organic Gardening and Lawn Care

Like most people, I grew up hearing a mixture of old wives' tales and so-called tried-and-true facts about gardening. We all followed a bunch of rules, the most important of which was to plant only over Memorial Day weekend (this was in New Hampshire). Some said to plant

leafy vegetables when the moon was waxing and root crops when it was waning. I'm sorry to say I didn't pay too much attention, and I missed all of my father's gardening wisdom. I remember his pitchfork, the compost pile, the smell of certain seeds, and his beautiful flowers but not the hows and whys. As an adult, with my father long dead, I've had a range of feelings toward gardening, not the least of which has been intimidation, as if I wasn't part of some secret club and was embarrassed not to know what damping-off meant, or overwintering. How silly of me. There are enough rules of thumb to last until the cows come home. There is more than one right way to make seeds grow. If you pare down gardening to the basics, you end up with the only real rule of thumb you need: Good soil, good mulch, and good fertilizer produce a great garden. A little humility doesn't hurt either, nor does a lot of common sense.

## MINI-GLOSSARY

**Annual.** A plant that lives for one growing season.

**Biennial.** A plant that produces leaves the first year and flowers the second and then dies.

**Damping-off.** A disease caused by soilborne molds that kill seedlings.

**Green Manure.** Green manure is a crop such as clover, winter rye, or alfalfa that is grown simply to be turned under the ground to increase the nutrient content of the soil. Green manuring is used to fertilize the soil and keep it from being bare and vulnerable to runoff.

**Humus.** Dark brown soil consisting of decomposed organic matter such as leaves, finished compost, and forest debris.

**Lime.** A mineral and source of calcium that is added to the soil to make it more alkaline. Ask for agricultural lime as opposed to mason's hydrated lime.

**Loam.** Sand, silt, and clay combination, equally balanced.

**Peat Moss.** Organic matter that is acidic, with a pH range from 3 to 5.

**Perennial.** A plant that lives for many years.

# Soil

Rich, loamy topsoil results in healthy plants and grass, and healthy soil is much less likely to grow diseased plants. Chemical fertilizers can kill earthworms and other microorganisms that make for favorable soil conditions. Some estimates are that we have lost up to 50 percent of our nation's topsoil with industrial farming techniques. Those who practice organic gardening and lawn techniques focus the vast majority of their attention on building healthy soil with compost, mulch, and organic fertilizers. The soil is the central concern around which everything else revolves.

The first step in establishing healthy soil is to know what your soil is made of. There are three types of soil: sand, clay, and silt. A loamy soil—the ideal soil—is made up of an equal balance of sand, clay, and silt, although some gardeners prefer to have a little less clay.

Now is a good time to develop a relationship with your county's cooperative extension service. The United States Department of Agriculture established a partnership with state colleges in 1914 to provide local expertise in activities related to gardening (including canning). We are lucky that this partnership is still in existence. I found the phone number for my cooperative extension service under the listings for my county in the white pages of the telephone book. Your county extension office can test your soil and tell you what kind you have and how to improve it.

**HOME SOIL TEST.** Soil tests will tell you if your soil has too much sand, clay, or silt. There is a simple way to test your soil at home. I learned about this test in *The Chemical-Free Lawn* by Warren Schultz (see Sources and Resources), and these directions are adapted from that book. Put 5 inches of dry soil into a large glass jar (such as a 1-quart canning jar). Add enough water to cover the soil, and securely screw on the lid. Shake and let set for 24 hours. After this time, the soil will have settled, and layers will have developed. Sand will be on the bottom, silt in the middle, and clay on the top. Measure the layers. If you have 1 inch of clay and 2 inches each of silt and sand, your soil contains 20 percent clay and 40 percent each silt and sand. That's perfect loam.

As the percentage of your layers gets too big in any direction, you will have clay, sandy, or silty soil. To improve sandy and clay soil, you'll want to add organic matter such as humus, peat moss, manure, and/or compost (see below for further instructions).

**TESTING SOIL pH.** Gardens, lawns, and soil bacteria all like a pH around neutral. If you have a lot of pine trees nearby, your soil may be acid. It is easy and cheap to test for your pH. You can buy simple kits at the hardware store, or call your cooperative extension. Soil should be neutral to slightly acidic for most plants. If your soil is too acid, add agricultural lime. If it is too alkaline, add wood ashes, pine needles, peat moss, or well-composted sawdust.

## BUILDING GOOD SOIL

You don't need to buy expensive topsoil; you can make it yourself using ingredients on your land, from your kitchen, and foraged from your community. Find a good source of manure, make compost, use grass clippings, track down sources of organic matter such as corncobs, leaves, and even sawdust and ground tree trunks. The more organic matter you use, the more organisms will thrive and make good soil. Add organic matter whenever you can, but make a point of it in spring and fall.

TYPES OF ORGANIC MATTER

**HUMUS.** See page 222.

**PEAT MOSS.** Acidic organic matter.

**MANURE.** Horse, cow, goat, sheep, rabbit, poultry, or pig. Fresh manure is too high in ammonia to safely use on a garden. Age the manure for six months before spreading it. Dried manure is much higher in nitrogen by weight than fresh.

**COMPOST.** Compost is the result of piling organic material (such as straw, hay, fruit and vegetable scraps, leaves, grass clippings, garden plants, manure, small branches, and chipped tree trunks) and turning it regularly for air circulation so that over time the pile decomposes. The resulting fine, dark dirt can be spread on a garden.

You can buy compost bins in most garden centers and through garden supply catalogs. Or you can build a boxlike structure with boards, with large spaces between them for air to circulate. Some people just have a pile near their garden that they throw things on. Do whatever you like that works. Just try to keep it downwind from your house.

- *Rule of Thumb for the Best Compost:* Ideally a compost pile should be 75 percent brown materials and 25 percent green materials (see below). A 50:50 ratio should be all right. The pile should be kept damp.

- *Turn the Compost:* Aerate the compost by turning it with a pitchfork every time you add new material.

- *Materials for the Compost:*
  *Brown Material:* Leaves, brush, twigs, dried weeds, straw, hay
  *Green Material:* Fruit and vegetable scraps, grass clippings
  *Don't Include:* Meat, fish, bones, dairy products, peanut butter, fats, pet waste, synthetic materials, or anything treated with chemicals, such as plywood. I don't recom-

mend including paper products due to inks, dyes, and chlorine.

*What About Diseased Plants?* The compost heats up to such a high temperature that almost all diseases found in plants die. The exception to this is diseases that affect tomatoes. Bury or burn diseased tomatoes and tomato plants.

Arriving at a successful composting system is just as much of a process as establishing a non-toxic home. I've had a lot of trouble establishing a good compost pile because I am so allergic to mold that turning the compost, which releases mold spores into the air, ruins my day. I am embarrassed to say that we have years of kitchen scraps piled high—we faithfully "compost"—but the pile has almost never been turned. We're keeping the scraps out of the landfill, but we can't use any of them on our garden. I am finally going to solve this problem—I hope—by buying a barrel-on-its-side composter with a handle turn. I can give the handle a good twirl and then run. If we keep the compost aerated from the beginning, it should smell a lot less. I've also realized that our compost has too many fruit and vegetable scraps and not enough leaves, twigs, and grass clippings. Too many kitchen scraps produces an odor. I'd been building a compost of about 75 percent kitchen scraps (it is amazing how many accumulate in a few days) and 25 percent leaves and other brown material. The ratio should be just the opposite.

Adding compost to gardens is an excellent way to add trace minerals. One way to make your compost as mineral balanced as possible is to include carrot tops, cornstalks, red clover,

## BUYER'S GUIDE

REAL Goods and the Gardener's Supply Company are just two catalogs where you can buy composting bins. The Gardener's Supply Company and Worm's Way offer natural fertilizers and sprays as well as gardening tools and bird-baths. Other organic gardening supply catalogs include Gardens Alive!, Peaceful Valley Farm Supply, and Smith & Hawken. Heirloom seeds can be ordered from the Abundant Life Seed Foundation, the Heirloom Seed Project, Seeds of Change, and United Plant Savers.

Concern and Safer are two brands of less toxic pest control products for gardening; they are available in gardening centers.

horsetail, alfalfa, maple leaves, chicory, nettle, chamomile, dandelion, yarrow, valerian, and oak bark.

### MULCH
Mulch is a protective soil covering. It helps retain moisture in the soil, reduces erosion during downpours, and smothers weeds.
TYPES OF MULCH
**ORGANIC:** Peat moss, cocoa hulls, corncobs, leaves, sawdust, wood chips, grass clippings, compost, dried manure, pine needles (too

many will make your soil acidic), hay, straw, seaweed

**PLASTIC:** Black plastic spread over the soil (adds no nutrients)

GUIDELINES FOR MULCHING

* *Rule of Thumb:* Don't let any bare soil show, not even a few inches. Put on enough mulch (at least two inches thick) to keep out the sunlight.

* Some old gardening books recommend mulching with tankage (animal residue), because it is high in nutrients. I do not recommend this method of fertilizing.

* Sewage sludge is an increasingly popular material for mulching, but I don't think it should be used because it is usually contaminated with heavy metals, and there are recent reports of contamination with excreted pharmaceuticals.

* Put mulch on in spring and after the ground is frozen in fall. Mulch helps retain moisture in the soil in summer and keeps down weeds.

* Cut up leaves so they don't mat and keep the soil from breathing.

* Plant a green manure crop in late summer or early fall; in spring, turn it over into the soil to add nutrients.

## FERTILIZERS

Recent research confirms that most chemically fertilized soils are unhealthy and are too high in nitrogen. The chemicals usually have killed off worms and microscopic bacteria essential to a healthy soil ecosystem. Read labels carefully to ensure that you are buying organic fertilizers.

**NPK RATIOS.** Commercially bagged fertilizer has a series of three numbers prominently displayed—for example, 5-4-5. These numbers refer to N (nitrogen), P (phosphorus), and K (potassium) in that order: the NPK ratio.

**RULE OF THUMB FOR DETERMINING IF FERTILIZER IS ORGANIC OR CHEMICAL.** If an NPK ratio adds up to more than 15, or if one of the numbers is more than 10, it is probably chemical, not organic. Natural, organic matter rarely has concentrations that high. The exception to this is fish meal, with an NPK of 7-13-4.

**WHEN TO APPLY.** There are varying opinions about when to apply fertilizer. Some people simply side-dress fertilizer (work it into the soil) in spring and fall; some top-dress with fertilizer (lay it on top of the soil) when plants in the garden are six to eight weeks old. Some fertilize all three times. Whatever rule you follow, don't overuse fertilizers. Test your soil, so that you add only the nutrients that your soil actually needs.

SAMPLE ORGANIC NPK RATIOS

Fresh Horse Manure: 0.7-0.25-0.55

Seaweed: 4 to 6-0.75-5

Cottonseed Meal: 8-2.5-2

Fish Meal: 7-13-3 to 4

Homemade Compost: 0.5-0.5-0.5 to 4-4-4

Grass Clippings: 0.5-0.2-0.5

Test your soil by working with your county cooperative extension service (see page 222).

**IF YOU NEED NITROGEN.** Nitrogen is almost always derived from organic matter. Add alfalfa meal, coffee grounds, cottonseed meal, eggshells, fish emulsion, fish meal, dried blood (blood meal), feathers, hair, or ground lobster shells.

**IF YOU NEED PHOSPHORUS.** Add bonemeal, compost, rock phosphate, ground coconut shells, or ground oyster shells.

**IF YOU NEED POTASSIUM.** Add potash rock, wood ashes, kelp, soybean meal, granite dust, ash of banana stalks and skins, corncobs, or cottonseed hulls. Hardwood ash gives 10 percent potash, whereas ash from softwoods gives 2 percent.

## WATERING

On average, a lawn or garden needs an inch of rain a week. I told my husband recently that we needed to buy a rain gauge. He looked at me with astonishment and asked why we couldn't just put out a pan. Ha! We compared how rainwater collects in pans, cups, and cylinders, and lo and behold we got the same height of water in each. The exercise reminds me of a friend's comment: "I wonder what my husband and I would talk about if we didn't have the garden?"

**RULE OF THUMB.** Water heavily every week instead of lightly every day. Add one to two inches of water a week for gardens and one inch for lawns. One inch of water should moisten to a depth of five inches.

If your soil is dry at a depth of three to four inches, it needs water.

# Gardens

## SEASONAL THINGS TO DO

### SPRING

* To extend the season in the North, you can start seedlings indoors under grow lights and outdoors in cold frames. There are many ways to make cold frames. We simply use old windows positioned over a simple rectangular wood frame slanted toward the sun. Garden supply stores and catalogs sell appropriate grow lights and materials for cold frames (see Sources and Resources).

* Work the soil as early as you can after it thaws. Rototill, let the weeds come up, and pull them out (it's easy when they are young). Rototill again if possible before planting, to allow another batch of weeds to grow. Weeds thrive in spring; by allowing weed seeds to germinate and grow then, you can remove them easily and have fewer weeds later on.

### FALL

* Consider planting a green manure cover crop of alfalfa, red clover, soybeans, white clover, ryegrass, or oats (see Mulch, page 224).

* Turn under your vegetable garden, or pull up the plants and compost them (except tomatoes; see page 224). If you don't plant a green manure crop, mulch with leaves after the ground freezes. (Shred the leaves first so they don't mat together and keep the soil from breathing.)

* After the first frost, remove dead leaves and flowers, and cut down the stems of perennials. Cover with mulch after the ground freezes.

## PROPAGATING SEEDS AND SEEDLINGS, AND SAVING SEED

Most seeds are F1 hybrids (F1 stands for first filial generation). They are "selfing" plants—

cloned, in a way—because the seed reproduces using its own pollen. This results in genetically identical plants. There is a hidden cost in using F1 hybrid seeds: After the first generation, seeds tend to be sterile. Using sterile seed creates a great loss of genetic diversity. This could actually threaten our food supply, because one blight could wipe out the entire worldwide crop of a hybrid plant-type vulnerable to that blight. If there were 400 varieties of corn growing around the world, the chances are that many varieties would be blight resistant.

Buy open-pollinated, organic heirloom seeds. Open-pollinated seeds are constantly modified in nature; they cross-pollinate, and the genes adapt to changing climate and soil conditions. Heirloom seeds have often been passed down for generations, preserving genes that would otherwise be lost. It is up to backyard gardeners and organic gardeners to preserve genetic diversity in our seed supply, because industrial farms use F1 hybrids and, more recently, genetically engineered seeds. See Sources and Resources for sources of heirloom seeds.

ZONES

Each location in the United States has a designated zone for growing temperatures. There are ten zones, determined by how cold it gets in winter. Seed packets provide information pertaining to zones; be sure to determine if the seeds you choose will grow in your zone. It is a good idea to buy seeds from a company in your own zone, because they are specialists.

Zone 1: −50°F
Zone 2: −40°F to −50°F
Zone 3: −30°F to −40°F

Zone 4: −20°F to −30°F
Zone 5: −10°F to −20°F
Zone 6: 0°F to −10°F
Zone 7: 10°F to 0°F
Zone 8: 20°F to 10°F
Zone 9: 30°F to 20°F
Zone 10: 40°F to 30°F

NOTE: Four-season gardening techniques—those that use greenhouses, grow lights, cold frames, and even underground tunnels to extend the growing season year-round even in very cold climates—are increasingly being developed. *Four-Season Harvest* by Eliot Coleman is an excellent book to introduce you to this subject.

**STARTING SEEDS.** Seed starter and potting mix are not the same. Seed starter can be simply peat moss without any added nutrients. After the first leaves sprout from the seed, it will need to be transplanted or fed a fertilizer.

TIPS

* Seeds germinate best in warm soil (at least 70°F).
* Soak seeds for a few hours in warm water before planting.
* Test the germinating capacity of old seeds by rolling up a few in a damp paper towel and seeing if they germinate in a few days.
* Don't use garden soil to start seeds, because it can cake and make it difficult for fragile seedlings to penetrate.
* Soil-less seedling mixes are free of soil-borne diseases. Seedling mixes made with topsoil should be sterilized. You can sterilize small amounts in your oven at 170°F for 30 minutes.

## SEEDLING MIX

Equal parts topsoil, peat moss, sand, and
compost

Combine the ingredients in a bucket, and use
the mixture to fill individual peat moss starter
pots. With your finger, push a $\frac{1}{2}$-inch-deep
hole into the center of the potted dirt, and
drop in the seed. Brush up to an inch of dirt
over the seed, less for small seeds.

*Preparation Time:* 15 to 20 minutes to make a
bucketful of mix
*Shelf Life:* Indefinite
*Storage:* Covered in a dry place

Variation
LOAM-RICH SEEDLING MIX: Add three times
as much topsoil to the mix.

## SOIL-LESS SEEDLING MIX

*This recipe is adapted from* Four-Season Harvest
*by Eliot Coleman. It makes a lot of seedling mix,
so you might want to halve the amounts.*

Three 8-quart buckets each peat moss and
compost
2 cups organic fertilizer
One 8-quart bucket perlite

Combine the ingredients in a big container
such as a garbage can. Thoroughly blend with
a pitchfork or shovel. Use the mix to fill individual peat moss starter pots. With your fin-
ger, push a $\frac{1}{2}$-inch-deep hole into the center of

the dirt, and drop in the seed. Brush up to an
inch of dirt over the seed, less for small seeds.
**Makes 32 quarts**

*Preparation Time:* About 20 minutes to make
the mix
*Shelf Life:* Indefinite
*Storage:* Covered in a dry place

## TRANSPLANT FERTILIZER

*Proving my point that there are many right ways
to make plants grow, I have read in some places
that transplant fertilizers are a mistake but in
other places that they are crucial. Since there are a
number of variables, you need to decide for yourself
from your own experience. Fish emulsion and seaweed extract are available at gardening supply
stores and through catalogs.*

1 tablespoon each fish emulsion
and seaweed extract
1 gallon water

Combine the ingredients in a gallon jug. Cover
and shake to blend. Pour about 1 quart of the
liquid into the hole before transplanting.
**Makes 1 gallon**

*Preparation Time:* A few minutes
*Shelf Life:* A week
*Storage:* Gallon jug

Variation
MANURE DRENCH: In a bucket combine 1
cup manure for each gallon of water. Add $\frac{1}{2}$

cup of the liquid to the hole before trans-planting; repeat a few times over the next week or two.

### Houseplant

T I P *Add 1 garlic clove to the potting soil of each potted plant to reduce disease.*

### SAVING SEEDS

* Be sure to choose nonhybrid varieties.
* Harvest the seeds when they are dry and breakable but before the pod has released them.
* For fruit seeds, choose seeds from overripe fruit.
* Wash seeds and soak them in water until they begin to ferment. Rinse and cover with clean water. Throw away any seeds that float.
* Dry seeds thoroughly by placing them on newspaper or towels. Once they are dry, place them in glass jars in a cool, dry, dark storage area.

### MAKING CUTTINGS

Parts of a parent plant—stems, roots, and even leaves—can be cut off and rooted in moist, well-drained soil or even plain water.

### DIVIDING PLANTS

Divide perennials that bloom in spring or early summer in August or September. Fall-flowering plants can be divided in spring; exceptions include iris, which should be divided right after it flowers.

Divide most plants every three to four years. To divide a plant, on a cloudy day when the soil is dry, dig up the plant and shake the soil from around the roots. Carefully pull the roots apart, or if necessary divide them with a knife or spade. Discard the old part of the plant. Divide and plant the fresh new roots.

### PLANTING BULBS

Most hardy bulbs bloom in spring.

* Plant in fall; plant tulips as late in fall as possible.
* Thin bulbs in June, making sure not to disturb the bulbs until their new leaves have withered.
* Divide bulbs every three to four years, if desired.

# Lawns

If you look at your lawn as a garden, you may be much more interested in its soil. A lawn is a garden of just grass. As with a vegetable or flower garden, a lawn needs good soil, good mulch, and good fertilizer in order to thrive. Much of my knowledge about lawns comes from two books by Warren Schultz: *The Chemical-Free Lawn* and *The Environmental Gardener* (see Sources and Resources).

### LAWN GUIDELINES

* What kind of grass do you have? If you don't know, ask your cooperative extension service. While you are speaking with them, ask what kind of grass they recommend for your area.
* How much of your lawn is grass and how much is weeds? Conventional wisdom says that if the lawn is more than 50 percent

weeds, you should dig it up and start over, or switch to a ground cover (see below).

* What is the history of your lawn? Have chemicals been used on it? Do you have thatch—a thick, spongy mat of strawlike grass? Experts think that thatch may be caused by overfertilizing.

* Just as with a garden, you need to determine the type of soil your lawn has. See Soil, page 222, for determining soil type.

* The pH of your soil should be around neutral.

* Use a mulching lawn mower.

* Cut grass only one-third of its height each time you mow. For example, if the grass is three inches high, cut only one inch. Too-short grass allows weeds to spread.

* For watering recommendations, see Watering on page 226.

* Use organic fertilizer. A good rule of thumb for fertilizing is to do it in early spring, early summer, and midsummer.

* Sow seeds in fall in the North and in spring in the South, so as not to compete with the weeds.

* If you have low rainfall, you might look into ground covers that thrive in drought as an alternative to a lawn. Call your county's cooperative extension for native grasses, ground covers, and wildflower meadow recommendations. Often ground covers and wildflower meadows need to be mowed only once a year if at all.

* Some standard alternative ground covers include pachysandra, ivy, periwinkle, ajuga, and cotoneaster. Most ground covers

are not suitable for high traffic areas. Be sure to plant ground cover thickly enough—every twelve inches or so on center—to discourage weed growth.

# Beyond Gardens and Lawns

## EDIBLE LANDSCAPES

An edible landscape has plants that you can eat. This is not just a vegetable garden but can be an area abundant with strawberries, herbs, edible flowers, blueberries, grapes, fruit trees, and so forth.

## NATIVE SPECIES GARDENING AND BACKYARD WILDLIFE

Scientists from the Smithsonian Institution, The Nature Conservancy, and the Environmental Defense Fund report that non-native species are the number-one threat to wildlife, followed by habitat destruction. Native species gardening is developing into a new art form. Native species are plants that are indigenous to the local environment, and they help support the native wildlife. Where to begin? With your cooperative extension service. They will know of local organizations that have lists and sources of native species in your bioregion.

Wild animals need what are called edges—the borders of a forest and field, for example—places where there is shelter, food, water, and a place for them to hide. The more diversity you can establish, the more diverse the flora and fauna you will have.

## ATTRACTING BUTTERFLIES

*Flowers:* Cosmos, impatiens, marigold
*Colors:* Purple, yellow, white, pink

## ATTRACTING BEES

*Herbs:* Thyme, catnip, lemon balm, marjoram, hyssop, sweet basil, mints

## ATTRACTING BIRDS

My mother, an excellent birder with fifty years of experience, provided me with these tips for attracting birds.

* Birds like and need water. If there is no nearby source (a pond or brook), provide a birdbath or devise a fountain with fresh water. Catalogs and bird stores sell drip birdbaths—those with a continuous trickle—which birds seem to relish (see Sources and Resources). In winter, melt snow once a day, or offer fresh water in a pan.

* Provide bird feeders. Black oil sunflower seeds have more protein than the striped variety, but both are good. Thistle seed can be hung in a special net feeder, too. In winter, suet attracts woodpeckers in addition to many other birds—nuthatches, chickadees, titmice, and crows. A mix of the above seeds with peanut kernels and millet is fine for ground-feeding birds that rarely use a feeder, such as sparrows, cardinals, and jays.

* Birds do not usually need feeders in summer, although feeders do attract birds for bird-watching.

* In winter, if you set up feeders for birds, it is important to keep them filled. Make arrangements for them to be filled if you are away on a trip; birds can become dependent on them. This is especially true in less urban areas where there are not many feeders around.

* Bird feeders should be hung near trees or bushes to provide cover, because birds are constantly alert to danger (the neighborhood cat, for instance) and will want a safe haven close by.

* Just about any kind of tree provides cover. Shrubbery with bright-colored berries also attract birds, who particularly like tart berries.

* Flowers attract birds. Hummingbirds are attracted to trumpet-shaped flowers, to red flowers such as beebalm, and to delphinium.

* Some plants, including weeds, attract birds for their berries and seeds: raspberries, blackberries, bayberry, highbush cranberry, mountain ash, holly, huckleberry, dandelions, thistle, chickweed, elderberry, honeysuckle, and juniper, for example. Birds are also attracted to trees because of the insects that live in their bark.

## ATTRACTING OTHER SPECIES

*Living with Wildlife,* a book by The California Center for Wildlife and published by The Sierra Club, offers many details about a wide range of wild animals, from rabbits to moose. Read this book, or others similar to it, to learn about habitats needed by animals in your community. Such books will give you clues about appropriate habitat restoration.

# Garden Pests

A few bugs won't hurt most plants. Nowhere does acting on common sense make more, well, sense than in coping with garden pests. Sometimes simple solutions are there if you just think long enough. Hosing bugs off a plant is often all that is needed.

### ALL-PURPOSE GARDEN PEST SPRAYS

There are many ways to use garlic, onions, strong-smelling roots, and spices for killing and repelling bugs. These ingredients have been used as repellents successfully for years. The following recipes can be adapted to what you have on hand, so you don't have to go out and buy something new. Mix and match ingredients as necessary.

Soap has been used for centuries as a pesticide. It disrupts the insect's cell membranes, killing the pest through dehydration. Dr. Bronner's peppermint liquid castile soap has worked well for many a friend.

### HANDS-ON

* Hand-pick the bugs.
* Place paper collars around plant stems.
* Place sticky bands on tree trunks by wrapping them in heavy paper such as poster board and brushing with a sticky substance such as honey. The bugs will get stuck.
* Broken eggshells are a deterrent to many bugs. They don't like to walk through them.
* Vacuum bugs off with a vacuum cleaner.

## GARLIC SPRAY ✄

1 head garlic
2 cups boiling water

Peel and mash the garlic. Place it in a pint mason jar and cover with boiling water. Screw on the lid and let set overnight. Strain. Freeze 1 cup of the infusion to use another time; place the other in a spray bottle with 1 additional cup of water. Spray on infested areas.
**Makes 4 cups spray**

*Preparation Time:* About 15 minutes
*Shelf Life:* Discard leftover spray
*Storage:* Freeze half the original infusion

### Variations

SOAPY GARLIC SPRAY: Add 2 teaspoons vegetable oil and 1 teaspoon liquid soap to the garlic infusion before dividing the batch in two.

SPICY INFUSION: Combine any of the following in the garlic infusion: garlic, scallions and onions, horseradish root, ginger, rhubarb leaves, cayenne, and other hot peppers. Add 1 teaspoon liquid soap.

ONION SPRAY: Combine an onion and a few hot peppers with the head of garlic in a blender with enough water to cover. Strain. Freeze what you don't use.

## NEEM OIL ✄

*Neem oil, a gum extracted from an evergreen tree, is an excellent all-purpose pesticide.*

2 teaspoons essential oil of neem
2 cups water

Combine the ingredients in a spray bottle. Spray on infested areas.
**Makes 2 cups**

*Preparation Time:* About 1 minute
*Shelf Life:* Indefinite
*Storage:* Leave in the spray bottle

## COMPOST TEA

1 cup finished (aged) compost
2½ quarts water

Combine the ingredients in a pail. Pour onto infested areas.
**Makes almost 3 quarts**

*Preparation Time:* A few minutes
*Shelf Life:* This is decomposed matter, and smelling awful is part of its character. It has already passed its shelf life.
*Storage:* Pail with a lid, outside the house

Variation
MANURE WATER: Substitute dried manure for the compost.

## WASHING SODA ✗

*Many pests don't like washing soda—a caustic, alkaline mineral.*

1 tablespoon washing soda
1 teaspoon liquid soap
1 gallon water

Combine the ingredients in a pail. Stir to blend. Pour some on infested areas, or put a few cups at a time in a spray bottle, and spray.
**Makes 1 gallon**

*Preparation Time:* 1 minute
*Shelf Life:* Indefinite
*Storage:* Covered container

## DORMANT OIL AND SOAP SPRAY

*This is a popular spray for orchards. The oil suffocates insect pests.*

½ cup vegetable oil
1 tablespoon liquid soap
2 quarts water

Combine the ingredients in a pail. Transfer 2 cups to a spray bottle. Spray infested areas.
**Makes about 2 quarts**

*Preparation Time:* About 1 minute
*Shelf Life:* The oil will go rancid eventually, but it doesn't really matter
*Storage:* Covered container

## CEDAR SPRAY

*Cedar contains a strong volatile oil that repels pests. It is often used as a clothing moth repellent.*

1 handful cedar chips or 1 teaspoon essential oil of cedar
4 cups boiling water

Place the cedar chips in a quart mason jar and cover with the boiling water. Let set overnight. (If using the essential oil, simply combine the oil and water in a mason jar.) Pour 2 cups into a spray bottle, and spray the infested areas.

**Makes 4 cups**

*Preparation Time:* A few minutes with the oil, overnight with the chips
*Shelf Life:* A few weeks
*Storage:* Glass jar with a screw top

## Variation

PYRETHRUM SPRAY: Substitute an infusion of chrysanthemum flowers; they contain pyrethrum, a broad-spectrum pesticide.

SEAWEED SPRAY: Substitute an infusion with seaweed extract. Some people swear by seaweed for pest control.

## SOAP SPRAY ✂

*Soap is used here as an insecticide. It kills pests by dehydrating them.*

1 to 2 tablespoons liquid soap
1 gallon water

Be sure not to use more than 2 tablespoons soap; too much can kill the leaves. Combine the ingredients in a pail. Transfer 2 cups to a spray bottle. Spray infested areas.

**Makes 1 gallon**

*Preparation Time:* A few minutes
*Shelf Life:* Indefinite
*Storage:* Covered container

## Variations

DISHWATER TREATMENT: Pour dishwater on plants.

PEPPERMINT SOAPY SPRAY: Use liquid castile soap with peppermint. Peppermint is a pest repellent in its own right.

SOAPY HERBS: Substitute an infusion of aromatic herbs (most highly scented herbs repel insects) for the water. Add 1 teaspoon soap per gallon of water.

PYRETHRUM SOAP SPRAY: Substitute an infusion of chrysanthemum flowers for the water.

## DIATOMACEOUS EARTH (DE) ✂

*These prehistoric skeletons are excellent pest repellents. The dust damages the pests' protective coating, drying them out. DE is available in many garden stores. Just be sure not to buy pool-grade DE; use natural DE.*

1 or more cups diatomaceous earth

Sprinkle the DE around the plants.

*Shelf Life:* Indefinite
*Storage:* Covered container

### ANIMAL REPELLENTS

HANDS-ON

* Scare away pests with loud noises such as from a radio.
* Build a scarecrow.

* Hang aluminum pie pans from trees. They shake and shift with the wind, startling animals.
* Hang soap bars from trees to ward off deer.
* Hair deters many predators. Use dog or human hair. Wrap in cheesecloth and hang near the garden.
* Have dogs; they can scare away deer.
* Build a fence eight feet high around your garden.
* Grow deer-resistant trees and plants. Deer usually don't like mint, basil, oregano, lavender, lemon balm, rosemary, thyme, juniper, cypress, stock, sunflowers, globe thistle, echinacea, chicory, lilac, jasmine, mulberry, and magnolia.
* Build wire cages around bulbs to protect them from deer and mice.
* Grow a lot of mint if you have a problem with mice. They don't like it.
* Moles don't like castor oil and water, so place bowls of a mixture of $\frac{1}{2}$ cup castor oil to 2 cups water around your garden.
* Make a spicy hot pepper infusion spray to deter squirrels and deer.

## Herbal Pest Repellents

Flowers that are reported to repel insects include marigolds, mints, rue, basil, tansy, pennyroyal, rhubarb, elder, garlic, yarrow, chamomile, St. John's wort, chives, oregano, sage, horseradish, hot peppers, stinging nettle, nasturtium, feverfew, lavender, catnip, anise, rosemary, hyssop, thyme, white geranium, jimsonweed, and zinnia.

## Traps and Baits

### BANANA TRAP

1 cup each vinegar and sugar
A few chopped banana peels
1 gallon water

Combine the ingredients and leave in open bowls or jars around the garden. Insects attracted to the smell will drown.
**Makes about 1 gallon**

*Preparation Time:* About 10 minutes
*Shelf Life:* It is supposed to ferment
*Storage:* Discard unused portion

### Variations

BEER TRAP: Substitute beer.
MOLASSES TRAP: Substitute $\frac{1}{2}$ cup blackstrap molasses, 1 package active dry yeast, and 1 gallon warm water.

## Rx for Mold, Mildew, and Plant Diseases

* Remove diseased plants immediately and bury, burn, or compost them. One exception is diseased tomatoes, which you should not compost.
* Sterilize the soil by covering it with black plastic for a few months. The heat buildup under the plastic will kill most organisms.

### BAKING SODA FOR MILDEW ✄

1 tablespoon baking soda
1 gallon water

Combine the ingredients in a pail. Stir to blend. Put a few cups in a spray bottle, and spray on the mildew.

**Makes 1 gallon**

*Preparation Time:* A few minutes
*Shelf Life:* Indefinite
*Storage:* Covered container

### Variation

WASHING SODA ✖: Substitute washing soda for the baking soda; add 1 tablespoon liquid soap, and use hot water. This makes a stronger formula than just using baking soda.

## HEAVENLY HORSETAIL

*The silicon in horsetail is antifungal.*

Handful of horsetail
4 cups boiling water

Put the horsetail in a quart mason jar, and cover with the boiling water. Let set overnight, then strain. Pour into a spray bottle, and spray on the mildew.

**Makes 4 cups**

*Preparation Time:* About 15 minutes
*Shelf Life:* A few days
*Storage:* Glass jar with a screw top

### Variation

NETTLE INFUSION: Substitute nettle for the horsetail.

## BENEFICIAL INSECTS, AMPHIBIANS, AND MAMMALS

- Bats and birds eat insects.
- Snakes and weasels eat mice.
- Dragonflies eat mosquitoes.
- Frogs and fish eat mosquitoes.
- Toads eat many kinds of insects.
- Beneficial insects include bees and praying mantises.
- Nematodes eat the larvae of many insect pests, including Colorado potato beetle grubs and Japanese beetle grubs.
- Milky spore (a naturally occuring microscopic bacteria) kills Japanese beetles.

## WEED CONTROL: ALTERNATIVES TO HERBICIDES

See Seasonal Things to Do, page 226, for suggestions for making weeds grow before you plant your garden.

## CHEAP AND SAFE NORTH DAKOTA VEGETATION KILLER ✖

*This preparation is for weeds growing in sidewalk cracks and between bricks, not in the garden.*

1 cup salt
8 drops liquid detergent
1 gallon vinegar

Combine the ingredients in a 2-gallon pail. Stir to blend. Pour some of the mixture into a spray bottle and spray weeds. The salt will kill

all the vegetation, so don't use this mixture in your vegetable garden.
**Makes 1 gallon**

*Preparation Time:* A few minutes
*Shelf Life:* Indefinite
*Storage:* Glass jar with a screw top

## NEEM OIL ✗

*Neem is an excellent broad-spectrum natural pesticide.*

2 teaspoons essential oil of neem
2 cups water

Combine the ingredients in a spray bottle. Shake to blend, and spray weeds.
**Makes 2 cups**

*Preparation Time:* 1 minute
*Shelf Life:* Indefinite
*Storage:* Leave in the spray bottle

# Pets and Pets' Pests

It is heart wrenching to see beloved pets with a flea infestation. They scratch, practically eat themselves alive, and have no peace for hours on end. To add insult to injury, many owners cover the pet in pesticides with sprays, dips, and flea collars, which may weaken the immune system even more and make the pet less able to fight off the fleas. In my early days of being chemically sensitive, we had an old dog that was allergic to fleas, and we struggled desperately to find a nontoxic way of ridding the house and the dog of fleas. After a lot of trial and error, I came to understand that many natural pest-control methods work as well if not better than synthetic pesticides, and to be a responsible owner of a pet with fleas does not mean using pesticides. I also learned that most pets hate to be fussed over with modern synthetic grooming products; they don't like the smells. The simplest products are all that are needed, and the more natural the better.

## PET SHAMPOO

### BASIC SOAP SHAMPOO FORMULA

10 ounces water
1 to 2 tablespoons liquid castile soap (the less the better)
1 teaspoon glycerin or ¼ teaspoon vegetable oil
2 to 3 drops essential oils (optional)

Combine the ingredients in a jar. Shake to blend. Dampen your pet's fur, and dab on enough shampoo to lather the pet. Work in with your hands. Rinse thoroughly.
**Makes 1¼ cups**

*Preparation Time:* About 5 minutes
*Shelf Life:* 6 months
*Storage:* Glass jar with screw top
NOTE: Be sure to use very little essential oil on pets. They are sensitive to it. Do double

duty with essential oils by choosing those that are flea repellent, such as lavender, eucalyptus, or rosemary, or rose geranium to repel ticks, for example.

## Variations

ALOE SHAMPOO: Substitute 2 ounces aloe vera gel for 2 ounces of the water. Aloe is soothing and healing for a pet's skin problems.
ANTISEPTIC CLOVE SHAMPOO: Add 5 drops essential oil of clove and an extra teaspoon vegetable glycerin.

## BASIC DETERGENT SHAMPOO FORMULA

10 ounces water
1 to 2 tablespoons commercial shampoo (the less the better)
1 teaspoon glycerin or ¼ teaspoon vegetable oil
2 to 3 drops essential oils (optional)

Follow directions for Basic Soap Shampoo Formula (page 237).
**Makes 1¼ cups**

*Preparation Time:* About 5 minutes
*Shelf Life:* 6 months
*Storage:* Glass jar with a screw top

## BASIC SOAP-FREE SHAMPOO FORMULA

3 ounces soap bark
10 ounces water
5 ounces vodka, rum, or brandy
1 ounce glycerin

⅔ teaspoon grapefruit seed extract
2 to 3 drops essential oils (optional)

Make a soap bark decoction with the water (see page 32). Let cool. Add the vodka, glycerin, grapefruit seed extract, and essential oils (if using); let set overnight.
**Makes 2½ cups**

*Preparation Time:* About 30 minutes, not including simmering time for decoction
*Shelf Life:* 2 to 4 months
*Storage:* Glass jar with a screw top

## BASIC DRY SHAMPOO FORMULA

½ cups each cornmeal (or other flour), almond meal, and orris root powder

Combine the ingredients in a glass jar. Shake to blend. Dust the powder into the hair, leave it on for an hour, then brush it out.
**Makes 1½ cups**

*Preparation Time:* A few minutes
*Shelf Life:* Indefinitely frozen; 4 months at room temperature
*Storage:* Glass jar with a screw top

### FUR CONDITIONERS

## GLYCERIN CONDITIONER

*Glycerin is a lubricant and humectant, and it draws moisture to the skin. Eliminate the lemon juice if you will be using this preparation on a cat.*

6 ounces herbal infusion or distilled water
2 ounces glycerin
1 ounce lemon juice (optional)

Make the herbal infusion (if using) with an emollient herb such as calendula: Place a few tablespoons of the herb in a pint mason jar, add 6 ounces boiling water, and let set overnight or for 8 hours; strain. Add the glycerin and lemon juice (if using). Massage into the dog or cat's skin. Rinse with warm water.
**Makes 1 cup**

*Preparation Time:* About 15 minutes
*Shelf Life:* Discard leftovers

Variation
ROSEMARY ANTISEPTIC CONDITIONER: Make the herbal infusion with rosemary, and add 2 to 3 drops rosemary essential oil to the blend.

## AFTER-SOAP VINEGAR RINSE

*Soap leaves behind an alkaline pH and, if you have hard water, a dull residue. Vinegar rinses off the soap and returns the skin to its natural acidic state.*

1 cup organic apple cider vinegar
3 cups water

Mix the vinegar and water. Rinse over the pet's fur, being sure to avoid the eyes.
**Makes 4 cups**

*Preparation Time:* 1 minute
*Shelf Life:* Indefinite
*Storage:* Glass jar with a screw top

## ALOE VERA GEL SIMPLE ✘

*Aloe vera is a powerful healing plant for the skin.*

Aloe vera gel

Massage the gel into the fur around irritated areas. Rinse with warm water.
*Preparation Time:* None

## PET MASSAGE OIL ✘

*The gentle antibacterial and antiseptic qualities of calendula add value to this oil blend. Calendula oil is a rich yellow color. Use this also on animals that have dry, lusterless fur (after making sure their diet is rich in essential fatty acids).*

1 cup olive oil infused with calendula
⅓ teaspoon grapefruit seed extract

Follow the directions for infusing oils on page 32. Massage the oil into the fur around irritated areas. Do not rinse off.
**Makes about 1 cup**

*Preparation Time:* 25 minutes
*Shelf Life:* 2 to 4 months refrigerated
*Storage:* Glass jar with a screw top

## CITRUS LOTION

*Lemon repels fleas and is an astringent skin softener. Don't use this preparation for cats.*

4 or 5 lemons and/or oranges
6 cups water
1 teaspoon glycerin

Cut up the fruit and cover with water in a pan. Simmer for a few hours, adding more water as it evaporates. Let cool. Strain, then add the glycerin. Shake to blend. Rub into the fur.
**Makes 6 cups**

*Preparation Time:* 20 minutes
*Shelf Life:* 1 week refrigerated
*Storage:* Glass jar with a screw top

### REPELLENT HERBAL PET BEDDING
Herbs sewn into pillows were popular during the Renaissance and Elizabethan periods. Called dream pillows, or sleep pillows, they are actually sachets, but the herbs were chosen for their restive qualities. A packet of fresh herbs known for promoting sleep, such as hops and chamomile, was inserted into the pillow, to be replaced when necessary. Some present-day herbalists still create dream and sleep pillows. They are easy to make and useful for times of stress and restless sleep. They are also excellent for dog beds.

Insert a large sachet (about eight inches by eleven inches) with insect repellent herbs into a dog bed pillow.
**REPELLENT HERBS.** Southernwood, rose geranium, palmerosa, rue, camphor, feverfew, lavender, rosemary, sage, catmint, pennyroyal, eucalyptus, black walnut tree leaves, neem, tansy.
*Caution:* Herbal pillows can irritate some dogs. If they avoid the pillow, remove it.

### GENERAL REPELLENTS FOR PETS' PESTS

## INSECT REPELLENT SPRAY FOR DOGS AND CATS

*Don't use citronella on cats.*

1 to 2 drops each essential oils of eucalyptus, citronella, tea tree, and pennyroyal
2 cups witch hazel extract

Combine the ingredients in a glass jar. Test the pet's tolerance for this herbal blend by putting only a few drops on the collar to see how the animal reacts. If it seems fine, place 1 teaspoon or so on the collar, and rub ½ teaspoon or so into the fur.
**Makes 2 cups**

*Preparation Time:* A few minutes
*Shelf Life:* Indefinite
*Storage:* Glass jar with a screw top

### FLEAS
**CITRUS PEELS AND FLEAS.** Two of the ingredients in citrus peels are linalool and d-limonene. d-limonene kills all stages of a flea's life cycle, from egg to adult. A study on rats and mice was conducted in 1990 to find out if d-limonene causes cancer. There was no evidence that it did in female rats or mice of either sex, but male rats developed cancer. The rat was fed very high doses of d-limonene, and the study is controversial. Citrus solvents, high in d-limonene and made primarily from

citrus peels and oil of orange, are strong VOCs. It is not without caution that I recommend using citrus peels and citrus solvents to eradicate fleas. But nothing else works as well. After a challenging flea infestation in our house, we washed the floors twice a week with 1/4 cup citrus solvent to 2 gallons water, and within a few weeks the fleas were gone. I felt the trade-off was worth it, because our dog was suffering greatly, and the alternative was more highly toxic flea pesticides (which I would never have used). Keep the windows open when you wash the floors with citrus solvents. It should also be noted that cats are very sensitive to citrus.

GENERAL CARE FOR FLEAS

* Use a flea comb.
* Brewer's yeast helps dogs and cats repel fleas by making them exude an odor that fleas don't like. Pet Guard brand of garlic and yeast wafers are available in health food stores. A ten-pound pet gets one wafer, a twenty-pound pet gets two wafers, and so on. Start with half that quantity for the first week.
* Add a couple cloves of garlic a day to your pet's food.
* Keep pets in good health by boosting their immune system. Give them a pet vitamin pill, and make sure they get enough essential fatty acids such as omega-3 and -6 in their diet (read the label of your pet food).
* Soap and water works as well as anything to repel fleas, and the fleas will drown in the water. However, if every part of the pet is submerged but the head, the fleas will

## GOOD HERBS THAT REPEL FLEAS

SOUTHERNWOOD, rue, camphor, feverfew, lavender, rosemary, sage, catmint, pennyroyal, eucalyptus, black walnut tree leaves, tansy

congregate there. Use a flea comb to remove them.

## CITRUS SHAMPOO

Follow the directions for Basic Soap Shampoo Formula (page 237), but add 1 teaspoon orange oil. Do not use on cats.

Variations

EUCALYPTUS AND PENNYROYAL SOAP: Instead of orange oil, substitute 5 drops each essential oils of eucalyptus and pennyroyal.

ROSEMARY WASH: Substitute 5 to 10 drops essential oil of rosemary for the orange oil.

## CITRUS LOTION WITH LAVENDER

*Citrus peels contain an ingredient that kills all stages of the flea. Don't use this preparation on cats.*

4 to 5 lemons and/or oranges
4 cups water
1 teaspoon glycerin
5 to 10 drops essential oil of lavender

Cut up the fruit and cover with water in a pan. Simmer for a few hours, adding more water as it evaporates. Let cool. Strain, then add the glycerin and lavender oil. Shake to blend. Rub into the fur.

**Makes about 4 cups**

*Preparation Time:* 20 minutes
*Shelf Life:* 1 week refrigerated
*Storage:* Glass jar with a screw top

**HERBAL FLEA RUBS**

### ROSEMARY RUB

½ teaspoon essential oil of rosemary
½ cup olive oil

Combine the ingredients in a glass jar. Shake to blend. Put a few drops on a cloth and rub into the fur.

**Makes ½ cup**

*Preparation Time:* About 1 minute
*Shelf Life:* Indefinite
*Storage:* Glass jar with a screw top

## Variation

EUCALYPTUS AND PENNYROYAL RUB: Substitute ¼ teaspoon each essential oils of eucalyptus and pennyroyal.

**FLEA POWDERS**

### FLEA POWDER I ✖

½ teaspoon each dried eucalyptus, fennel or rosemary, and pennyroyal
¼ cup cornstarch

Grind the herbs into a powder in a spice mill or a blender. Combine with the cornstarch in a glass jar. Shake to blend. Sprinkle on the pet and work into the fur.

**Makes ¼ cup**

*Preparation Time:* About 15 minutes
*Shelf Life:* Indefinite, although the herbs will lose their potency in a few weeks
*Storage:* Glass jar with a screw top

## FLEA POWDER II

*Do not use this preparation on cats.*

¼ cup baking soda
½ teaspoon orange oil

Combine the ingredients in a glass jar. Shake to blend. Dust onto the pet and work into the fur.
**Makes ¼ cup**

*Preparation Time:* About 1 minute
*Shelf Life:* Indefinite
*Storage:* Glass jar with a screw top

For ridding your house of fleas, see pages 240–41.

Flea Repellent Pet Beds

* Add flea repellent herbs such as southernwood, lavender, and pennyroyal to your pet's bedding. For directions, see Sachets, page 80.
* Line the dog bed with something washable, such as towels. Frequent washing will significantly reduce flea populations.

**Flea Collars.** Place a few drops of repellent essential oil on a cloth collar; repeat weekly. Recommended essential oils include orange oil, citronella, cedar, eucalyptus, or pennyroyal.

*Caution:* Pregnant women shouldn't use pennyroyal. Use only a few drops essential oils, because pets can be very sensitive to them.

### Ticks

We used to get twenty ticks a day off our dogs; they have none since we began putting a few drops—no more—of essential oil of rose geranium (or its near relative palmerosa) on the dogs' cloth collars every week. Nothing works as well as these essential oils, but it is important not to put too much on the dog, because essential oils can bother them.

Hands-On

* Check pets daily for ticks. Deer ticks are the size of poppy seeds at the nymph stage and very hard to see, so persevere.

# Natural Pest Control

NOTE: For insect repellents, see page 254.

Steps to Integrated Pest Management

1. Remove water.
2. Remove food.
3. Know your pest.
4. Remove their nests.

## TICK REPELLENTS

The Best Choice for Tick Repellent Essential Oil
Rose geranium or palmerosa.

Other Herbs and Essential Oils
Bay, eucalyptus, European pennyroyal, lavender, lemon balm (citronella), myrrh, rosemary, or tickweed (American pennyroyal)
*Caution:* Pregnant women should avoid pennyroyal.

# BUYER'S GUIDE
## CONTROLLING PESTS NATURALLY

**N**ATURAL pest control isn't as much going out and buying an alternative product as it is learning about what material or trap works to handle a pest, and using that instead. Most commercial pest control products, even if they are touted as natural, have inert ingredients that are toxic and should be avoided. If you find a product you like, call the company for information about the inert ingredients.

Victor Pest Control (see Sources and Resources) has a line of pest control products that are mint based and certified by Scientific Certification Systems as being poison free. Products include mouse- and ant traps, flying insect control, a mosquito barrier, ant and roach killers, and magnet pheromone traps.

### Pyrethrin, Pyrethrum, and Pyrethroids
Pyrethrum powder comes from ground chrysanthemum flowers and contains the active ingredient pyrethrin, which kills many insects. A lot of people are allergic to pyrethrum, so use it with caution. Pyrethroids are synthetic pesticides. Check Sources and Resources to find this powder without any added ingredients that may be harmful, such as piperonyl butoxide. Sesame seed oil is a much safer synergist than piperonyl butoxide. Also, pay close attention to labels: Don't buy synthetic pyrethroid pesticides.
*Caution:* Cats are very sensitive to even low doses of pyrethrin.

### Pheromones and Traps
Pheromones are secreted by animals and insects to attract attention. Sex pheromones in particular are used in natural pest controls as lures to bait insects to some sort of trap. See Sources and Resources for specific products.

### Ultrasonic Machines
There is no scientific evidence that these machines work, despite people's claims. I have found that mice do not spend much time in our kitchen when our ultrasonic machine is on, but about ten feet away the machine isn't very effective.

## ALL-PURPOSE NATURAL PESTICIDES

All-purpose pesticides work against flies, ants, fleas, and more. They also unfortunately kill honeybees, so avoid overuse.

HANDS-ON

* String hot peppers together and hang them in problem areas.
* Fill window boxes with herbs such as rue, thyme, mint, and oregano.

## PEPPERMINT ALL-PURPOSE CASTILE SOAP SPRAY ✄

2 tablespoons liquid peppermint castile soap
1 gallon water

Combine the ingredients and fill a spray bottle. Flies, ants, fleas, and mice avoid peppermint. Spray along baseboards, the backs of counters, and other areas of infestation. Do not rinse.

**Makes 1 gallon**

*Preparation Time:* A few minutes
*Shelf Life:* Indefinite
*Storage:* Covered container

Variations

CAYENNE CASTILE SOAP SPRAY: Add 1 teaspoon cayenne pepper. The shelf life is reduced to a few weeks.

PYRETHRUM INSECTICIDAL SOAP: Combine $\frac{1}{2}$ cup pyrethrum powder, 1 ounce liquid castile soap, and 1 gallon water. The shelf life is a few weeks.

## ALL-PURPOSE PESTICIDE POWDER

$\frac{1}{2}$ cup each bay and peppermint leaves
$1\frac{1}{2}$ teaspoons each citrus peels, garlic powder, diatomaceous earth, cayenne pepper, pyrethrum, and salt

Grind the ingredients into a powder in a blender or with a mortar and pestle. Dust along baseboards, the backs of counters, and other areas of infestation. Do not rinse.

**Makes 1 cup**

*Preparation Time:* About 20 minutes
*Shelf Life:* Indefinite, although the herbs will lose their potency.
*Storage:* Glass jar with a screw top

## ALL-PURPOSE PENNYROYAL AND EUCALYPTUS SPRAY ✄

1 teaspoon each essential oils of pennyroyal and eucalyptus
2 cups water

Combine the ingredients in a spray bottle. Shake to blend. Spray along baseboards, the backs of counters, and other areas of infestation. Don't rinse.

**Makes 2 cups**

*Preparation Time:* A few minutes
*Shelf Life:* Indefinite
*Storage:* Glass jar with a screw top

## Variations

CITRUS SPRAY: Use 2 teaspoons orange oil or citrus peel extract to 2 cups water.

CEDAR SPRAY: Use 1 to 2 teaspoons cedar oil to 2 cups water.

## DIATOMACEOUS EARTH (DE) FOR FLIES, FLEAS, ANTS, AND ROACHES ✘

Natural diatomaceous earth (as opposed to treated pool-grade DE)

Sprinkle diatomaceous earth anywhere pests are a problem.

*Preparation Time:* None
*Shelf Life:* Indefinite
*Storage:* Glass jar with a screw top

### ANTS (SUGAR AND CARPENTER)

HANDS-ON

* Locate the nest and, if outside, pour boiling water over it.
* Plant mint, pennyroyal, and tansy around the house; they repel ants.
* Remove water sources and fix dripping outdoor faucets.

## BORAX AND SUGAR ANT HOTEL ✘

*Use four screw-top jars a few inches in height (marinated artichoke heart jars are ideal).*

1 cup borax
1 cup sugar
3 cups water

Mix the ingredients in a bowl. Place a loose wad of toilet paper into the jars. Pour in the mixture until it is about an inch from the top. Screw the lids on the jars; with a hammer and nail, make 4 to 8 holes in each lid. Place the jars in areas where you have ants (but keep them away from children), and watch the ants line up in rows to march in. This trap will catch the workers but not the queen (see Note).

**Makes about 4 cups**

*Preparation Time:* About 20 minutes
*Shelf Life:* Indefinite
*Storage:* 4 small glass jars with screw tops
NOTE: To kill the queen, blend $1/4$ cup confectioners' sugar and 1 tablespoon borax. Sprinkle it in ant traffic areas. This is not enough borax to kill the worker ants immediately, so they take it back to the nest, which eradicates the whole nest. (If the worker ants die at the powder site, cut back on the borax.) Do not place the poison anywhere that children or pets could ingest it.

## HONEY TRAP

2 teaspoons honey
$1/2$ cup warm water

Dissolve the honey in the warm water. Pour into saucers. The ants attracted to it will drown.

**Makes $1/2$ cup**

*Preparation Time:* A few minutes
*Shelf Life:* Indefinite
*Storage:* Glass jar with a screw top

## MOLASSES TRAP

2 tablespoons each molasses and sugar
1 teaspoon active dry yeast
2 cups water

Combine the ingredients in a shallow, wide-mouthed jar. Pests will enter and drown.
**Makes 2 cups**

*Preparation Time:* A few minutes
*Shelf Life:* Fermentation is intended
*Storage:* Glass jar with a screw top

## GROUND CLOVES ✗

Ground cloves

Make a trail of ground cloves where there are ants. They avoid cloves.

*Preparation Time:* None
*Shelf Life:* Indefinite
*Storage:* Glass jar with a screw top

**CLOTHING MOTHS**
HANDS-ON

* Clean woolen items thoroughly before storage, and air in the sun for a few hours if possible before packing them away.
* If you discover moths, place items in a clothes dryer on high heat for about fifteen minutes if the fabric can handle the heat; if not, freeze for two days.
* Cedar chests help repel moths, but they must be sealed shut.
* Completely seal clean woolen items in bags, boxes, and chests.

## GOOD HERBS THAT REPEL CLOTHING MOTHS

LAVENDER, lemon, cloves, camphor, hyssop, winter savory, rosemary, cassia bark, cedar, sassafras

## NATURAL MOTH BALLS (REPELLENT SACHETS)

*These sachets are lovely to tuck into sweater drawers and hang in closets.*

2 ounces each dried rosemary and mint
1 ounce each dried thyme and ginseng
8 ounces whole cloves

Combine the ingredients in a large bowl. Blend. Make into sachets (see page 80).
**Makes about 14 ounces**

*Preparation Time:* About 2 hours
*Shelf Life:* Indefinite
*Storage:* Store leftover herbs in glass jars with screw tops

Variation
MOTH SACHETS: Combine any of the following herbs: rosemary, tansy, thyme, mint, southernwood, cloves, or sweet woodruff. Make into sachets or strew in drawers.

## CAMPHOR OIL

*The camphor plant produces a powerful volatile oil that is so antiseptic that it is used as embalming fluid and is even banned in some countries. Camphor oil is famous as a clothes moth insecticide, and it deters other pests as well.*

1 teaspoon camphor oil (not synthetic)
2 cups water

Combine the ingredients in a spray bottle and shake to blend. Spray drawers, closets, and anywhere moths might be found.
**Makes 2 cups**

*Preparation Time:* About 1 minute
*Shelf Life:* Indefinite
*Storage:* Leave in the spray bottle

### COCKROACHES
HANDS-ON
* Keep the house clean.
* Half fill a jar with beer and pieces of banana and/or apple. Rub the inside of the top of the jar with nonpetroleum jelly (to make it too slippery for the roaches to climb out). Wrap the jar with masking tape or newspaper to give the roaches "stairs" to climb on. The roaches will climb in and drown.
* Chickens and geckos love to eat roaches. You might consider getting a few.
* Herbs for use against cockroaches include tea tree oil, garlic, peppermint, bay leaves, and hot peppers. Add 2 teaspoons essential oil or

2 tablespoons ground herb to 2 cups water in a spray bottle and spray infested areas.

### TRIED AND TRUE ✖

*None of the ingredients given in the variations is better than boric acid, but you may have them more readily at hand.*

Boric acid

Sprinkle (don't pile) boric acid along baseboards, in cracks, behind the stove, under the sink, and so on, making sure it is inaccessible to pets and children.

*Preparation Time:* None
*Shelf Life:* Indefinite
*Storage:* Glass jar with a screw top

Variations
EPSOM SALTS: Substitute Epsom salts.
BAKING SODA AND SUGAR: Substitute equal amounts baking soda and sugar.
BORAX, COCOA, AND FLOUR: Substitute $1/4$ cup borax and 2 tablespoons each flour and cocoa.

### SOAP AND SALSA ✖

1 tablespoon each liquid castile soap and Tabasco sauce
4 cups water

Combine the ingredients in a spray bottle. Spray infested areas.
**Makes 4 cups**

*Preparation Time:* A few minutes
*Shelf Life:* About 2 months
*Storage:* Glass jar with a screw top

## DRUNKEN ROACHES ✘

Up to ½ cup beer

Place the beer in a saucer on the floor. Once the roaches are drunk, you can dispose of them easily.
**Makes ½ cup**

*Preparation Time:* None
*Shelf Life:* Replace every week or so
*Storage:* Discard

### Variation
STRANGE BREW: Combine beer with a few bay leaves and cucumber peels.

## ROACH KILLER

*Both of the ingredients in this preparation are often found in health food stores and gardening centers. Use natural, not pool-grade, diatomaceous earth.*

2 parts natural diatomaceous earth
1 part pyrethrin powder

Combine the ingredients. Dust infested areas.
*Preparation Time:* A few minutes
*Shelf Life:* Indefinite
*Storage:* Glass jar with a screw top

### FLEAS
HANDS-ON

* Suspend a lightbulb eight to ten inches over a pan of water at night. (A gooseneck lamp works well.)
* Citrus peel extract is an excellent flea repellent because its components—d-limonene and linalool—kill all stages of the flea's life cycle. (See page 38 for cautions about citrus solvent.) Put 2 teaspoons citrus peel extract in 2 cups water in a spray bottle and spray infested areas.
* Vacuum frequently; freeze the bags before throwing away to kill the fleas and larvae.
* Heating an environment to 103°F will kill fleas. During a heat wave, consider going to an air-conditioned hotel for a few days while you close all the doors and windows in your home to hold in as much heat as possible.
* For outdoor flea infestations, use predatory nematodes; they prey on flea larvae and pupae (see Sources and Resources).

## CITRUS SPRAY

2 teaspoons orange oil or citrus solvent
2 cups water

Combine the ingredients in a spray bottle. Shake to blend, and spray problem areas.
**Makes 2 cups**

*Preparation Time:* A few minutes
*Shelf Life:* Indefinite
*Storage:* Leave in the spray bottle

## PEPPERMINT CASTILE SOAP SPRAY ✕

2 teaspoons peppermint castile soap
2 cups water

Combine the ingredients in a spray bottle. Shake to blend, and spray infested areas.
**Makes 2 cups**

*Preparation Time:* A few minutes
*Shelf Life:* Indefinite
*Storage:* Leave in the spray bottle

Variations
EUCALYPTUS AND PENNYROYAL SPRAY: Substitute 1 teaspoon each eucalyptus and pennyroyal for the soap.
ROSEMARY SPRAY: Add 1 teaspoon essential oil of rosemary.

## CARPET AND UPHOLSTERY POWDER

2 cups natural diatomaceous earth (not pool grade)
1 cup each baking soda and cornstarch

Combine the ingredients. Dust on carpets and/or furniture. Let set for 1 to 2 hours, then vacuum.
**Makes 4 cups**

*Preparation Time:* A few minutes
*Shelf Life:* Indefinite
*Storage:* Glass jar with a screw top

## BOILED ONION SPRAY

2 onions
2 cups water, or as needed

Peel and slice the onions. Put in a pan, add water to cover, and bring to a boil. Reduce the heat and simmer for 30 minutes, adding more water as it evaporates. Let cool, then strain. Pour into a spray bottle and spray as needed.
**Makes 2 cups**

*Preparation Time:* About 30 minutes
*Shelf Life:* About 1 week refrigerated
*Storage:* Glass jar with a screw top

## CAYENNE FUMIGANT

2 teaspoons cayenne pepper

Burn the cayenne pepper as you would incense. Make sure that all people and pets are out of the house.

*Preparation Time:* None
*Shelf Life:* Indefinite
*Storage:* Glass jar with a screw top

## OUTDOOR FLEA CONTROL ✕

Agricultural lime

Dust lime in outdoor areas that pets frequent to deter the pests.
*Preparation Time:* None
*Shelf Life:* Indefinite

**FLIES**

HANDS-ON

* Cleanliness is the name of the game for keeping away flies. Remove compost to the compost pile, and don't leave food uncovered.
* Install window screens.
* Use flyswatters.
* Nurture your spider population; spiders eat flies.
* "Phannies" are fly predators—biological controls—that work beautifully for barns. See Sources and Resources.
* Hang pomanders on doors (citrus peel is a repellent).
* Dust the bottoms of trash cans with borax.
* Place potted basil plants in infested areas.

## HOMEMADE FLYPAPER

¼ cup corn syrup
½ cup sugar

Cut 4 or 5 long strips about 2 inches wide from brown paper bags. Mix the ingredients in a bowl, and spread on the strips with a knife. Hang the strips over a bowl to catch drips.
**Makes ¾ cup**

*Preparation Time:* About 20 minutes
*Shelf Life:* Indefinite
*Storage:* Glass jar with a screw top

## GOOD HERBS THAT REPEL FLIES

TANSY, cloves, basil, pine oil (hang a pine bough in your kitchen)

Variation

SWEETENED CASTOR OIL FLYPAPER: Substitute 3 tablespoons honey or molasses and 1 tablespoon castor oil (not synthetic).

## HANGING HERBAL SACHETS

Cloves
Eucalyptus leaves
Clover blossoms

Make sachets as described on page 80. Hang in infested areas.
*Preparation Time:* 1 to 2 hours
*Shelf Life:* Indefinite
*Storage:* Store remaining herbs in glass jars with screw tops

**FRUIT FLIES**

NOTE: Store all fruit in the refrigerator. Make sure there isn't any exposed compost in your kitchen.

## FRUIT FLIES HATE BASIL

1 pint packed basil leaves
Enough water to cover

Make a basil infusion in a pint mason jar; let set overnight. Strain, and spray infested areas.

**Makes 2 cups**

*Preparation Time:* 10 minutes
*Shelf Life:* 1 week refrigerated
*Storage:* Leave in the spray bottle

### Variation

BASIL OIL SPRAY: Add 2 teaspoons basil essential oil to 2 cups water in a spray bottle. The shelf life is indefinite.

### GRAIN MOTHS AND WEEVILS

## KEEP WEEVILS AT BAY ✄

Bay leaves
Water

Either sprinkle bay leaves around infested areas, or make a strong bay leaf infusion in a pint mason jar, strain into a spray bottle, and spray infested areas.

**2 cups spray**

*Preparation Time:* 15 minutes for infusion
*Shelf Life:* 1 week refrigerated for infusion; indefinitely for bay leaves
*Storage:* Spray bottle for infusion; glass jar with a screw top for leaves

### HEAD LICE

NOTE: See page 258 for how to rid hair of lice.

### MOSQUITOES

HANDS-ON

* Remove all sources of stagnant water; it serves as a breeding ground.
* Use mosquito netting and screens.

---

## GOOD HERBS THAT REPEL MOSQUITOES

BASIL, eucalyptus, cloves, geranium, peppermint, rosemary, lemon balm (citronella), onions, garlic, feverfew

---

### RATS AND MICE

HANDS-ON

* Use Havahart traps (release the rodents far from your home or they will return). Effective baits include peanut butter and bacon.
* Mice avoid mint. Place fresh mint boughs here, there, and everywhere you have mice.
* Store all food, including fruit and pet food, in containers, cupboards, or the refrigerator. Remove old boxes of clothes and magazines.

To kill mice without poisons, use a homemade vitamin D bait. Rats and mice cannot tolerate vitamin D because it disrupts their calcium metabolism. Rats die within two to four days of eating vitamin D. Vitamin $D_3$ is necessary for human metabolism, which is why it is added to all commercially sold milk. To make the bait, crush a vitamin-D pill and blend it with peanut butter or cheese, or sprinkle it on a piece of corn bread; place it in an area frequented by mice.

### TERMITES

NOTE: For identification purposes, the antenna on termites are not elbowed, whereas those of ants are.

HANDS-ON

* Determine what species of termite you have.
* Construct a barrier of eight- to ten-mesh sand at least five inches deep and one foot wide all around the house to keep the termites from tunneling.
* Remove all damp wood and moisture problems (for damp-wood termites).
* Use Tim-Bor, a boric acid compound, for permanent termite control.
* Nematodes (tiny worms) eat termites. Place them in the dirt surrounding the foundation. (See Sources and Resources: N-Viro Products.)
* You can electrocute dry-wood termites with an Electro-Gun. No fuss, no muss. Your local pesticide company can lease this equipment, if they don't already own it, by contacting ETEX, Ltd. (See Sources and Resources.)

## DIATOMACEOUS EARTH ✗

Natural diatomaceous earth

See Natural Pest Control, page 243.

*Preparation Time:* None
*Shelf Life:* Indefinite
*Storage:* Glass jar with a screw top

## Variations

PYRETHRUM ADDED: Use equal amounts diatomaceous earth and pyrethrum.
BORIC ACID AND DIATOMACEOUS EARTH: Use equal amounts boric acid and diatomaceous earth.

## TICKS
HANDS-ON

* Keep grass well cut, and remove brush and woodpiles, which harbor mice and small mammals that could carry ticks.
* Check pets daily for ticks.
* Carbon dioxide traps are Styrofoam containers holding dry ice (which releases carbon dioxide), with three-quarter-inch holes in each side of the Styrofoam. The containers are surrounded with about an inch-wide strip of sticky substance such as honey. Ticks are attracted to the carbon dioxide and can be vacuumed out of the container or will get stuck on the honey. Place the vacuum cleaner bag in a plastic bag; seal and freeze overnight before discarding. Call B.I.R.C. for the latest in this technology (see Sources and Resources).

## TICK SPRAY ✗ 🎁

2 teaspoons essential oil of rose geranium or palmerosa
2 cups water

Combine the ingredients in a spray bottle. Shake to blend. Spray dog beds and other areas where they sleep.
**Makes 2 cups**

*Preparation Time:* 1 minute
*Shelf Life:* Indefinite
*Storage:* Leave in the spray bottle

### Variation

ROSEMARY AND MYRRH SPRAY: Substitute 1 teaspoon essential oil of rosemary and teaspoon tincture of myrrh. The shelf life is 2 weeks refrigerated.

### WASPS AND YELLOW JACKETS

HANDS-ON

* Don't wear perfume, hair spray, scented deodorant, or brightly colored clothing outdoors.
* Remove compost and all sweet foods such as soda from the vicinity.
* Hire a professional pest control company to vacuum wasp nests and kill the wasps by putting the bag in the freezer.
* Traps can be used successfully to catch wasps. See Sources and Resources.
* Ground nests can be eliminated by sealing them off with an upside down bowl.
* Nematodes work well for eliminating ground nests.

# Natural Insect Repellents

The stakes are high for choosing effective means to repel insects. Deer ticks that carry Lyme disease, ehrlichiosis, and the amoebic parasite *Babesia* are now in almost every state, and outbreaks of encephalitis-carrying mosquitoes are increasing. It is easy to let fear of these bugs curtail your enjoyment of nature. The experience of my community, which is at the center of the tick epidemic, attests to this fact. But learning new ways to avoid insects can enable you to be outside as much as you want. We've learned that herbal repellents *combined* with some lifestyle changes is key to coexisting with bugs without coming to harm.

Repellent products are a help, but no matter what you use, a few bugs can get through any defense. Lifestyle changes include pulling your socks up over your pant cuffs and having a soapy shower after being in infested areas in the case of ticks. See specific insects, below, for more suggestions. Common sense is as good a guide as any. One of the rules is to know your insect. Mosquitoes like water at dusk, a place and time to avoid. My daughter found a deer tick on her after cross-country skiing in the woods near our house in upstate New York in January, when the trees were covered with an inch of ice. We weren't prepared for that, but now we know that we have to worry about ticks all year, even after an ice storm.

## BUYER'S GUIDE

### HERBAL INSECT REPELLENTS

GREEN Ban, Jungle Juice, Simmons Handcrafts, Nutribiotics, and Lakon Herbals are just a few of the companies selling pure essential oil–based insect repellents. Quantum has an excellent tick repellent containing rose geranium. Check in your health food store for more brands.

## HERBS AND ESSENTIAL OILS

Fortunately, most insects are innocuous, if irritating. Using herbal essential oils as natural repellents is often all you need to protect yourself from too many unpleasant bites. Folk wisdom from all over the world recommends similar plants to repel insects: Lemon balm (citronella) is used to repel mosquitoes everywhere, as is pennyroyal and lavender. There are many other herbs that are less well known but are reputed to be powerful. American Indians rubbed the juice of bloodroot on their skin for its insect-repellent properties.

NOTE: To reduce insects in your home and yard, see page 243.

## HOW TO MAKE REPELLENTS

A wide variety of combinations of herbs or essential oils make good insect repellents. Mix, match, and experiment. One herbalist I know recommends infusing many herbs and essential oils in oil for a potent "bug juice." I am more of a "simples" proponent—adding herbs and essential oils one at a time to find what does and doesn't work, and to isolate any possible allergies. Following are examples of repellent oils, vinegars, waters, and alcohols, all easily made at home. Essential oils are the strongest repellents, but never put essential oils directly on the skin, because they can burn.

**HOW TO MAKE REPELLENT SOAPS** ✗ 🎁. Add essential oils such as lemon balm (citronella), pennyroyal, lavender, and rose geranium to liquid castile soap, and wash before

## GOOD INSECT-REPELLING HERBS AND OILS

THIS list includes all the repellent herbs I have come across in my research. You never know when one obscure-sounding herb will work to repel an insect, as with rose geranium for ticks, for example.

Basil, bay, bergamot, bloodroot (never drink the poisonous red juice; just rub onto the skin), cajeput, cayenne pepper, chamomile, chives, citrus, cloves, coriander seeds, epazote, eucalyptus, feverfew (pyrethrum is the active ingredient), juniper berries, lavender, lemon balm (also called citronella; attracts honeybees), myrrh, mugwort, neem, peppermint, pennyroyal (don't use when pregnant or for mosquitoes; it attracts them), rose geranium, rosemary, rue, sage, sassafras, southernwood, tansy leaves, tarragon, tea tree oil, thyme, tickweed (American pennyroyal), wormwood

and after spending time outdoors. Add ten to fifteen drops essential oil per ounce of soap.

**HOW TO MAKE REPELLENT OILS** ✗ 🎁. It is tricky to get the right concentration of essential oils; in general, less is best. My dogs can tolerate only the smallest amount of essential oils on their collars each week—just one drop—but it is enough to repel the ticks. I use about one-fifth the amount of essential oils as most people do, because I find that a little goes a long, long way. To find the dosage necessary to repel the insects, start with a drop or two in your mixtures, and increase the amount as you find you can tolerate it.

Combining repellent essential oils and/or herbs with a fruit or nut oil carrier is a good technique when you want to dab a bit on your skin.

T I P *Almond oil contains sulfur, a repellent in its own right.*

## INSECT REPELLENT OIL I ✖

10 to 25 drops essential oil
2 tablespoons vegetable oil
1 tablespoon aloe vera gel (optional)

Combine the ingredients in a glass jar; stir to blend. Dab a few drops on your skin or clothing.
**Makes about 2 tablespoons**

*Preparation Time:* A few minutes
*Shelf Life:* 6 months
*Storage:* Glass jar with a screw top

## INSECT REPELLENT OIL II

1 to 2 ounces herbs
2 cups vegetable oil
⅔ teaspoon grapefruit seed extract

Infuse the herbs and oil in a Crock-Pot over low heat for 4 to 5 hours. Let cool, then strain. Stir in the grapefruit seed extract. Dab a few drops on your skin or clothing.
**Makes 2 cups**

*Preparation Time:* About 10 minutes, not including the infusing time
*Shelf Life:* About 6 months; discard if you see mold
*Storage:* Glass jar with a screw top

## HOW TO MAKE VINEGAR AND WATER INFUSION REPELLENTS

## REPELLENT I 🎁

1 to 2 ounces herbs
2 cups boiling water or organic apple cider vinegar
⅔ teaspoon grapefruit seed extract (for water infusion only)
¼ cup aloe vera gel (optional)

Infuse the herbs in a pint mason jar with the water or vinegar. Let set overnight for a water infusion or 4 to 6 weeks for a vinegar infusion. Strain completely. Add the grapefruit seed extract and aloe vera gel. Stir to blend. Dab on your skin.
**Makes 2¼ cups**

*Preparation Time:* About 15 minutes, not including the infusing time
*Shelf Life:* Indefinite for vinegar, 1 to 2 months for water (discard if you see mold)
*Storage:* Glass jar with a screw top

## REPELLENT II

25 drops essential oil
¼ cup water or organic apple cider vinegar

Combine the ingredients in a glass jar. Shake to blend. Dab some on your skin or clothing.
**Makes ¼ cup**

*Preparation Time:* A few minutes
*Shelf Life:* Indefinite
*Storage:* Glass jar with a screw top

**HOW TO MAKE ALCOHOL REPELLENTS** ✂ 🎁.
Follow the directions for making tinctures on page 32. An easy way to make alcohol repellents is to add ten to fifteen drops repellent essential oil per ounce of rum, vodka, or brandy. Dab a few drops on your skin or clothing.

**HOW TO MAKE WITCH HAZEL EXTRACT-BASED REPELLENTS**

## WITCH HAZEL REPELLENT ✂ 🎁

*This helps soothe bug bites as well as prevent more.*

10 to 25 drops essential oil
2 tablespoons witch hazel extract

Combine the ingredients in a glass jar. Stir to blend. Dab a few drops on your skin or clothing.
**Makes about 3 tablespoons**

*Preparation Time:* A few minutes
*Shelf Life:* Indefinite
*Storage:* Glass jar with a screw top

# Repelling Pests

TIPS AND TRICKS
Use the herbs listed in this section in repellent soaps, oils, and vinegars and in alcohol- or witch hazel extract–based repellents.

* If you are camping, throw some repellent herbs on the fire. Burning coriander seed is reputed to be a successful deterrent, as is burning lemon balm leaves.
* Put a few drops of an essential oil such as lavender in the rinse water of your outerwear.
* Drink a tablespoon or two of organic apple cider vinegar.
* Eat lots of garlic.
* Vitamin $B_1$ taken daily is supposed to help repel insects.

TICKS

CLOTHING
* Wear white or light-colored clothing so ticks are visible against it. Deer ticks are as small as poppy seeds in their nymph stage and are difficult to see under the best of circumstances.
* Wear long pants and long-sleeved shirts.
* Pull your socks up over your pant cuffs.
* Wear a hat or scarf.
* Place a few drops essential oil of rose geranium or palmerosa on clothing and on pet collars.

HABITAT
* Ticks like to live in grasses, trees, and shrubs and on warm-blooded animals such as cats, dogs, deer, and mice.

* Ticks are a problem twelve months a year even in the North, but less so when it is very cold.

PERSONAL HABIT TIPS

* Shower with soap after being in tick-infested areas, and get up a lather all over your body.

* Check each family member for ticks once or twice a day—especially under the armpits, behind the ears, in the genital area, and on the head.

* Be sure to remove ticks from pets daily, and don't allow pets on couches and beds.

FIRST CHOICE OF HERBS AND ESSENTIAL OILS FOR REPELLENTS

* Essential oil of rose geranium or palmerosa

OTHER CHOICES

* Bay, eucalyptus, European pennyroyal, lavender, lemon balm (citronella), myrrh, rosemary, tickweed (American pennyroyal)

## MOSQUITOES

CLOTHING

* Wear a hat with mosquito netting.
* Use repellent on clothes.

HABITAT

* Mosquitoes breed in stagnant water, such as is found in swamps, old tires, and bird-baths.

* Dusk in summer is the favorite hour for mosquitoes, so protect yourself.

FIRST CHOICE OF HERBS AND ESSENTIAL OILS FOR REPELLENTS

* Pennyroyal, lemon balm (citronella), thyme, lavender

OTHER CHOICES

* Bergamot, cajeput, eucalyptus, rose geranium, myrrh, peppermint, rosemary, oil of clove, oil of nutmeg, feverfew, cinnamon stick, mint

## BLACKFLIES

CLOTHING

* Flies reportedly avoid the color blue.
* Wear mesh headgear that ties under the chin and covers the entire head.

HABITAT

* Blackflies are the worst in spring and early summer.

CHOICE OF HERBS AND ESSENTIAL OILS FOR REPELLENTS

* Sassafras, lavender, eucalyptus, pennyroyal, bergamot, cajeput, cedar, myrrh, lemon balm (citronella), peppermint, camphor oil

## HEAD LICE

ACCESSORIES

* Metal nit comb

FIRST CHOICE OF HERBS AND ESSENTIAL OILS FOR REPELLENTS

* Tea tree, rosemary, lavender, eucalyptus, rose geranium, quassia bark

OTHER CHOICES

* Olive oil castile soap

HANDS-ON

*Steps to Remove Head Lice*

1. Lather hair with a coconut-oil castile soap. Adding a few drops of tea tree oil and neem oil to the lathered hair is also recommended.

2. Rinse and rewash with same.

3. After rewashing, do not rinse, but wrap a towel around the head and set for half an hour.
4. Again, do not rinse, but comb with a nit-removing comb (see Sources and Resources), strand by strand, until all nits are removed (this takes a while). Dampen hair as needed.
5. Wash and rinse the hair. Once dry, check thoroughly for any missed nits.
6. Thoroughly clean the comb, hands, bedding, and clothing. Pillows can be placed in the freezer overnight.
*Caution:* Be sure not to get soap with essential oils in the eyes. Rinse away from the face; children should be supervised by an adult.

## HERBAL LICE OIL

10 drops essential oil
1 ounce oil

Combine the ingredients, and comb through the hair. Wash with olive oil castile soap infused with essential oils (see below), then comb thoroughly with a metal nit comb. Makes enough for one shampooing.

*Shelf Life:* Enough for one treatment

## TEA TREE OIL SHAMPOO

10 drops tea tree oil
1 ounce shampoo

Combine the ingredients, and shampoo as usual. Makes enough for one shampooing.

*Shelf Life:* Enough for one treatment

## HERBAL CASTILE SHAMPOO

10 drops essential oils
1 ounce liquid olive oil castile soap

Combine the ingredients, and shampoo as usual. Comb hair thoroughly with a metal nit comb. Repeat daily. Makes enough for one shampooing.

*Shelf Life:* Enough for one treatment

# CHAPTER 6

# House Care and Hobbies

*Health for the body, peace for the spirit, harmony with the environment—*
*these are the criteria of the natural house.*

—DAVID PEARSON, *THE NATURAL HOUSE BOOK*

FOR years I've saved a magazine picture of a bathroom built primarily of bluestone, a gray-blue slate native to the Catskill Mountains in upstate New York. Fifteen-inch by fifteen-inch squares of the cool-hued slate cover the floor, reach shoulder high up the walls,

and encase a large, rectangular soapstone bathtub. A skylight provides soft, natural light, setting off the multihued colors in the slate and stone. A single bar of rich, creamy-looking natural soap rests on a spare wood soap dish by the tub, and plush natural-fiber towels lay folded and ready on a simple shelf. I've saved the picture all these years because it inspires me, gives me ideas for when I have more time and resources. The space looks more like a sanctuary than a bathroom, a place of repose and contemplation. It indicates balance with nature and

taps into our need for periods of peace and quiet. Bluestone is abundant in my community, which is probably why this bathroom has such an impact on me. A bathroom built of bluestone would truly make me feel at home.

Looking to nature will give us many more earth-oriented ideas for our homes similar to this bluestone bathroom. We can learn how to use native materials by looking at regional architecture from long ago, when people used what was close at hand. Arid climates are suited to building with earth—and what rich, warm, mellow colors—readily available and well suited to baking in the hot sun. Cedar—a wood that weathers well and lasts a long time even on exteriors and roofs of houses battered by salty ocean air on the eastern seaboard—can easily be made into shingles and shakes with the abundance of cedar trees growing nearby. Straw bale houses are increasingly being built in a variety of climates. One of the most comfortable houses I have ever been in was constructed entirely with poplar sustainably harvested from the surrounding ten acres. A house made of such natural materials breathes with the local environment. And it makes a home where its inhabitants fit in, an environment in which they belong. After all, we too are nature.

Fresh, clean inside air is the first and foremost priority for an ecologically sound home. We spend 90 percent of our time indoors, and the air inside our homes should rejuvenate and improve the quality of our lives and allow us to breath freely. A rule of thumb for clean indoor air is to choose the most inert natural materials available for building. These include stone, earth, minerals, and many kinds of wood. Inert materials don't have much of a smell, although this doesn't always mean they are safe, as in the case of rock that is contaminated with radon. Even natural materials are not always good choices for clean air. Freshly cut pine gives off strong terpenes, which aren't healthy in high concentrations and can be a serious problem in winter when many houses are closed up tight. But freshly cut maple, a wood with fewer strong terpenes, can

be substituted for pine. All building needs can be satisfied with materials that are safe for you and the environment.

Establishing a healthy home in balance with your natural surroundings doesn't happen overnight. It is a process. These days such a home is a rare place, with most such havens created to protect a chemically sensitive family member. They are established step by step and involve a continual process of evaluation and elimination. One month you might buy a water filter. Another month you might remove some carpet and add a window for more sun and a view of the trees. Whether you mix your own adhesives and paints or buy those that are ready-made, this chapter is meant to help you build and renovate in a safe, ecological way. You will learn how to use products that are the most inert and that "outgas" the fewest possible fumes. The guidelines provided will help you choose environmentally responsible and healthy natural materials. I urge you to take on the challenge—and a challenge it can be sometimes—to make your home an oasis of clean air, a sanctuary in balance with nature, a place to truly relax and breathe freely.

# New and Old Better Basic Materials

Most of us are aware of and concerned about indoor air pollution. Prestigious organizations such as the American Lung Association document the known health hazards such as cancer and sensitization to chemicals from materials such as particleboard and paint. Yet the majority of the products available in hardware and building supply stores don't yet reflect those concerns; the manufacturers and mainstream building trade haven't caught up. Most commonly available paints and stains contain pesticides and volatile organic chemicals (VOCs), carpets are adhered with toxic solvent–based glues, and pressure-treated wood is saturated with heavy metals. It is worth standing firm in your resolve to have clean air for your family. Nontoxic building products exist, but you have to look hard for them. You can also make your own.

I know that making your own paint—or caulk or glue—will be a stretch for most of you; it is for me most of the time. In this chapter I've provided a detailed list of guidelines to help you shop for safe materials and maintain a healthy home. But you may suddenly find yourself wanting to hang the wallpaper that has been gathering dust in the closet and don't feel like running to the store to buy paste. Most *Better Basics for the Home* formulas use materials you probably have on hand, and you can make the wallpaper paste on the spot, saving yourself time and money. What could be better than that?

# Guidelines for a Healthy House

Knowing how to evaluate the present-day health of your house is an important first step in learning about the pollutants you are living with and those to avoid in future building projects. The following guidelines were inspired by

## THE TOP SIX INGREDIENTS FOR HOUSE CARE

BEESWAX, mason's lime, linseed oil, natural pigments, the resin mastic, and glue are the main ingredients in these workshop formulas. Some of these may be less well known to the modern shopper, but almost all are readily available in local building supply and health food stores; you will rarely have to venture into mail order or chemical supply houses. Some ingredients, such as borax, are available in supermarkets. The initial gathering of supplies requires a bit of time, because you will need to go to a few different stores, but you'll find that once you have the necessary materials on hand, the supply will last. For example, mason's lime is commonly available in fifty-pound bags for as little as six dollars. You won't need to restock it very often.

the November/December 1991 issue of *Building with Nature,* edited and published by Carol Venolia, author of *Healing Environments.* These guidelines have been expanded and updated with Carol Venolia's generous help and permission. Also providing valuable insight was Mary

Oetzel, president of Environmental Education and Health Services. This overview will give you a starting point for assessing the health of your home.

Keep in mind that every person is different, and no one but you can choose what is healthiest for you, especially if you are hypersensitive. And just as every person is different, so too is every home. Be alert to problems of indoor air pollution that may be specific to your dwelling, such as spilled perfume or damp walls or pollution from your neighborhood such as contamination from a nearby orchard that uses pesticide sprays.

KEY

★★ Least Toxic/Best Choice for Those Sensitive to Chemicals

★ Acceptable Choice

✔ Cause for Concern

✖ Avoid/Generally Most Toxic

The five categories of chemicals described below refer to the designations in parentheses mentioned in the lists throughout this section.

**1. PESTICIDES.** Pesticides are toxic poisons designed to kill. The list of pesticides that are probable or possible carcinogens is extensive. Of the pesticides legally allowed to be used on food crops, the EPA considers to be potentially carcinogenic 60 percent of the registered herbicides, 90 percent of the fungicides, and 30 percent of the insecticides. Evidence is mounting that pesticides can alter the immune system's normal structure, reducing resistance to disease. There is also increased documentation

of endocrine disruption in wildlife caused by pesticides. Other concerns include central nervous system depression and the fact that organochlorine pesticides are long-lasting in the environment.

**2. TOXIC GASES, SUCH AS CHLORINE AND AMMONIA.** Most household bleach is sodium hypochlorite, a moderately toxic chlorine salt. Chlorine bleach is dangerous when combined with ammonia or acids such as vinegar, because toxic gases are released. In the wastewater stream, household bleach can bond with other chemicals to form simple organochlorines. Organochlorines can cause cancer and endocrine disruption. Ammonia is a suspected mutagen; is poisonous, corrosive, and explosive; and can cause chronic inflammation.

**3. HEAVY METALS.** Heavy metals are highly toxic. Lead, a common example, is a carcinogen, mutagen, and neurotoxic poison. Exposure can result in loss of IQ, headache, fatigue, sleep disturbances, aching bones and muscles, convulsions, brain and kidney damage, and death. Mercury poisoning can cause brain damage, irritability, memory loss, tremors, kidney disease, decreased fertility, and death.

**4. VOLATILE ORGANIC COMPOUNDS (VOCs).** Volatile organic chemicals are chemicals that evaporate into the air and react with sunlight to form ground-level ozone. Formaldehyde and solvents are VOCs and are some of the most dangerous pollutants in household building products. Volatile organic chemicals include carcinogens, endocrine disrupters, central nervous system disrupters, and sensitizers. You can

sidestep using solvents completely by not buying any VOC paints, using washing soda, and
making waxes and pastes by emulsifying water
and oil as if you are making face cream (see
Basic Cream Formula, page 30).

**5. PLASTICS.** The first clue that plastics cause
endocrine disruption came when it was discovered that the plastic tubing used in laboratories was estrogenic. To make plastics flexible,
the endocrine disrupter phthalate is added.
Phthalates are used in most plastics. Styrene is
another endocrine disrupter that is used in the
manufacture of many plastics.

VAPOR BARRIERS AND EXTERIOR
HOUSE WRAPS

Under the clapboards on most houses is a
vapor barrier or house wrap. Asphaltic
building paper is black, the same material
seen on tar paper shacks.

★ Plasticized papers such as Tyvek
(plastics)

★ Perforated aluminum foil

✖ Asphaltic building paper (VOCs)

*Tips for Improving an Existing Structure*
Old asphalt building paper, commonly used as
a vapor barrier and house wrap, won't outgas
too much unless it is exposed to the sun, and
most of the fumes outgas in a year or so.
Outgassing is less of a problem if these building materials are sealed off from the living area.

CABINETS

★★ Enameled metal

★★ Solid wood

✔ Exterior-grade plywood (sealed) (VOCs)

✔ Plastic-laminated cupboards (laminated on all sides) (VOCs)

✖ Interior-grade plywood (sealed only)
(VOCs)

✖ Particleboard (VOCs)

NOTE: Interior-grade plywood contains higher
levels of formaldehyde than exterior grade.

*Tips for Improving an Existing Structure*
Seal all particleboard to minimize outgassing
from formaldehyde. The surest way to do this
is with AFM's specially designed sealer (see
Sources and Resources). How old is old enough
so that the formaldehyde doesn't pose a problem? Probably never, although after ten years
the formaldehyde may have outgassed enough
to be negligible. You can test for formaldehyde
if you are concerned about it.

COUNTERTOPS

★★ Stainless steel

★ Granite

★ Marble

★ Ceramic tile (attached without admixtures) (see Flooring, page 265)

★ Metal

★ Corian (plastics)

★ High-pressure plastic laminates, such
as Formica (sealed on underside)

✔ High-pressure plastic laminates, such
as Formica (not sealed on underside) (plastics)

✔ Wood (hard to keep free of bacteria)

*Tips for Improving an Existing Structure*
If you have wood kitchen countertops, be sure
to clean them regularly with a natural disinfectant, as discussed in Chapter Two.

## DOORS

- ★ Metal
- ★ Solid wood (panelized)
- ✔ Solid-core doors (no particleboard)
- ✔ Hollow-core doors (no toxic glues or particleboard)
- ✘ Plastic laminates (plastics)
- ✘ Hollow-core or solid-core doors (particleboard) (VOCs)

*Tips for Improving an Existing Structure*

- ❧ Plastic-laminated doors should never be near a source of heat, or they will outgas higher levels of chemicals. If this is the case, replace them with something more inert, such as solid wood or metal.
- ❧ Doors that contain formaldehyde can be sealed with an AFM sealant (see Sources and Resources) to reduce formaldehyde outgassing.

## FLOORING

- ★★ Ceramic tile (mudset or Portland thinset without toxic additives; Portland cement grout without additives; and grout lines sealed with least toxic sealer)
- ★★ Brick
- ★★ Slate
- ★★ Marble
- ★★ Wood (least toxic paints or sealants and no glues; kraft paper substituted for asphaltic paper under flooring)
- ★ Natural linoleum (adhered with least toxic adhesive) (VOCs)
- ★ Concrete (without additives) (VOCs)

- ✔ Vinyl composition tile (least toxic adhesive; good carpet substitute for schools) (plastics)
- ✔ Wall-to-wall carpet (100 percent untreated natural fibers) (VOCs)
- ✘ Wall-to-wall carpet (plastics, VOCs)
- ✘ Soft vinyl (plastics)
- ✘ Treated fibers
- ✘ Vinyl asbestos tile (plastics)
- ✘ Laminated hardwood floors (VOCs)

*Tips for Improving an Existing Structure*

- ❧ An AFM sealant is available that helps reduce VOCs and pesticides outgassing from carpets, although it is not foolproof (see Sources and Resources). Replace rubber, urethane foam, or PVC carpet pads or backing with jute or recycled denim scrap pads (see Sources and Resources). If the carpet is tacked down rather than glued and is five years old or more, it has probably outgassed enough to be safe, although older carpets may have dust mites and mold. Indoor-outdoor carpeting that has been treated with pesticides should be removed because the pesticide used is long-lasting. Ideally, all carpets should be replaced with inert floor materials.
- ❧ Some laminated hardwood floors have high levels of formaldehyde. Look in your local Yellow Pages for laboratories that will test for formaldehyde.

## FOUNDATION

- ★ Stone
- ★ Concrete (no toxic admixtures and curing compounds)

★ Concrete block

✖ Wood that has been treated (pesticides)

✖ Pressure-treated wood (heavy metals)

✖ Material damp-proofed with asphalt-
based sealant (VOCs)

*Tips for Improving an Existing Structure*

∗ Do not plant fruits or vegetables near pressure-treated wood; arsenic and copper from
the treatment can leach into the soil and
be absorbed by the plants.

∗ Once dried and a year old or more,
asphalt-based sealant will not outgas much
unless it is in direct sun.

## GARAGE

★★ Detached or not used for cars

✔ Attached (no common attic or direct
access to house)

✖ Attached (used for cars) (VOCs)

*Tips for Improving an Existing Structure*

Do not leave cars in an attached garage if there
is a room above the garage, such as a bedroom
or an office. The car's exhaust can enter the
room. At the very least, seek means to control
the air in the upstairs room by using a vapor
barrier on the ceiling of the garage.

## HEATING SYSTEM

★★ Electric heat (best to minimize
indoor air pollution but not best
for the environment)

★★ Solar

★★ Wind

★★ Geothermal

★ Hot water baseboard or radiator (combustion unit ventilated in basement)

★ High-efficiency gas hot-water baseboard

✔ Hot water baseboard or radiator (combustion unit unventilated) (VOCs)

✔ Forced hot air with filter (lower rat-
ing due to fumes, dust, and mold)
(VOCs)

✔ Well-sealed woodstove (VOCs)

✖ Kerosene space heater (VOCs)

*Tips for Improving an Existing Structure*

∗ Investing in hot water baseboard heat is
highly recommended if family members
are sensitive to dust and mold.

∗ Remove combustion space heaters.

∗ If you heat with wood, invest in a contem-
porary woodstove, one designed to reduce
pollutants.

∗ If family members are sensitive to dust and
mold, install hot water baseboard heat or
use a central air filtration system.

## INSULATION

★★ Air-krete (foam sprayed into walls;
expensive)

★ Foil-faced bubble pack (VOCs)

✔ Cotton batt insulation (rodenticides,
fire retardants) (pesticides)

✔ Fiberglass (install with appropriate
vapor barrier; installers must be protected; avoid paper-faced type
because of asphaltic adhesive; only the
batts contain formaldehyde) (VOCs)

✔ Perlite (possible nuisance dust)

✔ Cork (some is chemically treated)

✔ Cellulose (contains inks and added chemicals) (VOCs)

✔ Rock wool (often contains coal or mineral oil)

✔ Vermiculite (best for horizontal applications; may contain small amounts of asbestos)

✖ Expanded polystyrene, polyurethane, phenolic, and polyisocyanurate (toxic if burned or heated) (VOCs)

✖ Urea-formaldehyde foam (VOCs)

✖ Phenolic rigid boards

✖ Asbestos

*Tips for Improving an Existing Structure*

Make sure that the insulation is separated from the living space with appropriate barriers.

## INTERIOR WALL AND CEILING FINISH

★★ Plaster (low-biocide paint)

★★ Ceramic tile (Portland thinset and Portland cement grout)

★ Gypsum board or drywall (least toxic joint compound and low-biocide paint)

★ Solid wood paneling

★ Natural-fiber fabric wallpaper (least toxic adhesives)

★ Metal foil wallpaper (least toxic adhesives)

✔ Paper wallpaper (applied without toxic glue) (VOCs)

✖ Wallpaper (vinyl and other plastics or paper applied with toxic glue) (VOCs, plastics)

*Tips for Improving an Existing Structure*

Remove plastic wallpaper, especially if exposed to heaters, which cause it to outgas.

## PLUMBING

★ Stainless steel pipe (lead-free solder or mechanical joints)

✔ Copper pipe (copper can leach zinc out of the body; use lead-free solder or mechanical joints)

✖ Cast iron supply pipe

✖ Galvanized steel supply pipe

✖ Polyvinyl chloride (PVC) supply pipe (plastics)

✖ Lead solder or pipes (heavy metals)

*Tips for Improving an Existing Structure*

Remove all lead, cast iron, galvanized steel, or PVC pipes and replace with copper, or drink only bottled water.

## PLYWOOD AND COMPOSITES

✔ Exterior-grade plywood, oriented strand board (outside an air barrier or sealed)* (VOCs)

✔ Foil-faced laminated cardboard sheathing

✔ Masonite (sealed)* (VOCs)

✔ Medium-density fiberboard (sealed)* (VOCs)

✔ Chipboard or waferboard (sealed)* (VOCs)

✖ Particleboard (VOCs)

*AFM has a VOC sealant that helps reduce the outgassing of formaldehyde. See Sources and Resources.

RETAINING WALLS
- ★★ Stone
- ★★ Masonry products (no additives)
- ★ Cedar (some people are sensitive to the terpenes)
- ✔ Recycled plastic lumber (plastics)
- ✔ Borax-treated lumber
- ✔ Low-arsenic pressure-treated lumber (heavy metals)
- ✖ Pressure-treated lumber (distinct pea green color) (heavy metals)
- ✖ Railroad ties or any wood treated with pentachlorophenol or creosote (pesticides)
- ✖ Folpet and tributyltin oxide (TBT) (VOCs)

ROOFING
- ★★ Metal
- ★★ Clay tile
- ★★ Slate
- ✔ Untreated cedar shakes (terpenes are a problem for some people)
- ✔ Concrete tiles that require sealant (VOCs)
- ✔ Asphaltic roofing* (VOCs)
- ✖ Built-up roofing (tar and gravel)

*Asphaltic roofing is the most economical but is a problem to apply. Construction and repairs should be done during a season when the windows are closed, and the attic must be well ventilated. Once dried, the roofing is usually not problematic except possibly on hot days near windows that open onto the roof, such as dormers. Asphaltic roofing is not a good environmental choice, due to the use of petroleum.

SHEATHING
- ★ Solid wood (laid diagonally for wall or subfloor)
- ★ Wood let-in lateral bracing (for shear resistance)
- ★ Diagonal metal straps (for shear resistance)
- ✔ Exterior-grade plywood, oriented strand board (outside an air barrier or sealed)* (VOCs)
- ✔ Foil-faced laminated cardboard sheathing
- ✔ Chipboard or waferboard (sealed)* (VOCs)
- ✔ Interior-grade plywood* (VOCs)

*Materials that require sealing to meet the "✔" criterion must be sealed thoroughly to reduce phenol and formaldehyde outgassing.

STRUCTURE
- ★ Earth (only in dry climates)
- ★ Concrete (without curing compounds)
- ★ Untreated wood (terpenes are a problem for some people)
- ★ Straw bale
- ★ Aluminum or steel (wash off coatings)
- ✔ Concrete block (VOCs)
- ✖ Treated wood

*Tips for Improving an Existing Structure*

Because most structural supports are separated from the living area, fumes are usually not an issue. That's a good thing, too, because there aren't many alternative structural materials.

## SIDING AND EXTERIOR VENEERS

- ★★ Stone
- ★★ Brick
- ★ Stucco (without toxic additives)
- ★ Cement board siding
- ★ Masonry (may require sealing)
- ★ Wood (painted) (pesticides, VOCs)
- ✔ Wood (stained) (pesticides, VOCs)
- ✔ Untreated cedar shingles and shakes (terpenes bother some people)
- ✔ Wood siding (water-based paint; no stains or sealants) (pesticides)
- ✔ Simulated wood siding (VOCs)
- ✔ Stucco (additives) (VOCs)
- ✖ Laminated wood products (VOCs)
- ✖ Vinyl (doesn't breathe; risk of mold) (plastics)
- ✖ Asbestos cement (VOCs)
- ✖ Aluminum siding*

*Although aluminum siding is vented, the vapor barrier may reduce air circulation and increase the risk of mold. How the metal siding interacts with electromagnetic fields is unknown.

*Tips for Improving an Existing Structure*

The "✖" category indicates serious problems that should be addressed by removal and replacement with safer materials.

## UNDERLAYMENT AND SUBFLOORS

- ★ Solid wood (laid diagonally for walls or subfloors)
- ★ Cement board (for tile work)
- ★ Exterior-grade plywood, oriented strand board (outside an air barrier or sealed)* (VOCs)
- ✔ Hardboard (toxic gases)
- ✔ Medium-density fiberboard (sealed)* (VOCs)
- ✔ Chipboard or waferboard (sealed)* (VOCs)
- ✔ Interior-grade plywood* (VOCs)
- ✖ Particleboard (VOCs)

*These materials must be sealed thoroughly to reduce phenol and formaldehyde outgassing.

*Tips for Improving an Existing Structure*

We bought a house that had particleboard underlayment throughout both floors of the house. Removal was the only safe option. We had it replaced with sealed exterior-grade plywood. It was a big and expensive job at the time, but it has been a healthy house ever since.

## VAPOR BARRIERS

- ★ Untreated building paper
- ★ Aluminum foil (not perforated)
- ✔ Polyethylene sheeting (seal behind interior finish) (plastics)

## WINDOW FRAMES

- ★★ Metal
- ★★ Untreated solid wood (custom windows)
- ★ Fiberglass
- ★ Clad wood
- ★ Manufactured wood (pesticides)
- ✔ Vinyl (plastics)

*Tips for Improving an Existing Structure*

Most window glass is held in place by synthetic materials that can be sealed. If contaminants from the windows seem to be a problem, seal them with paint or AFM sealants (see Sources and Resources).

## GUIDELINES FOR TESTING EQUIPMENT

### SMOKE DETECTORS

★ Photoelectric smoke detector

✔ Ionization smoke detector (emits alpha-ionizing radiation)*

✘ No smoke detector

*Return to manufacturer when discarded.

NOTE: Both types of smoke detectors are available in most hardware stores.

### LEAD TESTS

★ Professional X-ray fluorescence lead testing of paint

★ Laboratory testing (check Yellow Pages)

★ Flushing pipes for three minutes every morning

✔ Swab, or spot-testing, kits (available in most hardware stores)

✘ No testing

✘ Unaddressed lead water pipes; old peeling paint; exposure to antique toys; stained glass making

### CARBON MONOXIDE TESTERS

★ Wake-up detector

✔ Visual detector

✘ No detector

✘ Generator, kerosene space heater, or any unvented combustion appliance (do not use without carbon monoxide detector)

### RADON

★★ Long-term radon tests; continuous plug-in units

✔ Short-term tests

NOTE: If radon levels are above four picocuries per liter of air (pCi/l) in your home, the EPA recommends working with a contractor certified by its radon contractor proficiency program to correct the problem.

## ELECTROMAGNETIC FIELDS (EMFs)

If any testing can be fun, it is testing for electromagnetic fields (EMFs). These out-of-sight fields are present anywhere there is electricity. A few years ago, EMFs were Americans' number-one environmental health concern. Fear of them seems to have caught our collective imagination. The fields are measured in milligauss and can be gauged with a gaussmeter. There is controversy in the medical community as to how dangerous low-level EMFs actually are (high levels of EMFs have been cleared of causing leukemia in children), but prudent avoidance is warranted. "Hot" spots tend to be where electricity comes into the house, and near big appliances such as the refrigerator and dishwasher. (An askew building may have high EMF readings all over the house; in most cases faulty wiring is the problem. Gaussmeters cost around $160, but most electric companies will give you a free audit if you suspect a problem. Contact the EPA's EMF hotline for more information and current suppliers of gaussmeters.

How much EMF is too much? The standard agreed on by most environmental health practitioners is more than two milligauss.

### TESTING FOR PESTICIDES

Contamination from pesticides can last for years after application. Try to determine the pesticide history of the house. The National Coalition Against the Misuse of Pesticides (NCAMP) can offer an educated opinion about the longevity of specific pesticides (see Sources and Resources). Here are general guidelines.

- *Chlorinated Hydrocarbon Pesticides:* DDT, chlordane, heptachlor, lindane, aldrin, eldrin, endrin, and others: half-life more than fifty years
- *Other Pesticides Including Organophosphates such as Dursban:* half-life five years

### WATER TESTING

Getting your water tested is definitely advisable no matter where you live. In your list of contaminants to be tested, include lead and radon and as many pesticides and VOCs as you can afford. Look in your local Yellow Pages for laboratories in your area. Many experts believe that water is generally so polluted that everyone should have a water filter. This is good—though expensive—advice. Water pollution is a growing threat throughout the country. The results of the water tests, and the source of your water, will help you determine what kind of filter to get.

### WATER FILTERS

★ Carbon filters are a good choice for homes on a municipal water source, because they reduce chlorine and other chemicals. (They won't remove bacteria and viruses, problems common to wells.) Carbon filters do not reduce heavy metals as well as other types of systems.

★ Reverse osmosis filters are better for homes with wells because they remove bacteria and viruses plus chemicals and many heavy metals. Problems with reverse osmosis are that chemicals from plastic tubing can leach into the water, and the system uses a lot of water.

★ Distillers reduce chemicals, heavy metals, bacteria, viruses, and minerals. Make sure the unit is not made of aluminum; that metal can leach into the water. The biggest drawback with distillation is that it removes healthful minerals, such as magnesium.

# Adhesives, Glues, and Pastes

Gothic novels are full of horse carcasses being carried off to the "glue factory," where the bones, skins, intestines—hooves and hides, as they say—are boiled down to a gelatinous mass. Animal carcasses are still sent to rendering plants. The most impure by-product of this mass is dried to become glue and animal feed; the most pure becomes culinary gelatin. In the not too recent past, almost all glue was made from animal parts. The glue was sold in sheets and had to be soaked in water for many hours, then heated in a double boiler or electric glue pot. Other types of glues were made with plant pulp. Most modern-day glues, however, are made from synthetic polymers. They often contain highly toxic solvent VOCs and pesticides (biocides and fungicides).

## GLUES

THE safest ready-made glues to buy are all-purpose white glues, such as Elmer's Glue-All, although they are not usually waterproof. Yellow glue is sometimes waterproof, but it is not as safe as white glue because it contains additives. Pure hide glue is nontoxic and the best choice for wood musical instruments and delicate wood furniture because it expands and contracts with the wood, which prevents the wood from cracking. Most commercially available paste glues are also nontoxic, although you can easily make them yourself using everyday household staples. Glues to be avoided due to VOCs include those with solvents such as epoxy; standard carpet, panel, and construction adhesives; and rubber cement. Most experts I have spoken with believe that all-purpose white glues are all that is needed for the vast majority of jobs.

Glues and adhesives are synonymous: They are sticky concoctions used to attach objects to each other. Pastes have a different consistency, usually lumpy, and are easily made at home from a wide range of materials, many of which you may already have in your cupboard, such as cornstarch and flour.

### ANIMAL GLUES

Hide glue comes in sheets or granular flakes. They are soaked in water, then heated in electric glue pots that maintain a temperature of 130°F to 150°F, but a double boiler can be substituted for a glue pot. Hide glues are used nowadays only for making musical instruments or Shaker furniture reproductions. The beauty of hide glue for these purposes is that it expands and contracts, serving as a safety valve to prevent cracking of valuable wood pieces. Hide glue makes a bond that can be loosened when it is heated, which is a great advantage for easily dismantling and repairing wood musical instruments without breakage. Gregory Wylie, a violin maker I spoke with, varies the amount of water used to soak and heat hide glue, creating stronger glues (less water) or weaker glues (more water), depending on the part of the instrument he is working on. Glue strength also depends on its age. Glue that has been in the pot for a few days is weaker than that which has been freshly heated. Weak glue is valuable for some purposes, such as gluing on the top of the violin. Greg mentioned speculation that famous Italian instrument makers may have used casein glue, which is made with hide glue and casein (milk protein). Because casein is waterproof, it is helpful on violin parts that are stressed from repeated contact with body oils such as those found on the violinist's hands. See Sources and Resources for sources of hide glue, and follow the directions on the container for amounts of water needed for different strengths of glue.

NOTE ABOUT GELATIN: Gelatin is a refined hide glue, but the refining makes it less strong. I have experimented with substituting gelatin for hide glue with some success in glue recipes. Use half the amount of water required for making Jell-O; otherwise, follow the directions on the gelatin package. Let the gelatin set up overnight, then heat it to use as a glue.

## BASIC OLD-FASHIONED GLUE FORMULA

3 parts hide glue
8 parts water

Soak the glue in the water overnight. Pour off the water, and place the softened glue in an electric glue pot or double boiler, making sure that the glue temperature remains at 130°F to 150°F. You can leave the glue in the glue pot for several days before discarding. Apply the glue with a brush.

*Preparation Time:* 10 minutes
*Shelf Life:* Discard leftovers

### Variation

BOOKBINDING OR PHOTO MOUNTING GLUE: This glue lasts and doesn't damage the paper. Alum works as a preservative; use $3/4$ teaspoon alum per half cup hide glue. Remove the heated glue to a heatproof bowl, and stir in the alum. Use immediately. Reheat in a double boiler if it begins to gel.

## OLD-FASHIONED WHITE GLUE

*Zinc oxide or casein are added for their white color, and because zinc oxide is antibacterial and casein is waterproof.*

3 parts hide glue
8 parts water
Zinc oxide powder or casein

Follow the directions for Basic Old-Fashioned Glue Formula above. Remove the melted glue to a bowl, and add the zinc oxide or casein, $1/2$ teaspoon at a time, until the desired whiteness is achieved.

*Preparation Time:* 15 minutes
*Shelf Life:* Discard leftovers

### Variation

CASEIN HIDE GLUE: Casein hide glue is the most waterproof of all the glues. It is an excellent choice for furniture and wood instruments that are exposed to moisture. Combine 4 parts casein and 4 parts water; let soak for 12 hours. Do the same thing with 1 part hide glue and 4 parts water; heat as in Basic Old-Fashioned Glue Formula. Remove from heat and add the casein mixture. Stir to blend.

## PLANT AND MINERAL GLUES AND ADHESIVES

Mastic is resin from trees that grow in the Mediterranean region. I prefer mastic to other resins because it dissolves in alcohol, compared to other resins that require solvents to dissolve, such as turpentine, which causes indoor air quality problems when heated.

## WATERPROOF GLUE FOR GLASS AND CHINA

1 tablespoon mastic
1/8 ounce beeswax
1 tablespoon alcohol (such as vodka)

In a double boiler over medium heat, melt the mastic and beeswax in the alcohol. Remove from the heat, stir, and immediately scoop some of the mixture onto a popsicle stick or other similar tool. Spread the glue onto one side of the broken china. Attach the other broken half and press together firmly. Mastic hardens fast.

**Makes 2 tablespoons**

*Preparation Time:* 15 minutes
*Shelf Life:* Make only as much as you need at one time

### Variation

KNIFE HANDLE WATERPROOF GLUE: This is the traditional glue for inserting knife blades into handles. Follow the directions above to the point of removing the mixture from the stove. Meanwhile, in a small bowl, combine 1 tablespoon alcohol and 2 tablespoons plaster of

paris. Add the warmed mixture and stir to blend. Work quickly.

## GLUE FOR STONE

2 parts plaster of paris
1 part cornstarch
1/2 part sand
3 parts water

Combine the plaster of paris, cornstarch, and sand, stirring to blend. Add the water and let set for 5 minutes, then stir. Use before it dries.

*Preparation Time:* 10 minutes
*Shelf Life:* Indefinitely for dry ingredients; 15 to 30 minutes with water added

### PASTES

Grain pastes are old-fashioned white glue. The pastes were used for adhering paper, making papier-mâché, and applying wallpaper. Anyone-Can-Do-Them Grain Paste is still the best wallpaper paste, and you can make it with staples you have on hand.

## ANYONE-CAN-DO-THEM GRAIN PASTE ✗

*Alum, borax, and clove oil are natural preservatives; just one of them is enough to preserve the paste.*

1/2 cup flour (wheat, corn, or rice)
1 1/2 teaspoons alum or borax
Water
5 drops oil of cloves (optional)

Combine the flour and alum in a double boiler, and add enough water to make a consistency of heavy cream. Stir until the mixture is lump free, then heat until it is the consistency of thick gravy. Let cool, then stir in the clove oil (if using). Apply with a glue brush or a butter brush.

**Makes ½ cup**

*Preparation Time:* About 15 minutes
*Shelf Life:* About 2 weeks refrigerated
*Storage:* Glass jar with a screw top

### Variation

SIMPLE PASTE: Simply combine flour and water in a bowl, mix until the lumps are removed, and add more water as needed for the desired consistency: It should resemble a thick pea soup.

# Caulk and Putty

Caulk keeps water from migrating between cracks where materials are joined, such as where wall tiles meet the top of the bathtub. Putty covers up small holes in walls and conceals nails. Caulk and putty are not to be confused with joint compound, which is used to join sheets of drywall.

T I P *Add coffee, tea, or other natural earth pigments to putty to match the colors of stained woodwork and painted surfaces.*

## BASIC PUTTY FORMULA ✗

*This mixture is very spreadable. The oil provides some waterproofing qualities.*

Whiting
Raw linseed oil

Place the whiting in a bowl and add the linseed oil in a drizzle, stirring while you add, until the texture is like frosting. Scoop some onto a putty knife, and spread.

*Preparation Time:* A few minutes
*Shelf Life:* Indefinite; if the mixture dries out, add more linseed oil
*Storage:* Glass jar with a screw top

## SALT PUTTY ✗

*If you don't have any whiting to make basic putty, use this recipe instead.*

### BUYER'S GUIDE
#### BUYING CAULK AND PUTTY

THE safest caulk to buy is 100 percent silicone, available in most hardware stores. When it dries, it is inert. Other least toxic choices are linseed-oil putty, 100 percent silicone "rope" caulk, and acrylic caulk. Avoid products labeled "for use in kitchens and bathrooms," due to the addition of pesticides, including fungicides; also avoid high-VOC acrylic-solvent caulk, those made of polyurethanes, foam, and those that are oil based.

3 tablespoons cornstarch
2 tablespoons salt
2 tablespoons water

Blend the cornstarch and salt in a bowl. Add the water and stir until lump free.
**Makes almost ½ cup**

*Preparation Time:* A few minutes
*Shelf Life:* 1 week refrigerated
*Storage:* Glass jar with a screw top

## CORN CAULK

Equal amounts cornstarch, plaster of paris, and water

Combine the ingredients and stir thoroughly until the mixture is creamy and lump free.

*Preparation Time:* About 5 minutes
*Shelf Life:* If it dries out, add more water
*Storage:* Glass jar with a screw top

# Masonry Products: Concrete, Grout, Thinset, Mudset, and Mortar Mixes

Choosing additive-free masonry products helps you avoid chemicals such as fungicides that can outgas into your living area for years. Making masonry products from scratch is a dying art. Masons may enjoy having the formulas presented here; they may not know them. Or try your hand at them yourself. Laying tiles, for instance, is a manageable task for untrained do-it-yourselfers.

## MINI-GLOSSARY

**Air-Entrained Concrete.** Portland cement (see below) that has been filled with millions of microscopic air bubbles to help it expand when the water freezes. It also has chemical additives that maintain the air bubbles. For use in cold climates.

**Concrete.** A mixture of Portland cement (see below); sand, gravel, and other aggregates; and water. The ratio of water to cement affects the strength of the concrete. The more water, the weaker the concrete (but too little water makes the concrete hard to work with).

**Glue.** Hide glue, made from animal by-products, is the traditional glue used for many techniques, from making furniture to formulating paint. Modern white glue can be substituted for those who want to avoid animal products.

**Mortar.** Premixed product, typically Portland cement, sand, and aggregate. Used for rock and brickwork.

**Mucilage.** A watery, sticky solution (gum) used commonly as an adhesive. It is found in many plants and is made up of polysaccharides (one of the more complex carbohydrates, such as cellulose, starch, or glycogen) that soak up water, producing a sticky, jellylike mass.

**Mudset (or Thickset or Mudbed).** Masonry bed that tiles are placed on.

**Portland Cement.** Not a brand name, Portland cement is crushed and baked limestone.

**Portland Thinset.** Commercially premixed, used for laying ceramic tile on concrete or bare drywall.

**Portland Thinset with Latex Modifiers.** Commercially premixed, used for laying ceramic tile on concrete or bare drywall. Has latex additives to bond masonry tiles to wood, metal, and other surfaces.

**Stucco.** Combination of mason's hydrated lime (calcium hydroxide), sand, and Portland cement.

**Thinset.** See Portland Thinset.

**Varnish.** Used for finishing furniture, floors, and woodwork.

## CONCRETE

Concrete is used for basements, sidewalks, floors, molds, garden statuary, and more.

## BASIC CONCRETE FORMULA

*Ratios of the ingredients vary depending on the aggregate size. The following guidelines are for proportions by volume. If using a coarse aggregate ($1\frac{1}{2}$ inches maximum size), use 1 part cement, 3 parts aggregate, $2\frac{1}{4}$ parts sand, and $\frac{1}{2}$ part water. If using a finer aggregate ($\frac{3}{8}$ inch maximum size), use 1 part cement, $1\frac{1}{2}$ parts aggregate, $2\frac{1}{4}$ parts sand, and $\frac{1}{2}$ part water.*

Portland cement
Aggregate
Sand
Water

Combine the ingredients and mix thoroughly to a uniform color. If you have used too much

## BUYER'S GUIDE

### MASONRY PRODUCTS

THE most important rule of thumb when buying masonry products is to avoid admixtures, including fungicides, plastics, antifreeze, asbestos, and quick-drying chemicals. These materials will outgas for years. Ready-mixed products with admixtures are also much more expensive than those without them. Read labels carefully, watching out for ingredients besides the identifiable product you are buying. In particular, avoid asphalt-based products, those that use a "release oil" (it can be kerosene), vinyl, and mortars with additives. Portland thinset with latex is acceptable, but Portland thinset without latex that is water cured is preferable because it includes no admixtures. Choosing to make your own masonry products from scratch, although not at all hard, will take some determination, because the advertising slogans such as "fast-set," "swift-set," "ready-set," "instant," and "get-set-and-go" are compelling. If you can resist these, the results will be worth it.

water, a ridge or peak in the mixture won't hold but will instead slump back down, so you need to add more Portland cement and aggregate.

*Preparation Time:* About 20 minutes
*Storage:* Discard leftovers

## STUCCO

Stucco is a thick covering for walls, ceilings, floors, and cornices. It is applied over wire or metal lath, although sometimes it will adhere to concrete and other masonry. Like secret cake recipes, formulas for stucco are guarded by most masons, who still make stucco from scratch.

## BASIC STUCCO FORMULA

3 cubic feet sand
47 pounds Portland cement
12½ pounds mason's hydrated lime
Water

Combine the sand, Portland cement, and lime; blend well. Gradually add water until the desired consistency is reached.
**Makes enough to cover roughly 75 square feet, depending on how thickly it is applied**

*Preparation Time:* 20 minutes
*Shelf Life:* Discard leftover stucco before it hardens

## MORTAR

Mortar is used to bond bricks together. It is similar to concrete, but the lime helps increase its resistance to moisture.

## MORTAR MIX

100 pounds sand
16 pounds Portland cement
8½ pounds mason's hydrated lime
About 2 gallons water

Combine the ingredients in a large tub. The mixture should be the consistency of thick soup. Use before it dries.
**The square footage this covers depends upon what you are using it for and how thickly it is applied**

*Preparation Time:* About 30 minutes
*Shelf Life:* Discard leftover mix before it hardens

## ATTACHING TILES: MUDSET (OR THICKSET OR MUDBED) AND GROUT

A simple mudbed of Portland cement, sand, and water can be laid on wood or stone; tile is set into it, to be followed by a grout (with pigment to match the tile) that is then damp cured. This is far preferable to premixed petroleum-based or epoxy tile settings, which can outgas for years. I used the age-old technique of laying a mudset followed by a damp-cured grout for tiles on an island in our kitchen, and it was easy, looks beautiful, and has no odor.

**Step One**

## MUDSET

*Mudset (also called thickset or mudbed) is usually laid over underboards, then smoothed out.*

*You can put down a tile board on areas such as a countertop and spread the mudset on top of it. Lay the tiles into the mudset, and follow with a thinset or grout.*

3 parts sand
1 part Portland cement
Water
Natural earth pigment

Combine the sand and Portland cement in a tub. Slowly add water, stirring as you go, until the texture is like thick sludge. Add the pigment teaspoon by teaspoon, mixing as you go, until the desired color has been reached.
**Amount: 50 pounds covers about 75 square feet**

*Preparation Time:* 20 minutes
*Shelf Life:* Discard leftover mudset; it will dry out

**Step Two**

## GROUT

*The ratio of materials ranges between 1:1 and 1:3 Portland cement to sand, depending on how much space there is between tiles. More sand is used for wider gaps. Natural iron-oxide pigments are available (some iron oxides are synthetically derived), and these can be added to match the tile color.*

Portland cement
Sand
Water
Natural earth pigment

Combine the Portland cement and sand in a tub. Slowly add water, stirring as you go, until the texture is like thick sludge. Add the pigment teaspoon by teaspoon, mixing as you go, until the desired color has been reached.

*Preparation Time:* 20 minutes
*Shelf Life:* Discard leftover grout; it will dry out

**Variation**

LATEX-FREE PORTLAND THINSET: Commercially premixed, this is used for laying ceramic tile on concrete or bare drywall. Add natural oxide pigments to match the tile color.

**Step Three**

## DAMP-CURE

*Damp-cure grout to avoid chemical dryers. I like to damp-cure tile grout by wetting my fingers and rubbing them up and down the grooves. I did this whenever I thought of it for ten days, and the result was a strong cure. For large areas, such as floors, spray water onto the grout with a spray bottle, then cover with plastic to help hold in the water. Do that for a couple of days running. A ten-day damp-cure is the strongest.*

## GROUT SEALANT ✗

Waterglass

Follow the manufacturer's directions.

## Concrete Sealers and Damp Proofing

### WATERPROOFING CONCRETE

Healthy-house expert John Bower considers waterglass (sodium silicate) a viable concrete sealant, with the one caveat that you will not be able to paint over a waterglass seal. Use waterglass if you don't mind the natural concrete color. Waterglass is not always available locally; look in the Yellow Pages under chemical supply houses.

Waterglass is made by fusing washing soda (soda ash) and clean sand. It can be dissolved in water by prolonged exposure. Waterglass is used as a sealant to fill pores (but not cracks) where water is not a serious problem. Available in hardware and lumber supply stores.

### BUYER'S GUIDE

#### SEALING AND DAMP PROOFING CONCRETE

THE most important products to avoid for damp proofing and sealing concrete are those that are made with asphalt. They are slow-drying petroleum products and are very polluting. Choose instead cement sealers without added latex (unless used outside); waterglass (sodium silicate); and cement-based sealants. Or have your basement professionally protected with B-Dry, a process that uses no chemicals and that builds drainage right into the walls. Acceptable inside, although not the purest choice, are cement sealers with latex.

## Joint Compound

In the old days, a thick version of milk paint was used as a joint compound. Casein, the milk protein used as the base of milk paint, is waterproof and makes a good adhesive. Some people say that mold can grow on casein joint compound. In those cases, milk might have been used instead of the milk protein casein. I've found this error repeated frequently in old recipes. All my experiments using milk instead of casein turned green with mold in no time. Those with casein have never gotten moldy. For added protection, I've added borax as a mold inhibitor to the Casein Joint Compound formula below.

### CASEIN JOINT COMPOUND

1 part casein
4 parts water
½ part borax

Soak the casein in the water overnight. Dissolve the borax in just enough hot or boiling water to dissolve. Combine with the casein; stir to blend. Apply.

*Preparation Time:* 20 minutes
*Shelf Life:* Discard leftovers

# Lubricants

Petroleum oil lubricants are strong smelling and polluting. Jojoba is the best alternative; it is a natural liquid wax that never goes rancid.

T I P *If you want to substitute another oil for jojoba, choose olive oil (it is slow drying), and add a few drops lavender essential oil; it will help retard the drying even more.*

## JOJOBA 🗡

Jojoba

Use as you would a petroleum lubricating oil, such as for stuck doors, squeaky hinges, and machine lubrication (sewing machines, for example).

*Preparation Time:* None
*Shelf Life:* Indefinite

**Variation**
CASTOR OIL: Castor oil has an excellent reputation as a lubricant.

## BEESWAX OR SOAP

Piece of beeswax or bar of soap

Rub beeswax or soap along screw threads and squeaky hinges.

*Preparation Time:* None
*Shelf Life:* Indefinite

# Paints: Milk Paints, Whitewash, Fresco, Gesso, and Distressed Plaster

Paint has been made for centuries using simple ingredients available almost everywhere: milk, lime, and natural earth pigments. Barn red—that beautiful, multihued color still found on some New England barns—was made from milk protein (the curdled cheese known as casein) and an iron oxide earth pigment. I've heard that some farmers colored the casein with raspberries, and others used ox blood. Both could be true; the choices are consistent with the make-do approach of using whatever was around that worked. Milk paint was the interior paint of choice of Colonial America. It soaks well into wood and gives an antique look. Nowadays milk paint colored with natural pigments is frequently used in craft products and reproduction furniture and in the homes of the chemically sensitive. Milk paints have a lovely quality to them and, combined with natural pigments, offer a mellow look. Milk paints give wood a rich, deep, translucent color, staining the wood with the color of the paint but allowing the grain of the wood to show through.

Whitewash is a painting technique that was used for centuries for its luminous beauty and because its high alkaline content made it a natural insect repellent and disinfectant. Historically, it has been used as an exterior paint, although to this day many use it in the interior of barns. Whitewash reflects the light of the local environment—a dazzling white in the Mediterranean, a more mellow warm white in the North. Whitewash is made of lime, water, and sometimes the milk protein casein.

It is unfortunate that milk paint and whitewash have been left behind for modern synthetic paints. Both milk paint and whitewash

allow the underlying materials (such as wood beams and plaster walls) to breathe, permitting air circulation and moisture to be released and thereby preventing mildew and rot. Modern oil-based paints don't allow the building material to breathe, because they seal the material. If there is moisture underneath the paint, it will be trapped.

Why were milk paint and whitewash left behind if they are so good? I am increasingly convinced that the reason is because of the proliferation of incorrect recipes calling for milk instead of the milk protein casein. In my experimentation following the old recipes, all my attempts at milk paint using fresh or powdered milk (with or without additional lime) turned moldy in a few days. However, when I used homemade or ready-made casein (the curd of curdled milk), the paint has lasted, even outdoors in humid, wet weather. Casein is remarkably waterproof, especially when combined with lime. Another error I've frequently found in some old recipes was the addition of whiting, also known as calcium carbonate or chalk. Whiting changes the chemical composition of the casein and lime so that it won't emulsify properly, and the resulting paint is so chalky that it can easily be rubbed off.

As luck would have it, you can benefit from the considerable number of mistakes I've made in learning how to make milk paint and whitewash. One of the biggest mistakes I made was to buy the wrong kind of lime. A detailed glossary of the various ingredients used in recipes for milk paint and whitewash is given below. I've even provided information on materials I have learned you *don't* want in your products, so you will know why to avoid them if you stumble upon erroneous recipes. If you follow my directions carefully, you should be able to make a good product. And once you have gathered all the ingredients, making milk paint takes about the same amount of time (less than an hour of actual work) as making bread, minus the kneading. You have to be attentive to different components, and let things set here and there, but after you have made a few batches, the project will seem relatively easy.

Milk paints are extremely adhesive and will knuckle onto plaster so effectively that the paint can pull it right off. Milk paint is not designed to be used on exteriors, because it will water stain. However, many people use it on outdoor places where an antique look is desired. If used as an exterior paint, it should be combined with lime or sealed thoroughly with a waterproof sealant.

The most important health reason to make your own paints and stains is to avoid biocides (pesticides). Biocides are included in paint as a preservative and to kill mold, and in wood stains to kill insects. Just because you can't smell the pesticides in the paint doesn't mean they aren't there. A second important health reason to make your own paint is to eliminate your exposure to VOCs. The third reason is to ensure the use of natural dyes and pigments, free of toxic heavy metals.

## MINI-GLOSSARY

**Calcium Carbonate.** See Whiting and Lime.

**Calcium Hydroxide.** See Mason's Hydrated Lime.

**Calcium Oxide.** See Quicklime.

**Casein.** Casein is milk protein. It is the curd made from milk and an acid such as vinegar. Casein is used for making milk paint and some whitewashes. You can make your own casein with white distilled vinegar for small painting jobs (see the recipe on page 287). Buying dried casein is recommended for bigger painting jobs. I have had very little success drying homemade casein in the oven, so if you plan to use homemade casein, use it fresh, but you must add a fifth of its volume of mason's hydrated lime to dissolve the curds.

**Chalk.** See Whiting.

**Distemper.** Because the slaking of lime is so dangerous, limewash was sometimes replaced with distemper—a paint or whitewash of whiting, hide glue, water, and pigment. Whitewash is a strong paint. Because nowadays lime that has already been slaked is readily available, whitewash is preferable, more hygienic, and longer lasting than distemper.

**Emulsion.** A mixture of mutually insoluble ingredients, such as water and oil, where one is dispersed into the other.

**Formaldehyde.** A colorless, pungent preservative and a suspected carcinogen. See VOCs (page 263).

**Lime.** Lime is made by heating limestone (calcium carbonate) to high temperatures, resulting in quicklime, or calcium oxide. Quicklime is extremely caustic, like lye; when "slaked"—that is, combined with water—the temperatures can reach as high as 560° F. The process is dangerous and shouldn't be done by an amateur. Once the quicklime has been slaked and dried, it becomes calcium hydroxide, also known as mason's hydrated lime; it is the lime of choice for making milk paints and whitewash. Mason's hydrated lime is available in lumber supply stores.

**Agricultural Lime.** A mixture of calcium carbonate, calcium hydroxide, and often gypsum. This is *not* the type of lime to use for making paints.

**Lime Dust.** Found frequently in agricultural lime; contains calcium carbonate. Not to be used for milk paints or whitewash.

**Lime Paste.** A mixture of mason's hydrated lime and water. The general ratio for lime paste is 1 pound mason's hydrated lime to $1\frac{1}{4}$ gallons water. One 50-pound bag of mason's hydrated lime soaked in 6 gallons of water will result in 8 gallons of lime paste.

NOTE: Lime paste can also be made by slaking quicklime. The ratio for this paste is 38 pounds of quicklime to 8 gallons of water, which produces 8 gallons of lime paste. However, as noted above, slaking your own quicklime is dangerous and not recommended.

**Limewash.** See Whitewash.

**Mason's Hydrated Lime.** Quicklime that has been slaked and dried, resulting in calcium hydroxide.

**Quicklime.** The "original" material (calcium oxide, highly caustic and dangerous) that all lime products are made of. When water is added to quicklime, temperatures reach 560° F.

**Slaked Lime.** Water paste made with quicklime (calcium oxide) and water. Remember that adding water to quicklime is dangerous (see Lime).

**White Lime.** Mason's hydrated lime (calcium hydroxide).

**Linseed Oil.** Linseed oil is often added to whitewash and milk paint as an additional waterproofer. It also helps to "plasticize" paint. Linseed is chosen over other oils because it dries; olive oil, for example, doesn't dry. Use sun-bleached and thickened raw linseed oil (see page 22), or let the oil's vibrant yellow color tint the paint.

> *Rule of Thumb:* Add $\frac{1}{3}$ cup sun-bleached and thickened raw linseed oil for every 2 gallons whitewash or milk paint.

**Milk.** See Casein.

**Natural Pigment.** Made of plant dyes or natural earth minerals.

**Phenol.** A potentially toxic compound often used as a preservative in cosmetics. Phenols are also used as disinfectants. Phenols can irritate the skin. Some antiseptic essential oils have a high phenol content.

**Solvent.** Liquid substance capable of dissolving or dispersing one or more other substances.

**Stain and Sealant.** Besides darkening wood, stains also protect wood from the ultraviolet rays

# BUYER'S GUIDE

## PAINTS AND STAINS

**B**ESIDES containing fungicides to prevent mildew growth, paint contains biocides as preservatives to extend the shelf life. Biocides can be detected in the air five years after the paint containing the chemicals is applied. If you ask salespeople at a hardware store for a low-biocide paint, they may look at you blankly, not knowing that the cans of paint on their shelves are high biocide. You usually need to special order low-biocide paint. It is made on the spot, or in small quantities, and is meant to be used quickly. Special ordering this paint is well worth it, to avoid long-term exposure to pesticides. There are only a few commercial ready-made paints that meet all three better health requirements—low biocides, low VOCs, and natural pigments. See Sources and Resources for product recommendations.

A NOTE ABOUT NATURAL PAINTS: So-called natural ready-made paints are derived from terpenes such as citrus and balsam, and minerals. Although these paints are made with natural materials and are petroleum free, they can be high in VOCs. The smell of the terpenes can be strong for many months after the product has been applied, although, once dried, the natural paints and stains do not outgas biocides or fungicides.

## Exterior Paint

The best choice for an exterior paint is one that has zinc oxide as the fungicide. Next best choices are low- to zero-VOC paints, acrylic or latex paints, and recycled water-based paint. Low-biocide paints are not available for exteriors. All exterior paints have fungicides, and stains have even greater amounts of fungicides. Avoid oil-based paints as well as paint from old cans that may contain mercury or lead.

## Interior Paint

Low-biocide, low-VOC latex paint is the first choice for commercially available interior paint, as is milk paint. So-called natural paint is made with plant terpenes (instead of petroleum distillates) and natural pigments (instead of synthetics). Latex paint is safer for the environment than oil-based paint, but it needs to be used with great care due to the strong terpenes, which contribute to indoor air pollution. Acceptable paints, although containing biocides, include latex, acrylic, and recycled latex paints, assuming they don't contain mercury or lead. Avoid oil- and solvent-based paints. See Sources and Resources for product information.

of the sun. The more pigment, the more natural protection from ultraviolet light. Clear sealants exposed to the sun without ultraviolet protection won't last long. Clear stains are loaded with pesticides and wood preservatives; darker stains tend to be less toxic. Paint is preferable to stains.

**Terpene.** Any of various hydrocarbons found especially in essential oils, resins, and balsam.

**Whitewash.** Whitewash is made of mason's hydrated lime and water. It has been used throughout the world, indoors and out, on plaster, concrete, masonry, and stone. Limewash, as it is sometimes called, is a natural antiseptic and deters insects. Some formulas resemble milk paint.

**Whiting.** Calcium carbonate; chalk. This is what you *don't* want in your milk paint or whitewash, even though it is in some of the old formulas. It is very chalky and rubs off once dry.

## MILK PAINT AND LIME AND CASEIN PAINTS

### TIPS

MOLD PATROL

* Don't use fresh or powdered milk in milk paint recipes. Use only casein.
* Stir fresh milk paint every fifteen minutes or so; refrigerate overnight.
* Some recipes call for salt, borax, or alum as preservatives.
* Make milk paint with distilled water, which contains no bacteria.

WATERPROOFING

* Mixing whitewash with casein makes it more waterproof. Sometimes linseed oil is

added for the same reason. In the old days, people used tallow or other animal fat for the oil.

* As a rule of thumb, add 2 tablespoons raw linseed oil for every 2 gallons whitewash to increase its spreadability and waterproofing qualities.

GENERAL GUIDELINES

* Before application of milk paint or whitewash, the surface must be clean (but not glossy). If gloss is a problem, rinse the area with washing soda ($\frac{1}{4}$ cup to 1 gallon water).
* Do not apply milk paint over existing multiple layers of paint; when the paint dries, it will shrink in all directions and the undercoats could peel. According to the Old Fashioned Milk Paint Company (see Sources and Resources), you can test for this by cutting a one-inch-long X in the old paint with a sharp knife or razor blade. Position masking tape across the X, rub it, and pull it off quickly. If the old paint comes off, it has poor adhesion, and no water-based paint will stick to it. The old paint must be removed before you cover it with milk paint.
* Milk paint in powdered form can last indefinitely if kept dry.
* Paints made of casein, lime, and borax are resistant to fire.
* Milk paint needs to cure for up to a month before it becomes waterproof.
* Milk paint and casein whitewash are a rich, warm white. If you aren't adding pigment but want a cooler white, add 1 teaspoon laundry bluing per gallon of paint.

* For each pint of milk paint, add $\frac{1}{4}$ teaspoon alum; it helps the paint dry harder.
* To make a less translucent product, add the white pigment titanium dioxide (available from Kremer Pigments; see Sources and Resources).
* Milk paint and whitewash should be the consistency of thin cream.
* Dampen the surface to be whitewashed with water, and dampen again before subsequent coats.
* Whitewash doesn't stick to some synthetic surfaces, such as fiberglass, so be sure to test in advance.
* Apply milk paint to damp surfaces and in very thin layers. Don't be disturbed if you can see through the first few layers when they are wet. Each succeeding layer will be less translucent.
* Some pigments are destroyed by lime (and other highly alkaline materials) and others by acids. Be sure to ask which pigments are compatible with lime.

### GENERAL NOTES ON SQUARE-FOOT COVERAGE OF CASEIN AND WHITEWASH PAINTS

Be sure to make enough paint, especially if you add your own pigments. It is hard to match colors exactly.

The following recommendations are adapted from the Lime Institute's 1955 brochure *Whitewash and Cold Water Paints.*

Wood: 1 gallon covers 225 square feet
Brick: 1 gallon covers 180 square feet
Plaster: 1 gallon covers 270 square feet

Masonry (concrete): 1 gallon covers 250 square feet

**RULE OF THUMB.** Test your milk paint on the wall. If the paint is powdery after it has dried, you need to add more casein. If it cracks and flakes, you need less casein and more lime.

**CASEIN.** Casein is the milk protein in curdled milk.

## MAKE YOUR OWN CASEIN FOR SMALL JOBS ✗

1 gallon whole milk
$\frac{1}{2}$ cup white distilled vinegar

Pour the milk into a large pot. Add the vinegar, stirring to blend. Heat over low heat until the mixture curdles completely; the curd will float to the top, leaving greenish water underneath. Skim off the curd (casein). Using a colander and strainer, rinse thoroughly to remove all the vinegar. (The vinegar will react with the lime in the milk paint, interfering with the chemical combination of the casein and lime.) I have never successfully dried casein, but if you want to try, squeeze out as much water as possible from the casein, lay it on a baking sheet, and place it in a 200°F oven until just before it browns (3 to 4 hours), or in the sun.

**Makes about 1 cup**

*Preparation Time:* 20 minutes
*Shelf Life:* Indefinite if completely dried and powdered; a few days refrigerated if fresh
*Storage:* Plastic container

## Variation

SOUR MILK CASEIN: Instead of using vinegar, let the milk go sour naturally.

## MILK PAINT WITH FRESH CASEIN

*This recipe makes enough paint for small craft projects. If you have a larger project in mind, buy commercial casein.*

Freshly made casein from 2 gallons whole milk (see formula above)
About 2 cups mason's hydrated lime
Distilled water (if needed)

To the fresh casein, add the lime bit by bit, stirring as you add, until the casein has dissolved. If necessary add enough distilled water to make a texture like cream. (When I have made this, the lime dissolves the casein to such an extent that no more liquid is needed.)
**Makes about 3 cups**

*Preparation Time:* About 45 minutes
*Shelf Life:* Discard leftovers

## BASIC MILK PAINT INDOOR-OUTDOOR FORMULA (Dry Ingredients)

*This recipe is an adaptation of one found in the Lime Institute's 1955 brochure* Whitewash and Cold Water Paints. *The casein makes this paint adhesive.*

2½ pounds casein
7 gallons distilled water
25 pounds mason's hydrated lime

1½ pounds borax
Natural earth pigment (optional)

Soak the casein overnight in a large tub with 2 gallons of the water (heated). In a separate tub combine the lime and 3 gallons of the water; stir to blend. An hour or so before painting, dissolve the borax in 1 gallon of the water (heated), stirring to blend. After the mixture has cooled, stir it into the soaked casein. Add the lime mixture and blend thoroughly. Add pigment if desired. Add more water if the paint is too thick.
**Makes 8 gallons**

*Preparation Time:* Less than 1 hour
*Shelf Life:* Indefinite for dry ingredients; use liquid milk paint within a few days
*Storage:* Covered container
NOTE: Some brands of casein, such as that available from Kremer Pigments, suggest making milk paint with borax as a preservative and give specific instructions on how to do so.

## Variation

SALT PRESERVATIVE: Add about ¼ part salt to 1 part lime. Salt is used as a preservative.
MILK PAINT WITH LINSEED OIL: Add up to ⅓ cup bleached raw linseed oil (see Mini-Glossary, page 284) per 2 gallons finished product. The oil makes the paint more plastic and waterproof.

## SIMPLE OUTDOOR WHITEWASH FORMULA

*The salt adds antiseptic qualities to this whitewash.*

7½ pounds salt dissolved in 2½ gallons hot distilled water

25 pounds mason's hydrated lime mixed with
3 gallons distilled water
Natural earth pigment (optional)

In separate tubs, prepare the salt and lime mixtures. Combine, stirring to remove all lumps; add more distilled water if the paint is too thick. Add pigment if desired.
**Makes 6 gallons**

*Preparation Time:* About 20 minutes
*Shelf Life:* A few days (it doesn't decay; it loses texture)
*Storage:* Covered container

## SIMPLE WHITEWASH ✂

3 gallons distilled water
25 pounds mason's hydrated lime

In a mixing tub, add the water to the lime to make a paste. Blend well.
**Makes 4 gallons**

*Preparation Time:* About 15 minutes
*Shelf Life:* A few days (it doesn't decay; it loses texture)
*Storage:* Covered container

## LIGHTHOUSE WHITEWASH

*This preparation holds up well to weather; a variation was used in the past on U.S. lighthouses.*

25 pounds mason's hydrated lime dissolved in
3 gallons distilled water

7½ pounds salt dissolved in 2½ gallons
distilled water
1½ pounds rice flour
½ pound titanium dioxide
½ pound white glue
More distilled water as needed

In separate tubs, prepare the lime and salt mixtures. Add the flour and titanium dioxide to the salt mixture. Combine the salt and lime mixtures, stirring to remove all lumps. Add the glue and more distilled water if the paint is too thick.
**Makes 7 gallons**

*Preparation Time:* About 25 minutes
*Shelf Life:* A few days (it doesn't decay; it loses texture)
*Storage:* Covered container

## LINSEED LIMEWASH

*This is a "plastic" whitewash with waterproofing qualities.*

25 pounds mason's hydrated lime
3 gallons distilled water
¾ cup raw sun-bleached linseed oil

Combine the ingredients in a large mixing tub, and stir well.
**Makes 4 gallons**

*Preparation Time:* About 15 minutes
*Shelf Life:* A few weeks; stir to reblend
*Storage:* Covered container

## MASONRY WHITEWASH

### WHITEWASH FOR MASONRY

12 pounds each Portland cement and
mason's hydrated lime
3 to 4 gallons distilled water

In a mixing tub, combine the Portland cement
and lime with enough water to reach the consistency of paint.
**Makes 4 gallons**

*Preparation Time:* About 15 minutes
*Shelf Life:* Discard leftovers

### Variation
SALT WHITEWASH: For a more antiseptic
whitewash, add $1\frac{1}{2}$ pounds salt per 12 pounds
mason's hydrated lime.

## TEMPERA
See Hobbies, page 306.

## DISTRESSED PLASTER
This is an old-fashioned sealant for plaster.

### BASIC DISTRESSED PLASTER FORMULA ✗

3 parts white glue
1 part water
Natural earth pigment

Combine the glue and water in a mixing tub;
make a large enough batch to handle the surface area you want to cover. Add the pigment.
Use the mixture as you would a paint.

*Preparation Time:* 10 minutes
*Shelf Life:* Make only as much as you will use at
a time

# Pigments and Dyes

Natural pigments are made from minerals (earth
and clay, called iron oxides) and vegetables
(roots, bark, leaves, and fruit). The colors found
in nature are rich and mellow, never garish, integrating your home with its natural environment.
Making your own paint using pigments found in
nature will enable you to find unexpected beauty.
What colors you can find! Who knows, maybe
you will stumble across the famous but never
duplicated Pompeii red.

Not too far in the distant past, paint stores
carried barrels of pigments; the pigments were
added to a base of white lead or whiting. For
the recipes in this book, you can add earth pigments and dyes to milk paints and whitewashes and to water for stains. Finding a
source of natural pigments, or learning to
make your own, is crucial for establishing your
independence from toxic paints and stains. (See
Sources and Resources.)

### HOW TO MAKE YOUR OWN NATURAL DYES AND PIGMENTS
**Plant Dyes.** Experimentation is the name of
the game when making your own dyes and pigments. I matched the stain of our kitchen cabinets perfectly by simmering walnut hulls, then

## BUYER'S GUIDE

### COLORING PAINTS WITH PIGMENTS AND DYES

**N**ATURAL vegetable dyes and minerals are the first choice for coloring paints. Minerals should be screened for heavy metals (see Sources and Resources for companies that do this). Avoid organic or synthetic pigments contaminated with toxic heavy metals such as cadmium, cobalt, copper, mercury, lead, and arsenic, all of which are commonly found in artists' pigments. Most pigments available today are synthetic coal tar dyes, also called aniline dyes. Many coal tar dyes consist of aromatic hydrocarbons—organic chemicals that are increasingly found to be carcinogens—and contain heavy metals. When working with any powdered pigment, wear a NIOSH- (U.S. National Institute for Occupational Safety and Health) approved dust mask. Pigments are dangerous to breathe, and those with heavy metals are long-lasting in the environment.

adding a tad of alkanet root for a slightly reddish brown. There was no recipe, but I knew that walnuts made a beautiful brown and alkanet root made a vivid, slightly scarlet red. The starting point is the chart on page 292 to find materials that produce colors you are looking for.

T I P *When using natural materials, you may need more than you would expect.*
*Caution:* Wear gloves when making dyes.

## BASIC NATURAL DYE FORMULA ✂

*Natural dyes made of plants will make light to dark pastel colors when mixed with paint. Minerals can make darker dyes. Different natural dye materials will produce dyes of differing strength; when dying paint, for example, start with 1 cup pigment to a gallon of paint, and increase as desired. For stains, make a strong dye bath,*

*and use as many coats as necessary to reach the desired color.*

Handful of dye material (more for darker dyes, less for pastel dyes)
4 cups water, or as needed
1 teaspoon alum *or* 1 tablespoon white distilled vinegar

Combine the dye material and water in a pan and simmer for 2 hours, adding more water as it evaporates. Let cool, then strain. Stir in the alum or vinegar (as a mordant).
**Makes 4 cups**

*Preparation Time:* 15 minutes
*Shelf Life:* About 1 week refrigerated; 1 to 2 years frozen
*Storage:* Freeze leftovers (before adding to paint) in plastic containers

## NATURAL DYES AND PIGMENTS

| NAME | ORIGIN | COLOR |
|---|---|---|
| ALKANET ROOT | PLANT | SCARLET RED |
| BARBERRY ROOT | PLANT | YELLOWS AND GOLDS |
| BEET ROOTS | PLANT | SCARLET RED |
| BIRCH LEAVES | TREE | YELLOW |
| BLUEBERRY LEAVES AND BERRIES | PLANT | BLUES |
| CABBAGE, PURPLE | PLANT | PURPLES |
| CARROT TOPS | PLANT | YELLOW |
| CLAYS | EARTH | SIENNAS AND REDS |
| COCHINEAL | INSECTS | CRIMSON (CARMINE) |
| COFFEE | PLANT | BROWN |
| COLTSFOOT | PLANT | GREENS |
| CRANBERRIES | PLANT | PINK, RED |
| DANDELION FLOWERS | PLANT | YELLOW |
| DIRT | EARTH | OCHRES, GREENS, UMBERS |
| ELDERBERRIES | TREE | GRAY-BLUE |
| EUCALYPTUS | TREE | RUST |
| GALLNUTS | TREE | BROWN |
| GOLDENROD | PLANT | DEEP YELLOW |
| GRAPE LEAVES | PLANT | DEEP YELLOW |
| HAWTHORN BERRIES | TREE | BLUE/LAVENDER |
| HENNA | PLANT | REDS |
| INDIGO | TREE | BLUE |

| NAME | ORIGIN | COLOR |
|---|---|---|
| IRON OXIDES | MINERAL | OCHRES, SIENNAS, RED |
| IRON SILICATE | MINERAL | GREEN |
| LADY'S BEDSTRAW ROOTS | PLANT | RED TO PURPLE |
| LAPIS LAZULI | MINERAL | ULTRAMARINE |
| LICHEN | PLANT | VARIETY, INCLUDING ORANGES |
| LOGWOOD CHIPS | TREE | BLUE |
| MADDER ROOT | PLANT | RED |
| MULBERRIES | TREE | RED TO PURPLE |
| ONION SKINS | PLANT | RUSTS AND GREENS |
| PINE NEEDLES | TREE | GREEN |
| PITTOSPORUM | BUSH | PURPLE |
| PLUM LEAVES | TREE | LAVENDERS, GREEN |
| PURPLE GRAPES | PLANT | PURPLE |
| RED ONION SKINS | PLANT | LIGHT RED |
| ROSEMARY | PLANT | YELLOW-GREEN |
| SANDALWOOD | TREE | RED TO YELLOW |
| SPINACH | PLANT | GREEN |
| TEA, BLACK | PLANT | BROWN |
| TURMERIC | PLANT | GOLDEN YELLOW |
| VETCH FLOWERS | PLANT | BLUE-GREEN |
| WALNUT HULLS | TREE | BROWN |
| WALNUT LEAVES | TREE | BROWNS |
| WELD PLANT (NOT ROOTS) | PLANT | YELLOW |

## WALNUT STAIN ✘

*Walnut hulls make a rich brown dye. One woman I know uses walnut hulls to dye her hair. She makes the dye in a percolator coffeepot by placing crushed walnut hulls in the basket meant to hold the ground coffee. I haven't tried this method, but it makes sense. It is a good idea to look for 25-cup percolator coffeemakers at yard sales to use for this purpose.*

1 part crushed walnut hulls
4 parts water

Place the walnut hulls in a pan and cover with water. Simmer for 4 to 5 hours over very low heat, adding more water as needed.
**Makes 4 cups**

*Preparation Time:* 30 minutes
*Shelf Life:* 1 week refrigerated; 1 to 2 years frozen
*Storage:* Plastic container
NOTE: Walnut hulls can be ordered through the mail, such as from Kremer Pigments. See Sources and Resources.

## WALNUT AND ALKANET ROOT STAIN

*The combination of walnut hulls and alkanet root produces a warm, reddish brown dye.*

8 parts walnut hulls
1 part or more alkanet root
32 parts water

Follow the directions for Walnut Stain, above, but include alkanet root with the walnut hulls in the pan.

*Preparation Time:* 30 minutes
*Shelf Life:* 1 week refrigerated; 1 to 2 years frozen
*Storage:* Plastic container
NOTE: Don't use a coffee percolator with soft ingredients such as alkanet root, beets, and blueberries.

Variations
Depending on the desired color, beets, blueberries, and other dyestuffs can be substituted for alkanet root.

**EARTH PIGMENTS.** Earth pigments are derived from earth and rock. Called iron oxides, earth pigments are considered to be low in toxicity, and the colors are deep and earthy. Whereas most earth pigment colors are browns and rusts, in some parts of the world it is possible to find blues, greens, and purples. Colors available commercially include yellows, greens, umbers, gray, red, and even turquoise. Two mail order sources are The Natural Choice and Kremer Pigments (see Sources and Resources).

## RECIPE FOR MAKING YOUR OWN EARTH PIGMENT

*This recipe is for those of you who want to make earth pigment from your local region instead of buying it through a catalog. To find earth pigment, search in neighboring locales for dirt of interesting colors. The colors are the iron oxides. Collect a few bucketsful for testing purposes. Once you find colors you like, you can collect enough to make larger quantities.*

### Colored earth
### Water

Soak colored earth in water for 1 hour to saturate it. Strain and repeat. Transfer the mixture to a pot, bring to a boil, reduce the heat to medium-low, and simmer for a few hours. Let the sediment settle, then pour off the water. Let the sediment dry completely, then grind it into a powder with a mortar and pestle.

*Preparation Time:* About 1 hour
*Shelf Life:* Indefinite
*Storage:* Glass jar with a screw top

# Stains, Sealants, and Varnishes

TIPS

* You can achieve a range of colors on different woods depending on how much tannin is in the stain. The more tannin, the darker the stain.
* Water-based stains need to be sealed with shellac if they are to be waxed and polished.

## BASIC WATER-BASED WOOD STAIN FORMULA ✗

*The pigment in this recipe can be homemade (see recipe above) or commercial (available by mail order from The Natural Choice or Kremer Pigments; see Sources and Resources).*

### Water-soluble powdered pigment
### Warm water

Each pigment is different, so you'll need to do some testing to begin with. Start with 1 teaspoon pigment; add water, measuring as you go, until you reach the desired color. Once you have determined the ratios, you can increase them for a larger batch. Add water to the pigment slowly, mixing carefully so the powder doesn't disperse as you add the water. The more pigment, the darker the stain. Add enough water to produce the texture of paint.

*Preparation Time:* 10 to 15 minutes
*Shelf Life:* Indefinite
*Storage:* Glass jar with a screw top

### SHELLAC

Shellac, a by-product of insect secretions, is commonly used for finishing furniture and sometimes, although rarely, floors. Shellac is transparent and protective. French polish is a technique developed in the early nineteenth century: Layers upon layers of lac flakes are dissolved in alcohol; the resulting shellac is rubbed into the wood by hand.

Some experts feel that filling the wood pores with a pumice-stone paste filler is a must for a smooth finish. The paste is made by dissolving one part lac flakes in one part alcohol. Then one part or less of pumice stone powder is slowly stirred into the shellac until a paste-like consistency is reached. The surface is then sanded lightly.

## BUYER'S GUIDE

### STAINS AND SEALANTS

WATER-BASED stains and sealants without biocides and added dryers are the first choice among these products, as are those made with beeswax or carnauba wax. Acrylic urethanes manufactured without the addition of biocides are acceptable choices for those who aren't chemically sensitive. So is shellac (the alcohol evaporates). Avoid epoxies and oil-based formulations with dryers.

Besides darkening wood, stains also protect wood from the sun's ultraviolet rays. The more pigment, the more natural protection from ultraviolet light. Clear sealants without ultraviolet protection won't last long when exposed to the sun. Clear stains are loaded with pesticides and wood preservatives. Darker stains tend to be less toxic. Paint is preferable to stain due to the high level of pesticides in stain. Mary Oetzel, a national consultant on safer building materials and the president of Environmental Education and Health Services, believes we should never use clear or semitransparent exterior sealants; they have high amounts of fungicides and insecticides. As with stains, sealants with pigments are usually less toxic than those that are clear.

## FRENCH POLISH

*French polish consists of layers and layers of a lac-alcohol mixture. Some experts apply literally thousands of layers on one piece of furniture; they claim that, properly applied, the finish will last for twenty-five years.*

Lac flakes

Vodka, rum, or brandy

For the first layers, mix equal parts lac flakes and alcohol. For the last layers, mix 3 parts lac to 7 parts alcohol. The alcohol in each layer in between is increased gradually. Make each mixture by soaking the lac in the alcohol for 24 hours, or until dissolved. Dab some on a piece of soft cotton flannel or cheesecloth, and rub into the wood.

*Preparation Time:* Hours and hours
*Shelf Life:* Indefinite
*Storage:* Glass jar with a screw top
NOTE: Don't apply French polish to a waxed surface.

### VARNISH

Varnish is a furniture coating made of resin, resulting in a hard, shiny, transparent coat.

## VARNISH I

1 pound mastic resin
2 ounces beeswax
4 cups raw, sun-thickened linseed oil
2 cups vodka

Combine the mastic, beeswax, and oil in a double boiler over low heat and stir until melted. Remove from the heat and stir in the vodka.
**Makes about 2 quarts**

*Preparation Time:* 30 minutes
*Shelf Life:* Indefinite, although it will need to be reheated
*Storage:* Glass jar with a screw top

Variation
OIL-FREE VARNISH: Substitute alcohol for the linseed oil. This varnish will be thinner without the oil, which adds plasticity.

## VARNISH II

5 pounds lac
7 ounces mastic resin
5 to 6 pints vodka

Combine the ingredients in a double boiler over medium-low heat until dissolved. Remove from the heat, stirring constantly while the mixture cools. Apply with a clean brush.
**Makes about 1 gallon**

*Preparation Time:* About 45 minutes
*Shelf Life:* Indefinite, although the mixture will need to be reheated
*Storage:* Glass jar with a screw top

## SIMPLE VARNISH AND GLAZE

15 parts white glue
1 part pigment (optional)

Combine the ingredients in a jar. Mix well. Apply with a clean brush.

*Preparation Time:* 10 minutes
*Shelf Life:* Indefinite
*Storage:* Glass jar with a screw top

### BIRD'S-EYE EFFECT

## FAKE BIRD'S-EYE MAPLE

1 cup white distilled vinegar
4 cups water
As much natural earth pigment as desired

Combine equal parts of the vinegar-water combination and desired amount of the pigment. Wash the mixture over varnished surfaces. The vinegar will curdle the varnish to produce a bird's-eye effect.
**Makes 5 cups**

*Preparation Time:* A few minutes
*Shelf Life:* Indefinite
*Storage:* Glass jar with a screw top

# Paint Strippers

## PAINTBRUSH CLEANER

White distilled vinegar
Soap
Water

Heat the vinegar—enough to cover the paint-brushes—in a pan. Remove from the heat and pour into an old coffee can. Soak the brushes overnight. Wash them with soap and water, then let dry.

*Preparation Time:* About 10 minutes
*Shelf Life:* Discard

## WASHING SODA STRIPPER ✗

Washing soda
Water
Vinegar wash (1 cup white distilled vinegar
to 4 cups water)

Combine washing soda and enough water to make a thick paste. Spread it on the surface to be stripped. Misting with water occasionally to keep the paste very moist, let it damp-set for at least 6 hours. Scrape off the paint, which will have loosened and curled. To neutralize the remaining washing soda, rinse with the vinegar wash.

*Preparation Time:* 1 to 2 minutes
*Shelf Life:* Discard leftovers

# Wallpaper

Avoid wallpaper made with vinyl and other plastics due to outgassing of toxic VOCs and plastics. To find out more about wallpaper glues, see Adhesives and Glues, page 271.

T I P *To remove wallpaper, use steam, or hot water with a bit of baking soda added to it.*

## BUYER'S GUIDE

### STRIPPING PAINT

THE safest paint stripper is a thick washing soda and water paste. Be sure to wear gloves. Otherwise, choose the water-based stripper Safest Stripper, available in hardware and lumber supply stores. Avoid the carcinogen methyl chloride.

## WALLPAPER PASTE ✗

See recipe for wallpaper paste on page 274.

# Waterproofing

## NATURAL WOOD WATERPROOFER

Boiled linseed oil (see Note)

Paint a thin coat of linseed oil on the wood. Let it dry completely before repeating with another thin coat. You might need to wait up to a week between coats, but in dry weather a few days should be sufficient. Use 3 or 4 coats.

*Preparation Time:* None
*Shelf Life:* Indefinite
*Storage:* Glass jar with a screw top
NOTE: See Sources and Resources for a source of boiled linseed oil without added petroleum dryers.

**Variation**

WOOD WATER REPELLENT: Combine 1 cup boiled linseed oil and ½ ounce beeswax in a double boiler over medium heat until the wax is melted. Paint on the wood before the mixture hardens.

## WATERPROOFING LEATHER

### SOLVENT-FREE LEATHER WATERPROOFER WITH CLOVE OIL 🎁

½ ounce beeswax
1 cup boiled linseed oil
½ cup glycerin
½ cup water
2 to 3 drops clove essential oil

In a double boiler, heat the beeswax and oil over medium heat until the beeswax melts. Remove from the heat and add the glycerin, water, and clove oil. With an electric mixer, blend until emulsified. Pour into a glass jar. Let cool, then rub into leather with a cloth; wipe off excess.
**Makes 2 cups**

*Preparation Time:* 25 minutes
*Shelf Life:* Indefinite
*Storage:* Glass jar with a screw top

### SOLVENT-FREE LEATHER WATERPROOFER WITH COCONUT

½ ounce beeswax
¼ cup coconut oil
¼ cup olive oil
1 capsule (200 i.u.) liquid vitamin E

In a double boiler, heat the beeswax and oils until the beeswax has melted. Cut open the vitamin E capsule and add the contents to the mixture. Remove from the heat, pour into a glass jar, and let cool. Apply with a soft rag; wipe off excess.
**Makes ½ cup**

*Preparation Time:* 25 minutes
*Shelf Life:* 6 months
*Storage:* Glass jar with a screw top

### LANOLIN LEATHER PRESERVER

*This is an easy waterproofer for boots. Available at pharmacies, anhydrous lanolin usually comes in a tube.*

Anhydrous lanolin

Rub the anhydrous lanolin on boots and camping equipment.
*Preparation Time:* None
*Shelf Life:* Leave in the tube

## WATERPROOFING CLOTH
Some waterproofing sealants give off toxic VOCs. Here is an alternative.

### GLUE WATERPROOFER/CANVAS MILDEW PROTECTOR

½ cup each soap (liquid or a grated bar of soap) and white glue
¼ cup each salt and alum
1 gallon distilled water

Combine the ingredients. Boil cloth in this liquid for an hour or two; wring out the excess liquid and let dry.
**Makes 1 gallon**

*Preparation Time:* A few minutes
*Shelf Life:* Discard leftovers

## OILSKIN PROTECTOR

*Traditionally, plant oils were painted on heavy canvas to weatherproof the cloth and protect seamen from the elements. These days, plastics are usually used for foul-weather gear, but you may have some outdoor canvas that could benefit from this formula.*

Boiled linseed oil (see Note)

Paint a thin layer of boiled linseed oil on the cloth. Repeat as needed.

*Preparation Time:* None
*Shelf Life:* Indefinite
*Storage:* Glass jar with a screw top
NOTE: See Sources and Resources for boiled linseed oil without petroleum dryers.

### RUST AND CORROSION PROTECTION

TIPS
* Place chalk and/or uncooked rice in a toolbox to absorb excess moisture and prevent rust.
* Store nails and screws in screw-top glass jars.
* Place batteries in Ziploc bags in the refrigerator.

* Place a bucketful of sand where you store your gardening tools; insert the handles of hoes, shovels, and other implements into the sand for storage.

## NEW TOOLS PROTECTOR

¼ cup lanolin
¼ cup nonpetroleum jelly (see page 31)

Combine the ingredients in a bowl, and stir to blend. Dab some of the mixture on a cloth and rub onto new tools.
**Makes ½ cup**

*Preparation Time:* 25 minutes
*Shelf Life:* 6 months
*Storage:* Glass jar with a screw top

# Wood

### WOOD PRESERVATIVES
Wood preservatives are useful for wood exposed to the elements, such as wood used in gardens and outdoor furniture.

## ZINC OXIDE PRESERVATIVE

*Zinc oxide is available in powder form by the pound from herb suppliers.*

Zinc oxide powder
Water

Combine the ingredients in a bucket until the mixture is the consistency of paint. Apply 2 or 3 coats.
*Preparation Time:* 15 to 20 minutes

*Shelf Life:* Indefinite

*Storage:* Glass jar with a screw top

## CEMENT AND MILK PRESERVATIVE AND FIREPROOFER

*This formula makes a hard, thin sealant when painted onto wood. You can add a natural earth pigment if desired, or you can cover the preservative with paint.*

Cement

Water

Dried casein

Mix the cement with enough water to reach the consistency of thin paint. Don't add the water too fast or the mixture may be too thin. Stir in the casein slowly until the mixture is the consistency of thick cream. Apply 2 or 3 coats onto wood.

*Preparation Time:* 15 minutes

*Shelf Life:* Make only as much as you need at a time

### REPELLING INSECTS ON WOOD

## BORIC ACID SOLUTION

Boric acid powder

Water

Place the boric acid in a bowl or pail, depending on how much wood you need to cover. Stir in the water slowly just until the mixture is the consistency of thin paint. Paint on wood with a brush.

*Preparation Time:* Make only as much as you need at a time

### WOOD BLEACH

## LIME LIGHTENER

Mason's hydrated lime (1 cup will cover an area 4 feet square)

Distilled water

Vinegar wash (1 cup white distilled vinegar to 4 cups water)

Place the lime in a bucket and add water until the mixture is the consistency of paint. Brush the mixture onto wood. Leave it on for a few hours, misting it with water to keep it moist. Rinse with the vinegar wash to neutralize the lime if necessary.

*Preparation Time:* 15 minutes

*Shelf Life:* Discard leftovers

*Storage:* Covered container

### WOOD POLISH AND WAX

See Chapter Two.

# Shoes

T I P *For saddle soap, use real soap, not detergent.*

## SHOE WATERPROOFER

1 ounce beeswax

4 ounces oil (more for a soft salve, less for hard)

4 capsules (200 i.u.) liquid vitamin E

Melt the beeswax with the oil in a double boiler over medium heat. Remove from the

## BUYER'S GUIDE

### SUSTAINABLE SOURCES OF WOOD

BEFORE buying new wood, see if you can find salvaged or recycled wood. There are a number of salvage companies throughout the country. Another choice is to find sustainably harvested temperate timber that is not old growth and has been certified by a member of the Forest Stewardship Council (see Sources and Resources). Avoid all old-growth timber and tropical woods such as teak, lauan, rosewood, balsa, camphorwood, Brazilian redwood (bloodwood), canarywood, Spanish cedar, cocobola, damar, ebony, African and American mahogany, Central American oak, Pau d'arco, white mahogany, rosewood, and zebrawood. (You will find tropical woods in unexpected places. Lauan, a tropical wood, is commonly used as plywood or tropical veneer, for example.) This is a brief list of some of the more recognizable names of rain forest woods. For a comprehensive list, contact the Rainforest Action Network (see Sources and Resources).

heat, add the contents of the vitamin E capsules, and cream with an electric handheld mixer. Scoop some of the mixture onto a soft rag, and polish shoes.

**Makes about ½ cup**

*Preparation Time:* 25 minutes
*Shelf Life:* 6 months
*Storage:* Glass jar with a screw top

Variation
LANOLIN SHOE WATERPROOFER: Use anhydrous lanolin out of the tube. Dab some onto a soft rag, and polish shoes.

## LEATHER SHOE CLEANER AND SADDLE SOAP

*See Leather Cleaners, Chapter Two.*

SHOE POLISH

## BASIC SHOE POLISH FORMULA 🎁

*The ratio of ingredients here will be like nonpetroleum jelly (page 31). If you want stiffer polish, reduce the amount of oil.*

2 ounces oil (less oil for thicker polish)
½ ounce beeswax
½ to 1 teaspoon natural earth pigment
(see Note)

Combine the oil and beeswax in a double boiler over medium heat until the beeswax is melted. Remove from the heat and stir in the pigment, adding more for a darker color.
**Makes ¼ cup**

*Preparation Time:* 25 minutes
*Shelf Life:* 6 months
*Storage:* Glass jar with a screw top
NOTE: Natural earth pigments are available from The Natural Choice or Kremer Pigments; see Sources and Resources.

# Car Care

## SAFER ANTIFREEZE

There is a less toxic antifreeze available made of propylene glycol instead of the more common ethylene glycol. Propylene glycol is safe enough to be a food additive; ethylene glycol is toxic enough to be considered household hazardous waste. Quite a difference. Propylene glycol antifreeze is available from automotive supply stores.

*Caution:* Ethylene glycol antifreeze has a sweet smell that is attractive to animals but will poison them if they ingest it. Do not pour it down the drain if you have a septic system. If you are on municipal water, dilute the antifreeze with large quantities of water before pouring it down the drain. Some service stations recycle antifreeze; try to find one. Otherwise, save it for your community's household hazardous waste pickup day.

## WINDSHIELDS

**GLYCERIN WINDSHIELD FLUID.** A solution of 10 percent glycerin and 90 percent water has a freezing point of 28°F. If the glycerin percentage is increased to 58 percent, the solution's freezing point drops to −10°F. A solution of 5 percent denatured alcohol has a freezing point

of 25°F; if the percentage of alcohol is upped to 35 percent, the freezing point drops to −16°F. Combining glycerin and denatured alcohol in a 20 percent solution each with 60 percent water has a freezing point of −23°F.

HANDS-ON

* For overnight windshield freeze prevention, dampen bath towels in a water and salt solution. Lay them over the windshield, keeping in place with the windshield wipers. Remove in the morning.
* Conventional wisdom says that if water beads on the metal finish of your car, you may not need wax or polish. The surface of new cars may scratch or get hazy if treatment is applied before it is needed.
* If you do polish and wax, here are two general rules of thumb: The older the car, the more abrasive the polish should be; and the more you wash your car, the less you will need to wax.
* Synthetic fibers can scratch metal. Use soft cotton rags and chamois; some people even like to use silk for the final polishing.
* Cover up car scratches with crayons that match the color of the paint.

## WASHING THE CAR

### SUDSY SOAP ✗

¼ cup liquid detergent
1 gallon warm water

Combine the ingredients in a bucket. Saturate a sponge with the soapy mixture, and wash the car. Rinse. Dry the car with a soft cotton rag or a chamois. Polish with a chamois.

**Makes 1 gallon**

*Preparation Time:* A few minutes
*Shelf Life:* Discard leftovers

## TAR REMOVER ✗

¼ cup white distilled vinegar
½ teaspoon linseed oil

Combine the ingredients in a bowl. Dab some of the mixture on a cloth and rub on the tar spots. Polish with a soft cloth.

**Makes ¼ cup**

*Preparation Time:* About 1 minute
*Shelf Life:* Indefinite, although the linseed oil will go rancid
*Storage:* Glass jar with a screw top

## PETROLEUM AND TAR CLEANER ✗

¼ cup washing soda
4 cups warm water

Dissolve the washing soda in the warm water. Wearing gloves, saturate a cloth with the mixture. Rub off the spots. Rinse well.

**Makes 4 cups**

*Preparation Time:* 1 minute
*Shelf Life:* Indefinite; shake to reblend
*Storage:* Glass jar with a screw top
*Caution:* Washing soda can remove wax.

## WINDSHIELD CLEANER ✗

1 cup club soda

Pour the club soda into a spray bottle. Spray on the windshield; wipe dry. Do not use in the car windshield-spray reservoir because it might freeze.

**Makes 1 cup**

*Preparation Time:* None
*Shelf Life:* Indefinite
*Storage:* Leave in the spray bottle

Variation
WINDOW CLEANER: Combine 2 tablespoons white distilled vinegar, ½ teaspoon liquid dish detergent, and 2 cups water in a spray bottle; shake to blend.

## BATTERY CLEANER

Baking soda
Water

Sprinkle baking soda on battery terminals to neutralize the battery acid. Spritz with water to dampen. Let set for an hour or so, then sponge off the baking soda with water. Air-dry.

*Preparation Time:* None

## VINYL SMELL REDUCER AND NATURAL ENGINE DEGREASER

¼ cup washing soda
1 gallon warm water

Dissolve the washing soda in the water. Saturate a sponge with the mixture, and wash the vinyl. Rinse thoroughly. Wear gloves; washing soda is slightly caustic.
**Makes 1 gallon**

*Preparation Time:* 1 to 2 minutes
*Shelf Life:* Discard leftovers

### Variation

CITRUS SOLVENT ENGINE CLEANER: Blend ¼ cup citrus solvent with 1 gallon water. Spray onto the engine. Rinse. (Citrus solvents contain VOCs and should be used with adequate ventilation.)

## BUGS OFF

*This formula can be used on painted surfaces and chrome.*

½ cup baking soda
Enough liquid soap to make a paste

Combine the ingredients in a bowl. Scoop onto a sponge and scrub over splattered bugs until they are loosened. Rinse well.
**Makes ½ cup**

*Preparation Time:* A few minutes
*Shelf Life:* Make only enough to use at a time; it will dry out

### Variation

OIL AWAY BIRD DROPPINGS: Dab some vegetable oil on a rag and wipe off the droppings. Wash with soapy water, then rinse.

### LEATHER POLISHES
See Chapter Two.

### CAR WAX AND POLISH

## MILDLY ABRASIVE CAR POLISH 🎁

*Rottenstone, pumice, and emery powder are traditionally used for car polishes. Rottenstone is meant to be used after emery powder—it is a finer abrasive.*

Rottenstone, pumice, or emery powder
Raw linseed or walnut oil

Mix some of the powder with the oil until the mixture becomes a paste. Scoop onto a damp sponge or cloth, and apply to the metal. Rinse with warm water. Polish by rubbing the metal with dry rottenstone or pumice.

*Preparation Time:* A few minutes
*Shelf Life:* It will dry out eventually, but you can moisten it with more oil
*Storage:* Glass jar with a screw top

## CREME POLISH WITH CLOVE 🎁

1 ounce beeswax
1 cup walnut oil
½ cup glycerin
½ cup water
2 tablespoons rottenstone
2 to 3 drops clove essential oil
Vitamin E capsule (200 i.u.)

Combine the beeswax and oil in a double boiler over medium heat until the beeswax has melted. Remove from the heat and add the glycerin and water. Mix with an electric hand-

held mixer until creamy. Add the rottenstone, essential oil, and contents of the vitamin E capsule; stir to blend. Apply with a soft cloth, then buff to a high shine with a chamois.
**Makes about 1½ cups**

*Preparation Time:* 25 minutes
*Shelf Life:* 6 to 12 months
*Storage:* Glass jar with a screw top

### CLEANING POLISH

½ cup flakes of grated hand soap
½ cup water
½ ounce beeswax
½ cup jojoba

Dissolve the soap in the water by placing them in a jar or bowl overnight. Combine the beeswax and jojoba in a double boiler over medium heat until the wax is melted. Remove from the heat and add the soapy water; mix with an electric handheld mixer until creamy. Dab some onto a soft cloth, then buff to a high shine with a chamois.
**Makes 1½ cups**

*Preparation Time:* 30 minutes
*Shelf Life:* Indefinite
*Storage:* Glass jar with a screw top

# Art Supplies, Hobbies, and Kids' Projects

Making your own modeling clay, fingerpaints, or play dough is a fun project to share with young children. Toddlers can help make the material themselves and have the satisfying experience of playing with their creations afterward. Natural plant dyes from foods such as beets, blueberries, and purple cabbage can be used for color, and they add to the safety of the do-it-yourself product over its store-bought counterpart. As with many old folk recipes, formulas for children's art projects require ingredients that are already in most of our cupboards, such as flour, cornstarch, salt, and baking soda. Wear a smock and lay down lots of newspaper, because these projects can be messy.

Older children enjoy making their own silly putty and stretchy claylike material called goop. I found a fascinating recipe for how to write on the shell of an egg with an alum and vinegar ink so that the writing shows up on the egg white after hard boiling the egg for fifteen minutes. April Fool's Day can take on a whole new dimension with this trick. You don't need to be a child or have children to enjoy making your own simple crafts supplies. Clays, inks, and egg tempera paints are easily made at home.

### HOW TO MAKE JUICE DYES

¼ cup plant dyestuff
2 cups water

Combine the ingredients in a pan and simmer over low heat for 1 to 2 hours. Strain and let cool. Add a few tablespoons at a time to the item to be dyed until the desired shade is reached. Freeze what you don't use for another time.

## GOOD JUICE DYES

JUICE dyes are safe materials to use to dye children's art projects. Simple vegetables and trees growing in our backyards can provide a rainbow of colors for clays, finger paints, and play dough.

*Blue:* Blueberries, red onion skins

*Brown:* Walnut hulls, paprika

*Green:* Oak bark, crab apple leaves and bark

*Orange:* Yellow onion skins, oats

*Purple:* Purple grapes

*Red:* Cranberries, beets

*Tan:* Coffee and tea

*Yellow:* Apple tree bark, white onion skins, turmeric

**Makes about 1½ cups**

*Preparation Time:* 1 minute
*Shelf Life:* About a week
*Storage:* Glass jar with screw top; refrigerate

## ARTISTS' PAINTS

The pigments I call for in this section are natural earth pigments available from mail order sources such as The Natural Choice and Kremer Pigments (see Sources and Resources). Be sure to ask for natural earth pigments, and avoid those that are synthetic and may contain heavy metals.

## NONPETROLEUM OIL–BASED ARTISTS' PAINT

*This recipe was a true find. Commercial oil paints contain unhealthy petroleum solvents. Thanks to this adaptation of a recipe in the Kremer Pigments artists' catalog, I can paint again. Generally, figure on using up to three times as much pigment as oil by volume.*

½ ounce beeswax
3½ ounces raw, cold-pressed linseed oil
Natural earth pigments

In a double boiler heat the beeswax and oil over medium heat until the beeswax is melted. Don a dust mask and carefully place the powdered pigment on a glass plate with sloped sides. With a palette knife, slowly add the oil and beeswax mixture to the powdered pigment until you have made a firm paste. This can take up to 30 minutes. Be sure not to add too much oil; if the paste is too thin, the paint will crack.

**Makes ½ cup**

*Preparation Time:* Up to 45 minutes
*Shelf Life:* Indefinite
*Storage:* Glass jar with a screw top

## EGG TEMPERA

*Tempera paint is pigment mixed with linseed oil, egg yolk, and water. Tempera paints are natural emulsions. Water and oil usually separate, but the tempera process emulsifies the materials using ingredients such as egg. Many of the great masters*

## BUYER'S GUIDE

### ART SUPPLIES

ART supplies are often toxic with solvents and pigments and are frequently contaminated with heavy metals. For this reason, be sure to avoid oil-based paints, permanent felt-tip markers, synthetically scented markers, solvent-based glues, powdered paints and dyes, and paints sprayed from cans. Choose instead water-based paints, simple white glues, vegetable and plant dyes, and simple homemade formulas using safe materials, such as those found below.

The Art & Creative Materials Institute, Inc., certifies various art products for safety. It states that its certification seals mean that a product has been "certified in a program of toxicological evaluation by a medical expert to contain no materials in sufficient quantities to be toxic or injurious to humans or to cause acute or chronic health problems." It recommends that children in grades K through 6 and preschool children use only those products certified to be nontoxic. On special request, Art & Creative Materials Institute, Inc., (see Sources and Resources) will furnish you with a fifteen-page list of products that have received its seals.

Arts, Crafts, and Theater Safety (ACTS) offers a monthly newsletter called *Acts Facts,* updating health and safety regulations and research affecting the arts. Monona Rossol is the founder and president. See Sources and Resources for contact information.

---

*used tempera paints, and many wall murals are done in tempera.*

Equal parts by volume egg yolk, distilled
water, and natural earth pigment
5 drops per ounce oil of clove
(as a preservative)

Whip the egg yolks and distilled water. Mix with the pigment, following the directions in Nonpetroleum Oil–Based Artists' Paint (page 305). If the paint is too glossy, add more pigment. Stir in the oil of clove. Paint on a gessoed surface.

*Preparation Time:* Up to 45 minutes
*Shelf Life:* Discard leftovers

Variation
OIL-BASED EGG TEMPERA: Add an equal part by volume of cold-pressed raw linseed oil to make the tempera more plastic.

### WATERCOLORS 🎁

2 ounces ground gum arabic
1¼ ounces 1:1 honey-water mixture
1½ ounces glycerin
4 ounces distilled water

5 drops essential oil of clove (as a
preservative)
Natural earth pigment

In the top of a double boiler, combine the gum arabic, honey-water, and glycerin. Boil the distilled water and pour over the mixture, then heat to dissolve. Let cool, then add the clove oil. Strain. Carefully place the pigment on a glass plate. Slowly add the gum arabic mixture, working it into the pigment first with a spoon and then with a caulking spatula until it is thick and very smooth. Do not add too much of the mixture. The final texture should be that of a very thick paste.

**Makes 1¼ cups**

*Preparation Time:* Up to 45 minutes
*Shelf Life:* Indefinite
*Storage:* Glass jar with a screw top

### BLOWING BUBBLES

You can make your own ring for bubble blowing with wire from a hardware store, or use a coat hanger for big bubbles. Just make sure there aren't any sharp ends that could hurt a child.

## BASIC BUBBLES FORMULA ✗ 🎁

½ cup liquid dish soap
1 tablespoon glycerin
4 cups water

Blend the ingredients in a nonbreakable container. Dip the bubble ring into the bubbles; remove and blow through it to form bubbles.

**Makes 4½ cups**

*Preparation Time:* 1 minute
*Shelf Life:* Indefinite
*Storage:* Glass jar with screw top

### CLAY

See also Play Dough, page 312.

### TIPS

* After the clay shapes have been baked and cooled, paint them with water-based paints.
* Make holiday ornaments by punching a hole in each shape before baking. You can paint designs on the clay before or after baking.
* Incorporate shells and other found objects into the clay before baking. Don't use plastic or other materials that release toxic fumes when heated.

## NO-BAKE CLAY ✗

½ cup cornstarch, or more if needed
1 cup baking soda
⅔ cup water

Combine the ingredients in a pan and stir until smooth. Cook over medium heat to a dough-like consistency (about 10 minutes). Spoon onto a cutting board. Let cool, then knead for 10 minutes. The dough is ready to be worked when it holds its shape easily. Let dry for 2 days, then paint with water-based paints.

**Makes 1½ cups**

*Preparation Time:* 30 minutes
*Shelf Life:* 4 weeks refrigerated
*Storage:* Glass jar with a screw top

## HOMEMADE CLAY

2 cups flour
¾ cup water
½ cup salt
1 tablespoon cream of tartar
1 tablespoon vegetable oil

Combine the ingredients in a pan and cook over low heat until the mixture has thickened (about 10 minutes). Spoon onto a cutting board. Let cool, then knead for 10 minutes. The dough is ready to be worked when it holds its shape easily. After modeling, air-dry or harden in a 250°F oven for 2 hours.
**Makes 2½ cups**

*Preparation Time:* About 25 minutes
*Shelf Life:* 4 weeks refrigerated
*Storage:* Glass jar with a screw top

## MODELING CLAY ✄

1 cup salt
1 cup cornstarch
1 cup flour, or as needed
¾ cup water, or as needed
Juice dyes (see page 305)

Place the salt, cornstarch, and flour in a bowl. Stir to blend. Divide into 3 bowls for separate colors. Pour ¼ cup of the water into each bowl all at once, followed by the juice dye, and stir until completely blended. Let rest for a few minutes. If too dry, add a bit more water; if too moist, add a bit more flour. The texture should be like normal clay or play dough. Form into

shapes. If you want to keep them, place them on a baking sheet and bake at 250°F for 2 hours.
**Makes 3 cups dry mixture**

*Preparation Time:* About 25 minutes
*Shelf Life:* 4 weeks refrigerated
*Storage:* Glass jars with screw tops

## FLOUR AND SALT CLAY FOR RELIEF MAPS ✄

*Children often make relief maps in grade school. You can make them at home with this simple formula. Form the relief map on a board.*

1 cup flour
½ cup salt
Enough water to make dough

Combine the ingredients in a bowl. Stir thoroughly, then seal in a jar overnight. Scoop out of the jar and onto the board, and sculpt the map.
**Makes 1½ cups**

*Preparation Time:* About 3 minutes
*Shelf Life:* 1 week refrigerated
*Storage:* Glass jar with a screw top

### FINGER PAINTS

## HOMEMADE FINGER PAINTS 🎁

1 cup cornstarch
½ cup cold water
⅓ cup finely grated bar soap
½ cups boiling water
Juice dyes (see page 305)

Place the cornstarch in a large bowl and stir in the water. Place the grated soap in a separate, heat-resistant bowl; add the boiling water and stir until the soap has melted; then pour the mixture into the cornstarch mixture. Stir to blend. Let the mixture rest until it has become a thick, finger-paint texture. Divide into separate bowls and stir in juice dyes for color.
**Makes about 1 cup**

*Preparation Time:* About 20 minutes
*Shelf Life:* 1 week refrigerated
*Storage:* Glass jars with screw tops

## SIMPLE FINGER PAINTS ✂ 🎁

½ cup each cornstarch and soap flakes
1 cup water, or as needed
Juice dyes (page 305)

Combine the cornstarch and soap flakes in a bowl. Add water until the mixture is the consistency of thick paint. Divide into separate bowls; add the dyes and stir to blend.
**Makes about ½ cup**

*Preparation Time:* About 10 minutes
*Shelf Life:* 1 week refrigerated
*Storage:* Glass jars with screw tops

## SIMPLER FINGER PAINTS ✂ 🎁

Cornstarch
Water
Juice dyes (page 305)

Place the cornstarch in a bowl and add water slowly until the mixture is the consistency of thick paint. Divide into separate bowls. Add the dyes and stir to blend.

*Preparation Time:* 15 minutes
*Shelf Life:* 1 week refrigerated
*Storage:* Glass jars with screw tops

### GLUES AND PASTES
See page 271.

### GOOP
Goop is a children's crafts material similar to play dough.

## GOOP ✂ 🎁

*Goop is fun to play with because it feels slick and gooey at the same time.*

1 cup cornstarch, or more as needed
½ cup white glue

Pour the cornstarch into a bowl and add the glue a bit at a time, mixing first with a spoon and then with your fingers as the texture becomes too thick to stir with a spoon. The goop should not be sticky—that is a sign to stop adding glue and begin adding a bit more cornstarch.
**Makes 1¼ cups**

*Preparation Time:* 5 to 10 minutes
*Shelf Life:* About 1 week refrigerated
*Storage:* Glass jar with a screw top

## INKS

**TIP** *Make a homemade ink pad by using a small plastic container with a lid. Cut a sponge to fit and saturate with liquid tempera paint or homemade ink. Keep the lid on so it doesn't dry out.*

## BROWN INK (Tannin Ink) ✗

Black tea
Water

Make a very strong black tea infusion. Dip a quill pen into the tea and use as an ink.

*Preparation Time:* 10 minutes
*Shelf Life:* 1 week refrigerated
*Storage:* Glass jar with a screw top

### Variation
TANNIN-RICH GALLNUTS: Simmer gallnuts in water until the water is a rich brown. Strain. See Sources and Resources for a source of gallnuts.

## OLD RECIPE FOR INK

1 cup red wine
1 tablespoon grated bar soap
1 teaspoon glycerin

Combine the ingredients in a glass jar. Let set overnight, then shake to blend. Use with a quill pen.
**Makes 1 cup**

*Preparation Time:* A few minutes
*Shelf Life:* Indefinite
*Storage:* Glass jar with a screw top

## CRAZY EGGS I

*Make this invisible ink to inscribe eggs.*

1 white egg (raw)
¼ cup acid-based plant juice, onion juice, lemon juice, or milk mixed with
1/16 teaspoon alum

Write on the egg using the acid-based liquid and alum. Let dry. Drop the egg in water; the ink will show.
**Makes ¼ cup**

*Preparation Time:* A few minutes
*Shelf Life:* Discard leftovers

### Variation
CRAZY EGGS II: Using a small brush, paint an egg with the solution. Let dry thoroughly, then hard-boil the egg for at least 15 minutes. Crack the shell, the writing will be on the egg.

## PAPIER-MÂCHÉ

## BASIC PAPIER-MÂCHÉ FORMULA

Cardboard tubes, balloons, or other materials for a sturdy armature
1 cup flour
Up to ⅔ cup water
Newspaper

Build the armature to resemble the sculpture you have in mind. Mix the flour and water to make a paste. Tear newspaper into strips about

2 inches wide. Swipe the strips through the paste and apply to the armature until the shape is completed. Let set overnight or until dry. Paint with water-based paints.

**Makes 1 cup**

*Preparation Time:* A few minutes
*Shelf Life:* A few days refrigerated
*Storage:* Glass jar with screw top

## PLAY DOUGH

See also Clay, page 308.

### PRACTICAL PLAY DOUGH

2 cups flour
⅔ cup salt
3 tablespoons cream of tartar
2 cups water
3 tablespoons vegetable oil
A few tablespoons juice dyes
(optional; see page 305)

Place the flour, salt, and cream of tartar in a saucepan. Combine the water, vegetable oil, and juice dyes (if using). Pour the liquid into the flour mixture and stir together thoroughly. Cook over medium-low heat, stirring constantly, until the mixture is difficult to stir and is close to play dough texture (about 5 minutes). Let cool slightly, then knead until smooth.

**Makes almost 3 cups**

*Preparation Time:* 30 minutes
*Shelf Life:* 1 week refrigerated
*Storage:* Glass jar with a screw top

### Variation

PLAY DOUGH II: In a saucepan combine 2 cups flour, 1 cup salt, 1 teaspoon cream of tartar, 2 cups water, and 2 tablespoons oil. Cook over medium heat for 3 minutes. Let cool slightly, then knead.

## PLASTER OF PARIS

Hardware stores sell plaster of paris for crafts, primarily for mold making. When my daughter was young, I used to pour wet plaster of paris into aluminum pie pans, and she would decorate the wet plaster with found objects such as shells, feathers, and stones, resulting in interesting sculptures when dried. Make sure your children never put plaster of paris in their mouth—when wet or dry. Buy plaster of paris that does not contain harmful admixtures (look for warning labels on the package).

**T I P** *Add ½ teaspoon cream of tartar per gallon to help the plaster of paris set more slowly.*

### PLASTER OF PARIS FOR MOLDS ✗

1 part water
2 parts plaster of paris powder

Place the water in a container, then slowly add the plaster of paris. Let the mixture sit without stirring for 5 minutes, then blend. The mixture, like thick soup, will harden within 30 minutes.

*Preparation Time:* 6 or 7 minutes
*Shelf Life:* Indefinite for powder and hardened plaster
*Storage:* Covered container

# Sources and Resources

## Books

Ausubel, Kenny. *Seeds of Change: The Living Treasure.* New York: Harper San Francisco/HarperCollins Publishers, 1994.

Bakule, Paula Dreifus. *Rodale's Book of Practical Formulas.* Emmaus, PA: Rodale Press, Inc., 1991.

Berthold-Bond, Annie. *Clean & Green.* Woodstock, NY: Ceres Press, 1990.

Bower, John. *The Healthy House.* New York: Carol Publishing Group, 1991.

————. *Healthy House Building: A Design & Construction Guide.* Unionville, IN: The Healthy House Institute, 1993.

Bower, Lynn Marie. *The Healthy Household: A Complete Guide for Creating a Healthy Environment.* Bloomington, IN: The Healthy House Institute, 1995.

Brown, Alice Cooke. *Early American Herb Recipes.* New York: Charles E. Tuttle Co., Crown Publishers, Inc., 1966.

Cameron, Myra and Theresa Fay DiGeronimo. *Mother Nature's Guide to Vibrant Beauty & Health.* Paramus, NJ: Prentice Hall, 1997.

Carr, Anna, et al. *Rodale's Illustrated Encyclopedia of Herbs.* Emmaus, PA: Rodale Press, Inc., 1987.

Chase, Deborah. *Fruit Acids for Fabulous Skin.* New York: St. Martin's Press, 1997.

Colborn, Theo, Dianne Dumanoski, and John Peterson Myers. *Our Stolen Future.* New York: Penguin Group, 1996.

Coleman, Eliot. *Four-Season Harvest.* Post Mills, VT: Chelsea Green Publishing Company, 1992.

Daar, Sheila, Helga Olkowski, and William Olkowski. *Common-Sense Pest Control.* Newton, CT: The Taunton Press, 1991.

Dadd, Debra Lynn. *Home Safe Home.* New York: Penguin Putnam, Inc., 1997.

Dickey, Eugene and Pamela Wellner. *The Wood Users Guide.* San Francisco, CA: Rainforest Action Network, 1991.

Dickey, Philip. *Troubling Bubbles.* Seattle, WA: The Washington Toxics Coalition, 1998.

Emery, Carla. *The Encyclopedia of Country Living.* Seattle, WA: Sasquatch Books, 1995. (Available from Carla Emery, 3152 Parkway #13-221, Pigeon Forge, TN 37863.)

Environmental Health Coalition. *Toxic Turnaround.* San Diego: Environmental Health Coalition, 1998.

Facetti, Aldo. *Natural Beauty.* New York: Simon & Schuster, Inc., 1990.

Falconi, Dina. *Earthly Bodies & Heavenly Hair.* Woodstock, NY: Ceres Press, 1998.

Frazier, Charles. *Cold Mountain.* New York: Atlantic Monthly Press, 1997.

Graff, Debra. *Pest Control You Can Live With.* Sterling, VA: Earth Stewardship Press, 1990.

Grimes, Carl. *Healthy Habitats Guidelines.* Denver, CO: Healthy Habitats, 1998.

Hampton, Aubrey. *Natural Organic Hair and Skin Care.* Tampa, FL: Organica Press, 1987.

Harte, John et al. *Toxics A–Z: A Guide to Everyday Pollution.* Berkeley, CA: University of California Press, 1991.

Hiscox, Gardner D., ed. *Henley's Formulas for Home and Workshop.* New York: Crown Publishers, Inc., 1979.

Hochberg, Bette. *Fiber Facts.* Los Angeles, CA: Bette and Bernard Hochberg, 1993.

Jescavage-Bernard, Karen. *Gardening in Deer Country.* Croton-on-Hudson, NY: Daren Jescavage-Bernard, 1991.

Landau, Diane, ed. *Living with Wildlife.* San Francisco, CA: Sierra Club Books, 1994.

Lifton, Bernice. *Bug Busters: Poison-Free Pest Controls for Your House & Garden.* Garden City Park, NY: Avery Publishing Group. Inc., 1991.

Loe, Theresa. *The Herbal Home Companion.* New York: Kensington Books, 1996.

Lopez, Andrew. *Natural Pest Control.* Malibu, CA: The Invisible Gardener, 1994.

Mack, Norman, ed. *Back to Basics.* New York: Reader's Digest Association, Inc., 1981.

Miller, Judith and Martin Miller. *Period Finishes and Effects: A Step-by-Step Guide to Decorating Techniques.* New York: Rizzoli International Publications, Inc., 1992.

The National Lime Association, *Whitewash and Cold Water Paints.* Washington, D.C.: The National Lime Association, 1955.

Pearson, David. *The Natural House Book.* New York: Simon & Schuster, Inc., 1989.

Rose, Jeanne. *Jeanne Rose's Herbal Body Book.* New York: The Putnam Publishing Group, 1976.

———. *Kitchen Cosmetics Using Herbs, Fruit, and Flowers for Natural Body Care.* Berkeley, CA: North Atlantic Books, 1978.

Schultz, Warren. *The Chemical-Free Lawn.* Emmaus, PA: Rodale Press, Inc., 1989.

———. *The Environmental Gardener.* Emmaus, PA: Rodale Press, 1989.

Stein, Dan. *Dan's Practical Guide to Least Toxic Home Pest Control.* Eugene, OR: Hulogosi Communications, Inc., 1991.

Steingraber, Sandra. *Living Downstream.* New York: Vintage Books, 1998.

Tillotson, Betty. *Skills for Simple Living.* Washington: Hartley & Marks, Inc., 1991.

*2,000 Down Home Skills & Secret Formulas for Practically Everything.* Laguna Beach, CA: Gala Books, 1971.

Venolia, Carol. *Healing Environments.* Berkeley, CA: Celestial Arts, 1988.

Wailes, Raymond B., ed. *Manual of Formulas: Recipes, Methods & Secret Processes.* Bradley, IL:

Popular Science Publishing Co., Inc./Lindsay
Publications, Inc., 1932.

Wesley-Hosford, Zia. *Face Value: Skin Care for
Women Over 35.* San Francisco, CA: Zia
Cosmetics, Inc., 1990.

Wormwood, Valerie Ann. *The Complete Book of
Essential Oils and Aromatherapy.* San Rafael, CA:
New World Library, 1991.

# Newsletters

*ACTS FACTS*
Arts, Crafts and Theater Safety (ACTS)
Monona Rossol, editor
181 Thompson St. #23
New York, NY 10012-2586
Phone (212) 777-0062
E-mail: 75054.2542@compuserve.com
*Monona Rossol is the author of many books, most
notably* Artists Complete Health and Safety
Guide *(Allworth Press, NY). She has also written on
toxics in the theater* (Stage Fright: Health and
Safety in the Theater) *and is coauthor of*
Overexposure.

*Alternatives*
The Washington Toxics Coalition
Philip Dickey, Ph.D., editor
4649 Sunnyside Ave. N.
Suite 540 East
Seattle, WA 98103
Phone (206) 632-1545
Fax (206) 632-8661
Internet address: info@watoxics.org
*Alternatives is very informative. Philip Dickey, one
of the country's leading experts on toxics in consumer
products, is the author of* Buy Smart, Buy Safe: A
Consumer Guide to Less Toxic Products.

*The Amicus Journal*
Kathrin Lassila, editor
The NRDC
40 West 20th St.
New York, NY 10011
Phone (212) 727-2700
E-mail: amicus@nrdc.org
Internet address: http://www.nrdc.org

*The Bugs Flyer*
Biological Urban Gardening Services (BUGS)
P.O. Box 76
Citrus Heights, CA 95611-0076
Phone (916) 726-5377
E-mail: bugsirc@cwia.com
*A quarterly newsletter,* The BUGS Flyer, The
Voice of Ecological Horticulture; *natural land-
scape maintenance; research into natural and organic
horticultural products and techniques.*

*Building with Nature*
Carol Venolia, editor
P.O. Box 4417
Santa Rosa, CA 95402-4417
Phone (707) 579-2201
E-mail: CVenolia@compuserve.com
*Sixteen-page newsletter designed to "inform and
inspire designers, builders, and inhabitants of built
environments."*

*Canary News*
Lynn Lawson, editor
P.O. Box 1732
Evanston, IL 60201
Phone (847) 866-9630
E-mail: Lynnword@aol.com
*Canary News is an excellent newsletter for the chemi-
cally sensitive. Lawson is the author of* Staying Well
in a Toxic World.

*Co-op America Quarterly*
Co-op America
Alisa Gravitz, executive director
1612 K Street NW #600
Washington, DC 20006
Phone (202) 872-5307
Fax (202) 331-8166
Internet addresses: www.greenpages.org;
   www.coopamerica.org
   *Also publishers of the* National Green Pages, *the
   largest national directory of socially responsible busi-
   nesses.*

*Creative Downscaling*
Edith Flowers Kilgo, editor
Box 1884
Jonesboro, GA 30237-1884
Phone (770) 471-9048
   *Upscale, simplified living on a downsized budget; pub-
   lished bimonthly. Subscription $15 a year.*

*The Delicate Balance*
National Center for Environmental Health
   Strategies, Inc.
Mary Lamielle, editor
1100 Rural Ave.
Voorhees, NJ 08043
Phone (609) 429-5358
E-mail: WJRD37A@prodigy.com
   *Provides clearinghouse and technical services, educa-
   tional materials, support and advocacy for the public
   and those injured by chemical and environmental
   exposure.*

*Earth Island Journal*
Gar Smith, editor
300 Broadway, Suite 28
San Francisco, CA 94133-3312
Phone (415) 788-3666
Fax (415) 788-7324
E-mail: journal@eii.org
Internet address: http://www.earthisland.org/ei
   *A deep-green journal.*

*Earthword Journal*
Lynne Bayless, executive director
580 Broadway, Suite 200
Laguna Beach, CA 92651
Phone (714) 497-1896
Fax (714) 497-7861
E-mail: eos@igc.org
   *The newsletter of the EOS Institute for the study of
   sustainable living.*

*Eco-Home Network*
Julia Russell, executive director
4344 Russell Ave.
Los Angeles, CA 90027
Phone (213) 662-5207
   *A Los Angeles–based nonprofit organization dedicated
   to building a constituency for sustainable urban liv-
   ing. Quarterly newsletter,* Ecolution: The Eco-
   Home Newsletter; *354-page sourcebook,*
   Sustainable Cities.

*Ecology Action*
Bill and Betsy Bruneau
18001 Schafer Ranch Rd.
Willits, CA 95490-9626
Phone and fax (707) 459-6410
E-mail: bountiful@zapcom.net
   Ecology Action *newsletter,* The Bountiful Gardens
   Rare Seed Catalog, Bountiful Gardens Seeds,
   Organic Gardening with Bountiful Gardens.

*E Magazine*
Doug Moss, editor
28 Knight St.
Westport, CT 06881
Phone (203) 854-5559
Fax (203) 866-0602
E-mail: emagazine@prodigy.net
Internet address: http:www.emagazine.com
   *A nonprofit organization.*

*Environmental Building News*
Alex Wilson
28 Birge St.
Brattleboro, VT 05301-3206
Phone (802) 257-7300
Fax (802) 257-7304
E-mail: ebn@ebuild.com
Internet address: www.ebuild.com
*Sixteen-page newsletter on environmentally responsible
design and construction published ten times a year
($67 a year);* Environmental Building News
Product Catalog, $89; CD-ROM, "E Building
Library."

*Everyone's Backyard*
Center for Health, Environment and Justice
Lois Gibbs, executive director
119 Rowell Court, P.O. Box 6806
Falls Church, VA 22040
Phone (703) 237-2249
*Lois Gibbs is a famous figure from the Love Canal
disaster (she lived there). Other publications include*
Environmental Health Monthly.

*Focus on Pesticides*
c/o Environmental Advocates
353 Hamilton St.
Albany, NY 12210
Toll-free (800) SAVENYS

*The Global Citizen*
Donella Meadows, Ph.D., editor
Box 58
Plainfield, NH 03781
Phone (603) 646-1233
Fax (603) 646-1279
*An adjunct professor of environmental studies at
Dartmouth College, Donella writes a column, "The
Global Citizen," that is published in many newspa-
pers around the country. She is co-author of the 1970s
best-seller* Limits to Growth *and the more recent book*
Beyond Limits.

*The Green Guide*
Mothers & Others publication
40 West 20th St.
New York, NY 10011
Phone toll-free (888) ECO-INFO
*A nonprofit organization.* The Green Guide *is pub-
lished ten times a year.*

*Green Living*
953 Dover Rd., HCR 63, Box 29
South Newfane, VT 05351
Phone (802) 348-7441
E-mail: hipgl@sover.net
*A quarterly journal distributed free of charge through-
out southeastern Vermont, southwestern New
Hampshire, and northern Massachusetts.*

*Herb Companion*
c/o Interweave Press
201 East Fourth St.
Loveland, CO 80537
Phone (303) 669-7672

*The Human Ecologist*
H.E.A.L.
P.O. Box 29629
Atlanta, GA 30359-1126
Phone (404) 248-1898
Fax (404) 248-0162
E-mail: HEALnatnl@aol.com
Internet address:
http://members.aol.com/HEALnatnl/index.html
*Human Ecology Action League (H.E.A.L.) is the
national organization of the chemically sensitive. Fact
sheets, et cetera.*

*Journal of Pesticide Reform*
Caroline Cox, editor
NCAP
P.O. Box 1393
Eugene, OR 97401
Phone (541) 344-5044
Fax (541) 344-6923
E-mail: ncap@ipc.apc.org
Internet address: http://www.efn.org/~ncap/
 *A highly respected quarterly publication about pesticides.*

*Medical & Legal Briefs,* a referenced compendium
 of chemical injury.
Environmental Access Research Network
Cindy Duehring, editor
P.O. Box 1089
Minot, ND 58702-1089
Phone (701) 837-0161
 *Cindy Duehring is the winner of the prestigious
 Alternative Nobel Prize for her work in multiple
 chemical sensitivity. She is co-author of* The Human
 Consequences of the Chemical Problem.

National Coalition Against the Misuse of
 Pesticides (NCAMP)
530 Seventh St. SE
Washington, DC 20003
Phone (202) 534-5450
 *Information on pesticide dangers and alternatives;
 monthly newsmagazine,* Pesticides and You, *for $25
 a year including membership; technical reports.*

*News on Earth*
Phillip Frazer, editor
668 Greenwich St. #608
New York, NY 10014
 *Newsletter published twelve times a year. Covers the
 complex environmental issues facing the world in clear,
 easy-to-understand language.*

*Our Toxic Times*
Chemical Injury Network
Cynthia Wilson, editor
P.O. Box 301
White Sulphur Springs, MT 59645-0301
Phone (406) 547-2255
Fax (406) 547-2255
Internet address: http://biz-comm.com/CIIN
 *Pertinent topics about chemically induced health issues,
 problems with workplace exposure standards, risk
 assessment, medical ignorance, testing, and possible
 solutions.*

Permaculture
P.O. Box 2052
Ocala, FL 34478-2052
 *Newsletter, international directory, slide/script set,
 design course pamphlets, papers, distributor of perma-
 culture books, and more, all on permaculture.*

*Permaculture Drylands Journal*
Ann Audrey, executive director
P.O. Box 156
Santa Fe, NM 87504-0156

The Rachel Carson Council
8940 Jones Mill Rd.
Chevy Chase, MD 20815
Phone (301) 652-1877
E-mail: rccouncil@aol.com
Internet address: http://members.aol.com/
 rccouncil/ourpage/
 *Publications with help for less toxic pest control; exten-
 sive library; the quarterly "Rachel Carson Council
 News."*

*Rachel's Environment and Health Weekly*
Peter Montague, Ph.D., editor
P.O. Box 5036, Suite 101
Annapolis, MD 21403-3300
Phone (410) 263-1584
Toll-free (888) 272-2435
Fax (410) 263-8944
E-mail: erf@rachel.clark.net
Internet address: http://www.monitor.net/rachel
  *An excellent weekly newsletter distilling and analyz-*
  *ing information relating to the environment. Available*
  *free on the Internet.*

Scientific Certification Systems
Phone (510) 832-1415
E-mail: lbrown@scs1.com
  *A nationally recognized third-party certifier of envi-*
  *ronmental claims.*

*Talking Leaves*
1430 Willamette Street, #367
Eugene, OR 97401
Phone (541) 342-2974
Fax (541) 687-7744
  *Published three times a year by the Deep Ecology*
  *Education Project.*

*Toxinformer*
Sonya Holmquist, editor
Environmental Health Coalition
1717 Kettner Blvd., Suite 100
San Diego, CA 92101
Phone (619) 235-0281
Fax (619) 232-3670
E-mail: ehcoalition@igc.apc.org
Internet address: http://www.moosenet.com/~ehc/
  *Authors of* Toxic Turnaround.

*World Watch*
World Watch Institute
Lester Brown
1776 Massachusetts Ave., N.W.
Washington, DC 20036-1904
Phone (202) 452-1999
Fax (202) 296-7365

*Yes! A Journal of Positive Futures*
Sarah van Gelder, editor
P.O. Box 10818
Bainbridge Island, WA 98110
Phone (206) 842-0216
Toll-free (800) 937-4451
E-mail: yes@futureenet.org
  *This magazine about a sustainable future is well loved*
  *by many people.*

# Resources

Abundant Life Seed Foundation
P.O. Box 772
Port Townsend, WA 98368
Phone (360) 385-5660
Fax (360) 385-7455
  *One of the best native species seed-saving groups around*
  *the country.*

Acres, U.S.A.
P.O. Box 8800
Metairie, LA 70011
Phone (504) 889-2100
Toll-free (800) 355-5313
Fax (504) 889-2777
  *Interesting catalog of books on eco-agriculture.*

Allergy Relief Shop, Inc.
3371 Whittle Spring Rd.
Knoxville, TN 37917
Phone (423) 494-4100
Toll-free (800) 626-2810
E-mail: allergy@ix.netcom.com
Internet address: http://www.allergyreliefshop.com
  *A source for just about everything I recommend in*
  Better Basics for the Home. *The store also sells*
  *Bora-Care treatment for termites and carpenter ants.*
  *The owners consult about how to create healthy houses.*

The Allergy Store
P.O. Box 2555
Sebastopol, CA 95473
Phone (707) 823-6202
Toll-free (800) 824-7163

Alternatives for Simple Living
3617 Old Lakeport Rd.
P.O. Box 2857
Sioux City, IA 51106
Phone (712) 274-8875
*Produces and distributes award-winning video and print resources about voluntary simplicity and related products.*

American Council for an Energy-Efficient
  Economy
1001 Connecticut Ave., N.W.
Suite 801
Washington, DC 20036
Internet address: acee.ix.netcom.com
*Publishers of the excellent* Consumer Guide to Home Energy Savings and the Most Energy-Efficient Appliances *[order from Berkeley, CA, at (510) 549-9914].*

American Environmental Health Foundation
8345 Walnut Hill Lane, Suite 225
Dallas, TX 75231
Phone (800) 428-2343
*Catalog of products for those who are chemically sensitive. The catalog is an offshoot of the famous Rea detox clinic.*

American Formulating and Manufacturing (AFM)
Samuel Goldberg, president
350 West Ash St.
Suite 700
San Diego, CA 92101
Phone (619) 239-0321
Fax (619) 239-0565
*Manufacturer of safe paints, stains, and cleaning products pristine enough for the chemically sensitive.*

Anderson Laboratories, Inc.
Rosalind Anderson, Ph.D.
773 West Hartford Main St.
P.O. Box 323
West Hartford, VT 05084-0323
Phone (802) 295-7344
E-mail: anderson.lab@connriver.net
*Lab that analyzes carpets, bedding, et cetera, for toxics.*

Art & Creative Materials Institute, Inc.
1280 Main St.
2nd Floor
P.O. Box 479
Hanson, MA 02341
Phone (781) 293-4100
Fax (781) 294-0808
Internet address: http://www.creative-industries
  .com/acmi

Aubrey Organics
4419 N. Manhattan Ave.
Tampa, FL 33614
Phone (813) 877-4186
Toll-free (800) 282-7394
*A 100 percent natural, certified organic line of hair and skin care products, including shampoos without sodium lauryl sulfate. These products are as pure as they get. They are the brand I chose for my newborn—and no one paid me to say that.*

Auromere Ayurveda Imports
2621 West Highway 12
Lodi, CA 95240
Toll-free (800) 735-4691

Auro Natural Plant Chemistry
P.O. Box 857
Davis, CA 95617-0857
Phone (916) 753-3104
*Importers of beautiful building and renovating supplies made of natural materials; paints, waxes, and so forth are their specialty.*

Autumn Harp, Inc.
61 Pine St.
Bristol, VT 05443
Phone (802) 453-4807
Toll-free (800) 886-5432
Fax (802) 453-4903
*Un-petroleum products. Plant-based skin care products including lip gloss, lip balm, un-petroleum jelly, and skin moisturizers. Available in health food stores and mail order through* Environmentally Sound Products *at (toll-free) (800) 886-5432.*

The Aveda Corporation
4000 Pheasant Ridge Dr.
Blaine, MN 55449
Toll-free (800) 283-3224
Internet address: www.aveda.com
*Although Aveda products—everything from permanent lotions to hair dyes—aren't perfect, they are far and away less toxic than any other line sold in salons. I highly recommend them.*

Avena Botanicals
219 Mill St.
Rockland, ME 04856
Phone (207) 594-0694

Best Paint Co., Inc.
5205 Ballard Ave. NW
Seattle, WA 98107
Phone (206) 783-9938
*VOC-free paints.*

Better Pest Management
Toll-free (888) 589-6531
Internet address: www.betterpestmgt.com
*Phannies for fly control.*

Bio Designs
557 Burbank St., Suite K
Broomfield, CA 80020
Phone (303) 438-0600

Bio-Integral Resource Center (B.I.R.C.)
Sheila Daar, Ph.D.
P.O. Box 7414
Berkeley, CA 94707
Phone (510) 524-2567
*B.I.R.C. is the leading international research center for less toxic pest control options. Their book,* Common-Sense Pest Control, *is the bible of the field.*

The Boston Jojoba Company
P.O. Box 771
Middletown, MA 01949
Phone (508) 777-9332
Toll-free (800) 2-jojoba
E-mail: jojobabob@aol.com
*Hobacare 100 percent pure jojoba extract.*

Brookside Soap Company
P.O. Box 55638
Seattle, WA 98155
Phone (206) 742-2265
E-mail: brksdesoap@aol.com

Burt's Bees, Inc.
P.O. Box 90157
Raleigh, NC 27612
Phone (919) 510-8720
*Natural body care products.*

Cabinetmakers
Charles Bailey
H.C. 62 Box 29
Flippin, AK 72634
Phone (870) 453-3245
Internet address: http://www.southshore.com/~crbslf
*Second Life Furniture, specially designed for the multiply chemically sensitive, with hopes that nontoxic furniture will give the owner a second life.*

Center for Resourceful Building Technology
P.O. Box 100
Missoula, MT 59806
Phone (406) 549-7678
Fax (406) 549-4100
E-mail: crbt@montana.com
Internet address: http://www.montana,com/crbt
   *The center educates the public on issues relating to
   housing and the environment, with particular empha-
   sis on innovative building materials and technologies.
   Publishes the* Guide to Resource Efficient
   Building Elements *(112 pp., $28).*

Chem-Safe Products
Box 33023
San Antonio, TX 78265
Phone (210) 657-5321
   *VOC and preservative-free paints.*

Church and Dwight Co., Inc.
469 N. Harrison St.
Princeton, NJ 08543
Phone (609) 683-5900
   *Baking soda and washing soda.*

The Cotton Place
P.O. Box 59721
Dallas, TX 75229
Phone (214) 243-4149
Toll-free (800) 451-8866

Dancing Willow Herbs
960 Main Ave.
Durango, CO 81301
Fax (970) 247-1654
Toll-free (888) 247-1654
E-mail: dwillow@frontier.net
Internet address: http://www.creativelinks.com/
   dancingwillow/
   *Single herb tinctures, essential oils, ready-made herbal
   products.*

The Dasun Company
P.O. Box 668
Escondido, CA 92033
Phone (619) 480-8929
Toll-free (800) 433-8929
Fax (619) 746-8865
   Air and Water: The Essence of Life *catalog fea-
   tures zeolite powder, used for carpets, flooring, furni-
   ture, vehicles, pets, laundry, et cetera, and zeolite
   breather bags, used in offices, closets, and basements.*

Desert Essence
9510 Vassar
Chatsworth, CA 91311
Phone (818) 709-5900
   *Distributor of tea tree oil, a broad-spectrum fungicide.*

Dial Corporation Information Center
15101 N. Scottsdale Rd.
M.S. 5028
Scottsdale, NY 85254
Phone (800) 457-8739
   *Borax.*

Dr. Bronner
Box 28
Escondido, CA 92033
Phone (619) 743-2211
   *Liquid castile soaps.*

E. B. Botanicals, Inc.
1133 Route 23
Wayne, NJ 07470
Phone (973) 696-7766

The EcoMall
E-mail: ecomall@internetmci.com
Internet address: http://www.ecomall.com
   *The site has an activist center, a news center, and
   information on environmental organizations. It will
   link you to other sites as well.*

Eco-Source
P.O. Box 1656
Sebastopol, CA 95473
Phone (707) 829-7562
Toll-free (800) 274-7040

EcoTimber International Corp.
1020 Heinz Ave.
Berkeley, CA 94710
Phone (510) 549-3000
E-mail: ecotimber@igc.apc.org

ECOWEB
On-line address:
  http://ecosys.drdr.virginia.edu/EcoWeb.html
  *EcoWeb's Links (WWW Virtual Library
  Environment Subject Page), divided alphabetically
  and by subject.*

Edwin and Ocarina Textiles
P.O. Box 744
N. Bennington, VT 05257
Phone (802) 442-9871
  *Beautiful handwoven organic textiles.*

Envirolink Network
On-line address: http://www.envirolink.org
  *The web's most complete environmental service. Key
  word searchable. Sustainable Electronic Environmental
  Library for newsletters, magazines, and journals.*

Environmental Building Supply
1314 NW Northrup
Portland, OR 97216
Phone (503) 222-3881
  *Less toxic and nontoxic building supplies.*

Environmental Construction Outfitters
190 Willow Ave.
Bronx, NY 10454
Phone (718) 292-0626
Toll-free (800) 238-5008
Internet address: www.environproducts.com
  *A wide range of building and furnishings designed for
  good health.*

Environmental Consultant
John Banta
P.O. Box 3217
Prescott, AZ 86302
Phone (520) 445-8225
  *John, former owner of a hardware store with products
  for safer homes, is an electromagnetic field (EMF) spe-
  cialist and a good source for information.*

Environmental Education and Health Services
Mary Oetzel
P.O. Box 72004
Austin, TX 78709-2004
Phone (512) 288-2369
Fax (512) 288-9538
  *Mary is a building consultant for the chemically sensi-
  tive and is extremely knowledgeable about nontoxic
  building materials.*

Environmental Home Center
1724 4th Ave. S
Seattle, WA 98134
Phone (206) 682-7332
  *Nontoxic and less toxic building supplies.*

Environmental Technologies Company
P.O. Box 10395
Prescott, Arizona 86301
Toll-free (800) 757-0993
  *Source of Envirocloth, a fiber woven so that fibers work
  to clean surfaces, to be used instead of detergents and
  other cleaning products. These cloths work well.*

Essential Applications
P.O. Box 1104
Kapa'au, Hawaii 96755
Phone (808) 889-6749
E-mail: ss.enterprise@juno.com
  *Source of plumeria flower essence.*

ETEX, Ltd.
Phil Holt
3200 Polaris Ave., Suite 9
Las Vegas, NV 89102
Phone (702) 364-5911
Toll-free (800) 543-5651
Fax (702) 364-8894
Internet address: http://www.Etex-Ltd.com/
  *Electro-Gun, which is 100 percent effective in killing
  dry-wood termites.*

Falcon Formulations
Dina Falconi
468 County Route 2
Accord, NY 12404
  *Herbal remedies, body and hair oils, salves, and nat-
  ural skin and hair care line from the author of* Earth
  Bodies and Heavenly Hair *(see p. 314).*

Forest Stewardship Council
Avenida Hidalgo 502
68000 Oxaca, Mexico
Internet address: http://www.fscoax.org/

Gardener's Supply Company
128 Intervale Rd.
Burlington, VT 05401
Phone (802) 863-1700
  *Organic gardening supplies.*

Gardens Alive!
5100 Schenley Place
Lawrenceburg, IN 47025
Phone (812) 537-8651
  *Organic gardening supplies.*

Garrett Wade Co.
161 Avenue of the Americas
New York, NY 10013
Phone (212) 807-1155
Toll-free (800) 221-2942
  *Natural pigments, hide glues, and so on.*

Granny's Old Fashioned Products
P.O. Box 660037
Arcadia, CA 91006
Phone (818) 577-1825
  *Body care and housekeeping products without perfumes,
  dyes, and other additives.*

Green Ban
Mulgum Hollow Farm
P.O. Box 986
Nowra NNSW 2541
Australia
  *Herbal insect repellents for pets and people.*

Green Mountain Spinnery
P.O. Box 568C
Putney, VT 05346
Phone (802) 387-4528
  *Wholesale and retail natural-fiber yarns and blan-
  kets. The company developed a vegetable oil substitute
  for the petroleum lubricant generally used in yarn pro-
  duction.*

Green Seal
Arthur Weissman, Ph.D., president
1400 16th St. NW, Suite 300
Washington, DC 20036-2215
Phone (202) 588-8400
Fax (202) 588-8465
E-mail: aweissman@greenseal.org
Internet address: http://www.greenseal.org
  *The organization provides Green Seal standards and
  evaluates products for recycled materials.*

Green Terrestrial
328 Lake Ave.
Greenwich, CT 06830
Phone (203) 862-8690
  *High-quality herbs.*

Harmony
360 Interlocken Blvd., Suite 300
Broomfield, CO 80021
Fax (800) 456-1139
Toll-free (800) 869-3446
*Natural cotton, bedding, cleaning products.*

Healthy Habitats
Carl Grimes
1811 S. Quebec Way, #99
Denver, CO 80231
Phone (303) 671-9653
E-mail: grimes@habitats.com
*Carl is a consultant and author of* Healthy
Habitats.

The Healthy Home Center
1403A Cleveland St.
Clearwater, FL 34615
Phone (813) 447-4454
Fax (813) 447-0140
E-mail: healthy123@aol.com
Internet address: www.healthyhome.com
*Nontoxic paints, flooring, insulation, filters, et cetera.*

The Healthy House Institute
John and Lyn Bower
430 N. Sewell Rd.
Bloomington, IN 47408
Internet address: www.hhinst.com
*An independent resource center offering books and
videos containing practical information for designers,
architects, contractors, and homeowners interested in
making houses healthy places in which to live. Due to
time constraints, they no longer consult.*

Heart of Vermont
P.O. Box 612
Barre, VT 05641
Phone (802) 476-3098 or (802) 476-2075
*Natural and organic bedding: mattresses, pillows,
body pillows, organic wool comforters.*

Heirloom Seed Project
Landis Valley Museum
2451 Kissel Hill Rd.
Lancaster, PA 17601-4899
*Heirloom seed reference guide and seed catalog.*

Herb Growing and Marketing Network
P.O. Box 245
Silver Spring, PA 17575
Phone (717) 383-3295
E-mail: herbworld@aol.com
Internet address: www.herbworld.com
*Publisher of* The Herbal Green Pages, *the premier
herbal resource guide for retail and wholesale.*

HerbPharm
P.O. Box 116
Williams, OR 97544
Phone (503) 846-7178
*Herbal products and essential oils.*

Hermana Herbal Products
381 Snyderville Rd.
Elizaville, NY 12523
Phone (518) 537-6086
E-mail: hermana@epix.net
*A line of herbal body care products.*

Household Hazardous Waste Project
P.O. Box 108
Springfield, MO 65804
Phone (417) 836-5777
*Wrote and published the excellent booklet* Guide to
Hazardous Products Around the Home *and other
educational information.*

Hummer Nature Works
HCR 32, Box 122
Uvalde, TX 78801
Phone (830) 232-6167
E-mail: hummers@hctc.net
*Distributor of all sorts of "green" product lines.*

Infinity Herbal Products
Division of Jedmon Products, Ltd.
333 Rimrock Rd.
Downsview, Ontario M3J 3J9
Canada
Phone (416) 631-4000
*Concentrated all-purpose detergent, Heavenly
Horsetail, pH 4.5, for washing wool.*

INFORM
120 Wall St.
New York, NY 10005-4001
Phone (212) 361-2400
E-mail: Inform@igc.apc.org
*A nonprofit environmental organization that identifies
state-of-the-art preventive strategies to protect natural
resources and public health.*

Insect Aside
P.O. Box 7
Farmington, WA 99128
Phone (509) 287-2200
*Less toxic pesticides.*

The Institute for Bau-biologie Newsletter
Helmut Ziehe
Box 387
Clearwater, FL 34615
Phone (813) 461-4371
Fax (813) 441-4373

Institute for Sustainable Forestry
P.O. Box 1580
Redway, CA 95560
Phone (707) 247-1101
Fax (707) 247-3555
E-mail: info@isf-sw.org
*Promotes forest management that contributes to the
long-term ecological and economic well-being of forest-
based communities in northwest California and
beyond. Administers the Pacific Certified Ecological
Forest Products certification program.*

Janice Corporation
198 Rte. 46
Budd Lake, NJ 07828-3001
Phone (973) 691-5459
Toll-free (800) 526-4237
E-mail: JSwack@worldnet.att.net
*High-quality cotton everything, from mattresses to
shower caps.*

Jantz Design
P.O. Box 3071
Santa Rosa, CA 95402
Toll-free (800) 365-6563
*Natural bedding.*

Jean's Greens
119 Sulphur Spring Rd.
Norway, NY 13416
Phone (315) 845-6500
*Palmerosa, rose geranium, zinc oxide, PABA, attrac-
tive glass jars, essential oils, herbs, and more.*

Karen's Nontoxic Products
1839 Dr. Jack Rd.
Conowingo, MD 21918
Phone (410) 378-4621
Toll-free (800) 527-3674

Kiss My Face
P.O. Box 224
Gardiner, NY 12525-0224
Toll-free (800) 262-KISS
Internet address: www.kissmyface.com
*Pure olive oil soap.*

Kremer Pigments Inc.
228 Elizabeth St.
New York, NY 10012
Phone (212) 219-2394
Toll-free (800) 995-5501
Fax (212) 219-2395
Internet address: www.kremer-pigments.de/.
*Casein powder, hide glues, bone glues, pigments, rice
starch, beeswax, carnauba wax, larch turpentines,
natural resins, shellac, and pigments.*

Lead Check
P.O. Box 1210
Framingham, MA 01701
Toll-free (800) 262-LEAD
*Consultants.*

Life Tree Products
Division of Sierra Dawn
P.O. Box 1203
Sebastopol, CA 95472
*Life Tree Herbal Ultra dishwashing liquid, premium dishwashing liquid, premium laundry liquid, Fresh and Natural bathroom cleaner, Home-Soap all-purpose cleaner, Fresh and Natural all-purpose spray cleaner, automatic dishwashing liquid.*

Logona
544-E Riverside Dr.
Asheville, NC 28801
Toll-free (800) 648-6654
*Very pure body care products, including plant hair dyes.*

The Masters Corporation
Paul Bierman-Lytle, architect, consultant
P.O. Box 514, 189 Mill Rd.
New Canaan, CT 06840
Phone (203) 966-3541
Fax (203) 966-2807
*One of the leading pioneers in nontoxic building, Paul is an architect and the author of a number of books with gorgeous pictures of gorgeous nontoxic homes.*

M. H. Design
519 Lincoln Way #2
San Francisco, CA 94122
Phone and fax (415) 664-9014
*Organic cotton bedding, including comforters and pillowcases. Lovely and expensive.*

Miller Paint Co.
317 SE Grand Ave.
Portland, OR 97214
Phone (503) 233-4491
*VOC- and biocide-free paints. Specify "low-biocide" when ordering.*

Mountain Rose Herbs
20818 High St.
North San Juan, CA 95960
Toll-free (800) 879-3337
*Herbs, herb seeds, essential oils, bottles, complete line of materials for making herbal body care products.*

Murco Wall Paint Products, Inc.
300 NE 21st St.
Ft. Worth, TX 76106
Phone (817) 626-1987

National Environmental Health Association
720 South Colorado Blvd., Suite 970 Tower South
Denver, CO 80222
Phone (303) 756-9090
Fax (303) 691-9490
*This group provides a list of doctors who practice environmental medicine.*

National Institute of Environmental Health
  Sciences (NIEHS)
100 Capitol Drive, Suite 108
Durham, NC 27713
Phone (919) 361-9408
Toll-free (800) 643-4794
Internet address:
  http://ehpnet1.niehs.nih.gov/EHPhome.html/.
*NIEHS is a "world center for toxicological and environmental health science research." Information for concerned citizens, environmental justice groups, and grassroots organizations.*

The National Lime Association
200 North Glebe Rd.
Suite 800
Arlington, VA 22203
Phone (703) 243-5463
Internet address: www.lime.org
*Local sources of lime.*

National Testing Laboratories, Ltd.
6555 Wilson Mills Rd.
Suite 102
Cleveland, OH 44143
Phone (440) 449-2525
Toll-free (800) 458-3330
Fax (440) 449-8585
*Water-checking product with pesticide option: Tests 74 contaminants plus 20 pesticides and PCBs.*

Natural Animal Health Products, Inc.
P.O. Box 1177
St. Augustine, FL 32085
Phone (904) 824-5884
Toll-free (800) 274-7387
*Safe pet products.*

The Natural Choice/Eco Design Co.
Rudolf Reitz
1365 Rufina Circle
Santa Fe, NM 87505
Toll-free (800) 621-2591
*Extensive line of natural earth pigments, milk paints, Sodasan cleaning supplies, and Bioshield natural paints, stains, and sealers.*

Natural Lifestyle
16 Lookout Dr.
Asheville, NC 28804-3330
Phone (800) 752-2775
*Products for natural living, from body care to cleaning to water filters.*

The Natural Pet Care Company
8050 Lake City Way
Seattle, WA 98115
Toll-free (800) 962-8266

Naturals for Animals
514 37th St. N
St. Petersburg, FL 33713
Phone (813) 327-2356
*Nutritional, holistic products for pets.*

Naturlich Flooring Interiors
Natural Home
P.O. Box 1677
Sebastopol, CA 95473
Phone (707) 824-0914
Toll-free (800) 329-9398
*The leading national source of nontoxic flooring: linoleum, cork, grass, natural wool carpets, area rugs.*

N.E.E.D.S.
527 Charles Ave., 12-A
Syracuse, NY 13209
Toll-free (800) 634-1380
*An excellent store for nontoxic products, particularly paints and filters; also supplements.*

New York Coalition for Altenatives to Pesticides (NYCAP)
353 Hamilton St.
Albany, NY 12210-1709
Phone (518) 426-8246
Fax (518) 426-3052
*NYCAP is a long-standing organization with good resources available to the public.*

Nontoxic Environments
P.O. Box 384
Newmarket, NH 03857
Phone (603) 659-5919
Toll-free (800) 789-4348
E-mail: nontoxic@ici.net
Internet address: http://www.nontoxicenviron-ments.com
*Catalog of nontoxic-living products, such as paints, finishes, adhesives, stains, vacuum cleaners, purification systems, and organic cotton beds.*

Nutricology, Inc.
P.O. Box 489
San Leandro, CA 94577
Phone (510) 639-4572
Fax (201) 445-7068
Internet address: http://www.ayslcorp.com
  *Manufacturer of grapefruit seed extract, an EPA-registered herbal disinfectant.*

N-Viro Products Ltd.
610 Walnut Ave.
Bohemia, NY 11716
Phone (516) 567-2628
  *Nematodes for control of termites.*

Old Fashioned Milk Paint Company
P.O. Box 222
Groton, MA 01450
Phone (978) 448-6336
Fax (978) 448-2754
  *A wide array of old-fashioned milk paint in Colonial colors.*

Pace Chem Industries, Inc.
P.O. Box 1946
Santa Inez, CA 93460
Phone (805) 686-0745
Toll-free (800) 305-2912
  *Less toxic paints, et cetera.*

Peaceful Valley Farm Supply
P.O. Box 2209
Mill Valley, CA 95945
Phone (916) 272-4769
  *Catalog for organic gardeners.*

Perfectly Safe
7245 Whipple Ave. NW
North Canton, OH 44720
Toll-free (800) 837-KIDS
  *Simple pest control products.*

Pesticide Education Center
Marion Moses, M.D., consultant
P.O. Box 420870
San Francisco, CA 94142-0870
Phone (415) 391-8511

Pet Care Systems, Inc.
P.O. Box 1529
Detroit Lakes, MN 56502
Phone (218) 846-9610
Fax (218) 846-9612
E-mail: swheat1@northernnet.com
Internet address: www.sweatscoop.com
  *Manufacturer of wheat cat litter, free of silica dust.*

Pet Sage
4313 Wheeler Ave.
Alexandria, VA 22304
Phone (703) 823-9714
Toll-free (800) PET-HLTH
E-mail: info@petsage.com
Internet address: www.petsage.com
  *Natural pet care product catalog, many herbal insect repellents, and more.*

Planetary Solutions
2030 17th St.
Boulder, CO 80302
Phone (303) 442-6228
Fax (303) 442-6474
  *Building products including true linoleum, cork and bamboo flooring, wool carpets, low-VOC paints.*

Praxis
2723 116th Ave.
Allegan, MI 49010
Phone (616) 673-2793
E-mail: praxis@datawise.net
Internet address: www.datawise.net~praxis
  *This company will log in your pest problems for $50 and mix and match their nontoxic pest control treatment programs to meet your needs.*

Prestige Proteins
Hugh Henley
Phone (561) 495-8710
Fax (561) 495-7043
E-mail: casein@casein.com
Internet address: www.casein.com
*Suppliers of wholesale casein.*

Quantum
20 DeWitt Drive
Saugerties, NY 12477
Toll-free (800) 348-8398
Internet address: http://www.maine.com/herbs/
*An effective tick repellent containing rose geranium.*

Rainbow Henna
170 Wilbur Place
Bohemia, NY 11716
*Henna products.*

Rainforest Action Network
221 Pine St., Ste. 500
San Francisco, CA 94104
Phone (415) 398-4404
E-mail: rainforest@ran.org
Internet address: www.ran.org/ran/

Rainforest Alliance
Ivan Ussach
270 Lafayette Ave.
New York, NY 10012
Phone (212) 941-1900

Raintree Marketing, Inc.
1601 W. Koenig Lane
Austin, TX 78756
Phone (512) 467-6130
Fax (512) 467-6822
Toll-free (800) 780-5902
E-mail: info@rain-tree.com
*Sustainably harvested soap bark (quillaja bark).*

Real Goods
555 Leslie St.
Ukiah, CA 95482-5576
Toll-free (800) 456-1177
E-mail: realgoods@realgoods.com
Internet address: www.realgoods.com
*Catalogs of energy efficient products, solar energy products, and basic green products.*

Real Purity Inc.
Anne Fiske
8200 E. Phillips Place
Englewood, CO 80112
Phone (303) 770-8808
Fax (303) 843-9188
*Product lines of water filters, air filters, vacuums, Real Purity natural skin care products.*

Sage Mountain Herb Products
P.O. Box 294
Montpelier, VT 05641
*Herbs and essential oils.*

San Francisco Herb Company
250 14th St.
San Francisco, CA 94103
Phone (415) 861-7174
Toll-free (800) 227-4530
Fax (415) 861-4440
Internet address: www.sfherb.com
*Herbs, spices, teas, essential oils, and potpourri.*

Sappo Hill Soapworks
654 Tolman Creek Rd.
Ashland, OR 97520
Phone (541) 482-4485
Toll-free (800) 863-7627
Fax (541) 482-2556
E-mail: sappohill@aol.com
*Homemade soaps with glycerine.*

Seeds of Change
Kenny Ausubel
1364 Rufina Circle, No. 5
Santa Fe, NM 87501
Phone (505) 438-8080

*The excellent book* Seeds of Change *(Harper San Francisco, 1994) is by Kenny Ausubel, one of the founders of this wonderful organization that protects and tends to seeds, including heirloom seeds.*

Seventh Generation
Jeffrey Hollender, CEO
1 Mill Street, Box A26
Burlington, VT 05401-1530
Phone (802) 658-3773
Fax (800) 456-1139
Toll-free (800) 456-1177

*Cleaning products with some of the best and safest ingredients available.*

Simmons Handcrafts
42295 Highway 36
Bridgeville, CA 95526
Phone (707) 777-1920

*Homemade soaps; body care tools such as cleansing stones and ayate skin scrubbers; natural shaving kit, shampoo without sodium lauryl sulfate, natural insect repellents, and more. A wonderful catalog.*

Smith & Hawken
25 Corte Madera
Mill Valley, CA 94941
Phone (415) 383-4415

*The Rainforest Alliance has certified many Smith & Hawken products as being made from sustainably produced tropical materials.*

Southern Wood Herbs
Cathy Smith
305 East Lincoln Ave.
Melbourne, FL 32901
Phone (407) 729-0104

*Herbs, spices, and essential oils.*

Sunfeather
1551 State Highway 72
Potsdam, NY 13676
Phone (315) 265-3648
Toll-free (800) 771-7627

*A wonderful catalog full of soaps and body care accessories.*

Thursday Plantation
330 East Carillo St.
Santa Barbara, CA 93101
Toll-free (800) 848-8966

*Australian tea tree oil products.*

Tim-Bor, U.S. Borax and Chemical Group
3075 Wilshire Blvd.
Los Angeles, CA 90010
Toll-free (800) 989-6267

*Borax-based termite control.*

Tom's of Maine
Box 710
Lafayette Center, 3rd Flr.
Kennebunk, ME 04043
Phone (207) 985-2944
Internet address: www.tom's-of-maine.com

*Most well known for their herbal toothpaste.*

TerrEssentials
2650 Old National Pike
Middletown, MD 21769-8817
Phone (301) 371-7333

Traditional Products Company
P.O. Box 564
Creswell, OR 97426
Phone (503) 895-2957

*Plant-fiber bristle brushes for bath, sauna, hands, nails, and teeth; sisal for body scrubs.*

United Plant Savers
P.O. Box 420
East Barre, VT 05649
Phone (802) 479-9825
Fax (802) 476-3722
E-mail: info@www.plantsavers.org
Internet address: www.plantsavers.org
*A nonprofit organization dedicated to preserving native medicinal plants.*

Vermont Country Store
P.O. Box 3000
Manchester, VT 05255
Phone (802) 362-2400
Internet address: www.vermontcountrystore.com

Victor Pest Control Products
59 North Locust St.
Lititz, PA 17543-0327
Phone (914) 591-5516
*Nonpoisonous, mint-based pest control for many kinds of insects. Certified poison free by the Scientific Certification Systems.*

Vreseis Limited
P.O. Box 66
Wickenburg, AZ 85358
Phone (520) 684-7199
*FoxFibre is the naturally colored cotton bred by Sally Fox; Natural Cotton Colors grows, breeds, and markets naturally colored cotton. Vreseis Limited is the retail mail order company through which Sally Fox first sold cotton lint to hand-spinners.*

The Water Quality Association
4151 Naperville Rd.
Lisle, IL 60532
Phone (708) 505-0160
*Consultants.*

Wise Woman Center
P.O. Box 706
Mt. Marion, NY 12456
*Herbs.*

Wise Woman Herbals, Inc.
P.O. Box 279
Creswell, OR 97426
Phone (541) 895-5152
Fax (541) 895-5174
*An excellent source for many herbal products, in particular all the antiseptic essential oils recommended frequently in* Better Basics *for cleaning, preserving, and body care.*

Woodcraft
210 Wood Country Rd.
P.O. Box 1686
Parkersburg, WV 26102-1686
Toll-free (800) 225-1153
*Source of powdered pigments, hide glue, et cetera.*

Woodstock Natural Products
2337 Lemoine Ave.
Fort Lee, NJ 07024
*Herbal toothpaste.*

Woodworkers Alliance for Rainforest Protection
John Shipstad
Box 133
Coos Bay, OR 97420
Phone (503) 269-6907

Worm's Way
7850 North Highway 37
Bloomington, IN 47404
Phone (800) 274-9676
*Urban Farming Source Book.*

# Index

# About the Author

Annie's northern New England roots of independence of spirit, thrift, care for the environment, self-reliance, and Yankee ingenuity
have all contributed to her longstanding fas-
cination with folk remedies and formulas that
are based on natural materials rather than
chemicals. This interest was heightened when
her own health was compromised and she
developed chemical sensitivity. Turning her
kitchen into an informal lab, and filling her
bookshelves with nineteenth-century formula
books, she has spent years learning about
herbs and testing and researching natural
solutions for everyday problems such as carpenter ants, lip balm, and cleaning the bathtub. She is a frequent contributor to many
periodicals as a writer and editor, provides
how-to information on her Web site
www.betterbasics.com, and is the author of
*Clean & Green* and *The Green Kitchen
Handbook.*

VISIT WWW.BETTERBASICS.COM TO:

* Read "Ask Annie," the on-line column to
answer your practical questions.
* Watch videos and slide shows of Annie
demonstrating recipes.
* Read updates to *Better Basics for the Home*'s
Sources and Resources.
* Post *your* hints, tips, and recipes (they are
always welcomed).